Parliaments and Legislatures Series

U.S. Senate Exceptionalism

Edited by
Bruce I. Oppenheimer

The Ohio State University Press
Columbus

Library of Congress Cataloging-in-Publication Data

U.S. Senate exceptionalism / edited by Bruce I. Oppenheimer
    p. cm.—(Parliaments and legislatures series)
Includes bibliographical references and index.
ISBN 0-8142-0915-7 (hardcover : alk. paper)
1. United States. Congress. Senate. I. Oppenheimer, Bruce Ian. II. Series.
JK1161.S447 2002
328.73′071—dc21
2002005676

Text and jacket design by Sans Serif, Inc.
Type set in Times by Sans Serif, Inc.
Printed by Thomson-Shore.

The paper used in this publication meets the minimum requirements of the American
National Standard for Information Sciences—Permanence of Paper for Printed Library
Materials. ANSI Z39.48-1992.

9 8 7 6 5 4 3 2 1

CONTENTS

ACKNOWLEDGMENTS

This book is the outgrowth of a conference on Senate Exceptionalism that I hosted at Vanderbilt University in October 1999. Support for the conference was provided through the Norman Thomas Lectures with support from the Mary L. Armistead Fund.

The presentations at the conference, beginning with Richard Fenno's keynote talk and ending with David Rohde's and Lawrence Dodd's overview summary perspectives and including fourteen papers, were of such high quality and so well integrated around the conference theme that I believed it worthwhile to share with the broader audience of legislative scholars and students. Thus the impetus for this volume. A major purpose of that conference and of this book is to stimulate additional research on the U.S. Senate—both to focus attention on the unique nature of the Senate as a legislative institution and to compare the Senate with the House of Representatives and with other legislatures.

It has been my good fortune that Pat Patterson, the general advisory editor of the Parliaments and Legislatures Series at The Ohio State University Press, shared my enthusiasm for this project. Given Pat and Anthony Mughan's book in that series, *Senates: Bicameralism in the Contemporary World,* this book seemed like a natural companion. In addition, in his role as series editor, Pat made a number of valuable suggestions that influenced the final manuscript in most beneficial ways.

A number of people at The Ohio State University Press have contributed their time and effort to the success of this project. Malcolm Litchfield, the director of the press, was most helpful in marshaling this project through various hurdles. Eugene O'Connor, the managing editor, has taken great care in overseeing the production of this book. Shawn Mann, the assistant to the director, helped with many of the administrative tasks in managing a book with a large number of contributors. Linda Patterson Aselton demonstrated great concern in preparing for the marketing of this book. In particular, the work of the book's copyeditor, Elisabeth Magnus, was particularly skilled. Bringing a consistent hand to a many-authored volume and doing so without having contributors complain is simply amazing.

Several colleagues in the Department of Political Science at Vanderbilt were most helpful in ensuring that the conference was a success. In particular, John Geer, Geoff Layman, and Brad Palmquist provided important contributions in our ability to host the conference. Rosalyn Cooperman volunteered her organizational abilities, attention to detail, and common sense and proved absolutely invaluable. The department's administrator, Peter Carney, cut through the under-brush of the university bureaucracies.

The success of the conference and of this book, however, is largely the product of the conference participants. Tom Mann, though not a contributor to this volume, agreed to serve in a critic-at-large role during the conference. He not only offered his perspectives, but he helped keep us focused. My biggest thanks are reserved for those who wrote papers for the conference and are the authors of the chapters of this volume. Not only did they make first-rate research contributions, but they are as cooperative and delightful a group of scholars as one could be fortunate enough to gather together. They epitomize the wonderful collegial spirit that exists in the legislative studies community.

As always, Susan and Anne have been most understanding, especially when conference and book deadlines have competed for my attention.

FOREWORD

During October 1999, Bruce Oppenheimer convened a "Norman Thomas Conference on Senate Exceptionalism" at Vanderbilt University in Nashville, Tennessee. His purpose was to assemble the leading American experts on the U.S. Senate—its constituency basis, structural features, policy processing, and patterns of consensus and cleavage—in order to establish better understanding of the Senate institution. The papers, prepared by a stunning cast of scholars and presented at that conclave, constitute the chapters of this book. The excellent empirical inquiries embraced in the following chapters underscore the extraordinary nature of the U.S. Senate—its "exceptionalism," if you will—and open avenues of new appreciation, both theoretical and empirical, of Congress's upper house.

That the U.S. Senate is a wondrous, remarkable political institution can hardly be gainsaid. It emerged from the founding era a secretive, contentious, transient, innocuous body. But the institution steadily evolved into a legislative body with substantial influence upon Washington politics and national policy making. Ultimately, the Senate came to equal and sometimes even exceed the House of Representatives in its leverage upon national politics. While the U.S. Senate may not literally be "the greatest deliberative body in the world," as some have claimed, there is no doubt of its distinctiveness among the world's upper legislative chambers.

Above all, the U.S. Congress is a *bicameral* representative institution. Fundamental to understanding how Congress is organized and how it operates is the fact of two legislative houses, a House and a Senate. In this respect, the U.S. Congress is in the minority among the world's parliamentary bodies. About two-thirds of the parliaments of the world are *unicameral*—they have only one house, and that one house exercises all of the constitutional or political power available to parliament. At the same time, Congress is not unique in being bicameral. In most of the world's largest democracies—France, Germany, and Italy; countries of the Western Hemisphere including Canada, Mexico, and most South American countries; and countries elsewhere like Australia or Japan—the national legislative assembly is organized as two chambers, a lower house and an upper house.

In many bicameral legislatures the lower house has the upper hand. It is the body, often named the House of Representatives, directly elected by the people, bearing the main load in establishing and succoring a government in parliamentary systems, and dominating policy making, especially in formulating and finalizing the national budget. But in a few democracies the two houses of the bicameral legislature are, on balance, co-equal. Action by both bodies is required by the lawmaking process. In the case of the United States of America, the House of Representatives and the Senate must ultimately adopt legislative proposals in the same form for them to become the law of the land. Accordingly, we say that the U.S. Congress is institutionally "symmetrical" in the sense that its two houses have essentially co-equal legislative power.

Of course, this does not mean that the U.S. House of Representatives and Senate are the same, tweedledum and tweedledee. To mention only the most obvious differences, lower house members are elected from a multitude of single-member districts delineated according to state populations, while each state is represented equally by two senators irrespective of state population disparities. The House is more than four times larger than the Senate. And, while laws must be endorsed by both houses, each house enjoys some distinctive constitutional powers (for instance, in regard to impeachment, approval of presidential appointments, processing tax legislation, or affirming treaties). But the symbiotic linkages between House and Senate are profound despite some functional differences.

It is, therefore, axiomatic that the two components of the U.S. Congress cannot be well analyzed in isolation. Studies of the House must take some account of the looming reality of the Senate, and vice versa. The contributions in this book, although focusing on the Senate, have the House of Representatives in mind. The convenor of the Vanderbilt conference and editor of this anthology points out the common analytical thread tying together the several contributions. Then each contributor investigates and analyzes the institutional features of one legislative body, the U.S. Senate, so as to establish how the Senate is similar to, and different from, other legislative bodies, especially the congressional lower house. A summary of major findings from the studies opens important new lines of appreciation and inquiry.

"Analysis of the Senate in light of the House" produces a rather new understanding of the Senate. We learn of the Senate's striking polarization along political party lines, grounded in ideological cleavage, and the effectiveness on the choices voters make in Senate elections; we discover the ideological basis of senators' campaigns in which media markets fit candidates for the Senate better than candidates for the House; we see that Senate elections are more nationalized than elections to the House.

The basis of representation for the two congressional bodies differs, with the House based on population equality and the Senate anchored in equal representation of the states. We note that, despite important representational differences, there is some convergence between the House and Senate in their "electoral sensitivity"; although the states are multimember constituencies in the sense that each state's voters choose two senators (usually at different times), senators from the same state tend to divide the territory; Senate leaders and their rank and file seek to influence and manage the media agenda so as to promote their own party and purposes.

Interesting, important structural and policymaking differences prevail inside the two congressional houses. Although there are notable parallels in the committee organization of the House and Senate, Senate committees did not develop historically in the same way as House committees; procedures such as bill introduction emerged differently in the two houses; and party leadership evolved differently in the Senate compared to the House, affected by variations in party competition and intercameral disparities in making rules changes. Senate policy making is profoundly shaped by delaying tactics (filibustering, holds, the requirement of unanimous consent) not to be found in the House; Senate leaders have less control over the policy agenda than their House counterparts; distributive policies are shaped by different forces in the Senate than in the House. Finally, some policy arenas engender unusual House and Senate decision making, such that, for instance, impeachment processes are particularly notable for unmasking intercameral differences.

The authors of this book have a great deal to teach us about the U.S. Senate. Doubtless, scholars will debate the appropriate conceptualization of the Senate as a lawmaking institution, contending over questions of its uniqueness or exceptionalism. Inquiries focusing on the world's family of representative assemblies in which the U.S. Senate is a towering member will enrich knowledge of institutions at the very center of democratic polities. In the vortex of the U.S. Congress, the nexus of Senate and House provides the focus for fruitful theorizing, enriching empirical awareness, and possibly even wisdom. This book offers a wealth of important new knowledge about the U.S. Senate and presents valuable stimuli for more intensive study of parliaments in general.

Samuel C. Patterson
General Advisory Editor

Introduction

· 1 ·

Let's Begin with the Senate: An Introduction to *U.S. Senate Exceptionalism*

Bruce I. Oppenheimer

The U.S. Senate is an exceptional political institution in an exceptional political system. It is exceptional in the sense of being different, deviating from the norm, and in its rareness and uniqueness compared to other legislatures. Most obviously, the U.S. Senate differs substantially from senates in other national legislatures. As Barbara Sinclair (1999a) observes: "Three characteristics make the U.S. Senate unusual among upper chambers: it shares legislative power equally with the House of Representatives; it operates under a set of rules that vest enormous power in each senator; and when majorities rule in the Senate it is only by leave of minorities" (32). In their volume on upper chambers, Anthony Mughan and Samuel Patterson (1999) conclude that the U.S. Senate differs from its counterparts in other countries in terms of its position in "the larger political system" (338). They state that the U.S. Senate "has come to enjoy remarkable prestige and power" but that the same is not the case of upper houses generally. Even in those rare instances where a constitution establishes equality with the lower house, such as Italy, the Senate assumes a lesser role (338).

In part, the exceptionalism of the U.S. Senate compared with upper chambers in non-American legislatures may reflect something about the nature of what has become known as "American exceptionalism." Although scholars who have written on the topic of American exceptionalism refer to the Senate only in passing, they do note its role in making American government "a weak and internally conflicted political system" (Lipset 1996, 39), both through its place in an elaborate system of separation of powers and checks and balances and through its "manifestation of the federal system" (Kingdon 1999, 9). As Kingdon searches for institutional prescriptions to the difficulties of mobilizing and leading in the American governing context, his one specific suggestion is that the

Senate "could act to trim the considerable ability of individual senators to tie the institution up in knots if it were to adopt a rules change to end filibusters more easily and abandon the practice of allowing individual senators to put holds on nominations and bills" (90). In saying this, Kingdon acknowledges the uniqueness of the U.S. Senate as a legislative institution and its epitomizing the unusual qualities of American government.

In another sense, however, the Senate and many other "active" legislatures (the U.S. House of Representatives, American state legislatures, and some non-American lower houses) are very much alike. For all of them lawmaking is a primary function. Although most cannot guarantee the enactment of a law, no bill can become law without their approval. Thus, in the bicameral U.S. Congress, the House and the Senate are functionally the same in fulfilling their most important governing role. They both have the same basic power in the lawmaking process.

Given that shared, coequal responsibility, one might assume that this underlying sameness would outweigh other differences. But to make such an assumption would ignore the array of ways in which the Senate and the House either were purposively designed to be different or have become different in ways the Framers did not anticipate. And the Senate not only differs from the House but also is an outlier among influential legislatures. The purpose of this collection, however, is not to deny the similarities between the Senate and the House or the Senate and other lawmaking legislatures. (In fact, some of the contributors to this volume find similarities between the two bodies that have not previously received emphasis.) Instead, the goal is to explore more fully the unique features of the Senate and their consequences.

One should not misconstrue the meaning of the concept of exceptionalism as it is applied here to the U.S. Senate. Others may talk or write of the Senate's exceptionalism in terms of its being superior to other legislatures. In this volume, however, our concern is not with accuracy of long-voiced claim that the Senate is the world's greatest deliberative body or whether William S. White's (1956) view of the Senate as "the one touch of authentic genius in the American political system" (ix) is something more than hyperbole. Whether the Senate is also exceptional in the sense that "exceptional children" are thought to be brighter or more talented than other children is not the focus of this book. Instead, we ask whether the unusual nature of the Senate as a legislative institution deserves more scholarly attention than it has previously been given and whether a focus on "exceptionalism" is a useful vehicle in developing fuller understanding of the Senate as a political institution.

The stimulus for my interest in the broader topic of U.S. Senate exceptionalism resulted from my work with Frances Lee on the effects of the Senate's apportionment scheme (Lee and Oppenheimer 1999). One of the Senate's most

4

obvious, important, and unique features had gone largely unstudied. In terms of deviation from the representational norm of "one person, one vote," no other meaningful national legislature in a representative democracy is more extreme. Yet as Lee and I demonstrated, a broad array of consequences result from having each state, regardless of population, equally represented, especially given the broad range and distribution of state population sizes. Senate apportionment affects the representational relationships between senators and their constituents, the competitiveness and funding of Senate elections, the strategic behavior of senators, and the way the Senate designs policies.

If apportionment were the only unique feature of this legislature, a study of institutional exceptionalism might not be justified. Clearly, however, the apportionment basis of the Senate is just one of the most obvious features that set it apart from other legislatures. The fact that two members are elected from each constituent unit, the relatively long and staggered terms of office, and some of its specific constitutional powers and responsibilities are among the attributes that make the U.S. Senate unique. Individually, these features and others make the Senate stand out on a variety of dimensions. Any one of them may be worthy of exploration. It is accordingly surprising that so little research has focused on the consequences of each of these and other facets. Yet like the apportionment basis, they have not received much attention. Scholars freely acknowledge these features but rarely bother to investigate their implications. Nor has there been the recognition that taken together these attributes of the Senate may have greater significance for our analysis of it as an institution than has previously been admitted.

A focus on Senate exceptionalism does not mean viewing the Senate in isolation. An ability to understand an institution requires a grasp of variation across institutions. Accordingly, most of the contributors to this book make direct comparisons between the Senate and the House of Representatives.

Further, I do not mean to claim that we are without truly excellent scholarly studies of the U.S. Senate. The Senate books by Matthews (1960) and Sinclair (1989), for example, can be found on nearly everyone's list of the most important studies in American politics. Yet as Richard Fenno, the preeminent legislative scholar of the modern era, freely confesses in the conference keynote, his efforts at "finding the Senate" have proven a far more elusive, and perhaps frustrating, undertaking than his research on the House. And though he has uncovered a great deal more of the Senate than he modestly claims, no doubt many legislative scholars who have tackled both institutions in their research endeavors agree with Fenno's conclusion. Collectively, the understanding of the House that legislative scholars have developed over the past half century far outstrips their understanding of the Senate. Why is this the case? Can a focus on Senate exceptionalism assist in unlocking the puzzles that the Senate presents?

5

One might reasonably ask why the exceptional features of the Senate have not received more research attention. After all, if a focus on them has path-breaking potential, one would assume that the active community of legislative scholars would have trod those routes already. Let me suggest two key reasons why Senate exceptionalism has not received the attention that it warrants. First, because of a number of factors, congressional scholars have focused their research more heavily on the House of Representatives than on the Senate. Although Ralph Huitt, the father of the modern political science study of Congress, devoted his attention to the Senate, his offspring (and subsequent generations) did not follow (Huitt 1990). The House presented certain research advantages. Just as House members are more accessible to their constituents than senators, they have also been more accessible and generally more willing to visit with scholars. In addition, the study of Congress at first, and perhaps still, was very much focused on committees (Fenno 1966; Manley 1970; and Jones 1961, among others). And there was the widespread, and correct, perception that committees were more important to the workings of the House than they were to the Senate. Thus, with two notable exception (Price 1972; Evans 1991), the study of Senate committees was auxiliary in the research undertakings on committees. Finally, I speculate that from the standpoint of incentives for scholarly inquiry the House, with its larger membership, was more attractive for performing data analysis, allowing for the consideration of a larger number of variables and capable of producing statistically significant results. In sum, simply because congressional scholars did not devote the same level of research attention to the Senate, knowledge about the Senate, including knowledge about its unique features, lagged behind that of the House.

A second and related reason for the failure to focus on the exceptional features of the Senate is that much of the research on the Senate had its origins in research based on the House. Thus, upon completing research on the House, one would ask if the same findings held for the Senate. Although such lines of inquiry might yield different results and explanations based on differences between the two institutions (e.g., because the Senate had fewer members or longer terms of office) and thus might hint at a unique feature, the research questions tended to have their basis in the study of the House. The House not only served as the benchmark for evaluating findings of similar research on the Senate but also biased the nature of the questions that researchers asked. Questions about an institution where the members served the same-sized constituencies did not tend to lead to questions about variation in constituency size when transferred to the Senate. Questions about congressional elections in an institution in which there were no staggered terms naturally did not generate an investigation of the effects of staggered terms. And questions about those policy areas in which the House had a special constitutional and/or traditional role (revenue and appropriations bills) did not generate scholarship about subjects where the Constitution provided unicameral power to the Senate. Instead, scholars, tended, quite naturally and legitimately, to look respectively at home styles of senators, incumbency advantage in Senate elections, and taxing and spending politics in the Senate. The size of the constituency or the longer term of office or going second in the process might come into play in these analyses, but often it was only in an auxiliary component of the research. Differences between the House and Senate might serve as the bases for findings on each of these topics, but they did not necessarily lead to a broader investigation of what made the Senate different or a recognition that the Senate not only was different from the House but might also be unique.

In his concluding essay in this collection (chapter 18), Lawrence Dodd takes this point a step further and argues that the theoretical approaches that have general acceptance in the study of the House may be inappropriate in developing an understanding to the Senate. One wonders whether a research agenda that did not borrow so heavily from House scholarship and instead was stimulated more directly by questions about the Senate itself might lead scholars in new directions, to a better grasp of this complex institution, and to new theoretical approaches to understanding political institutions.

It is not my claim here, nor is it that of the contributors to this volume, that a focus on Senate exceptionalism will answer all or even most of the unresolved questions about this important legislative institution. But it may assist our efforts in developing a fuller picture of the Senate as an institution and in comparison with other legislatures, as well as generating alternative theories of legislative behavior. Nor should one think that we reject the idea of making comparisons with the House or that we are dismissive of findings that emphasize the similarities between the two bodies. In fact, investigating U.S. Senate exceptionalism clearly involves an understanding of what about the Senate is unexceptional. Thus, some of the findings in this collection will point to the lack of institutional differences, even where such differences may have been hypothesized, and to trends that have made the House and Senate more alike.

The organization of this volume is an accurate reflection of the flow of the Senate Exceptionalism Conference. Like the conference, the book begins with Richard Fenno's keynote lecture to the conference participants and the broader audience of attendees (chapter 2). In an edited version of that presentation, Fenno discusses the rewards, frustrations, and pitfalls that an experienced congressional scholar confronts as he grapples with making systematic sense of the Senate. This good-humored yet insightful talk offers unusual guidance to veteran legislative researchers as well as new graduate students embarking on studying the Senate. It reminds us that good theory and good questions drive the best research efforts and that even the most successful scholars are more than occasionally confronted with dead ends.

Following this keynote, the book is organized into five sections that mirror the five conference panels and cover the range of research topics that concern legislative scholars: elections, representation, development of internal organization, process-policy linkages, and specific powers. The first of these contains three chapters that address various aspects of the same central issue, the role of national issues and ideology in Senate elections. In one way or another all three attest to the greater role of issues and ideology in Senate elections than in House elections. Alan Abramowitz (chapter 3) investigates the change in the extent to which national issues and ideology have come to influence voter behavior in Senate elections since the 1960s. He finds not only that the changing ideological composition of the Senate parties has affected the sources of influence on voter decisions but that the increase in the role of ideology has been greater in Senate than in House elections.

The chapter by Kim Kahn and Patrick Kenney (chapter 4) nicely complements the Abramowitz chapter. In effect, the authors provide an explanation for the Abramowitz findings. They argue and present data demonstrating that Senate campaigns include far more ideological and policy information than House campaigns. Part of this difference is due to the themes and amount of news media coverage given to Senate campaigns. These provide voters with sufficient ideological and issue position information about the candidates even when ideology and issue are not central to presentation by the candidates. Because House campaigns are for less important offices (more members serving shorter terms and usually representing smaller constituencies) and are less competitive, they receive less media coverage. This creates a differential cost for voters in obtaining ideological information about senators compared to House members and in turn affects the factors that influence voter decisions.

Robert Erikson (chapter 5) is similarly concerned with the influence of ideology plus the influence of partisanship in Senate as opposed to House elections. Because of less insular constituencies, Senate elections are less immune to shifts in public opinion than are House elections. Moreover, Erikson demonstrates how the data from Senate elections fit nicely with a theory of ideological balancing (with the preferences of voters in presidential elections). Thus, in all three of these chapters the authors establish the increasingly close linkage between national political events (ideology, issues, and partisan shifts) and the outcomes of Senate elections.

In a piece that provides a transition between a focus on elections and one on representation, John Alford and John Hibbing (chapter 6) find a convergence between the House and the Senate and the diminution of the exceptional nature of the Senate that the Founders intended. In particular, they discover that the

Senate has become an electorally sensitive institution and no longer provides the insulation necessary for it to be a defense against "temporary errors and delusions." Through an analysis of data on membership turnover and length of service, they demonstrate how this historic shift has eroded the distinctive quality that the Founders envisioned for the Senate.

One continuous and unique feature of the Senate's representational arrangement, the dual composition of each state's membership, provides the framework for Wendy Schiller's chapter (chapter 7). She explores how holding the same geographic constituencies leads same-state senators to develop differing representational bases of electoral support within the state. Even senators of the same party seek to attract support from different geographic regions, demographic groups, and interests in a state.

In the concluding chapter on Senate representation, Patrick Sellers (chapter 8) analyzes how representational conflicts affect the nature of media coverage. Sellers's concern is with how Senate party leaders cope with the goals of senators to serve their individual electoral concerns with news coverage tailored to their states while the leaders want to publicize a unified message reflecting party legislative priorities. His analysis is based on a range of sources including senator press releases, interviews with Senate press secretaries, and notes as a participant-observer in a leadership office.

Three historical pieces compose the section of the book devoted to the internal organization and workings of the Senate. Instead of merely accepting the notion that institutional development occurred in the Senate much the way it did in the House and at about the same time, the authors of these chapters find that the distinctive character of the Senate played a far larger role than previous conventional wisdom would have us believe. Simply translating House-based explanations for internal structures and procedures does not provide a satisfactory or accurate understanding of the internal arrangements in the Senate. Rather, a grasp of the unique nature of the Senate is needed for understanding how Senate structures and procedures emerged.

In their examination of the evolution of Senate standing and select committees, David Canon and Charles Stewart (chapter 9) pinpoint the start of partisan dominance of the committee system. Although they argue that there is a great deal of similarity between the House and the Senate in the development of their committee systems, Canon and Stewart also find that the Senate, not the House, was the first to establish a standing committee system. Similarly, Joseph Cooper and Elizabeth Rybicki (chapter 10) find that the Senate preceded the House in making bill introduction a prerogative of members instead of committees and that the consequences of this change were very different in the Senate, where the change in bill introduction accompanied other rule changes that preserved other member prerogatives. Senators did not allow committees and party leaders to obtain other powers in exchange for gaining control of bill introduction, as was the case in the House. Cooper and Rybicki compare self-interest, party strength, and contextual theories as bases of explanation for understanding these changes.

While previous explanations based on careerism, membership turnover, and workload increases have been thought to be related to the development of party organizations and the creation of formal Senate leadership positions, Gerald Gamm and Steven Smith (chapter 11) find these explanations wanting. They find that rather than mirroring factors related to party leadership emergence in the House, the Senate, because of unique institutional attributes, did not change its rules to adjust to its needs. Instead, the Senate parties created new structures to cope with collective action problems, especially when the parties were evenly divided and most competitive.

The exceptionalism of the U.S. Senate might be intriguing in and of itself. But unless those features that give the Senate uniqueness have consequences for the way it legislates and the legislation it produces, they may merely attest to its institutional quaintness rather than to something of substantive significance in the "who gets what, where, when, and how" of politics. Beginning with Barbara Sinclair's study of the filibuster (chapter 12), the chapters in Part V of this book offer ample support for the claim that the Senate differences make a difference. Through an investigation of the strategic uses of the filibuster and data on its impact on the enactment of legislation, Sinclair shows that the way in which senators and parties now use the filibuster has implications for legislative output. Moreover, she finds that the frequency and manner in which the filibuster was used were largely responsible for the higher rate at which measures failed in the 1990s than in earlier decades.

C. Lawrence Evans (chapter 13) explores three major piece of legislation in the 106th Congress to understand better how senators make eventual roll call decisions and how qualities of the institution influence that process. His study yields preliminary findings about the capacity, means, and effectiveness of Senate party leaders to influence the decisions of the members. In addition, he raises new questions about the capacity of the Senate to preserve the quality of deliberation, once thought to be an institutional hallmark.

In an outgrowth of her previous work, Frances Lee (chapter 14) analyzes the effect of Senate apportionment on distributive policy. Not only have most previous studies of distributive policy neglected the Senate's role, but none before Lee's have considered the effect of apportionment. Compared to the traditional variables used to understand pork barrel politics, which produced only modest findings, Senate apportionment is shown by Lee to play a major role in explaining variation in the federal transportation dollars that states receive.

Two perspectives on the Senate's role in the impeachment process not only give insights into this infrequently used constitutional power but, more importantly, offer opportunities to view institutional incentives that mute partisanship. In studying the differences between the way the Senate and House dealt with the Clinton impeachment, Ross Baker (chapter 15) argues that institutional patriotism still remains an important norm because of the close link between the reputation of members and the reputation of the institution. While institutional patriotism has declined substantially in the House, its continued presence in the Senate remains a key restraint on partisanship. In a complementary chapter to Baker's, Burdett Loomis (chapter 16) examines the components of explanation that senators offered for their votes in the impeachment trial of President Clinton. In efforts not to be seen as partisan, senators employed various themes to justify their decisions. Yet senators' party affiliations were closely tied to the explanatory themes they employed.

In the final panel at the Senate Exceptionalism Conference, David Rohde (chapter 17) and Lawrence Dodd (chapter 18) offered their summary perspectives on the papers, on the conference theme, and on the direction of future research. Following the conference, and with sufficient opportunity to digest the materials, they formalized their comments in the two chapters that complete this collection. Rohde reflects on the substantive findings of the papers and the questions they raise and makes a range of suggestions for the future direction of research. Among other things, Rohde reminds us how important it is that legislative research continue to emphasize variation across institutions. He observes that the willingness of papers in this collection to make Senate-House comparisons demonstrates that the study of Senate exceptionalism requires that the Senate be compared with other legislatures. Dodd's emphasis is on the conceptual approaches of legislative scholars. He asks whether the ones that have proved so useful in understanding the House are as appropriate for guiding research on the Senate. Dodd contends that the relatively unstructured and more unpredictable environment of the Senate is less suited to the rational-choice perspectives. Instead, he speculates that social psychology theories of adaptive social learning may assist legislative scholars in coping with the elusiveness and distinctiveness of the Senate.

The research issues and findings in this volume are not meant to provide the last word on the unique qualities of the U.S. Senate and how to study them. Rather, they should be read as first words. The success of this volume, accordingly, should be measured by its effectiveness in stimulating research and scholarly debate about the Senate rather than in ending it. Hopefully, giving more attention to the Senate exceptionalism will make this important legislative institution more hospitable to systematic understanding.

▪ 2 ▪

Looking for the Senate:
Reminiscences and Residuals

Richard F. Fenno, Jr.

When Bruce invited me to come give a public, preconference talk, my first thought was this: I am not studying the Senate, I have nothing to present, and so I can't do it. My second thought, however, was this: while it is true that I have nothing to present, I can't pass up the opportunity to be in the same place with such a great group of congressional scholars. So here I am—naked to my colleagues—with no data, no findings, no results, no theories, no generalizations, no conclusions, no research agenda of my own, and, rest assured, no intention of prescribing agenda items for tomorrow's conference.

My credential, as Bruce mentioned, is that I have, indeed, been a student of the Senate—off and on for a number of years. But very much a sometime student of the Senate, while focusing my research—along with the great preponderance of congressional scholars—on the House of Representatives. Many of you, I dare say, have been weaned on that large body of political science research devoted to the House and are—quite self-consciously—trying to redress what we might call "the great imbalance" in studies of Congress.

As a historical note, when *my* research cohort got interested in Congress, the balance was tipped in the opposite direction. We were weaned on the Senate-centered research of Ralph Huitt (1990) and Donald Matthews (1960)—not to mention the Senate-centered journalism of William White (1956) and Alan Drury (1963). When I began studying the appropriations process in the House in the late 1950s, the House was the less well-understood body; and I was imbued with the same pioneering spirit that has animated a lot of recent research on the Senate. So I resonate, instinctively, to the remedial aspects of this conference.

But what do I have to say about its subject matter—the U.S. Senate? Well, I've thought about that, and I have concluded: on the one hand, not much; but on the other hand, let's face it, for most of my professional life, I've been an explorer and a storyteller, someone who ventures out into the political world and reports back to his colleagues, so why not tell stories about my off-and-on Senate explorations.

I can tell you, in advance, the outcome of those explorations. I always wanted to "write a book about the Senate"—something that would match the defining quality of the Donald Matthews study, but I never did. That is why I label this talk "Looking for the Senate." Since I haven't found "the Senate" and doubtless never will, since I've now gone back to the House, I'm going to seize the opportunity to do a little retrospective storytelling about one person's search for the Senate—using some unreported explorations, some pieces of the mosaic I never could put in place, and some tales I never got to tell—mostly about people. Hence the subtitle "Reminiscences and Residuals." In all of this, I confess, I'm exercising, even abusing, the privileges of my seniority—so I invite you to think of this talk as falling somewhere between a "hold" and a filibuster.

All of my research on the Senate has been motivated by research on the House and began, implicitly or explicitly, with the intent of comparing some idea or activity that I had studied in the House with that same idea or activity in the Senate. My first encounter with the Senate came as a strictly secondary matter in a research project on appropriations politics in Congress. In the formal appropriations process, the House normally acted first, the Senate second; and this sequence made the House Committee on Appropriations *the* dominant money committee in Congress. For that reason, the House committee commanded most of my attention.

So I was not "looking for the Senate" at the time. But I did talk, in 1960 and 1961, with members of the Senate Appropriations Committee. The picture I got would surely have fit nicely with Barbara Sinclair's (1989) authoritative portrait of the transforming—yet still clubby—Senate of the 1960s. Looking back, I have one untold tale that might underscore her transitional theme.

I interviewed Republican Appropriations Committee member Margaret Chase Smith, the only woman in the Senate; and my tale of her quiet battles to secure and protect her senatorial rights has been untold because she explicitly asked me not to write about it. I didn't. Nor have I ever talked about it. But I'm reluctant to let it gather dust, since it might enrich our view of an earlier Senate and provide another benchmark in the evolution of what remains a male-dominated institution. Smith is certainly a different and less studied kind of Senate *outsider* than our research favorites of that period—reformer Joseph Clark and iconoclast William Proxmire. But in the long run, precisely because Smith did not *choose* to be an outsider, she may be an equally instructive one.

My interview summary describes Smith as "friendly, insecure, worried about her prerogatives, not really at home in the club, seems to need constant reassurance . . . worried to see if her responses were jibing with others." Her worries dominated our brief interview.

On winning her assignment to the Appropriations Committee, for example, she stated, "You have to watch things very closely on your committee assignments. I worked awfully hard on it. One of the senior members challenged me as to why I wanted two major committees—Armed Services *and* Appropriations. He, already having his two major committees, was questioning my right." "On Armed Services," she added, "[Sen.] Schoeppel was placed ahead of me [in seniority. But] I came from the House and he had once been a governor, so I outranked him. I went before the Committee on Committees to get it settled and I pressed my rights. It may seem picayune, but it could mean the matter of a chairmanship later on." With respect to her acute sensitivity to slights and rights, she complained, too, that Sen. Karl Mundt—elected the same day she was but sworn in three days earlier, had more seniority than she. "Everywhere I go, he outranks me and it bothers me. It's not right." These concerns reflect, of course, the never-ending battle for position and prerogative inside each party's ranks.

And across party lines, too. In a discussion of the practice of allowing ex officio members to sit with her Subcommittee on Defense Appropriations, she told this story:

> We were having an appropriations hearing and the Joint Chiefs were before us. . . . Senator Chavez [a Democrat] was presiding . . . and there were [Senators] Thye and Smith on the Republican side and [Senator] Symington ex officio on the Democratic side. When Thye finished speaking, I should have been next because I was a member of the committee, even though I was on the same side as the previous speaker. But Chavez turned to Mr. Symington instead. Well, I didn't know what to do. It seems like a little matter, but I had prepared some important and necessary questions to ask. I always do that. . . . I knew that if I didn't get this question of the rights of committee members settled right there, it could cause problems later on. So I interrupted and called him on it. Of course, he turned to me and I asked my questions. To this day, whenever I walk into that room, Senator Chavez knows I'm there. I'm glad I did it.

Her generalization was careful, understated, unaggressive, but clear. "I think maybe because I'm the woman, I have to fight harder to get what's rightfully mine. But I don't know. Sometimes I think some of the men get gypped, too." And she followed that comment with a firm request that I not mention any of her complaints.

When she talked about "the men" on the committee, her overall sense of separateness, of not belonging, set her apart from my other interviewees. In her description of the Democratic leaders on the committee, for example: "Some of these men, they know so much about their subject—Hill, he's an expert on health, a real expert, and Russell, a brilliant man. And they are such gentlemen. They will sweet-talk you and cut your heart out while they are doing it if you don't watch out." When we talked, she had already been in the Senate for twelve years. Yet she conveyed the sense that she was still an observer, on the outside looking in—in the Senate, but not wholly a part of it. "If you could get a camera and a tape recorder and take it into an [Appropriations] mark-up session . . . with all the personalities and all, it would make a wonderful novel. If you could listen to Hayden, Chavez, and Russell and Bridges and Saltonstall . . . going back and forth . . . you'd have the choicest bit of material you could imagine." And so it went, the sensitivities, challenges, and perceptions of the only woman in the untransformed men's club—and some benchmarks, perhaps, for the study of gender politics in and around today's Senate.

Smith served in the Senate for twenty-four years, until 1972, and there is a noteworthy career to be studied. In her gutsy and much admired "declaration of conscience" criticizing her Republican colleague Joe McCarthy—while her male Republican colleagues hunkered down in partisan self-protection—there is more evidence of her outsiderness and her well-developed sense of right and wrong. The public resonance of that highly individualistic adventure, including her formal nomination for president at the 1964 Republican Convention—a first for women—was a signpost on the road to the transformed Senate.

In Irwin Gertzog's (1995) categorization of women in Congress, Smith represents what he calls the transitional figure, a woman "professional," coming between the earlier women "amateurs" and the later women "colleagues." It was in this transitional, women-as-professionals spirit that she wrote later, in referring to her important work for women in the Armed Services: "It left the impression, I'm afraid, that I was a feminist concentrating on legislation for women. And if there is one thing I've attempted to avoid, it is being a feminist. I definitely resent being called a feminist" (Smith 1972). As I say, "transitional."

My one sustained search for the Senate also began as a derivative of my research on the House. It grew out of a six-year study I had done of some House members—not about what they did in Washington but about what they did when they were at home in their constituencies (Fenno 1978). During that study of the constituency activities of House members, I was often asked whether senators would behave similarly when they were back in their home states. And when an opportunity to pursue that comparison unexpectedly appeared, I decided to have a look. One of the House members in my study decided to run for the Senate. He became the pivotal figure in moving me to look directly at the Senate. But because he lost, he disappeared from my subsequent Senate studies—another untold tale I wish to tell.

Philip Hayes was a Watergate baby from Evansville, Indiana, a state legislator who had defeated a three-term, die-hard Nixon supporter in 1974. He was one of Burdett Loomis's "new politicians" (Loomis 1988), a cocky, bright, articulate, aggressive, and energetic thirty-four-year-old who was profiled on the front page of the *Wall Street Journal* as typical of the reform-oriented freshmen class.[1] A year into his first term, he decided to run against Indiana's senior senator Vance Hartke in the Democratic primary. And I went out to watch—my first exposure to a home-based, Senate-oriented activity.

For those in the audience who are not political scientists, I should note that my research method places heavy emphasis on learning by interviewing, watching, and hanging around members of Congress wherever they work—whether in Washington or with their constituency. Participant-observers, I might add, are perversely slow to accept congressional reality until they can see, hear, touch, and talk to real live members.

By following Hayes, I found three differences from my House member experience that became especially real for me because I was experiencing and learning about them at the same time as Hayes himself was experiencing and learning about them. *First,* statewide constituencies are bigger and more complex than congressional districts. In his fourteen-county congressional district, Hayes could get any place from his home in a little more than an hour. In his Senate campaign, however, we had to campaign one day in a rented four-seater airplane from South Bend to Gary to Fort Wayne, something I had never done in a House campaign. The next day, we drove till 2:30 in the morning across northern Indiana with three of us taking turns at the wheel—another "hands-on" learning experience. Culturally, too, it was light-years between poverty-stricken, majority-black Gary, and comfortably Lutheran and white Fort Wayne—a greater complexity within a single constituency than I had ever seen in my House member travels.

In an area eight times more populous than his congressional district, Hayes had 6 percent name recognition. Constituency size and complexity thus combined to underscore a *second* House-Senate difference—a quantum change in the importance of the media. Running for the Senate in Indiana was overwhelmingly different for him from running for Congress in Indiana. It was the difference between personal contact campaigning and media market campaigning.

One morning after meeting and greeting some union members in a small South Bend factory, Hayes flatly refused to do any more handshaking that day. "So what if we condescended to go to that small plant," he said. "Thirty people came through the gates, and there won't be any follow-up PR. So who will ever know about it? Mine is a media campaign. I can't afford to do that personal campaigning. That would be okay if I were running in a state Senate district, but not in a U.S. Senate race. I need media time in all these little towns who don't know my ass." By way of contrast, I vividly recalled an evening two years before when Congressman Hayes had spent two hours socializing with a different thirty factory workers at their union hall in Evansville. When we left, he had said, "Maybe I overstayed my welcome, from my point of view, but they are so used to having someone scooped up and whisked away in a limousine. [Senator] Birch Bayh comes in, shouts, bangs the table for 10 minutes and leaves. I want them to feel they'll have someone they can talk to." I reminded him, in Gary, of his earlier Birch Bayh comment. "I finally figured out," he said, "that I'm running a Birch Bayh style campaign. I zip into an area, get media coverage, and zip out. The difference is Birch Bayh is known and I'm not."

With Hayes, every mention of the media led seamlessly into the subject of money. And that was my *third* introduction to House-Senate differences. The very first event of my visit with Hayes the Senate candidate was a fund-raiser. By contrast, I could not recall, in my thirty-six visits to House districts, having attended more than a half-dozen fund-raisers. Hayes had no money to pay for media. "My media budget is sagging," he said, "that's my problem."

Without paid media, he was running a campaign that depended on the free media. "I'm an imaginative, creative person, and I figured we could run a media campaign that was a kind of freak show that would attract attention." He had, for example, been standing in front of travel agencies in each of the state's seven media markets, attacking Hartke for excessive junketing and demanding that he return the money. When the state's biggest paper, the *Indianapolis Star,* reported his junketing charge, he believed that his campaign "had turned the corner." And when NBC-TV covered the performance I watched in front of a travel agency in South Bend, he was ecstatic. "There we were with the wind blowing the hair, the Robert Redford bit with cameras grinding. It's street theater. . . . We're up. We're going to win this one." He didn't. The odds were all against him. It was a crazy but influential three days—and made more memorable because of Hayes himself.

In my interview notes, I compared him to Billy Marvel, a favorite comic strip character of my youth who, when he uttered the magic word *shazam,* produced lightning bolts that turned him into Captain Marvel—the invincible, heroic defender of the oppressed. Hayes spoke of himself as someone who "makes things happen," "turns people on," "is tough," "has balls," "has nerve," "has guts" and is "a mean son of a bitch." Hartke, in Hayes' eyes, was "corrupt," "an old bag," "a dead horse," "a zip gun," "a clunk," "a stiff," "a turkey," "a frigging psychotic." "I'm going to blow him out of the water," he said, "bang him like a drum," "give him a shot," "dynamite him," "jet him," "hit him," "zap him." It was the language of lightning bolts—zip, zap, biff, bop, wham, "shazam!" But he never turned into Captain Marvel.

Months later, after a postmortem luncheon in Washington, he asked me, "Are you going to follow us to our graves?" "No," I said, and I haven't heard of him

17

since. Now, however, I feel I have, at last, given Billy Marvel and his madcap campaign a proper burial in just the right place—Nashville!

My experience with Hayes, however, convinced me to turn my research focus to the Senate, to House-Senate differences; and to do it by focusing on Senate campaigns. So, in 1978, I began traveling around with some Senate candidates—some incumbents, some not—in their home states. Pretty quickly, however, I became less and less interested in House-Senate comparisons of complexity, media, and money and more and more interested in the ways in which a senator's activity at home might relate to his or her activity in Washington—a relationship I had never pursued with House members.

This change in my research question was propelled by firsthand exposure to an important House-Senate institutional difference—the six-year Senate term (Fenno 1982). It gives senators a longer, uninterrupted stretch of Washington activity, and it gave me the incentive to use this longer time period to study their Washington activity. So, after adding more guinea pigs to my Senate roster during the 1980 campaign season, I spent the academic year of 1981–82 in Washington following several of them around in their institutional contexts, as I had already done in their constituency contexts.

Participant-observation research, by its very nature, has to be conducted over time, and because of that, the most commanding ideas for organizing your observations tend to be ideas that incorporate some sense of time, of sequence, and of change. In trying to connect the home activity and the Washington activity of U.S. senators, the most available such idea was the six-year sequence—of campaigning activity at home, governing activity in Washington, and campaigning activity at home again.

For five senators whose activities I was able to follow in both places, I used these ideas about the six-year cycle as the organizing framework for individual case studies of their activity and of their development as individual senators. The idea of their individual development over time and across cycles was conveyed in the very titles of those five case studies. There was the *making* of a senator for Dan Quayle, the *learning* of a senator for Arlen Specter, the *emergence* of a senator for Pete Domenici, the *odyssey* of a senator for John Glenn, and the *failure* of a senator for Mark Andrews. Making, learning, emerging, questing, failing—all were about sequence and about change over time (Fenno 1989a, 1990, 1991a, 1991b, 1992).

The concept that threaded together the macro-level campaigning-governing-campaigning sequence and the micro-level individual developmental sequence was the idea of the *career.* Thus, my projected "book about the Senate" mutated into the study of senatorial careers—or more accurately, of senatorial career segments—with segments covering their governing and campaigning activity over a specified period of time. I had found senators; but I had not found the Senate.

What was missing from all this was any idea about how the Senate worked as an institution. I had no particular theory about the institution that I had come to Washington to work with—no specific activity I wanted to explain. As I followed the governing activity of "my" senators, however, I developed a vaguely defined interest in the sequencing of the institution's business—in what we might call the internal decision-making rhythms of the institution.

From the outside, so much internal activity seems to be a matter of sequence—of timing, of speeding up business or slowing down business, of lazy starts and logjams and hasty endings—of *when* something gets done as much as what gets done—the sorts of use-of-time problems Bruce Oppenheimer (1985) has written about. From the Senate gallery, you could observe the perpetual preoccupation with scheduling and time agreements and deadlines—all day, all week, all session—obviously the result of some familiar institutional features of the Senate.

I initiated several exploratory projects to capture various matters of internal sequence—none of which came to fruition. They are the residuals of eleven months of my daily visits to the Senate. For example, I got two of Majority Leader Howard Baker's assistants, Marty Gold and Jim Range, to agree to periodic meetings to discuss the flow, the planning, and the unplanning of business. It started well, deteriorated when Gold left, and broke down when Range got busier as the session progressed.

On the theory that the sequencing of constituent mail flows might relate to the sequencing of issue activity inside the Senate, I collected two years' worth of month-by-month mail records for six senators. My ward boss Larry Evans and two fellow graduate students identified issues and issue areas common to the six senators and compared the two-year mail flow patterns by timing and by issue area for each senator and for all combined. They produced interesting and diverse issue flow patterns. But I dropped the effort to relate them to the timing of individual or institutional schedules and actions. As part of that study, I also had plans to compare the early agenda planning of the same six senators to see how their personal agendas dovetailed or conflicted with the development of the institutional agenda. But that monitoring problem foundered.

One view of the Senate's internal rhythm, by Senator Fritz Hollings, went this way: "In January, we wait to get the president's budget, then there's the Lincoln and Washington Day recess, then we're off for the spring holidays—Easter and Memorial Day—then we're off for the Fourth of July, then we're off for the summer, and then Labor Day and then, of course, Thanksgiving and Christmas" (Miller 1986, 34). During the February 1982 Lincoln Day recess, I visited 59 Senate offices, asking staffers what their senator was doing that week and why—in an effort to fit patterns of recess activity into the flow of work. I got a lot of information; but I never followed it up. It, too, perished. (For starters, however, thirty-three spent the entire recess in their states, thirteen spent part of the recess there, and thirteen spent no time there.)

I began to follow some coalition-building sequences that would differentiate the timing of individual senator decisions to join—differentiating among early joiners, later joiners, and last-minute joiners. I published one such qualitative study—of the decision to sell AWACS planes to Saudi Arabia (Fenno 1986). But no others followed, so I got no comparative leverage.

I wanted to think about the campaigning-to-governing sequence as it affected staff. Watching campaigns convinced me of the great electoral value of a "quality campaign team" to the making of what we call a "quality candidate." I wanted to think about the differences between that kind of team and a quality governing team—and to look at hiring patterns involving campaign staff and noncampaign staff. My idea was that campaign staffers would dominate the original Senate staff and gradually give way to people without campaign experience. I began looking at staff turnover data among senators and collecting stories, but that project, too, got overrun by the five case studies.

I kept blow-by-blow records, too, of a unique event during my stay—the expulsion trial of Senator Harrison Williams. It wasn't the ethical problem that interested me but the way in which the institutional reputations of various senators were affected in the course of this internal, problem-solving drama—where many senators would be closely watched and evaluated in a context of full attendance on the floor and maximum media coverage. But that miniproject, too, died aborning.

During the year, I also interviewed nineteen senators with whom I had not traveled, but the interviews failed to cumulate into anything like a dominating view of the Senate—undoubtedly because I did not know what to ask.

Well, that's the underside of a one-year effort to find the Senate—a series of tentative exploratory efforts that never turned into a mosaic. That's a familiar research story, of course. But confronted here with a room full of Senate scholars, I felt especially compelled to demonstrate that I had, indeed, once gone looking for the Senate as an institution and could not find it!

Which brings me to the point in my saga at which I stopped looking for the Senate as a collectivity, left Washington, and went back to my original senatorial research site—the home state constituency. There, the research focus changed from the emphasis on governing back to an emphasis on campaigning. The overall subject was still Senate careers, but the central career-building activity I was studying changed from legislating in the Washington context to representing in the home state context.

Again, the sense of sequential activity over time dominated the study of representation—the pursuit of a career, the flow of a campaign, the influence of one campaign on another, the development and the durability of constituency connections. Moreover, the idea of sequence became embedded in the basic conceptualization of *representation as a process,* a process of continuous negotiation—personal negotiation and policy negotiation—between the performance of senators and the expectations of their constituents, with an important chunk of these negotiations taking place at home (Fenno 1996).

When this study of senators' careers in their home constituencies was published, I had nothing left to say about senators—nothing of general interest to my colleagues, that is. So I closed my senator files and went back to thinking about House members. Buried in the Senate research files, however, was a lot of unused material—the unexamined residuals of my research. Bruce's invitation triggered my interest in who or what I had left behind and why. So I dug out some notes and took a look.

Among the left-behind senators were Pat Moynihan and Bill Cohen. With Moynihan, it was a case of too little and too much exposure. On the one hand, I spent only a day with him on the trail. On the other hand, we had known each other as friends, and we had talked off and on in a variety of contexts over a long period of time. That mixed relationship was sufficiently complex to consign him to permanent research limbo.

My notes do record, however, an instructive part of my one campaign day:

We walked up Fifth Avenue from the Century Club on West 43rd to the Oyster Bar at the Plaza on West 59th. People stopped him all along the way—to wish him well, to tell him his picture hung on their daughter's wall, to ask him to autograph a dictionary, to tell him that although they were AFT [American Federation of Teachers, currently squabbling with him] members, they supported him. All the way up, he stopped to talk—to truck drivers, taxi drivers, a young man wheeling his baby daughter. Met and talked with [newsman] Sander Vanoccor. People patted him as he strode briskly along wearing his Irish walking hat, tipping his hat to the women. "Good afternoon to you, ma'am. It's a wonderful afternoon, isn't it." "He's feeling pretty good," said one man. "He's pretty chipper today," said another. People wanted to take his picture. It was a warm, bright, happy day. He's a known personality.

For him, it was a reassuring stroll, that he had a personal relationship with his constituents, that he was "in touch." "I've gotten through to those people, haven't I," he said at lunch. "They think I'm all right. They are glad I'm there. And they think the Republic is working all right." He stopped himself. "Well, that last synapse may not be correct." For me, the walk up Fifth Avenue was exactly like walking down Main Street with a House member. And it had the same effect on the elected official. The similarity was a clear disincentive for my proposed study of House/Senate differences.

Bill Cohen qualifies as a Senate residual because I had so much more to say about him than I ever said. I had traveled with him earlier and more often and over a longer period of time than with any other senator. I wanted to fit him into my governing-centered case studies, but I couldn't because his policy preoccupation was national defense, intelligence, and foreign affairs and because security reasons kept me from observing so much of his governing activity.

If I had followed up my Phil Hayes experience by studying the media relationship of senators, Cohen would have been Exhibit A. He was a child of the media, which carried him to prominence during Watergate. As a poet and novelist, he lived, as media people did, by the written—as well as the spoken—word. No one with whom I traveled talked more about his media relationships than he did. His ruminations were fascinating; but I found no place for them.

Nor could I find a useful way to include his interesting Maine constituency—small enough yet diverse enough for an outsider to analyze its various political and economic subcultures. Of special interest were what he called Maine's "little industries"—geographically locatable, economically and symbolically crucial, independently minded, yet under severe competitive pressures. As his campaign manager put it, electorally, "The good part [of Bill's support] is that it's diffuse—2 percent for shoes, 2 percent for fishing, 2 percent for blueberries, 2 percent for potatoes, 2 percent for defense. His strength is across the board."

The little industry I followed—beginning with a meeting in Lewiston, Maine, and ending with a meeting in the White House—was the wooden clothespin industry. It provided 500 jobs that kept three small towns alive, and it was being threatened by competition from Chinese imports. "I saved the clothespin industry," Cohen said. "I went to the White House and I almost got down on one knee and kissed the ring. I begged the president to give us three years of [quota] relief and he did." It was, he said, the "only thing I ever got from Reagan." It was a rich case study; and I spent a lot of time on it for six weeks. I wanted the senator and the "little industries" of his constituency to be part of a larger Cohen story—but no larger, governing-centered study ever took shape. So the parts gathered dust.

Other Senate residuals consisted of cases where senators lost their elections before I could take hold of their careers, stopping an emerging research project dead in its tracks. The two main cases were Senator Robert Morgan in North Carolina and Senator Donald Stewart in Alabama. Their defeats were costly for me, and I want to reminisce a little about them.

I traveled with Robert Morgan for four days in his first reelection campaign in 1980—during which time I had begun to develop a picture of him as an "unsenator," as someone who had not learned how to be, or did not want to be, a U.S. senator. He was ambitious, having previously been elected as North Carolina's Attorney General. He had a depth of knowledge about his state's history and a deep emotional attachment to his state—a combination that many senators, I discovered to my surprise, do not have. He was a poor country boy who placed the highest value on old-fashioned hard work, personal humility, and good character. He cared little about material well-being. All of this was exemplary. But he did not act like a modern-day U.S. senator.

He was self-effacing to a fault. He was a team player who willingly made himself hostage to the Democratic Party—a passive partisan who supported President Jimmy Carter through thick and thin on all the hard votes. He had great difficulty engaging in any form of self-advertisement—for himself, his accomplishments, or his votes. He was a public relations flop—and a terrible campaigner. He exercised no discipline or control over his staff, even though he recognized that his campaign was running out of control. He was simply unable to make decisions in the face of the relentlessly negative battering he was absorbing from the Jesse Helms organization on behalf of his opponent, John East. While I was there, candidate Morgan was doing all the things campaigners do—except extolling his own virtues or attacking his opponent. As a politician, he seemed unaggressive, submerged, and confused. In an age of self-propelled candidacies and celebrity politics, he was totally cast against type.

My exemplary Morgan story came from a monster party unity rally at the Charlotte Coliseum where all the statewide candidates, including Morgan, had gotten up to whip up support for the Democratic party ticket and President Carter. The moderator was winding it up when Morgan suddenly stepped up and said, "Let me say something for *me*"—the audience clapped, and he asked for their votes.

When I asked him about this incident, he said,

My mother didn't raise me to be a politician. She taught me never to ask anyone to do anything for you if you couldn't do it yourself. She wouldn't even let us go to the neighbors to borry sugar when we ran out. And she would whup us if we bragged. If you can't ask your friends to help you and if you can't brag on yourself, you aren't going to be successful as a politician. My staff got tired of hearing me talk about the party all the time, so they wrote a speech for me telling people all the things I had done. I gave it twice and stopped. It just didn't feel natural. Besides, you can't do things by yourself. You've got to run with the party. People ask me, "Are you supporting Jimmy Carter?" Of course I'm supporting Jimmy Carter. I can't do it without him anymore than he could do it without me.

His was a campaign that mattered; and he lost it by six-tenths of a percentage point.

When it was over, we talked at length in his Senate office. He was relaxed, gracious, and forthright—and pleased that his self-respect was intact.

I'm not surprised that I lost. . . . It wasn't a catastrophe for me. I do think it was a catastrophe for the state and the country. . . . I don't know what else we could have done. Maybe we could have put on a negative TV campaign attacking him in the last few days. If I had done that, my friends would have said that I had gotten right down on his level. I'm glad I didn't do it. All the newspapers agreed this was the dirtiest, most unfair campaign in the history of the state. All of them praised my campaign. I feel good about that.

"The president called me," he went on, "and told me that he had told his staff that if he had the power to reverse one result in the election, the one he would have chosen was mine. Then he started to take the blame on himself for my defeat—[but] I stopped him. 'Mr. President,' I said. 'I voted for your proposals because I believed in them.'"

During the campaign, Morgan had gone out of his way to show me the office he had occupied when he was Attorney General. And he had said, "I should be back there. They were the most enjoyable years I ever spent. If I could arrange it so it would work, I would exchange with the present occupant." And indeed, on a plane ride, I heard him actually propose such a swap—in jest—to Attorney General Rufus Edmisten. So I asked him during our postmortem talk, "Will you miss the Senate?" "No," he said. "I never liked the job. It has its compensations, but I never liked the job." Any persuasive description of Morgan as a senatorial misfit, about the what, the why, and the so-what of this "un-senator," required, of course, that he win reelection and that I watch him in Washington. He didn't; so I couldn't; and my idea, intriguing though it was—that not all senators are cut out for the modern-day Senate—went nowhere.

Another unexamined residual was Democrat Donald Stewart of Alabama. He became a target of opportunity when I was contemplating House/Senate comparisons because he had been elected to fill the last two years of an unexpired term: that is, he was a U.S. senator with a House member's term of office. I could vary the office but hold length of term constant. Alabama Senator Jim Allen had died; his wife had been appointed till the next election; Stewart, a state senator, had challenged her and won; and he had served for two years. He had, indeed, acted like a new House member—working his tail off, coming home every weekend for two years, and breaking a record by visiting all 165 counties.

When I arrived, he was running hard for the full six-year term, but he had three opponents—one named Stewart—in the Democratic primary. Obviously, he was thought to be vulnerable—and he was. He ran far ahead in the primary, but failed by 1.4 percent to win a majority. And he subsequently lost in the runoff primary. So all he ever got was a House member's term! He was very bright and very hard working, attributes that are often necessary but never sufficient.

The story I wanted to write would have explained his vulnerability by emphasizing the insufficiency of the two-year time period for a relative unknown to negotiate support in a statewide constituency of four and a half million people. When he came under attack in the primary, he had developed no cushion of support—much less trust—available to him. A part of that problem was his own inexperience, overconfidence, and miscalculations. He conducted his primary campaign against his prospective general election opponent instead of his primary opponent—and he picked on the wrong general election opponent to boot. In his meteoric political career—one term in the Alabama House, one term in the Alabama Senate, and two years in the U.S. Senate, he had left behind a reputation for arrogance–a young man in too big a hurry—that he himself either could not recognize or could not change.

My exemplary Stewart story is *his* account of his relationship as a freshman member of the Alabama House with his own state senator—the man he had succeeded in the House—whom we will call Fred. "I was fighting against a loan company bill in the House," Stewart said,

> because I didn't think higher interest rates would be of help to the people. Fred had pushed for it very hard in the Senate and it had passed there. You can't filibuster in the House, but I was proposing a lot of amendments. I ended up with 11 votes on the final vote. I had really gotten my butt kicked. And I had almost been censured. They couldn't censure me, but they kept declaring all my amendments out of order. I had been humiliated. I was feeling an inch high. That's when Fred came over to me and said, "Tell me, how's the 'people's man' doing now?" I don't know why he did that to me. We had been friends. I had worked for him, organized his campaign for him the first time he ran for the House. But there I was. I literally could not get anyone to go to the bar with me and have a drink afterward. I had thought that someone would have stood up with me, but no one did. So I went home that night feeling low. My belly was dragging on the ground. My wife asked me, "How did it go today?" I told her, "I got my butt whipped today," and I told her what Fred had said, "How's the people's man doing now?" She said, "Hang in there." I said to her, "I've made one decision today. I've done one positive thing. I've decided to run against Fred and take that seat away from him." I trailed that a——— for the next six months. And I whipped his butt. I got 67 percent of the vote. I carried every box and beat him with more than two-thirds of the vote. I wanted to ask him how he thought "the people's man" was doing now. But I didn't have to. The people had given their answer.

In self-confidence, aggressiveness, and hardball politics, Donald Stewart was at the far end of the scale from Robert Morgan.

There was also an interesting contextual factor that I perceived but could not fathom in my five days with Donald Stewart—and that was an Alabama populist subculture in which a standard and punishing political argument was that one's opponent was beholden to special interests and was, or would become, part of the Washington crowd and had lost, or would lose, touch with the home folks. Stewart had used it in his winning election; his opponents used it against him in his losing election. It was partly because of this intriguing contextual factor and partly because I just couldn't write off my initial investment that I decided to go back to Alabama and hang out with the Democrat who had defeated Stewart in the primary.

He was Jim Folsom, a Public Service commissioner and son of a famous Alabama governor, "Big Jim" Folsom. I spent three days on the trail with "Little Jim." But he, too, lost—in the general election. So I never got to think further about an Alabama subculture and its effect on governing. Thus, my two-part adventure in Alabama has sat in a pretty large, but very dead, file.

Two postscripts. Jim Folsom's defeat was as crushing a research blow as I have ever suffered. He was an engaging, storytelling, guitar-playing, seat-of-the-pants, country-shrewd, friends-and-neighbors, little guy–populist politician who was ignorant of and unconcerned with national issues, who fairly clung for advice and support to his extended family, and who was scared to death of the media. I cannot tell you how I salivated at the prospect of following Little Jim into the U.S. Senate. Even thinking, now, of that lost opportunity, makes me drool and weep—just imagining Mayberry RFD in the Senate.

As for Donald Stewart, his story did have a large component of self-destruction. And its effects on him personally were unmatched by any of my other Senate cases. Because I was surprised by the results of his initial primary, and because political science research told me that the front runner often loses in the runoff, I went back to Alabama on the eve of the runoff primary. I helped put up decorations for the election night party, and I planned to talk with him about it afterward. But the defeated and shell-shocked candidate disappeared and, much to the displeasure of his supporters gathered there, never even made an appearance at the party that evening. Nor was he anywhere to be found the next day. So when I went to D.C. in November to talk with my other 1980 incumbent losers, I made an appointment to talk with him.

When I went to his Senate office at the appointed hour, his secretary told me he'd be with me in "a few minutes." After a half-hour, she went into his office, came out, and told me, "He just isn't ready." A half-hour later, she went in, again, came out, and said, "He doesn't think he can talk about it. But wait." By that time, his wife—who had been very friendly in Alabama—had come to the office. "He's having a very hard time with things right now," she said. His secretary went in to his office a third time, came out, and said, "I'm sorry, he just can't talk about it with you." And he stayed holed up in his office till I left. His wife suggested, "Why don't you write to him in a couple of months and come down to Alabama and talk there." I said I would. I wrote to him twice—no answer.

Ten years later, I had a chance to chat with a prominent Alabama Democrat. "What's Donald Stewart up to," I asked. "I guess he's still around in Alabama," the man said, "probably practicing some law. But I *never* see him." Donald Stewart, perhaps, has remained deeply affected by what had been for him an unexpected and unexplainable end to a meteoric political career.

Why his response to defeat should have been so completely different from that of Robert Morgan would be a matter for psychological speculation—and that is not my field. In my postmortem with Morgan, he had said to me, "I called Donald after his defeat, and they told me he had gone off somewhere by himself. I thought that was strange. If I had lost, I would want to be with my friends." Which takes me to a point where political science gets off; and I do too. Taken together, however, the two cases remind me of a generalization attributed to Speaker John McCormack that "members of Congress are often elected by accident but are seldom reelected by accident." That is to say, U.S. senators can be accidents. Maybe I had chosen two of them.

As you can see, I've enjoyed this chance to reflect informally on some unreported aspects of a doomed Senate research saga. As you can see, too, I've left the field absolutely untouched! I have offered no generalizations; I have preempted nobody's research. And I tender absolutely no advice, except this: that you savor the opportunity to do research within a scholarly community that has always been remarkably collegial and productive and has, for that reason, been a lot of fun. That said, I will lift the hold and end the filibuster. Thanks for listening.

Note

1. John Pierson, "A Freshman Lawmaker Finds Few of His Ideas Get through Congress," *Wall Street Journal,* June 17, 1975.

Senate Elections

▪ 3 ▪

Party Realignment, Ideological Polarization, and Voting Behavior in U.S. Senate Elections

Alan I. Abramowitz

The U.S. Senate today is a very different body from the Senate of the 1960s and 1970s. The Senate today is much more sharply divided along partisan and ideological lines than it was twenty or thirty years ago. Party line votes occur more frequently, and party cohesion is much greater. Regional divisions within the parties are much less prominent. There are fewer moderates in both parties, and cross-party coalitions are less common. As a result, it is more difficult to forge compromises on controversial legislative issues (Owens 1998).

The central argument of this chapter is that these changes in the makeup and decision-making processes of the Senate, along with parallel changes in Senate campaigns, have had important consequences for voting behavior in Senate elections. I will argue that an ideological realignment of the parties within the Senate and the growing salience of national issues and ideology in Senate campaigns have significantly increased the influence of ideology and presidential evaluations on voter decision making. As a result, the parties' electoral coalitions have themselves become more socially distinctive and ideologically polarized since the 1970s, thus reinforcing the partisan and ideological divisions within the chamber.

Ideological Realignment in the Senate

The growing influence of party leaders and organizations and the increase in party voting in both the House and Senate since the 1970s have been amply documented by David Rohde and other congressional scholars (Rohde 1991; Cox and McCubbins 1993; Smith 1993; Sinclair 1995; Foley and Owens 1996; Dodd and Oppenheimer 1997; Owens 1998). I will briefly summarize the evidence concerning changes in the makeup and decision-making processes of the Senate in this section.

The 1990s witnessed a substantial increase in both the frequency of party line votes and party cohesion in the Senate. Between 1990 and 1998, an average of 57 percent of all Senate roll call votes produced party divisions—votes in which a majority of Democrats opposed a majority of Republicans. In contrast the average proportion of party divisions in the Senate was only 44 percent during the 1980s, 42 percent during the 1970s, 42 percent during the 1960s, and 43 percent during the 1950s. In 1995, following the Republican takeover of the House and Senate, 69 percent of Senate roll call votes produced party divisions, the highest proportion of party divisions since Congressional Quarterly had begun compiling statistics on congressional roll call votes in the early 1950s (Ornstein, Mann, and Malbin 2000, 201).

Just as impressive as the increase in the frequency of party divisions has been the increase in party cohesion on roll call votes. The proportion of Senate Republicans voting with their own party on party divisions averaged 85 percent during the 1990s, compared with 79 percent during the 1980s, 72 percent during the 1970s, and 76 percent during the 1960s. The average party unity score for Senate Democrats was also 85 percent during the 1990s, compared with 78 percent during the 1980s, 74 percent during the 1970s, and 75 percent during the 1960s. Party unity scores reached record levels in the four years following the Republican takeover of Congress in 1994, with Senate Democrats averaging 87 percent and Senate Republicans averaging 90 percent (Ornstein et al. 2000, 202–3).

Increases in both the frequency of party divisions and party cohesion reflected an ideological realignment within the congressional parties during the 1980s and 1990s. During the 1960s and early 1970s, the membership of the Senate included a substantial number of Democrats and Republicans whose positions were far out of line with the dominant ideology of their own party. Conservative Democrats, mainly but not exclusively from the South, still composed a substantial proportion of the Democratic caucus and often held key committee chairmanships. Liberal Republicans, mainly from the Northeast, formed a smaller but still influential bloc within the GOP. By the 1990s, however, very few conservative Democrats or liberal Republicans remained in the Senate. In fact, very few moderate Democrats or Republicans remained in the Senate (Cohen 2000).

We can use the ratings given to senators by the liberal Americans for Democratic Action (ADA) to compare the ideologies of Senate Democrats and Republicans in 1972 with the ideologies of Senate Democrats and Republicans in 1998. In 1972, the average ADA rating for Senate Democrats was 55, while the average rating for Senate Republicans was 23. In 1998, the average ADA rating for Senate Democrats was 88, while the average rating for Senate Republicans was 9. In 1972, twenty-one Democrats received ADA ratings below 50, and five Democrats—John Stennis and James Eastland of Mississippi, John Spark-man and James Allen of Alabama, Herman Talmadge of Georgia, and John Mc-Clellan of Arkansas—received ADA ratings of 10 or below. At the same time, eleven Senate Republicans received ADA ratings of 40 or higher, and three Republicans—Clifford Case of New Jersey, Jacob Javits of New York, and Edward Brooke of Massachusetts—received ADA ratings of 80 (Barone, Ujifusa, and Matthews 1973). In 1998, not a single Democrat received a rating below 50, and only four Republicans received a rating of 40 or higher. The most liberal Republican in the Senate, James Jeffords of Vermont, received a rating of 55, while the most conservative Democrat in the Senate, Ernest Hollings of South Carolina, received an identical rating of 55 (Barone and Ujifusa 1999).

Changes in Senate Campaigns

Recent changes in Senate campaigns have reinforced the effects of ideological realignment within the Senate. During the 1990s, several major developments in campaign finance, including the rise of soft money, the growing involvement of state and national party organizations in congressional campaigns, and issue advertising, have increased the salience of ideology and national issues in Senate campaigns. Soft money—contributions to party organizations that are not restricted by current campaign laws—has increased dramatically since 1992, and this has allowed party organizations to play a much larger role in supplementing campaign spending by individual House and Senate candidates (Sorauf 1998). Soft money expenditures are supposed to allow party organizations to engage in "party-building activities" such as registration and get-out-the-vote drives. In fact, however, much of this money has been spent on television ads attacking the opposition party's record and positions.

Since 1992 there has also been a dramatic increase in spending on issue advertising by interest groups and political parties. Issue advocacy campaigns avoid contribution limits and disclosure requirements by not explicitly recommending a vote for or against a specific candidate. However, while not endorsing or opposing a specific candidate, these issue ads are usually highly critical of the voting record or issue positions of one of the candidates in the race (Ornstein 1997; Sorauf 1998). Like soft money expenditures, issue advocacy campaigns by interest groups and parties probably serve to increase the salience of ideology and national issues in House and Senate campaigns.

Hypotheses: Consequences of Ideological Realignment for Voting Behavior in Senate Elections

In this chapter, I will test four major hypotheses concerning the consequences of ideological realignment for voting behavior in Senate elections:

1. *Social Divergence.* I expect the social characteristics of Democratic and Republican voters to become more distinctive over time, especially after 1992, as groups with liberal policy preferences align themselves with the Democratic party and groups with conservative preferences align themselves with the Republican party.

2. *Ideological Divergence.* I expect the ideologies of Democratic and Republican voters to become more distinctive over time, especially after 1992, with Democrats becoming more liberal and Republicans becoming more conservative.

3. *Ideological Voting.* After controlling for party identification, incumbency, and presidential performance evaluations, I expect to find an increase in the influence of ideology on voter decision making in Senate elections since the 1970s, and especially since the election of Bill Clinton in 1992.

4. *Presidential Performance Voting.* After controlling for party identification, incumbency, and ideology, I expect to find an increase in the influence of presidential performance evaluations on voter decision making in Senate elections since the 1970s, and especially since the election of Bill Clinton in 1992.

I expect to find similar but weaker trends in House elections. Many of the forces affecting Senate elections since the 1980s have also affected House elections. The House, like the Senate, has seen an increase in ideological polarization between the parties as liberal Republicans and conservative Democrats have gradually disappeared (Rohde 1991). At the same time, the national parties and organized interest groups have become increasingly involved in House campaigns. The major difference between Senate and House elections, however, is that these trends have mainly affected the small minority of House races that are truly competitive. The large majority of House races remain uncompetitive, with only a small minority of incumbents facing serious, well-financed challengers. In these uncompetitive contests, voters may learn little or nothing about national issues. As a result, I would not expect either ideology or national issues to have as strong an influence on voting decisions in House elections as in Senate elections.

Data and Measures

Data for this chapter came from the American National Election Studies Cumulative Data File. This data set consisted of selected variables from the 1948 through 1996 American National Election Studies (NES). For this study, however, the main focus was on the years 1972 through 1996, for which measures of ideology and presidential performance were available.

The dependent variables used in this chapter were the party direction of the vote for U.S. Senate and House of Representatives. Only major party voters were included in this measure. Independent variables included ideological identification, presidential job evaluation, and incumbency status. Ideological identification was measured by a 7-point scale ranging from extremely liberal to extremely conservative. Respondents who could not place themselves on this scale were excluded from the analysis. Presidential job evaluation was measured by a question asking respondents whether they approved or disapproved of the president's performance. I used the dichotomous approve-disapprove measure because the 4-point approval scale was not available until 1980. Finally, incumbency status was measured by a 3-point scale on the basis of whether a House or Senate race included a Democratic incumbent, no incumbent, or a Republican incumbent. Unfortunately, the incumbency status variable was not provided by the NES for Senate races before 1978. In addition to these measures of voting behavior and political attitudes, I included a variety of social characteristics in my analysis of the party coalitions, including gender, race (white vs. African American), religious affiliation (Protestant, Roman Catholic, or Jewish), family income (measured in quintiles), union membership, and region (South vs. North).

In analyzing change over time, I chose to use the presidential administration, rather than the individual election or the decade, as the unit of analysis. The time period of this study included the Eisenhower (1956–60), Kennedy-Johnson (1962–68), Nixon-Ford (1970–76), Carter (1978–80), Reagan-Bush (1982–92) and Clinton (1994–96) administrations. Presidential administrations are more politically meaningful time divisions than decades—significant changes in American politics often coincide with changes in party control of the White House. Combining data from all of the elections during an administration makes it easier to separate long-term trends from short-term fluctuations in electoral behavior.

Trends in Party Support

Figure 3.1 shows the trend in the Republican share of the national popular vote in U.S. Senate elections from the Eisenhower administration through the Clinton administration. The election of Bill Clinton as president turned out to be a major boon to the Republican Party in the Senate. Even though Republicans were able to maintain control of the Senate from 1981 until 1987, GOP candidates received only 45 percent of the national popular vote in Senate elections during the Reagan-Bush years. In the two elections following the election of Bill Clinton, however, Republican Senate candidates received an average of 52 percent of the national popular vote in Senate elections—their best showing since the Eisenhower administration.

According to the social divergence hypothesis, Republican gains in Senate

FIGURE 3.1. Trend in Republican Proportion of U.S. Senate Vote

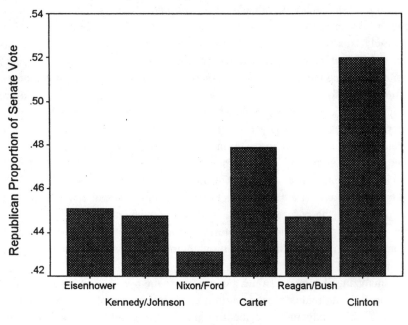

elections since 1992 should be greatest among social groups with conservative policy preferences and limited or nonexistent among social groups with liberal policy preferences. To test this hypothesis, Table 3.1 displays the trend in the Democratic percentage of the vote for U.S. Senate among African Americans and several subgroups of white voters that are generally considered to hold relatively liberal or conservative policy preferences. The more conservative white subgroups include males, upper-income voters, southerners, and Protestants. The more liberal white subgroups include females, lower-income voters, union members, and Jews.

The data in Table 3.1 are generally consistent with the social divergence hypothesis. Among whites, the most dramatic Republican gains in Senate voting since 1992 have occurred among males, upper-income voters, southerners, and Protestants. In contrast, Republicans have made smaller gains or lost ground among women, lower-income voters, union members, and Jews. As a result, the social characteristics of Democratic and Republican voters have become somewhat more distinctive since 1992. For example, the gender gap among whites increased from 4 points during the Reagan-Bush years to 12 points during the Clinton years, while the gap between lower and upper income voters increased

TABLE 3.1. Trend in Percentage Voting Democratic for U.S. Senate among African Americans and White Demographic Groups

Demographic Group	Administration				
	Ike-JFK-LBJ	Nixon-Ford	Carter	Reagan-Bush	Clinton
African Americans	82	90	82	89	80
All whites	53	53	49	51	45
Gender					
Female	52	54	46	53	51
Male	53	52	53	49	39
Income					
Lower	53	58	61	58	60
Upper	50	49	46	46	36
Labor Union					
Members	63	63	61	61	60
Nonmembers	49	50	45	48	42
Region					
North	49	51	52	51	47
South	74	60	43	60	42
Religion					
Jewish	74	75	76	78	86
Catholic	67	60	54	57	54
Protestant	46	48	45	46	38

Source: American National Election Studies, 1952–96.

Note: Based on major party voters. Income categories based on upper two quintiles and lower two quintiles.

from 12 points during the Reagan-Bush years to 24 points during the Clinton years.

The most dramatic change in Senate voting, however, involved the behavior of southern whites. During the Reagan-Bush years, Democratic Senate candidates received an average of 60 percent of the vote among southern whites. Since 1992, however, Democratic candidates have averaged only 42 percent of the vote among southern whites. As a result, there has been a reversal of the traditional regional bases of the parties—southern whites have gone from 9 points more Democratic than northern whites during the Reagan-Bush years to 5 points more Republican than northern whites during the Clinton years.

The only group in Table 3.1 whose behavior seems to conflict with the social divergence hypothesis is African American voters. Despite their generally liberal policy preferences, African Americans were slightly less likely to vote for Democratic Senate candidates during the Clinton years than during the Reagan-Bush years. Nevertheless, African Americans remained more loyal to the Democratic Party than any other major social group. The slight dip in Democratic voting among African Americans after 1992 may reflect the declining salience of racial issues in American politics, or it may be due to chance factors—the 1994 and 1996 samples included a total of only 123 African Americans who voted in a Senate election.

A more direct test of the ideological realignment theory involves looking at trends in the ideological composition of the party coalitions. Table 3.2 displays trends in the size of each major ideological group (liberals, moderates, and conservatives), the Republican share of the vote in each group, and the contribution of each group to the Democratic and Republican electoral coalition in Senate elections. The contribution of a group to a party's electoral coalition is simply the proportion of the party's voters who belong to that group. For example, during the Nixon-Ford years, liberals made up 15 percent of the Republican coalition and 35 percent of the Democratic coalition, moderates made up 36 percent of the Republican coalition and 38 percent of the Democratic coalition, and

TABLE 3.2. Contributions to Republican and Democratic Coalitions by Ideological Groups in U.S. Senate Elections

Ideological Group	Administration	Size of Group	Republican Percentage	Contribution to Rep	Contribution to Dem
Liberals	Nixon-Ford	25	20	15	35
	Carter	23	27	12	33
	Reagan-Bush	25	23	13	36
	Clinton	20	13	6	39
Moderates	Nixon-Ford	37	46	36	38
	Carter	31	46	28	33
	Reagan-Bush	32	40	28	36
	Clinton	27	42	20	35
Conservatives	Nixon-Ford	38	61	49	28
	Carter	47	63	60	34
	Reagan-Bush	43	66	60	28
	Clinton	53	78	75	26

Source: American National Election Studies, 1972–96.

Note: All percentages are based on voters placing themselves on the liberal-conservative scale. Liberal = 1–3, Moderate = 4, Conservative = 5–7. Contribution of Group to Party Coalition = (Size of Group x Party % of Group Vote)/Party % of Total Vote.

conservatives made up 49 percent of the Republican coalition and 28 percent of the Democratic coalition.

The data in Table 3.2 show that there was a substantial increase in both the size of the conservative voting bloc and the Republican share of the conservative vote between the 1970s and the 1990s. Conservative identifiers made up only 38 percent of all voters in Senate elections during the Nixon-Ford years. By the Clinton administration, however, conservative identifiers composed 53 percent of the entire Senate electorate. Republican candidates received only 61 percent of the conservative vote during the Nixon-Ford years. By the Clinton administration, however, Republican candidates were winning 78 percent of the conservative vote.

While the conservative voting bloc was growing and becoming increasingly Republican, the liberal bloc was shrinking and becoming increasingly Democratic. Between the Nixon-Ford years and the Clinton years, the proportion of liberal identifiers in the Senate electorate fell from 25 percent to 20 percent, while the Republican share of the liberal vote declined from 26 percent to only 13 percent.

The net result of these changes was a dramatic increase in ideological polarization between the Democratic and Republican electorates due primarily to the increasing conservatism of Republican voters. During the Nixon-Ford years, 51 percent of Republican Senate voters were moderates or liberals, and only 49 percent were conservatives. By the Clinton years, only 25 percent of Republican Senate voters were moderates or liberals, and 75 percent were conservatives.

The increasing ideological polarization of the Democratic and Republican electorates over time is shown very clearly in Figure 3.2. This figure displays the mean location of Democratic and Republican Senate voters on the 7-point liberal-conservative scale between 1972 and 1996. Over this period, the ideological distance between the Democratic and Republican electorates tripled in size—growing from approximately 0.5 points in 1972 to approximately 1.5 points in 1994 and 1996.

Explaining Vote Choice

The increasing ideological polarization of the Democratic and Republican electorates is consistent with the ideological realignment theory. However, to determine whether ideology and presidential evaluations have become more important factors in voter decision making, it is necessary to control for other potential influences on the vote, such as party identification and incumbency. In this section, I test the following model of vote choice in Senate and House elections:

FIGURE 3.2. Average Ideological Position of Republican and Democratic Voters in U.S. Senate Elections, 1972–1996

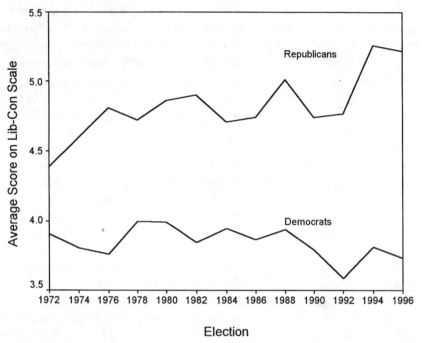

Election

$$V = b_1*PID + b_2*INC + b_3*JOB + b_4*IDEO + e,$$

where V represents the party direction of the vote, PID represents party identification, INC represents the incumbency status of the race, JOB represents evaluation (approval vs. disapproval) of the president's job performance, IDEO represents ideological identification, and e is an error term. This model will be estimated for Senate and House elections, using data on the Carter (1978–80), Reagan-Bush (1982–92), and Clinton (1994–96) administrations.[1]

Table 3.3 presents data on the zero-order correlations between each of our independent variables and vote choice in Senate and House elections over time. The results are consistent with the ideological realignment theory. The correlation between ideology and vote choice increased dramatically between the Reagan-Bush administration and the Clinton administration, going from .42 to .59 in Senate elections and from .38 to .51 in House elections. At the same time, the correlation between presidential evaluation and vote choice rose from .42 to .54 in Senate elections and from .37 to .47 in House elections. These results suggest that both ideology and presidential evaluations were becoming more influential factors in voter decision making. However, a more definitive test of the ideological realignment theory requires a multivariate analysis of vote choice.

TABLE 3.3. Correlations between Vote and Independent Variables by Administration

Independent Variable	Administration	Senate Vote	House Vote
Ideology	Nixon-Ford	.328	.298
	Carter	.330	.296
	Reagan-Bush	.418	.385
	Clinton	.588	.509
Presidential Job	Nixon-Ford	−299	-.360
Evaluation	Carter	.266	.231
	Reagan-Bush	−424	-.374
	Clinton	.536	.467
Party	Eisenhower-Kennedy	.755	.747
Identification	Nixon-Ford	.610	.627
	Carter	.610	.534
	Reagan-Bush	.627	.594
	Clinton	.715	.712
Party of	Eisenhower-Kennedy	NA	.324
Incumbent	Nixon-Ford	NA	.324
	Carter	.181	.499
	Reagan-Bush	.232	.468
	Clinton	.125	.397

Source: American National Election Studies, 1952–96.

Note: Dependent variable is party direction of vote. Incumbency variable not available for Senate elections before 1978. Correlation coefficient is Kendall's tau-c. All coefficients significant at .001 level based on one-tailed t test.

Tables 3.4 and 3.5 present the results of logistic regression analyses of vote choice in Senate and House elections during the Carter, Reagan-Bush, and Clinton administrations. Our independent variables are ideology, presidential approval, party identification, and incumbency status. Once again, the results are consistent with the ideological realignment theory. The influence of ideology on Senate voting decisions increased dramatically during this time period—the coefficient for the ideology variable in the Senate vote equation increased by 65 percent between the Clinton administration and the Reagan-Bush administration and then doubled between the Reagan-Bush administration and the Clinton administration. These results indicate that ideology was a relatively minor factor in Senate voting during the 1970s but had become a major influence by the mid-1990s. During this same period, the influence of ideology on House voting decisions rose much more modestly. The coefficient for the ideology variable in the House vote equation increased by 10 percent between the Clinton administration and the Reagan-Bush administration and by 25 percent between the Reagan-

41

TABLE 3.4. Logistic Regression Analyses of Senate Voting Decisions by Administration

Independent Variable	Carter B	(SE)	Reagan-Bush B	(SE)	Clinton B	(SE)
Party Identification	.603	(.051)***	.524	(.027)***	.510	(.048)***
Ideology	.134	(.070)*	.222	(.040)***	.447	(.075)***
Presidential Job Evaluation	.441	(.187)**	−.940	(.108)***	1.095	(.189)***
Incumbency	.276	(.056)***	.366	(.027)***	.279	(.052)***
Constant	−4.430		-2.966		−6.281	

Source: American National Election Studies, 1978–96.

Note: Dependent variable is party direction of vote. Significance levels based on one-tailed *t* test.
*p < .05; **p < .01; ***p < .001.

TABLE 3.5. Logistic Regression Analyses of House Voting Decisions by Administration

Independent Variable	Carter B	(SE)	Reagan-Bush B	(SE)	Clinton B	(SE)
Party Identification	.565	(.048)***	.511	(.025)***	.655	(.047)***
Ideology	.245	(.066)***	.269	(.037)***	.336	(.068)***
Presidential Job Evaluation	.262	(.169)	−.767	(.103)***	.798	(.178)***
Incumbency	.702	(.048)***	.620	(.026)***	.603	(.046)***
Constant	−5.552		−3.965		−6.715	

Source: American National Election Studies, 1978–96.

Note: Dependent variable is party direction of vote. Significance levels based on one-tailed *t* test.
***p < .001.

Bush administration and the Clinton administration. These results indicate that during the Clinton years, ideology was a significant influence on voting in House elections but was less important than in Senate elections.

The data in Tables 3.4 and 3.5 show that presidential performance became a more important factor in Senate and House voting during the time period covered by the table. However, the largest increase in the influence of presidential evaluations occurred between the Carter administration and the Reagan-Bush administration. The impact of presidential evaluations increased only modestly between the Reagan-Bush administration and the Clinton administration. Nevertheless, these results indicate that presidential evaluations had a strong influence on voter decision making in both Senate and House elections during the Clinton years. As expected, the impact of presidential evaluations was stronger in Senate elections than in House elections throughout the period under examination. Moreover, the magnitude of this difference increased over time, with the largest difference occurring during the Clinton years.

Discussion and Conclusions: Conditional Party Government and the Electoral Environment

The findings presented in this chapter support the argument that an ideological realignment within the Senate since the 1960s and the growing salience of ideology and national issues in Senate campaigns have caused significant changes in the behavior of voters in Senate elections. Ideology and evaluations of presidential performance have become more important factors in voter decision making, especially since 1992. Although similar trends were evident in House elections, the effects of ideology and presidential evaluations on House voting were weaker and increased less dramatically during the 1990s. The continuing absence of meaningful competition in the large majority of House races may serve to limit the influence of ideology and national issues on voter decision making.

As a result of the growing influence of ideology and presidential evaluations on Senate voting, the Democratic and Republican electoral coalitions have become more socially and ideologically distinctive, thus reinforcing the partisan and ideological divisions within the chamber. There is much less overlap between the reelection constituencies of Democratic and Republican senators now than there was during the 1960s and 1970s. The reelection constituency of the average Democratic senator today, regardless of region, is disproportionately nonwhite, poor, female, and moderate to liberal in ideology; the reelection constituency of the average Republican senator today, regardless of region, is disproportionately white, affluent, male, and conservative in ideology.

Scholars have long described party and constituency as the most important forces influencing the behavior of members of the House and Senate. The traditionally low level of party cohesion in Congress has been explained largely by the frequency with which members perceive conflicts between their constituents' views or interests and the positions taken by their party's leaders. Since 1992, however, such conflicts have become less frequent due to the increased social and ideological homogeneity of each party's reelection constituency. Today's senators are much more likely to perceive party and constituency pressures as reinforcing each other rather than conflicting.

43

The findings presented in this chapter indicate that some previous explanations of conditional party government in Congress require modification. Cox and McCubbins (1993), Sinclair (1995), Foley and Owens (1996), and Dodd and Oppenheimer (1997) have emphasized internal explanations for the development of conditional party government during the 1980s and 1990s. According to these scholars, the increase in party voting and cohesion in the Congress reflected the growing internal homogeneity of the parties and the emergence of activist leaders who took advantage of the new internal environment by building strong party organizations. However, the findings presented in this chapter suggest that to understand the development of conditional party government in the 1990s, one must also consider changes in the electoral environment of Congress. The most important such change was the growing social and ideological division between the reelection constituencies of the two parties—a division that reflected the increasing influence of ideology and presidential evaluations on voter decision making.

Note

1. Data on the incumbency status of Senate races were not provided by the NES for elections before 1978, and the ideological identification question was not asked before 1972.

• 4 •

Ideological Portrayals during
U.S. Senate Campaigns

Kim Fridkin Kahn and Patrick J. Kenney

In the fall of 1992, as Bill Clinton's campaign appeared poised to defeat incumbent President George Bush, Senator Bob Dole, Clinton's eventual challenger in 1996, was easily reelected to the U.S. Senate in Kansas. By 1992, Dole had become a highly visible conservative Republican senator, not just in Kansas, but across the nation. He was first elected to the U.S. House of Representatives in 1960 and subsequently elected to the U.S. Senate in 1968. He cast many ardently conservative votes in the Senate in the late 1980s and early 1990s. His Americans for Democratic Action (ADA) scores were always under 10, sometimes reaching 0. Across this time period, few Republican senators were consistently as conservative as Bob Dole. His philosophy guided his actions in the U.S. Senate and was an excellent predictor of how he voted.

Yet he did not talk about his ideological beliefs during his reelection bid in 1992. He failed to mention that his staunchly conservative beliefs would guide his decisions in the future. Instead, his main campaign themes stressed his personal characteristics. He touted his experience in politics, he emphasized his leadership in the Senate. Most of all, he reminded Kansans that for years he had been "in touch" with their worries and that he always "got the job done." The only significant policy discussion during the campaign was about agriculture. This was hardly surprising, since the well-being of most Kansans is tied to agriculture, wheat mostly, in one way or another.

Dole's main message, "care for the state," was quite evident in the press coverage of the 1992 campaign.[1] In the *Wichita Eagle,* the largest circulating newspaper in the state, Dole's efforts were evident in headlines during the fall. For example, on September 12, 1992, the *Eagle* reported, "Russell Gets $1.5 Million

45

Grant to Develop New Industrial Park." Russell, of course, is Dole's hometown. Other examples included headlines on September 14, "Dole's Hometown Chosen for Wheat-Processing Plant"; on September 18, "Senate Panel OKs Military Work for Wichita Planemakers"; and on October 15, "Bob Dole's Continued Services Are Great for This Nation and This State."

While Dole's work for the state received ample coverage, Dole's ideological views were barely mentioned. The word *conservative* was mentioned in only three articles from Labor Day to Election Day in the press. On September 26, on October 4, and on November 4, the *Eagle* referred to Dole as a "fiscal conservative." In each article the phrase was used to describe Dole's tireless efforts at balancing the federal budget.

His opponent, Gloria O'Dell, lacking resources, political skills, and campaign experience, ran a lackluster campaign. She spent a mere $250,000 to unseat Dole. Her message, although not presented in commercials or by the press, focused primarily on Dole's largesse as a Washington insider. She stressed Dole's rides on corporate jets, his support for senatorial pay raises, and his excesses in terms of raising PAC money. She chose not to emphasize Dole's conservative philosophy during her campaign.

In the end, of course, Bob Dole was returned to the Senate. His voting record remained the same after his successful reelection campaign. His ADA score in 1993 was 10 and his score in 1994 was 0. Dole's 1992 campaign was not unusual for an incumbent U.S. senator. Senators, at least on the campaign trail, rarely utter the words *liberal* or *conservative* when delivering their campaign messages. In fact, an analysis of senatorial elections between 1988 and 1992 revealed that these terms were virtually absent from the lexicon of contemporary U.S. Senate campaigns. A content analysis of 266 advertisements produced by seventy of the eighty incumbents seeking reelection during this period revealed that the words *liberal* and *conservative* were mentioned in less than 1 percent of the senators' political commercials. And interviews with incumbents' campaign managers indicated that none of the managers mentioned ideology as a "main theme" of their campaigns. Not one.

Yet 80 percent of constituents, at least those interviewed by the National Election Study/Senate Election Study (NES/SES), placed incumbents on the traditional 7-point liberal-conservative continuum during the same time period. And, quite remarkably, a full 48 percent were approximately correct in the placement of their senators as judged against senators' ADA scores.[2] In addition, scholars examining voters' decision rules in senatorial elections routinely find that ideological compatibility between voters and incumbents is an important predictor of vote choice (Abramowitz 1980, 1988; Abramowitz and Segal 1992; Kahn and Kenney 1997; Krasno 1994; Westlye 1991; Wright and Berkman 1986).

The acumen of voters, in terms of incumbents' ideologies, is puzzling considering the dearth of ideological discussion by candidates. On what basis do voters arrive at their judgments? Where do they acquire their information? The answers to these questions are the focus of this chapter. We explore several factors that may affect voters' awareness of their senators' ideological views.

First, the press may invoke ideological talk to fill the void left by senators. This discussion may eventually find its way to citizens. Second, voters may infer ideological positioning of incumbents from discussions of policy matters by the candidates, or the press, or both. Third, the campaign environment itself may cause citizens to take notice of political discourse and develop ideological impressions of their incumbent senators. Intense campaigns, characterized by a steady stream of press coverage, ample candidate activity, and polls, suggesting a horse race, motivate citizens to watch, listen, and absorb political messages. Such a campaign setting may encourage citizens to draw conclusions about their senators' ideological views.

While we are interested in examining how campaigns affect voters' understanding of their senators' ideological profiles, we need to take into account preexisting information citizens may hold about senators. For example, it is important to consider the seniority of the senator, since the length of service of some senators may make their ideological proclivities familiar to many constituents. In addition, citizens differ dramatically in their understanding of politics, and citizens who follow politics closely will have little difficulty placing their senators on ideological scales.

It is exciting to explore the possibility that campaigns—via the news media and the candidates—disseminate relevant and useful information that informs potential voters. Campaigns have a distinct educative function in large-scale representative democracies. For most constituents, they are the only link of communication between representatives and the represented. It is vital to examine this link to better understand what information girds the ties between politicians and the mass public. For students of representation, campaigns allow us to investigate whether the messages disseminated by representatives are assimilated and accepted by citizens.

An examination of the informational role of U.S. Senate campaigns may be more fruitful than an exploration of U.S. House races. Compared to U.S. House races, Senate races often are more competitive, generate more news attention, and attract more qualified challengers (Clarke and Evans 1983; Goldenberg and Traugott 1984; Kahn and Kenney 1999; Westlye 1991). Therefore, campaigns for the U.S. Senate generate more information to potential voters and may be more likely to perform an educative function.

We focus on ideological messages, since senators' philosophies are excellent predictors of their actions in Congress. Ideological information, while providing crucial clues about the senators' behavior in office, is unlikely to be available outside of the campaign. For the vast majority of citizens, "opportunity costs" for acquiring such ideological information are high, maybe prohibitive. However, campaigns that are filled with either clear ideological discussions or generous amounts of policy debates can provide voters with the information they need to assess their senators' ideological views. If voters are able to glean enough information from campaigns to make ideological evaluations, then we can feel more assured that campaigns enhance representation by providing key bits of political data for constituents.

Design

In the most thorough analysis to date, Franklin (1991) discovered that campaigns affect where citizens place U.S. senators on the ideological continuum. Franklin cleverly compared respondents' placements of senators seeking reelection to senators not facing the electorate because he lacked "fine-grain measures of candidate behavior" (1206). We spent considerable amounts of time acquiring these "fine-grain measures," allowing us to identify the amount and type of information available in the campaign environment. Specifically, we assembled three sets of data for the 1988–92 period: (1) information regarding senators' voting records that delineate an overall ideological picture of senators; (2) issue and ideological discussions during campaigns; and (3) citizens' understanding of the senators' ideological views after the campaigns.

To begin, we obtained data on the ideological backgrounds of U.S. senators running for reelection in 1988, 1990, and 1992. Following a rich research tradition, we relied on ADA scores as measures of ideological views (Bullock and Brady 1983; Elling 1982; Erikson 1990; Erikson and Wright 1980, 1997; Franklin 1991).[3] We obtained ADA scores for each of the six years leading up to the senators' reelection campaigns. We calculated an average ADA score for the six years before the election.[4]

Candidate Discussion of Issues and Ideology

To measure the senators' ideological discussions during campaigns, we conducted a telephone interview with the senators' campaign managers. We were successful at completing fifty-nine interviews for the eighty senators running for reelection (a response rate of 74 percent). We specifically asked campaign managers to identify the ideological location of the senator on the traditional 7-point scale.[5] In addition, we asked campaign managers to identify the main themes of the campaign. Managers were allowed to articulate up to six messages.[6] As we already noted, none of the campaign managers mentioned ideology as the main theme of their campaigns.

Furthermore, we conducted a content analysis of the television advertisements aired by the senators—and their opponents—during the campaigns. We examined *televised* political advertisements, since these commercials are a central component of U.S. Senate campaigns (Herrnson 1995; Krasno 1994) and since television advertising represents the single biggest expenditure by Senate candidates (Ansolabehere, Behr, and Iyengar 1993). In addition, television advertisements, compared with newspaper advertisements, are considered significantly more effective in swaying voters' opinions and are used much more frequently during statewide and national campaigns (Abramowitz and Segal 1992; Goldenberg and Traugott 1984; Jacobson 1997; Luntz 1988; Westlye 1991).

We relied on the Political Commercial Archive at the University of Oklahoma to obtain our sample of political commercials. The archive has the largest collection of U.S. Senate advertisements publicly available. We stratified the population of ads by candidate and randomly selected four advertisements for the senators running for reelection in 1988, 1990, and 1992. We obtained a sample of 266 advertisements for the senators examined in this study. We also content-analyzed 209 advertisements for their challengers.

To measure the ideological information in the candidates' commercials, we focused on two types of content. First, we simply recorded the number and direction of ideological mentions in the advertisements (e.g., "I am a fiscal conservative"). As we discussed earlier, incumbents and challengers almost never used the terms *liberal* and *conservative* in their commercials. Second, we coded the number and direction of issue positions in the incumbents' commercials (e.g., "I support a woman's right to choose"). We also examined how the challenger described the issue positions of the senator.[7]

The News Media's Focus on Ideology and Issues

Voters may also receive ideological information from the news media's coverage of the senator's campaign. To measure the news media's messages, we conducted an extensive content analysis of press coverage in each state where senators ran for reelection in 1988, 1990, and 1992. We selected the largest circulating newspaper in each state for analysis simply because more potential voters read these newspapers.[8] In addition, large and small newspapers across the state routinely "pick up" the same news stories about local campaigns from the wire services. For example, in Minnesota, similar stories about a campaign will appear in newspapers in the Twin Cities, in Duluth, in St. Cloud, in Rochester, or in Moorhead.[9]

News coverage was examined between September 1 and Election Day.[10] We examined every other day from September 1 to October 15 (Monday through

Saturday) and every day from October 15 through Election Day.[11] In addition, every Sunday was included for the entire time period. We selected all articles that mentioned either candidate in the first section, state section, and editorial section of the newspaper. We did not restrict our analysis to campaign-related stories, since citizens often acquire issue information about senators in stories that are not directly related to the ongoing campaign (e.g., stories detailing a senator's work on legislation relevant to the state). In total, 5,533 articles were coded for the eighty races where senators sought reelection.

When conducting the content analysis of media coverage, we measured how the news media presented issue and ideological information to voters. We coded the amount and substance of ideological discussion in the news.[12] In addition, we assessed media coverage of the senators' positions on issues and created a liberal-conservative policy index based on the coverage of the senators' positions on different issues.[13]

Voters' Understanding of the Senators' Ideology

To assess citizens' understanding of the messages disseminated during Senate campaigns, we relied on the NES/SES. As Krasno (1994) points out, the NES/SES is "unique because, like the Senate itself, it includes (roughly) equal numbers of respondents from all fifty states" (10). National surveys, in contrast, are problematic because most respondents in a nationwide survey are drawn from the largest states, leading to an overrepresentation of competitive Senate contests (Krasno 1994; Mann and Wolfinger 1980; Westlye 1991).[14]

The NES/SES survey includes questions assessing people's ideological impressions of the senators. The survey also includes measures assessing respondents' attention to the news media, interest in political campaigns, and knowledge about the candidates. Finally, the NES/SES includes a number of political questions (e.g., party identification, ideological placement) and demographic questions (e.g., education) about the respondents.

In summary, the NES/SES contains the most extensive collection of information available about voters' perceptions of senate candidates. With the NES/SES data in hand, coupled with information about the content of candidates' messages and the substance of news coverage, we turn to examining the abilities of the press and the candidates to influence citizens' views of the ideological positions of senators seeking reelection.

Searching for Evidence

We are interested in understanding how voters arrive at their ideological impressions of senators. As discussed above, candidates rarely discuss their views in ideological terms during campaigns. However, the press may present ideological discussion, filling the void left by senators. We look at this possibility first.

The News Media's Discussion of Ideology

During campaigns, citizens rely on the information disseminated by the news media when forming impressions of senatorial contestants (e.g., Abramowitz and Segal 1992; Jacobson 1992; Kahn and Kenney 1999; Westlye 1991). Voters may learn about the senators' ideological views from the news media *if* the press discuss senators in ideological terms. While this was not the case for Bob Dole of Kansas, we turn to our content analysis of newspapers for the incumbent races to make more authoritative conclusions. According to our analysis, the terms *liberal* or *conservative* were used to describe sitting senators an average of six times (with a standard deviation of almost seven) between Labor Day and Election Day. Clearly, this is not a dramatic amount of ideological coverage. However, there were several races where ideological discussion in the press was significant, averaging more than twenty paragraphs during the campaign, such as the Lautenberg versus Dawkins race in New Jersey in 1988 and the Metzenbaum versus Voinovich campaign in Ohio in 1988.[15] The race with the most ideological discussion (i.e., thirty-eight paragraphs) appeared in the *Raleigh News and Observer*'s coverage of the heated battle between Jesse Helms and Harvey Gantt in North Carolina in 1990.[16]

The fact that the press provides information about the ideological views of sitting senators is interesting, since incumbents rarely mention these terms while campaigning. Why do editors and reporters use these terms at all? We conducted an OLS analysis to explain the variation in ideological mentions by the press.[17] According to our analysis, the most important factor explaining the press emphasis on the senator's ideological profile is the ideological record of the senator. The likelihood that the press will use ideological labels increases with the ideological extremity of senators. When senators behave as extreme ideologues, according to their ADA scores, reporters are more likely to mention ideological terms in their coverage of the senators' reelection bid.

In addition, press coverage of senators' ideological views is affected by how senators describe themselves during their campaigns. As mentioned above, we asked campaign managers to describe the ideological positioning of their candidates. We then compared this "campaign representation" with the senators' ADA scores, averaged across the six-year term. The more senators misrepresented their voting record, the more the press focused on the senators' ideological views in their coverage of the campaign.

Finally, and consistent with prior research (e.g., Graber 1997; Kahn and Kenney 1999; Westlye 1991), the seniority of the senator, campaign spending during the campaign, and the size of the newspaper all affect the amount of ideological coverage in the newspaper. For example, in races where incumbent senators spend more money on their reelection campaign, newspapers publish more ideological information about the senators. Similarly, senior senators who tend to emphasize personal traits rather than their policy orientation receive less ideological coverage than their more junior colleagues. In addition, larger newspapers, with more space for news, publish more ideological information than smaller newspapers.

Inferring Ideology from Issue Discussion

Although ideological talk is nonexistent by incumbents and infrequent in the press, research indicates that there is considerably more discussion of issues by candidates and in the news media. This is especially true in competitive races (Kahn and Kenney 1999; Westlye 1991). As senatorial campaigns become more competitive, candidates are more likely to discuss their policy agenda, more willing to declare positions on matters of public policy, and more willing to discuss controversial topics. Furthermore, as candidates increase their discussions of issues, the news media tend to present more coverage of policy matters (Kahn and Kenney 1999). The discussion of issues generally, and position taking by candidates in particular, provides extensive clues that voters can use to place candidates on the ideological spectrum.

The ability of voters to make inferences from broad political labels (e.g., party or ideological affiliations) and social characteristics (e.g., gender, religion, or race) to specific issue stands (e.g., a stand on abortion) is well documented (e.g., Huddy and Terkildsen 1993; Kahn 1996; Milburn 1991). Likewise, researchers have noted that voters can make links from candidates' specific issue positions to broad political labels (e.g., Rahn 1993). Thus, social psychologists and political scientists have concluded that voters can rely on cues in their political environment to make political judgments about candidates (e.g., Conover and Feldman 1989; Feldman and Conover 1983; Bartels 1988; Krosnick 1988; Kinder 1978). Given citizens' abilities to draw inferences, it is possible that voters can assess the ideological leanings of senators when the candidates and the press provide extensive details about the senators' positions on issues.

We expect that when candidates are portrayed as consistently liberal or consistently conservative in their positions on a variety of issues, citizens will become more adept at placing the candidates on an ideological scale. To assess whether liberal-conservative consistency across issues affects voters' understanding of the ideological profile of senators, we looked at three sources of information: issue consistency in the senator's own advertisements, portrayal of the senator in the opponent's advertisements, and how the senator's issue positions were presented in the press.

When examining issue consistency, we scored senators on twenty different issues on the basis of their reported positions.[18] For example, in commercials that focused on education and where candidates took clear positions, we scored candidates espousing more federal spending on education as advocating a liberal position and candidates who wanted less federal spending as taking a conservative position. Or in ads where candidates took clear positions on abortion, for example, we scored candidates advocating a women's "right to choose" as a liberal belief and those stressing "right to life" as espousing a conservative attitude. Liberal positions were scored −1 and conservative positions were coded +1. We then summed these scores and calculated the absolute value across the twenty issues, creating a measure assessing the consistency of the senator's issue positions.

For the senators' advertisements, the liberal-conservative issue scale ranged from 0 (no difference in the number of liberal and conservative positions on issues) to 4 (four more conservative positions than liberal positions or four more liberal positions than conservative positions). The mean of the scale was .64 and the standard deviation was .90. In the opponents' advertisements, the mean score for senators on the liberal-conservative scale was .23, with a standard deviation of .74 and a range of 0 to 4.

We followed a similar procedure when analyzing press coverage. We examined the same twenty issues and used the same scoring procedures. Senators received either a −1 or +1 in paragraphs where they were linked to an issue and a clear position was reported.[19] We then summed these scores and took the absolute value, once again measuring the ideological consistency of U.S. senators. This scale ranges from 0 to 100, with a mean of 12.9 and a standard deviation of 17.7.

In addition to looking at the specific discussion of issue positions during campaigns, we examined senators' general emphasis on policy during their reelection bids. Senators often ignore policy matters in their reelection campaigns, preferring to focus on their experience and tout their work for state, as Dole did in his 1992 campaign. However, some senators do emphasize their issue concerns, as Rockefeller emphasized affordable health care in his 1990 reelection race. By focusing primarily on issues, senators may encourage a more thorough discussion of policy matters during the campaign and more interest in policy matters by voters. When issues are at the forefront of a campaign, citizens may be more adept at making ideological judgments about the senators.

We relied on answers to the campaign manager survey to determine whether senators focused on policy matters in their campaigns. In particular, if the majority of the "main themes" of the campaign were policy oriented, the senator was classified as emphasizing issues. In our sample, 34 percent of the incumbents' campaigns were mainly about issues.

The Context of the Campaign

Several additional aspects of campaigns influence what people know about candidates (e.g., Jacobson 1997; Kahn and Kenney 1999; Krasno 1994). Campaign spending, which can be viewed as a surrogate for candidate activity, affects voters' knowledge of the candidates (e.g., Jacobson 1997).[20] The level of competition in a race may also increase voters' knowledge of the candidates by intensifying voters' attention to the messages produced by the candidates and the press (e.g., Kahn and Kenney 1999).[21] And the amount of coverage devoted to a campaign in the news media is likely to increase general understanding of the candidates as well as increase interest in the campaign (e.g., Kahn and Kenney 1999; Krasno 1994; Westlye 1991).[22]

In addition, the quality of the challenger may influence what citizens know about the sitting senator.[23] Prior work examining Senate campaigns has shown that quality challengers mount a more rigorous campaign than less experienced candidates (e.g., Jacobson 1997; Kahn and Kenney 1999; Squire 1989, 1992; Westlye 1991). Therefore, in races with quality challengers, more ideological information about the senator may be presented, influencing citizens' abilities to place senators on the liberal-conservative continuum.

Just as the quality of the challenger may influence people's understanding of incumbents' ideological profiles, the characteristics of senators may also be important. Certain senators, because of sheer longevity in office, are well known in their home states. And, in the wake of several campaigns, numerous speeches over the years, and countless press releases, people tend to know their ideological leanings. Therefore, we needed to control for years in the Senate so that the ideological savvy of respondents in some states would be attributed properly to the longevity of the senator (e.g., Kennedy from Massachusetts, in the Senate since 1962, or Thurmond from South Carolina, in the Senate since 1954) and not to issue discussion during campaigns.

Finally, we added a variable tapping the size of the state. First, the size of the state allowed us to estimate the impact of campaign spending by holding constant wide variations in spending that resulted from extreme differences in state size. But in addition, state size is related to voters' levels of awareness and contact with their senators. For example, respondents from smaller states are more likely to hold information about their senators, due to the simple fact that they have more contact with and exposure to their senators (e.g., Hibbing and Brandes 1983; Lee and Oppenheimer 1999; Oppenheimer 1996).

The Characteristics of Voters

The habits, preferences, and skills of citizens also influence their knowledge about U.S. senators. People differ dramatically in their levels of political sophistication about politics (e.g., Converse 1962, 1964; Dalager 1996; Krosnick 1990; Lodge and Hamill 1986). Some citizens have an extensive understanding of politics and a great deal of stored information about policies and political candidates. Others know very little about political affairs. We expect people's levels of political expertise to affect whether they are aware of their senator's ideological leanings.[24]

Similarly, citizens who rely heavily on the news media are likely to have more information about their senator, including ideological information. Prior research indicates that people who watch television news and regularly read the local newspaper are much more knowledgeable about political events and political figures (Brians and Wattenberg 1996; Drew and Weaver 1991; Larson 1990; Zhao and Chaffee 1995).[25]

In addition, people who are more interested in politics are likely to know more about their sitting senator (Dalager 1996; McLeod and McDonald 1985; Robinson and Davis 1990). These "political junkies" pride themselves on learning the most esoteric details about politicians.[26] Beyond mere interest in politics, formal education also influences attention to and involvement in elections and politics generally (Rosenstone and Hansen 1993). Schooling eases an individual's ability to acquire information about all topics, including ideological information.[27]

Voters also vary in the strengths of their attachments to political parties and to ideological philosophies. Citizens with entrenched partisan beliefs routinely acquire news about political events and political figures (Miller and Shanks 1996). And people with extreme ideological attitudes will most likely be able to identify the ideological leanings of senators, especially compared to citizens who rarely place themselves on scales measuring ideology.[28]

Findings

Placing Senators on the Ideological Scale

We begin our analysis by looking at whether the rhetoric of campaigns affects citizens' ability to place senators on the liberal-conservative continuum. The dependent variable was constructed from the NES/SES 7-point scale measuring the incumbents' ideological positions. We gave individuals who were willing to place the senator a score of 1, while those who did not place the senator received a score of 0.[29] The results of our analysis are presented in Table 4.1.

The model performs well, predicting correctly 84 percent of the cases. In addition, thirteen of the eighteen variables in the analysis reach traditional levels of statistical significance. We are most interested in the set of variables tapping campaign discussion. These variables represent the information produced during the campaign that might assist respondents in developing ideological

TABLE 4.1. Logit Analysis Explaining Respondents' Ability to Place Senator on Ideological Scale

	Unstandardized Coefficient (SE)	Standardized Coefficient
Campaign Discussion		
Media Discussion of Ideology	−.006 (.005)	−.08
Media Discussion of Issue Positions	.007 (.002)***	.30
Senators' Discussion of Issue Positions	.06 (.03)**	.14
Opponents' Discussion of Senators' Positions	.06 (03)**	.11
Senators' Focus Primarily about Issues	.08 (.07)	.08
Campaign Characteristics		
Amount of News Attention	−.00007 (.00007)	−.12
Campaign Spending	.03 (.04)	.08
Challenger Quality	−.005 (.01)**	−.03
Competition	−.003 (.002)	−.13
Seniority	.007 (.004)*	.12
Voting-Age Population	−.002 (.0009)**	−.21
Citizens' Attitudes		
Strength of Party Identification	.04 (.02)**	.10
Strength of Ideology	.17 (.03)***	.41
Interest	.07 (.02)***	.01
Education	.02 (.01)**	.15
Attention to News	.02 (.005)***	.21
Knowledge of Senator's Party	.18 (.06)***	.22
Sophistication about Politics	.36 (.02)***	1.47
Constant	−.54 (.39)	

$N = 3,401$

84 percent of cases predicted correctly
Chi-square statistic = 3551.58***

Note: The dependent variable is 1 = respondent placed the senator on the ideological scale; 0 = otherwise. The standard errors are in parentheses.
*** $p < .01$; ** $p < .05$; * $p < .10$

impressions of their senators. The first variable, media discussion of ideology, does not reach statistical significance. Its coefficient is nearly the same size as its standard error (−.006/.005). As we discussed above, the newspapers do not use the terms *liberal* and *conservative* very often when describing the candidates. Therefore, the inability of ideological discussion in the news to affect ideological understanding of the senators is probably due to the lack of variance in ideological coverage.

However, each of the variables tapping issue position taking is statistically significant ($p < .05$). These variables measure the consistency of the senators' positions on issues from several sources. In each case, as consistency increases, voters' likelihood of placing candidates on the ideological scale also increases. In other words, when senators are described as taking consistently "liberal" or "conservative" stands on a range of issues, respondents are more likely to place the senators on the liberal-conservative continuum. Regardless of the sources of information—the senators' campaigns, the opponents' campaigns, or the news media—information on the senators' issue positions affect people's willingness to place them on the ideological scale.

A comparison of these three variables suggests that the news media's discussion of issue positions is by far the most important. As the media's portrayal of the senator becomes more abundant and more consistent, citizens are more willing to offer an ideological assessment of the senator. The standardized coefficient for the media measure is .30, twice as large as senators' own discussions of their policy stands.[30] We illustrate the impact of the news media's discussion of issue positions by converting the logit coefficients to probabilities.[31] In particular, we find that individuals who are exposed to campaigns with no media discussion of the candidates have a .84 probability of placing the senator on the ideological scale. In contrast, when coverage is much more extensive (i.e., 100 paragraphs about the senator's issue position in the news), respondents have a .92 probability of offering an ideological assessment of the senator.

The greater impact of the news media's message may be due to the fact that citizens have greater exposure to this source of information, compared to advertisements aired by the senate candidates. Overall, these results suggest that citizens are quite adept at using discussions of specific issue positions to make inferences about the senators' ideological views.

We also find that the more general aspects of campaign environment affect people's willingness to place incumbents on the ideological scale. For instance, it appears that citizens are more willing to place senior senators on the ideological scale. Similarly, people from smaller states are more able to place their senator on the ideological scale.

Finally, and consistent with a large literature, the characteristics of voters are vitally important when it comes to understanding which voters are confident enough to discuss the senator's ideological views. Each of the respondent characteristics significantly affects a people's willingness to place incumbents on the left/right continuum. Both long-term characteristics (e.g., strength of party attachment) and short-term measures of campaign interest (i.e., attention to the news) are strongly related to placing senators. The real star in this galaxy, however, is the citizen's level of sophistication about politics. This measure, unrelated to the ongoing campaign, is the most powerful factor in the model. The standardized coefficient for political sophistication is three and a half times larger than its nearest rival (1.47 vs. .41 for strength of ideological beliefs).

Accurately Placing Senators on the Ideological Scale

The general pattern of findings from Table 4.1 suggests that campaigns increase the likelihood that citizens will place senatorial candidates along an ideological continuum. But what about their accuracy? Are citizens close to reality? Clearly, there are forces at work to lead them astray (e.g., lack of knowledge; absence of basic information; actions by the opponents to distort the senators' records; the ambiguity of the senators' own messages). In this analysis, we seek to examine how the campaign affects people's abilities to *accurately* place senators on the ideological continuum.

As we mentioned at the outset, a sizable number of citizens are quite accurate when placing their senators. We used the senators' six-year average of their ADA scores as our measure of reality. We then computed the absolute distance between the ADA scores and the citizens' placements of the senators on the 7-point continuum. Thus, the respondents' placements could range from completely accurate to 6 places off the mark. In fact, 17 percent of citizens were correct in their placement, 31 percent missed by a mere 1 point, 25 percent missed by only 2 points, 14 percent missed by 3 points, 8 percent missed by 4 points, 3 percent missed by 5 points, and 2 percent missed by the maximum 6 points.

To explain people's ability to gauge accurately the senators' ideological position, we included variables measuring campaign discussion, campaign characteristics, and citizen characteristics. In the present analysis, we relied on OLS regression given the interval nature of the dependent variable. The results are presented in Table 4.2. The model performs well. The R^2 is .13, acceptable for survey data, and fourteen of the eighteen independent variables reach traditional levels of statistical significance.

Turning first to the variables that represent campaign discussion, we find that four of the five variables tapping campaign discourse are statistically significant. Two of these coefficients (media discussion of ideology, senator's focus on issues) are negatively signed, indicating that these types of campaign messages lead to more accurate assessments by citizens. These messages produce a closer connection between the respondent's placement of the senator on the ideological scale and the senator's actual ADA score. However, two of the coefficients capturing campaign discussion (media discussion of issue positions, opponents' discussion of senators' positions) are statistically significant *and* positively signed, indicating that other types of campaign messages produce greater inaccuracy.

We begin our discussion by looking at the variables that generate more accuracy. As the news media increase their use of ideological terms in campaign coverage, citizens are more correct in their placement of senators. These results indicate that people can process information about ideological terms when it is appears in their press. While the news media often avoid ideological discussion

TABLE 4.2. OLS Analysis Explaining Respondents' Ability to Accurately Place Senator on Ideological Scale

	Unstandardized Coefficient (SE)	Standardized Coefficient
Campaign Discussion		
Media Discussion of Ideology	−.009 (.005)*	−.05
Media Discussion of Issue Positions	.005 (.002)**	.07
Senators' Discussion of Issue Positions	−.02 (.03)	−.01
Opponents' Discussion of Senators' Positions	.08 (.04)**	.04
Senators' Focus Primarily about Issues	−.30 (.07)***	−.09
Campaign Characteristics		
Amount of News Attention	−.0004 (.000007)***	−.21
Campaign Spending	.08 (.04)**	.07
Challenger Quality	.03 (.01)***	.06
Competition	.02 (.002)***	.20
Seniority	.01 (.004)**	.05
Voting-Age Population	−.002 (.0008)**	−.05
Citizens' Attitudes		
Strength of Party Identification	.003 (.03)	.002
Strength of Ideology	−.06 (.03)**	−.04
Interest	−.03 (.02)	.03
Education	−.02 (.01)**	−.05
Attention to News	.009 (.007)	.02
Knowledge of Senator's Party	−.13 (.05)**	−.04
Sophistication about Politics	−.20 (.02)***	−.22
Constant	1.59 (.42)***	

$N = 2,710$
$R^2 = .13$
F statistic = 38.51***

Note: The dependent variable is absolute distance between the senator's ADA score and the respondent's placement of the senator. The standard errors are in parentheses.
***$p < .01$; **$p < .05$; *$p < .10$.

when covering campaigns, when the labels are presented, citizens' understanding of the senators' ideological views improves.

In addition, when senators focus their campaigns mainly on issues, as opposed to personal characteristics, citizens become more adept at placing senators on the liberal-conservative scale. The senators' focus on policy matters leads to a more informed public. In fact, the standardized coefficient (−.09) for this variable is the strongest among the campaign discussion variables and the third highest in the model. Most assuredly, when senators spend time and money discussing issues, compared to other topics, voters become more knowledgeable about incumbents' ideological leanings.

While some types of campaign discussion lead to a more attuned citizenry, other campaign messages lead to confusion. In particular, the news media's discussion and the opponents' discussion of issue positions lead to greater inaccuracies by citizens. In both cases, senators have limited control over the content and stream of this information. Information disseminated by challengers is likely to paint an unfavorable picture of the senators' issue stands. These messages may conflict with the senator's own self-depiction as well as with reality. The results in Table 4.2 indicate that the presentation of discordant information is likely to produce confusion among citizens.

Likewise, the news media's presentation of the senators' policy stands produces a "disconnect" between the respondents' views of the senators' ideological stands and senators' actual positions. As the news media increase their discussion of senators' issue positions, citizens become less accurate in placing their senators on the ideological continuum. While the news media may not be working to discredit incumbents, the press may be disseminating information that conflicts with the senators' own messages. In addition, the press may be producing stories about issues that run counter to the opponents' messages, heightening confusion for voters. Finally, a biased press (Kahn and Kenney 1999; Page 1996) may be distorting the incumbents' records, thereby producing an ambiguous picture of the senators' ideological profiles. For any or all of these reasons, the news media's messages about issues befuddle voters; as newspapers print more stories about the issue positions of sitting senators, respondents become less able to place senators accurately on the left-right scale.

Other aspects of the campaign also affect people's abilities to accurately assess the senators' ideological views. The closeness of the race, the amount of campaign spending, and the quality of the challenger all inhibit people's accuracy. As races become more hard-fought, as candidates spend more money, and as challengers become more experienced and more effective, the amount of discordant information is likely to escalate. In such a setting, the sitting senator does not control the content of the campaign discourse. Instead, the campaign environment is full of loud and conflicting voices. Such a campaign setting seems to confuse citizens, leading respondents to misrepresent the ideological profiles of sitting senators.

We also find that the seniority of the senator affects people's ability to accurately place senators. While we expected respondents to be more adept at recognizing the ideological profile of senior senators, we found the opposite effect. In particular, as seniority increases, inaccuracy in ideological placement increases. Senior senators may be viewed less accurately because, compared to their junior colleagues, they are less likely to present ideological and issue information during campaigns (Kahn and Kenney 1999). Senior senators (like Robert Dole in his 1992 reelection campaign) present citizens with few clues about their ideological preferences during campaigns. Instead, they tend to emphasize their service to the state and their personal characteristics during their reelection bids.

In addition, the overall amount of information presented in the news appears to help citizens develop more accurate assessments of the ideological leanings of senators. While press attention on the senators' issue positions confuses voters, the greater coverage given to the race, in general, enhances people's understanding of the senators' ideological views. Information, for example, on senators' issue priorities (e.g., "The senator views affordable child care as an important national priority") and news about senators' policy work in Washington (e.g., "The senator has authored legislation to insure citizens are not 'thrown off' welfare") encourages citizens to accurately place senators on the liberal-conservative continuum.

Finally, several characteristics of citizens affect their ability to place senators accurately on the ideological scale. Strength of ideology, education, knowledge of the senator's party, and voter sophistication all lead to greater accuracy. As in Table 4.1, voters' sophistication about politics continues to be an important explanatory variable; its standardized coefficient (−.22) is the largest in the model. In addition, the negative sign for strength of ideology is interesting, suggesting that as individuals become more extreme in their own ideological self-placement, they are more likely to know the ideological beliefs of their senators.

The Conditioning Effect of Seniority

The results presented in Table 4.2 suggest that campaign information sometimes clarifies the senators' ideological views, while other campaign messages (i.e., issue messages delivered by the news media and the opponent) confuse voters, leading citizens to misinterpret the senators' ideological positions. However, the impact of campaign information may vary for different types of senators. In particular, we expect the seniority of the senator to condition the influence of campaign information on voters' understandings of the senator's ideological views.

When a senator has been serving a state for a number of years, citizens are likely to be familiar with him or her and may have a store of information about the senator's views on issues. Such a store of information will make it easier and more efficient for voters to process the new information disseminated during campaigns (e.g., Krosnick 1990; Lau and Sears 1986; Zaller 1992). Furthermore, since voters have more preexisting information about senior senators, these citizens will be in a better position to discount discrepant information.

To illustrate, John Chafee was a fixture of the Rhode Island political landscape when he ran for reelection in 1988. Before beginning his tenure in the U.S. Senate in 1976, Chafee served as governor of Rhode Island for three terms during the 1960s. Given Chafee's long electoral history in the state, citizens of Rhode Island should have had an easy time processing the campaign information presented during the 1988 reelection campaign. When Chafee discussed his own issue and ideological views during the campaign, voters probably could understand and easily assimilate the information. Furthermore, when Chafee's opponent tried to distort the Senator's record (e.g., calling Chafee a "right-wing conservative"), citizens could "counterargue" the information given their long acquaintance with the senator.

In contrast, when a first-term senator, like Frank Lautenberg in New Jersey in 1988, faced his first reelection campaign, voters were less familiar with the senator's ideological views. Unlike Chafee, Lautenberg was a newcomer to politics when he first captured a seat in the U.S. Senate in 1982. In 1988, a well-financed challenger, as well as unfriendly press, may have been effective in distorting the senator's positions on issues, since voters did not have well-established attitudes about the senator.

Given the possibility that seniority may mediate the influence of campaign information, we reestimated the equation in Table 4.2 with a series of interaction terms. In particular, we include five multiplicative terms to see if the seniority of the senator affected how campaign information influences people's ability to place senators accurately on the ideological scale. The results in Table 4.3 indicate that three of the five interaction coefficients are statistically significant ($p <$ .01). Furthermore, these three coefficients are negative, suggesting that as seniority increases, campaign information leads people to make *more* accurate assessments of their senator.

To illustrate the conditioning influence of seniority, we examine more closely the interaction between the opponent's discussion of a senator's issue positions and the seniority of the senator. In particular, we examine respondents' ability to accurately place the senator when the senator's opponent is presenting extensive information about the senator's position on issues (i.e., opponent's discussion of senator's issues = 4). Relying on the model in Table 4.3, we estimate citizens' ability to place senators accurately on the ideological scale under two conditions: (1) when an opponent discusses the issue positions of a *junior* senator (the senator has served one year in the Senate); (2) when an opponent discusses the issue positions of a *senior* senator (the senator has served eighteen years in the Senate).[32] On average, citizens' assessments of the ideology of the *junior* senator is inaccurate—with an estimated score of 4 on the ideological scale ranging from 0 (an accurate placement) to 6 (a totally inaccurate placement). In contrast, citizens' placement of the *senior* senator is far more accurate, approaching 0 on the ideological scale. In this example, challengers are able to shape citizens'

TABLE 4.3. OLS Analysis Examining How Seniority Conditions the Impact of Campaign Discussion on Accuracy of Ideological Placement

	Unstandardized Coefficient (SE)	Standardized Coefficient
Campaign Discussion		
Media Discussion of Ideology	.002 (.02)	.01
Media Discussion of Issue Positions	.03 (.006)***	.38
Senators' Discussion of Issue Positions	.10 (.08)	.07
Opponents' Discussion of Senators' Positions	.61 (.15)***	.31
Senators' Focus Primarily about Issues	.14 (.17)	.04
Media Discussion of Ideology * Seniority	.0005 (.001)	.01
Media Discussion of Issue Positions * Seniority	−.002 (.0006)***	−.41
Senators' Discussion of Issue Positions * Seniority	−.007 (.006)	−.08
Opponents' Discussion of Senators' Positions * Seniority	−.09 (.02)***	−.30
Senators' Focus Primarily about Issues * Seniority	−.04 (.01)***	−.15
Campaign Characteristics		
Amount of News Attention	−.0003 (.00008)***	−.16
Campaign Spending	.11 (.05)**	.09
Challenger Quality	.03 (.01)***	.06
Competition	.01 (.003)***	.15
Seniority	.04 (.006)***	.20
Voting-Age Population	−.0008 (.0009)	−.02
Citizens' Attitudes		
Strength of Party Identification	−.001 (.03)	−.01
Strength of Ideology	−.06 (.03)**	−.04
Interest	−.03 (.02)	−.03
Education	−.02 (.01)**	−.04
Attention to News	.01 (.007)	.03
Knowledge of Senator's Party	−.12 (.05)**	−.04
Sophistication about Politics	−.20 (.02)***	−.23
Constant	1.13 (.41)***	

$N = 2,710$
$R^2 = .15$
F statistic = 66.32***

Note: The dependent variable is absolute distance between the senator's ADA score and the respondent's placement of the senator. The standard errors are in parentheses.
*** $p < .01$; ** $p < .05$; * $p < .10$.

63

views of the ideological beliefs of junior senators—distorting the senators' ideological profile. In contrast, challengers have a difficult time distorting respondents' understanding of the ideological positions of senior senators.

In summary, these findings, coupled with the results presented in Table 4.2, show that the impact of campaign messages depends on the seniority of the senator. Seniority is an important mediating force aiding citizens in their interpretation of campaign information.

Conclusion

Informed citizens constitute the foundation of a functioning representative democracy. Whether to guide vote choice or to shape the interactions between legislators and constituents, the accumulation of accurate information by citizens concerning the beliefs of representatives enhances the quality of our democratic system of government. In this chapter, we demonstrate that campaigns can bolster people's understanding of their senators' ideological stands. We show that some of the information produced during campaigns can go beyond simply introducing candidates to voters. It appears that the messages generated by the senators help voters identify the political philosophies of the incumbents. Maybe most surprising, we find that potential voters are able to infer from senators' stated policy positions and draw conclusions about more general ideological beliefs.

However, not all campaign information is educative. We find that issue information presented by the senator's opponent and by the press confuses voters concerning the ideological beliefs of senators instead of informing them. But we find that such information is less confusing when citizens are asked to evaluate more senior senators. As seniority increases, issue information presented by challengers and the news media begins to clarify voters' impressions of the incumbents' ideological stands. Our results indicate that the seniority of the senator is an important conditioning force that aids voters in interpreting campaign information.

While we find that campaign information influences people's understanding of U.S. senators, are these findings applicable to the "people's House"? We think not. Most campaigns for the U.S. House of Representatives simply do not provide enough information to citizens. Policy and ideological information is lacking in House races for two reasons. First, races for the U.S. House are less competitive than U.S. Senate campaigns. Less than 10 percent of House races are competitive in any given year; whereas, approximately 40 percent of U.S. Senate races are close. When contests are not competitive, candidates—especially incumbents—stay away from emphasizing policy matters (Kahn and Kenney 1999). Furthermore, news coverage of noncompetitive campaigns is extremely limited, since media elites focus their attention on interesting races with uncertain outcomes (Clarke and Evans 1983; Goldenberg and Traugott 1984; Westlye 1991).

Second, the so-called "media-market fit" is much better for Senate races than House campaigns. Most readers of major metropolitan newspapers, for example, are likely to live in the same state and pay attention to one race for the U.S. Senate. Yet a newspaper's circulation is are likely to be spread across different congressional districts. Therefore, newspapers spend more time focusing on Senate campaigns and allocate resources to only the most interesting and competitive House campaigns.

The media-market fit also has ramifications for the advertisement strategies of candidates. Television stations, like newspapers, do not necessarily coincide with House district boundaries. Thus, House candidates running commercials on television know that viewers exposed to their commercials may not reside in their districts. Therefore, it is not "cost effective" for House candidates to air political advertisements in these media markets. This is not the case in most U.S. Senate races. The inefficiency of the media-market fit in House districts limits the amount of commercials aired by House candidates, especially compared to Senate candidates. Fewer commercials translates into less information for voters.

In the end, it is easy to see why the relevant issue and ideological information is likely to be sparse in House races compared to Senate campaigns. Thus, campaigns for the U.S. House are less likely to provide enough ideological and policy information to affect citizens' understanding of the ideological views of House incumbents. Voters cannot draw inferences about sophisticated abstract concepts such as ideology without clues. Citizens are only as clever as the information at hand. It is ironic that constituents are more likely to hold ideological information about representatives from the upper chamber, since institutional designs (e.g., size of constituencies, length of time between elections) were intended to produce more information about members of the lower chamber.

Notes

1. Lee and Oppenheimer (1999) find that small state senators often pursue a strategy of emphasizing their "care for their state."

2. The ADA scores were converted to the 1-to-7 liberal-conservative continuum (0 to 12 = 7), (13 to 27 = 6), (28 to 42 = 5), (43 to 57 = 4), (58 to 72 = 3), (73 to 87 = 2), (88 to 100 = 1). We considered a correct placement as any score within 1 point of the ADA score.

3. For a discussion of the validity and reliability of ADA scores, see Smith, Herrera, and Herrera (1990) and Herrera, Epperlein, and Smith (1995). One concern with the ADA

scores is that they measure only a single dimension of policy choice. Indeed, Poole and Rosenthal (1991b) establish the existence of a second dimension, yet this dimension adds very little explanatory power in predicting roll call votes. Thus, we follow the lead of Wood and Andersson (1998) and consider only the dominant dimension, liberalism-conservatism. In relying on the ADA scores, we correct for absences in the senators' voting record (see Elling 1982).

4. While many researchers have explored whether senators become more moderate in their voting as their reelection campaign approaches, the evidence for moderation is mixed (Ahuja 1994; Amacher and Boyes 1978; Hibbing 1984; Thomas 1985; Wright and Berkman 1986). Furthermore, we find little evidence for moderation in the 1988–92 period. For example, the correlation between ADA scores in the sixth year with ADA scores for the first through third years (averaged) is .94, and the correlation between the sixth-year ADA score and the fourth- and fifth-year scores (averaged) is .94. Franklin's (1991) assessment for 1988 and 1990, relying on American Conservative Union scores, is strikingly similar to ours.

5. The ideological question was one of several questions asked on the "campaign manager survey." Its exact wording was: "We hear a lot of talk these days about liberals and conservatives. Think about a ruler for measuring political views that people might hold, from liberal to conservative. On this ruler, which goes from 1 to 7, a measurement of 1 means very liberal political views , and a measurement of 7 would be very conservative. Just like a regular ruler, it has points in between, at 2, 3, 4, 5, or 6. Where would you place the senator on this scale where 1 means 'very liberal' and 7 means 'very conservative'?"

6. The exact wording of the question was, "What were the main themes that you tried to stress in [SENATOR'S NAME] campaign for the Senate?"

7. The interviews were conducted by 14 Arizona State University (ASU) students and one of the authors using the ASU Survey Research Lab. Interviewers were trained before talking with managers, and interviews were continually monitored. All open-ended comments were coded and categorized by the authors and one graduate assistant. Reliability checks were conducted to assess the coding of the open-ended comments; intercoder reliability never fell below 95 percent agreement.

8. To see whether alternative newspapers from the same state would cover Senate campaigns differently, we compared coverage patterns in 1988 in the *Miami Herald* and *Tampa Tribune,* the *Houston Chronicle* and *Dallas Daily News,* the *San Francisco Chronicle* and *Los Angeles Times,* and the *New York Times* and *New York Daily News.* In general, coverage patterns across newspapers were strikingly similar in content and amount.

9. Newspapers, instead of television news, were chosen to represent news coverage for substantive and practical reasons. Among the substantive reasons, studies demonstrate that newspapers allocate more resources and more space to their coverage of statewide campaigns, compared with television, thereby producing more

comprehensive coverage (Leary 1977). Westlye (1991) finds that, compared with local broadcast news, "newspapers present an amount of information that more closely approximates what campaigns are issuing" (45). In addition, while people rely heavily on television news to keep informed about national politics, they depend on local newspapers for coverage of senatorial and gubernatorial campaigns (Mayer 1993). Similarly, statewide campaign officials consider newspapers more effective than local television news for communicating with potential voters (Graber 1993). People also learn more about statewide campaigns from newspapers than from local news broadcasts (Clarke and Fredin 1978). Practical considerations also influenced our decision to examine newspapers. Newspapers are routinely saved on microfilm, which makes them easily accessible for analysis. Tapes of local television news, in contrast, are seldom available after a campaign, making a systematic examination of television news more difficult.

10. In those cases where the state's primary election was held after September 1, coding began the day after the primary.

11. To avoid problems associated with periodicity, we alternated sampling Monday, Wednesday, Friday (i.e., first week), and Tuesday, Thursday, and Saturday (i.e., second week).

12. Ideological descriptions of the senator in the press were coded on a 3-point scale: 1 = liberal, 2 = moderate, 3 = conservative.

13. The coding of the articles was a labor-intensive enterprise. Coders were trained to copy articles from microfilm, and another set of coders were taught how to content-analyze the articles. In all, 20 coders were trained and participated in the media project. Intercoder reliability was assessed repeatedly during the coding process. On average, there was 92 percent agreement across the content codes.

14. In the conducting of the NES/SES, about 60 respondents in each state in each year were randomly selected to be interviewed. The interviews were done by telephone and took place within two months of the 1988, 1990, and 1992 elections. The interviews averaged just over 35 minutes in length. For the Senate races examined for this study, 3,401 respondents were interviewed.

15. Over 20 paragraphs translates into an ideological mention appearing every third day or so. In reality, most press coverage occurs after October 1. So the 20 or more paragraphs are typically spread across about 30 days from early October to early November, averaging about one paragraph per day. In these particular races, it is altogether possible that the press provided some clues for voters.

16. In the next section of the chapter, when we attempt to explain people's impressions of the senators' ideological views, we will examine whether press discussion of the incumbents' ideology matters.

17. The dependent variable in this analysis is the number of ideological mentions in the press. The unstandardized coefficients, standard errors, and standardized coefficients of the statistically significant variables in the model are ideological extremity, 3.30

(1.11), .35; ideological distortion, 1.28 (.85), .17; seniority, −.16 (.11), −.17; incumbent spending, 3.69 (2.30), .19; competition, −.08 (.05), −.21; and size of the newspaper, .002 (.0007), .33. The R^2 was a healthy .42 for the 59 races were included in the analysis. The corresponding F statistic was 3.68 ($p < .001$).

18. Coders looked at 37 issues overall. We restricted our analysis to 20 issues where a liberal or conservative position could be clearly identified. The 20 issues were spending on defense, foreign aid, health care, the elderly, welfare, education, farm issues, AIDS, day care, support for "big government" involvement in Central America, regulation of trade, the environment, business, energy, position on abortion, civil rights, prayer in school, the death penalty, and support for the Gulf War.

19. In the content analysis of press coverage, the unit of analysis was the paragraph.

20. The campaign spending of the two candidates was summed, thus tapping the total amount of spending in the race.

21. Competition was captured by the last available poll reported statewide. Competition ranged from 28 (extremely noncompetitive) to 100 (extremely competitive).

22. The amount of press coverage was the total amount of paragraphs given to both candidates, irrespective of where it was placed in the paper and whether it was directly about the campaign or not.

23. The quality of the challenger was measured by using prior elective experience and establishing a 9-point scale. Following prior work by Squire and Smith (1996) and Squire (1989, 1992), we ranked nonincumbents as follows: 1 = no prior elective experience; 2 = no prior elective experience but high name recognition due to celebrity status in the state; 3 = local electoral experience; 4 = state legislator; 5 = state legislative leader; 6 = mayor of a major city; 7 = first-term statewide officeholder or U.S. House member; 8 = multiple-term statewide officeholder or U.S. House member; 9 = governor.

24. We measured political sophistication with six questions from the NES/SES. First, we coded respondents as correct if the respondent said George Bush was more conservative than Michael Dukakis (in the 1988 and 1990 survey) or Bill Clinton (in the 1992 survey). Similarly, if the respondent said the Republican party was more conservative than the Democratic party, the answer was coded as correct. We also measured people's knowledge about the senator *not* up for reelection, since it was important to develop a knowledge measure independent of the current political campaign. We relied on the following NES/SES measures. First, we measured correct recognition of the senator's name. Second, we measured knowledge of the senator's name and party. Respondents who correctly recalled the senator's party *and* name received a score of 2, respondents who recalled only the senator's name (and not party) received a score of 1, and respondents who could not recall the name or the party of the senator received a score of 0. We also measured correct ideological placement of the senator. To measure correct ideological placement, we recoded ADA scores to range from 1 to 3 (1 = liberal, 2 = moderate, 3 = conservative) and averaged the scores for the two years before the respondent's interview date. Each respondent's answer to the ideological

placement of the senator was also recoded from 1 to 3 (1 = liberal, 2 = moderate, 3 = conservative). If the difference between the respondent's recoded score and the recoded ADA score was 0, the respondent correctly identified the ideological placement of the senator. If the score was different from 0, the respondent incorrectly identified the ideological placement of the senator. With these six questions, we created a sophistication index ranging from 0 to 7.

25. To assess attention to the news, we relied on the NES/SES questions asking voters how often during a week they watched a news program on TV or read a newspaper. We combined these two measures into one index tapping attention to the news. The questions were "How many days in the past week did you watch news programs on TV?" and "How many days in the past week did you read a daily newspaper?" Thus, the index ranged from 0 to 14, with 14 representing an individual who reported reading a newspaper every day and watching a news program every day.

26. The measure of interest was the standard NES question, "Some people don't pay much attention to political campaigns. How about you? Would you say that you were very much interested, somewhat interested, or not much interested?"

27. Education was measured as years of schooling.

28. To measure strength of partisan attachment, we relied on the standard 7-point party identification scale. We folded the scale to create four categories: strong partisans, weak partisans, leaning partisans, and independents. To measure extremity of ideological beliefs, we used the standard NES 7-point ideological scale. We folded the scale to create four categories ranging strong ideologues (extreme liberals, extreme conservatives) to moderates.

29. Since the dependent variable was dichotomous, we relied on logistic regression to derive the parameter estimates for the model.

30. Standardized coefficients provide estimates for the relative importance of independent variables in a multivariate regression analysis for a single sample (Lewis-Beck 1980).

31. In calculating these probabilities, we relied on the procedure described in King (1989) by varying the amount of news coverage of issue positions from the minimum (i.e., 0 paragraphs about issues) to the maximum number (i.e., 100 paragraphs about issues) and holding all the remaining variables in the model at their means.

32. In our calculations, all remaining variables in the model were placed at their means so that the influence of rival hypotheses would be held constant.

· 5 ·

Explaining National Party Tides in Senate Elections: Macropartisanship, Policy Mood, and Ideological Balancing

Robert S. Erikson

Each election year brings the prospect of partisan turnover in the Senate. Although the amount of the partisan shift is typically modest, there have been notable exceptions. These include the Democratic surge of 1958 and the Republican surges of 1980 and 1994 that put the Republicans in the majority. Most recently, a modest Democratic surge in the 2000 election brought an end to the Republican majority.

What accounts for the changing partisan composition of the Senate? Are partisan shifts merely the residue of thirty-three or so individual Senate contests decided by purely local forces, with each new partisan division representing nothing more than chance variation? Or are they generated by uniform tidal surges exerting a common partisan energy across all the American states at once? And if the latter, what causes these transformations of the national partisan verdict? Part of the mystery is that Senate elections draw little scrutiny as a political barometer. Far greater attention is given to U.S. House elections. Senate seats are up for election only every six years, whereas all 435 House seats are up every two years. It follows that in any election year, only about thirty-three Senate seats are at stake.[1]

This chapter argues that the study of Senate elections should be rescued from its state of relative neglect. Senate election outcomes actually are highly volatile and sensitive to national political forces—more so even than House election outcomes. Ironically, although the Constitution designed the Senate to be insulated from popular passions, when senators do face reelection their fates are more tied to shifts in public opinion than are the fates of House members. The reason lies in the difference between House and Senate constituencies. Whereas House members typically are elected from safe seats insulated from national partisan tides, Senators must face statewide constituencies. In most states, each party has at least a fighting chance to capture a Senate seat when the circumstances are right.

The Volatility of Senate Elections

Measuring Senate election outcomes in terms of a national partisan verdict is more of a challenge than might be evident at first glance. The standard method is to simply monitor Senate partisanship as the time series of the Senate's party composition. While the Republican-Democrat division in the Senate is certainly a useful indicator for understanding policy making, it is deceptively smooth as an indicator of electoral change. This is because party composition is a moving average of election outcomes for three elections spanning six years. Adding to the confusion, attention is often concentrated on the change in party composition from one election to the next (e.g., Abramowitz and Segal 1986; Waterman 1990; Lewis-Beck 1992; Grofman, Brunell, and Koetzle 1998). This makes sense for House elections, where partisan gains and losses have an exact, clear meaning. For the Senate, however, change from one election to the next is complicated by the six-year term. Net change in party composition over two years actually represents a muted rendition of electoral change from six years previously to the present.[2]

The solution is to measure the national Senate election outcome as the partisan division for the thirty-three or so Senate seats that are up for election in the specific election year. Since the selection of the thirty-three or so states with a Senate contest any year is quasi-random, there is no need to worry about bias in the selection of different states and electoral contests in successive election years.[3] Moreover, as we will see below, the partisan division among seats up for election is not dependent on the parties' seat strengths going into the election or even the partisan division of election outcomes decided six years earlier. Measured as the seat division in the seats up for reelection, each election outcome is determined by the key variables measured for the year at hand and, apart from continuity of the key predictors, is independent of election outcomes that came before.

Figure 5.1 displays the post–World War II party division of the Senate over time in two ways—as the division of the entire Senate and as the division for seats freshly elected. The former is a moving average of the latter and makes a far smoother appearing time series. By isolating the time series of seats up for election, we see tremendous variation in electoral fortunes. In the best Democratic years (e.g., 1958, 1964), Democrats win over two-thirds of the seats up for election. In the best Republican years (e.g., 1946, 1980, 1996), Republicans win

FIGURE 5.1. Party Composition of Senate Seats over Time: All Seats vs. Seats Up for Election

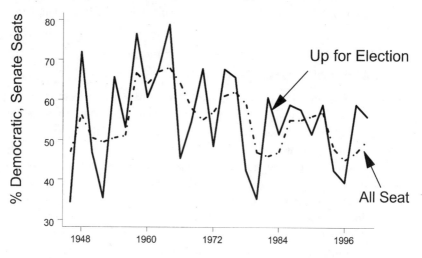

over 60 percent of the seats. Note also that a party's gain or loss in overall composition is due as much to its performance six years before as to its performance in the year at hand. (Witness the Democrats' resurgence of 2000 following their 1994 debacle.)

Measured in terms of seats up for election, the percentage of Senate seats

FIGURE 5.2. Partisan Division of House and Senate Seats up for Election

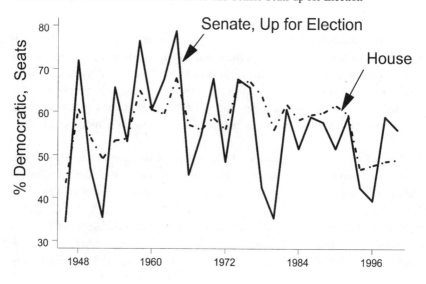

won by Democrats moves in far wider swings than that of House seats. This pattern is shown in Figure 5.2. Senate elections are far more responsive to national forces than are elections for the House. The reason, of course, is that House outcomes tend to be insulated from national forces by one-party districts and a strong incumbency advantage. Senate constituencies (states) are by far the most competitive from a partisan standpoint and hence display a stronger seat swing per shift of the national vote.

The next task is to account for the variation over time that we observe in the partisan division of Senate elections. As shown below, much of the variance—about 75 percent, in fact—can be accounted for by four independent variables—the national division of party identification, the nation's ideological mood, presidential coattails (or their absence at midterm), and ideological balancing (in midterms or in presidential years when the presidential winner is widely anticipated). The analysis of the effects of partisanship and ideological mood are drawn from chapter 7 of *The Macro Polity* (Erikson, MacKuen, and Stimson 2002), covering the twenty-three elections over the period 1952–96. The analysis is extended for this volume to cover coattails and ideological balancing.

Performance and Ideology: Macropartisanship and Mood

Previous attempts to account for the partisan division of seats in the House or Senate have centered their attention on performance indicators such as the president's popularity and the state of the economy. The standard hypothesis has been that for Congress, the presidential party is helped when the president is popular and good economic times roll. With the focus on House contests, the literature has debated whether presidential popularity and prosperity actually make much discernible difference apart from the indirect influence via presidential coattails (e.g, Erikson 1990; Jacobson 1990). Of course, the idea that good times help the presidential party is fully rooted in common sense. Yet this preoccupation with the goodness or badness of the times narrows our understanding of voter motivations. As we will see, there is more to accounting for Senate election outcomes (and those for the House) than simply whether the president's approval rating is high and the economy growing during the run-up to the election.

When election scholars account for votes at the individual level using survey data, they usually start with two crucial individual-level indicators—the respondent's party identification and some measure of the respondent's liberalism-conservatism. People who call themselves Democrats and have liberal political attitudes vote Democratic; people who call themselves Republicans and have conservative attitudes vote Republican. It might seem to follow, therefore, that if the aggregate division of partisanship or ideology were to shift from one election to the next, the election results would also change accordingly. Convert more voters to Republicanism and conservatism for example, and one would expect more Republican votes. Despite the logic of this argument, until recently the nation's partisan and ideological divisions were ignored in analyses of electoral time series.

There were two reasons for this neglect. First, their effects could not be tested: the nation's macro-level partisanship and ideological preferences had not been measured systematically as time-series data. Second, there was thought to be little reason for testing: it was widely believed that even if these variables were measured, they would behave more like constants than variables. Seemingly the variables that explain partisan differences from one election outcome to another would be a different set from the variables that explain one voter's choice from another's in the same election.

In *The Macro Polity* (Erikson et al. 2002) and in earlier writings we reported on our measurements of partisanship (macropartisanship) and ideology (policy mood) over time. Both macropartisanship (MacKuen, Erikson, and Stimson 1989, 1992; Erikson, MacKuen, and Stimson 1998) and liberal-conservative mood (Stimson 1991, 1999) are variables, not constants, displaying palpable movement over time. Moreover, we understand much of the dynamics underlying these crucial indicators of the public temperament. Macropartisanship responds to performance: the same shocks that move consumer sentiment and presidential approval also affect partisanship (see especially Erikson et al. 1998, 2002, chaps. 4, 5). Mood responds to economic maladies (with unemployment boosting liberalism, inflation boosting conservatism) and is also affected by current policy, with liberal policy reducing the demand for further liberalism, and so on (see Erikson et al. 2002, chaps. 6, 9). Macropartisanship and mood are now measured and show real and predictable variation. To be relevant, partisanship and ideology must pass the additional test of electoral relevance. Do shifts in these variables signal electoral change or not? This test is applied here for Senate and House elections: we ask, Do Senate (and House) election outcomes vary over time as a response to the electorate's shifting of its collective party identification and its ideological demands?

Macropartisanship

Macropartisanship largely reflects the cumulative permanent record of the public's evaluation of the parties. The economic shocks and political shocks that influence consumer sentiment and presidential approval also add to and subtract from the public's identification with the presidential party. By this interpretation, all past inputs into the electorate's collective partisanship are permanent. The current division of the parties has been influenced by such events as the current economy, the Gulf War, Watergate, and probably even ancient history like

Roosevelt's court-packing scheme. In terms of major stimuli, current partisanship reflects the permanent influence of the New Deal (helping the Democrats) and the Reagan era (helping the Republicans).[4]

Macropartisanship is measured here as the Democratic percentage of partisans in the third quarter of the election year. Following Erikson et al. (1998), macropartisanship is subdivided into two components: equilibrium partisanship and transient partisanship.[5] Equilibrium partisanship is the long-term fundamental component of partisanship, measured as the cumulation of economic and political shocks manifested in consumer sentiment and presidential approval. Transient partisanship is the residual, the portion of observed partisanship unaccounted for by equilibrium partisanship. According to Erikson et al. (2002, chap. 7), both components of macropartisanship are powerful predictors of presidential voting. As we will see here, only equilibrium partisanship appears to affect Senate and House outcomes.

Ideological Mood

Consider a simple model of ideological representation that works as follows. The public's demand for liberalism versus conservatism rises and falls as a function of the public's changing taste plus the policy response from Washington to past ideological demand. The more liberal the taste, the more liberal the demand; but also, liberal policies lower the demand for more liberalism. Politicians respond to the public's ideological demand because they perceive an electoral threat if they fail to do so. Republicans moderate because they believe the electorate votes Democratic when in a liberal mood, while Democrats moderate because they believe the electorate votes Republican when in a conservative mood (Erikson et al. 2002, chap. 9). For this electoral threat to be credible, the electorate's vote must actually translate its ideological demand into a partisan choice.

Electoral ideology is measured as Stimson's (1991, 1999) policy mood, the annual measure of the public's net policy preferences, 1952–96. The mood score for a given year is an estimate of the public's liberalism on policy issues for the year. Percentages can be interpreted as weighted means of survey responses where the percentage is the liberal percentage of liberal and conservative responses. Responses are adjusted to reflect year-to-year movement by item but be unaffected by the survey items asked the public in the given year.

Macropartisanship, Mood, and Senate Elections

Table 5.1 presents a set of regressions predicting the national partisan verdict in Senate (and House) elections, 1952–96. As independent variables, the equations

TABLE 5.1. Predicting Democratic Seats from Macropartisanship, Mood, Midterm

	House			Senate			
	(1)	(2)	(3)	(4)	(5)	(6)	(7)
Macropartisanship	0.68			1.29**	1.24***		
	(4.37)			(3.49)	(3.05)		
Equilibrium		0.96***	0.99***			2.37***	2.39***
		(4.61)	(4.73)			(5.02)	(5.27)
Short-term		0.33				0.19	
		(1.59)				(0.33)	
Mood	0.37*	0.59***	0.63***	1.38**	1.44***	2.14***	2.17***
	(2.75)	(3.84)	(4.13)	(3.86)	(4.19)	(6.15)	(6.56)
Midterm	−10.65***	−10.52***	−10.16***	−21.30***	−19.49***	−16.17**	−15.58***
	(−4.88)	(−5.00)	(−4.84)	(−3.77)	(−4.02)	(−3.69)	(−3.98)
Lagged Seats, t-2	0.53**	0.64***	0.73***	0.09			
	(3.48)	(4.24)	(5.38)	(0.52)			
Lagged Seats, t-6					0.06		
					(0.45		
Constant	−31.76*	−69.26**	−78.48***	−100.87**	−101.24**	210.81***	214.41***
	(−2.38)	(−3.25)	(−3.93)	(−3.05)	(−3.05)	(−4.72)	(−5.07)
Adjusted R Squared	.727	.754	.749	.606	.604	.718	.731
SEE	3.04	2.89	2.91	7.69	7.71	6.51	6.36

N = 23 elections, 1952-1996. * = significant at .05, ** at .01, *** at .001. T-values in parentheses.

include macropartisanship and mood plus a midterm variable and, in some instances, a variable reflecting lagged seats. The midterm variable is used to give a preliminary accounting for the midterm effect—the strong tendency of the presidential party to lose seats in midterm years. It is scored 0 for presidential years, +1 for midterms with a Democratic president, and −1 for midterms with a Republican president.

In all seven equations for the Senate and House, we see significant effects for macropartisanship and mood. The size of the evident effect depends on the exact specification. Equations vary by whether lagged seats are controlled and by whether macropartisanship is subdivided into its two components. One difference between Senate and House equations is the contribution of lagged seats. For House equations, lagged seats matter, most likely because seats held going into an election reflect the aggregate partisan incumbency advantage. For Senate elections, lagged seats show no effect—whether from two or six years earlier—

as if neither the incumbency lineup nor recent partisan track records mattered.[6] For both chambers, more variance in seats is explained when macropartisanship is measured by its equilibrium component alone. Equilibrium partisanship represents the permanent cumulation of economic and political shocks, while short-term partisanship represents transient effects on the division of Democrats and Republicans. In a quite visible difference, the former but not the latter contributes to Senate and House seats; evidently partisan change affects legislative elections only when the partisan change is long-lasting.[7]

The "best" equations in table 5.1 are equations 3 and 7, predicting seats parsimoniously from equilibrium partisanship, mood, the midterm variable, and (for the House only) lagged seats, with each predicting over 70 percent of the variance in seats. At the moment, our interest is on the coefficients and t values for equilibrium partisanship and mood. These variables show strong and highly significant coefficients for both chambers, but particularly the Senate. According to the estimates, each percentage point change of equilibrium partisanship or mood creates a change of over 2 percent of the Senate seats up for election. Translated from percentages to numbers won or lost, each three points of macropartisanship or mood generates a corresponding shift of about two additional Senate seats.[8]

With the dependent variables calibrated in terms of the percentage of seats up-captured by the Democrats, we see that Senate outcomes are much more responsive to public opinion than House outcomes. This makes considerable sense. First, in terms of votes, there is no reason why Senate contests should be any less responsive to national forces than House contests. Second, as a group, Senate constituencies (states) are much more competitive than House constituencies. Clearly, small perturbations in national partisanship or liberalism-conservatism can change the makeup of the new Senate class.[9]

Adding Presidential Approval

Presidential approval is one variable often thought to be a good predictor of congressional elections. Here we briefly examine the fate of our equations when approval is entered on the right hand side. Because the test is whether approval is related to presidential party success, we multiply approval times a presidential party variable (1 if Democrat, −1 if Republican) and include presidential party as a control, along with the usual midterm variable. Table 5.2 shows the result. Equations 8 and 10 include approval but not equilibrium partisanship or mood. As expected, these equations show "significant" approval effects. In equations 9 and 11, equilibrium partisanship and mood are entered. Their coefficients continue to retain most of their original value and continue to be statistically

TABLE 5.2. Predicting Democratic Seats from Macropartisanship, Mood, Midterm, and Presidential Approval

	House		Senate	
	(8)	**(9)**	**(10)**	**(11)**
Equilibrium Macropartisanship		0.72*		2.16***
		(2.87)		(3.82)
Mood		0.43*		1.92***
		(2.38)		(4.65)
Presidential - Party	−10.04*	−5.59	−24.00**	−7.33
	(−2.55)	(1.78)	(2.87)	(−1.03)
Pres. Approval *Pres Party. .	0.21*	0.11	0.44*	0.10
	(2.85)	(0.87)	(2.80)	(0.75)
Midterm	−10.69*	−10.49**	−21.30***	−11.40
	(−2.48)	(−3.52)	(−3.77)	(−2.09)
Lagged Seats, t-2	0.50*	0.73***		
	(2.67)	(5.26)		
Constant	−34.78*	−49.57	63.95	−187.15**
	(−3.52)	(−2.00)	(14.20)	(−3.39)
Adjusted R Squared	.481	.764	.377	.730
SEE	4.52	2.80	10.11	6.37

N = 23 elections, 1952–1996. * = significant at .05, ** at .01, *** at .001. T-values in parentheses.

significant. Approval now is no longer significant. Its seeming effect is largely spurious, largely because it is superseded by equilibrium partisanship.[10]

Approval no longer matters (or at least does not matter to a statistically convincing degree) because it is incorporated into equilibrium partisanship. Although perhaps not obvious at first blush, this distinction is an important nuance. The next Senate election will be somewhat predictable from current approval, but only in the sense that the same shocks that cause a president's approval (and consumer sentiment, which predicts approval) to go up and down also add to the permanent record of equilibrium partisanship, which predicts the next election.

Why the Effects of Macropartisanship and Mood Are Obscured

We have seen that Senate seats are greatly affected by macropartisanship (the national division of party identification) and mood (the liberalism-conservatism of public policy preferences). Although these effects show up strongly in multivariate equations, to show this result more is required than simply measuring these variables and observing the correlations. The Democratic share of contested Senate seats correlates only modestly, at .25 and .45 respectively, with equilibrium partisanship and mood. The underlying strength of the effects of these variables on Senate seats is obscured by the strong negative relationship ($r = -.55$) between equilibrium partisanship and mood. Aggregate partisanship and aggregate ideology are decidedly different in the national time series, each obscuring the effect of the other. Why these two aggregate-level variables are negatively related is an interesting question, but one that is beyond the scope of this chapter.[11]

Balancing and Coattails

So far the discussion has failed to comment on the significant negative coefficient for the "midterm" variable. This variable is necessary to capture the congressional losses the presidential party typically receives at midterm. But why do presidential parties suffer at midterm? Understanding this phenomenon can only sharpen our understanding of Senate elections.

The two prominent explanations for midterm loss are "ideological balancing" and "withdrawn coattails." By the balancing argument (Alesina and Rosenthal 1994; Fiorina 1992), moderates vote against the presidential party because adding more Congress members from the opposite ideological persuasion provides a welcome moderation in policies. The "withdrawn coattails" argument, with its longer history, argues simply the withdrawal of the winning president's coattails.

The persistently negative coefficient for the midterm dummy signifies that at midterm each party is better off not controlling the presidency. This result is as if the electorate tilted to the out-party at midterm to ideologically offset the influence of the president. Note that this interpretation is not simply a restatement of the law of "midterm loss," whereby the seat change for the presidential party almost always declines at midterm. For House elections, the regularity of midterm loss is often attributed to a natural decline from the winning presidential party's exceptional seat strength going into the midterm election, whether in terms of surge and decline, regression to the mean, or seats exposed. This interpretation is incomplete at best because midterm loss persists even when previous seat holdings are held constant. And the "withdrawn coattails" explanation contains a logical flaw when applied to Senate elections. As Grofman et al. (1998) point out, Senate midterm loss cannot plausibly be attributed to a party's fortunes in the previous presidential election for the simple reason that Senate seat loss at midterm is a function of the election six years earlier, which as often as not did not even favor the current presidential party.

This reasoning makes the highly significant −15.58 midterm coefficient for Senate seats all the more remarkable. A presidential party loses about five Senate seats at midterm that it otherwise would hold if it did not control the White House. This is controlling for the electorate's partisanship and ideology and ignoring the seat divisions from two or six years earlier.[12] The earlier seat divisions do not matter anyway, as the current division of Senate seats is quite independent of partisan history and is solely a function of the key variables in the election year.[13]

Clearly, the midterm electorate is influenced by which party controls the presidency, favoring the party out of power. But why? The explanation offered here is ideological balancing: knowing the ideology of the presidential party causes centrist voters to give extra consideration to the opposite party at midterm. Among political scientists, balancing theory is controversial, since it is difficult to sell the idea that even a modest share of the public is capable of ideologically strategic voting. As we have seen, the public's collective determinations of the partisan divisions of the Senate and House are predictable from the public's net ideological preferences. If people vote Democratic to get liberal policies and Republican to get conservative policies, surely some could also be capable of voting against the presidential party to restore ideological balance.[14]

Still, the balancing interpretation faces one interesting challenge. Do voters also balance in presidential elections? According to Alesina and Rosenthal's initial theory, voters do not balance in presidential years because they do not know who the president will be. However, in many election years the identity of the incoming president is obvious to attentive observers by Election Day. Where is the evidence of their presidential-year balancing? Alesina and Rosenthal (1994) suggest a possible answer: ideological voters can be balancing on the basis of expectations of the presidential outcome but be offset by coattail voters voting a straight ticket.

Thus, we add a further complexity to the Senate vote in presidential years. Do some presidential-year voters engage in anticipatory balancing, tilting against the presidential party for Congress when the anticipated presidential outcome is a near certainty? We must also ask, do some presidential year voters behave as coattail voters, casting congressional votes as if influenced by the party of their presidential choice? It may be noticed that these two propositions are potentially in contradiction to each other: Does an anticipatory landslide make one vote against the party of the anticipated winner; and/or does an actual presidential landslide carry extra voters for the presidential party on the president's coattails?

To sort this out empirically requires separate measures of the presidential

TABLE 5.3. Predicting Democratic Seats from Presidential Vote Margin and Probability of Democratic President.

	House			Senate		
	(12)	(13)	(14)	(15)	(16)	(17)
Equilibrium	0.99***	0.91***	0.82**	2.39***	2.20***	2.03***
Macropartisanship	(4.73)	(4.15)	(3.65)	(5.27)	(4.68)	(4.37)
Mood	0.63***	0.55**	0.54**	2.17***	2.00***	1.96***
	(4.13)	(3.41)	(3.27)	(6.56)	(5.70)	(5.69)
Midterm	−10.16***	−10.15***		−15.58***	−15.36***	
	(−4.84)	(−4.90)		(−3.98)	(−3.99)	
Presidential		0.17	0.70***		0.40	1.36**
Vote Margin		(1.23)	(3.88)		(1.30)	(3.53)
Probability of			−8.93***			14.64***
Democrat Win			(−4.79)			(−4.15)
Lagged Seats, t-2	0.73***	0.74***	0.67***			
	(5.38)	(5.52)	(5.19)			
Constant	−78.48***	−69.10**	−59.16*	−214.4***	−192.1***	−179.1***
	(−3.93)	(−3.27)	(−2.77)	(−5.07)	(−4.27)	(−4.03)
Adjusted R Squared	.749	.756	.749	.731	.740	.750
SEE	2.91	2.87	2.91	6.36	6.25	6.03

N = 23 elections, 1952–1996. * = significant at .05, ** at .01, *** at .001. T–values in parentheses.

vote margin (to estimate coattails) and the probabilities of Democratic and Republican presidential victories, as seen by ideological voters on Election Day. Could presidential-year balancing be hidden by countervailing behavior by coattail voters? And could coattail voting be obscured by the countervailing behavior of balancers?

Estimating the presidential vote margin, of course, is easy. For presidential years, it is measured as the Democrats' two-party vote for president minus 50 percent in presidential years; for midterms it is set to 0. Estimating the expected probability of a Democratic win is more complicated. For midterms, the probabilities, of course, are 0 if a Republican president and 1 if a Democratic president. For presidential years, the estimated probability of a Democratic win is based on the final report of the Gallup Poll. To convert poll margins to probabilities, it is assumed that informed voters act as if they know the regression equation predicting the actual vote margins from final poll margins and decipher the probability of a Democratic victory by assuming the standard error of estimate to be the sampling error.[15] This is not as ridiculous as it might seem at first glance; it is just an approximation of the electoral odds that informed voters would obtain by paying attention to the experts.

Table 5.3 presents the relevant regressions for both the Senate and House. Equations 12 and 15 provide the base, predicting seats from equilibrium partisanship, mood, midterm, and (for the House) lagged seats. Next, we add presidential coattails as measured by presidential vote margin (equations 13 and 16). By itself, this variable contributes nothing to predicting the seat divisions. If we stopped here, we would conclude that presidential voting had no effect on the outcomes of lower offices, that presidential coattails were a myth. But as equations 14 and 17 show, that would be the wrong conclusion.

The purpose here is to see if there is equal balancing in presidential years when the outcome is known with near certainty as at midterm. The appropriate critical test is whether we get a similar coefficient for probability of a Democratic win as we do for the original midterm variable. We do, as equations 14 and 17 clearly show. With both of our new variables in the equation, we see a significant positive coattail effect and a significant negative effect from the expectation of presidential victory.

The implication of the probability of Democratic win coefficient of equation 17 is that when the probability of a presidential victory is nearly 1.0, the expected seat division is virtually identical to the expectation when the party holds the presidency at midterm, given the same independent variables. The trick is that coattails are held constant at 0 in midterms but are a major factor in presidential races. Given an expected presidential landslide, the presidential party holds more seats than two years later at midterm; but the difference is made up by the presence of coattails in the presidential year and their absence two years later. The impact of strong coattails is often obscured because of the early balancing in the presidential year. The best set of circumstances for a victorious presidential party would be a strong landslide (coattails) that was unexpected (no balancing)—such as the 1980 Reagan shock. The worst set of circumstances for the victorious presidential party would be a tepid victory (few coattails) that was expected (balancing)—such as the weak Republican congressional showing when Bush ascended in 1988.

Discussion

We have seen that Senate (and House) elections are largely determined by the electorate's partisanship (macropartisanship), the ideological demand of the electorate (mood), and the expected party of the president. If this analysis is correct, then political parties are in a certain sense in control of their electoral fate.

The national division of partisanship is a cumulation of political and economic shocks, with the president's party gaining from good times and punished for the bad. Thus, a party helps itself by producing and maintaining good times when it controls the presidency and suffers when it does not. The president's senatorial ticket-mates share the ride when times go good or bad, but with the partisan fate determined as much by events past as events present.[16]

Similarly, the electoral importance of mood suggests that parties can control their electoral fate by their balance of kowtowing to public opinion versus engaging in ideological indulgence. Other analysis (Erikson et al. 2002, chaps. 8, 9) indicates that liberal policies cause mood to move in the conservative direction and vice versa. Thus, to the extent that mood matters electorally, the majority congressional party must decide how much policy to consume at the cost of what electoral risk. Similarly, the minority congressional party must decide how much electoral reward it will buy at the price of bowing to ideologically distasteful policy.

Finally, we see strong evidence that the vote is affected not only by the president's party at midterm but by the expected presidential party in presidential years. Here again, parties control their fate in the sense that congressional parties gain by conceding control of the presidency while at the same time avoiding adverse coattails. In this sense, the pathway to Senate (and House) electoral success may be via losing the presidency. And whether or not it is exactly what they want, the voters may get divided government as the result.

Notes

1. For studies that focus specifically on the party composition over time in the U.S. Senate, see Abramowitz and Segal 1986; Lewis-rock and Rice 1992; Waterman 1990; Grofman, Brunel, and Koetzle 1998.

2. That is, assuming 100 seats and ignoring the occasional short-term replacement,

$$\Delta\%Dem._t = \%Dem._t - \%Dem._{t-2}$$
$$= \left\{ \left(\frac{D_t + D_{t-2} + D_{t-4}}{100} \right) - \left(\frac{D_{t-2} + D_{t-4} + D_{t-6}}{100} \right) \right\} \times 100$$
$$= D_t - D_{t-6}$$
$$\cong \frac{(\%D_t - \%D_{t-6})}{3}$$

where $\%Dem._t$ = the Democratic percent of seats in year t, D_t = the number of Senators elected in year t, and $\%D_t$ = the percent won by Democrats in year t of those up for election in year t.

3. In addition to regularly scheduled elections, the database includes elections for short terms to fill vacancies.

4. Consider that in surveys into the 1980s, the pre-Depression generation was more Republican than the immediate post-Depression generation. This persistence of this

generational divide into old age is due to the older cohort's pro-Republican stimuli from the pre-Depression years that the post-Depression voters lacked.

5. Because the division into the two series begins with 1953, for 1952 equilibrium partisanship and transient partisanship are measured by their 1953:1 values.

6. Not shown, lagged Senate seats do not contribute to the House seats equation, and vice versa.

7. This distinction does not apply to presidential elections. Transient and equilibrium partisanship contribute about equally to the presidential vote (Erikson et al. 2002).

8. Following any one election, the net partisan division of all 100 senators reflects mood and macropartisanship over three successive elections. We can predict 78 percent of the partisan variance for 100 seats from pooling the forecasts for the three relevant election years.

9. Possibly, the effects of the independent variables are concentrated in open seats. To test this possibility, we divide the seat change into that due to partisan shifts in incumbent races and that due to partisan shifts in open seats (with appropriate weighting for the relative number of incumbent/open seats). The coefficients are larger for open seats than incumbent races, since open-seat contests are usually tighter. Yet for both incumbent races and open seats, the effects of all three independent variables are highly significant. Another surmise is that much of the change is not due to the electorate at all but to strategic retirements. However, this hypothesis fails spectacularly. The net partisanship of retirees is totally unrelated to the independent variables.

10. We could also add consumer sentiment or some other economic measure to the mix on the right-hand side. Like approval, consumer sentiment does not add significantly. This variable is on the border of significance if entered when macropartisanship and mood are omitted. However, even this hint of an effect is swamped when approval is included.

11. One conjecture is that favorable macropartisanship leads to electoral success, which brings policy changes that yield negative ideological reactions in terms of mood.

12. To the extent that midterm seat loss is a function of lagged party strength in the prior presidential election, party control at midterm explains only seat change and not seat holdings at midterm. Strong midterm effects on seat holdings without controlling lagged seats only emphasize that the midterm effect is due to conditions at midterm, not the previous election.

13. Recall, however, that the division of Senate seats does depends on current equilibrium partisanship, which is a cumulation of past political and economic shocks. In that sense, when current voting is a function of equilibrium partisanship it indeed depends on partisan history.

14. It is not required that voters make a conscious conditional judgment of the sort "I will vote Republican because the president is a Democrat, but I would vote Democrat if the president were a Republican." All that is required is that the presidential party be one influence—one consideration—on their vote choice.

15. The assumption is that informed voters consider the prediction as the mean of a normal distribution with a standard deviation equal to the standard error of estimate for the prediction equation. Informed voters then locate the point on this scale where the vote is a tie. The percentage of the distribution to the left of this point is the probability of a Democratic win. The regression equation is $Y = 0.82 + 0.83\ X$, where Y is the Democratic vote and X is the Gallup estimate. The R^2 is .85. The N is 14 elections, from 1948 to 2000. As an alternative, we could assume a normal distribution centered at the Gallup prediction as the mean, with a standard deviation based on sampling theory and survey sample sizes of, say, 1,500. The two estimates correlate at .96 for presidential years and yield similar results.

16. Coattails add to the steepness of the ride in presidential years.

The Senate as a
Representative Institution

· 6 ·

Electoral Convergence in the U.S. Congress

John R. Alford and John R. Hibbing

> The federal Senate will never be able to transform itself, by gradual usurpations, into an independent . . . body. . . . If such a revolution should ever happen . . . the House of Representatives, with the people on their side, will at all times be able to bring back the Constitution to its primitive form and principles.—James Madison, Federalist #62

As a result of the 1980 elections, the 97th Congress consisted of a House of Representatives controlled by the Democrats and a Senate controlled by the Republicans. While this situation produced a good deal of commentary about the hazards of a divided Congress, it was hardly a novel occurrence. Divided control of the Executive and Congress had become commonplace by 1980, and Congress itself had been divided three times in the previous 70 years. But there was a truly novel aspect to the events of 1980. For the first time in the history of the Republic, the Senate rather than the House had taken the lead in responding to a partisan tide. This independent, responsive role of the Senate was evident again in 1986 when another partisan switch occurred in the Senate but not in the House. And then, in 1994, partisan control of the Senate switched in lockstep with that of the House—not years later.

These recent events are particularly noteworthy in light of the distinctive architecture of Senate and House elections. The constitutionally specified electoral arrangements of the House and Senate were based on the clear desire of the Framers to make the Senate more insulated than the House from electoral responsiveness. The events of the 1980s and 1990s are inconsistent with these intentions, constituting a reversal of the Framers' carefully crafted electoral design. Are these events flukes, or are they indicative of more fundamental and longer-lasting changes in the relationship of the two houses to the people? Has

89

the Senate actually become as sensitive to vote shifts as the House? If so, when did this change occur and why?

We believe that, rather than being an aberration, recent relative sensitivity of the Senate is actually the culmination of a long-term trend toward the elimination of the electoral distinction between the House and the Senate. In the pages that follow, we marshal three forms of historical evidence to support this statement: (1) the nature of switches in the partisan control of the two houses; (2) the levels of turnover in the two bodies; and (3) the respective swing ratios of the House and Senate. Analysis of these three diverse measures should provide sufficient basis for confirmation or rejection of our thesis. In the final portions of this chapter we speculate on the causes and consequences of the disappearance of the central structural component of Article 1. But first, we present a brief discussion of the Founders' intent and the reasons for it.

Founders' Intentions

The expressed desire of the Founders was to create a system in which the lower house would be sensitive to changes in the public mood while the upper house would provide insulation from rapid swings in popular sentiment. The Senate was to be "the saucer that cooled the coffee" (see Fenno 1982, 5). At the constitutional convention, Madison (1987) remarked on the need for the Senate to "protect the people against the transient impressions into which they themselves might be led" (193). He continued: "Men chosen for a short term and employed but a small portion in public affairs, might err from the same cause" (193–94). Madison thus felt that the second branch of the proposed government should be "sufficiently respectable" to stop the most egregious of these errors and that toward this end "considerable duration ought to be given to [terms of service in the Senate]" (195).[1] Similarly, Gouverneur Morris stated that the purpose of the second house (the Senate) was to "check the precipitation, changeableness, and excesses of the first branch" (Madison 1987, 233).

Madison expanded on these concepts in Federalist #62: "The necessity of the senate is not less indicated by the propensity of all single and numerous assemblies, to yield to the impulse of sudden and violent passions, and to be seduced by factious leaders into intemperate and pernicious resolutions. . . . A body which is to correct this infirmity ought itself to be free from it, and consequently ought to be less numerous. It ought, moreover, to possess great firmness and consequently ought to hold its authority by a tenure of considerable duration" (Madison, Hamilton, and Jay 1965, 379). Elsewhere in #62, Madison decried the "mutability in the public councils, arising from a rapid succession of new members" and argued for the need to have "some stable institution in the government" (380). Madison clearly felt that the Senate should be this institution, for regarding the House he speculated that "every new election [would] change one-half of the representatives" (381). Such large changes in membership would increase the likelihood of similarly large changes in opinion and consequent changes in measures. Madison saw this as unfortunate, since "continual change even of good measures is inconsistent with every rule of prudence and every prospect of success" (381).

The mechanics by which the second house would be made "less precipitous, changeable, and susceptible to excess" were eventually agreed upon. Senators were to be elected indirectly by state legislatures rather than directly by the people. Clearly, however, the Founders felt that indirect elections alone would be insufficient to shield the Senate properly from the vicissitudes of popular opinion. After all, the state legislatures themselves could be subject to rapid change. Thus, two other insulating features supplemented indirect election. Senators were presented with a six-year term—three times longer than that of a House member and half again longer than that of the president—providing them both an opportunity to acquire experience at the national level and a period of at least a few years in which securing their return to the Senate would be a fairly distant concern. Moreover, by incorporating a staggered term, the Founders extended this insulation to the institution itself. In the most precipitous of circumstances, only a third of the membership could be changed in a single election. Even assuming complete turnover, at least two election cycles would be required to install a new majority in the Senate. Our intention is to examine the degree to which these features do in fact provide some measure of decreased electoral sensitivity for the Senate relative to the House and to assess whether any insulating capabilities have eroded over the decades. We turn first to a careful look at the issue that initially caught our attention: the pattern of changes in House and Senate party control.

Switches in Partisan Control

The differentiated structure of Senate and House elections outlined in Article 1 was intended to produce one of two patterns of congressional response to changes in public sentiment. One type of anticipated change occurred if a shift in the public mood brought about the election of a new majority in the House of Representatives but left the Senate in the hands of the previous majority, though perhaps less securely. Assuming that the new public mood survived until the subsequent election, when another one-third of the Senate seats were being contested, the recently installed House majority would be retained and the Senate would now come into line with both the House and the public mood. We refer to this sequence of events as a *House-initiated* pattern of change, and an example of it occurred when the Whigs lost control of the House of Representatives to the Democrats in 1842 but retained control of the Senate until the 1844 election (see Table 6.1).

The second intended pattern is what we refer to as a *House-truncated* pattern. Here, as with the House-initiated pattern, a shift in public mood brings about the election of a new majority in the House but not the Senate. Two years hence, however, the public mood shift proves to be ephemeral. The switch, rather than being consummated with a new majority in the Senate, is undone by the return of the House to the old majority. Such a House-truncated pattern occurred in 1846 when the Whigs gained control of the House only to see it recaptured by the Democrats in the 1848 elections. No such flip-flop took place in the Senate, which remained in Democratic hands throughout. This is an example of what the Founders were hoping for when they attempted to design the Senate as a "defense to the people against their own temporary errors and delusions."

For better or worse, the defenses built into the structure of Senate elections are not foolproof. In the context of a well-developed two-party system, narrow partisan majorities in the Senate could be supplanted by the same tide that turned the House, even with elections affecting only one-third of the Senate membership. The result would be an unintended pattern, reflecting a breakdown in Senate insulation. This *simultaneous* pattern occurs when a shift in public mood produces simultaneous change in the control of both the House and the Senate. Such a pattern was evident in the 1840 election, in which both the House and the Senate switched from Democratic control to Whig control.

In Table 6.1, we apply the above typology to a history of change in partisan control of the House and the Senate for the period from 1836 to 1998.[2] If the structure of Senate elections provides the buffer the Founders intended, we should see two things: a disproportionate number of House switches and a predominance of truncated and delayed patterns as opposed to simultaneous patterns. To provide a rough feel for how the patterns have evolved, the figures at the bottom of the table summarize the House-Senate changes for the approximately eighty-year periods before and after the most notable alteration in Senate elections structure, the shift to universal direct elections in 1914.

In the first period (1836–1914) the constitutionally provided electoral structures performed as intended. House switches were nearly twice as likely to occur as Senate switches (14 House to 8 Senate), but, more importantly, the patterns were almost always of the constitutionally intended House-initiated (6 of 11) or House-truncated (3 of 11) rather than constitutionally unintended simultaneous (2 of 11) or Senate-led (0 of 11) variety. In the second period (1914–98), the results were quite different. Senate switches actually occurred more frequently than House switches (7 House to 9 Senate). Most importantly, only one of the nine switch patterns after the advent of direct elections was of the intended sort, and even this exception would not have occurred except that the Republicans

TABLE 6.1. Switches in Partisan Control

Year	House	Senate	Pattern	Nature
1840	Dem. to Whig	Dem. to Whig	Simultaneous	Unintended
1842	Whig to Dem.			
1844		Whig to Dem.	House initiated	Intended
1846	Dem. to Whig			
1848	Whig to Dem.		House Truncated	Intended
1854	Dem. to Rep.			
1856	Rep. to Dem.		House truncated	Intended
1858	Dem. to Rep.			
1860		Dem. to Rep.	House initiated	Intended
1876	Rep. to Dem.			
1878		Rep. to Dem.	House initiated	Intended
1880	Dem. to Rep.			
1882		Dem. to Rep.	House initiated	Intended
1880	Rep. to Dem.			
1888	Dem. to Rep.		House truncated	Intended
1890	Rep. to Dem.			
1892		Rep. to Dem.	House initiated	Intended
1894	Dem. to Rep.	Dem. to Rep.	Simultaneous	Unintended
1910	Rep. to Dem.			
1912		Rep. to Dem.	House initiated	Intended
1918	Dem. to Rep.	Dem. to Rep.	Simultaneous	Unintended
1930	Rep. to Dem.			
1932		Rep. to Dem.	House initiated	Intended
1946	Dem. to Rep.	Dem. to Rep.	Simultaneous	Unintended
1948	Rep. to Dem.	Rep. to Dem.	Simultaneous	Unintended
1952	Dem. to Rep.	Dem. to Rep.	Simultaneous	Unintended
1954	Rep. to Dem.	Rep. to Dem.	Simultaneous	Unintended
1980		Dem. to Rep.		
1986		Rep. to Dem.	Senate truncated	Unintended
1994	Dem. to Rep.	Dem. to Rep.	Simultaneous	Unintended

SUMMARY

Time Period	Intended Pattern	Unintended Pattern	House Switches	Senate Switches
1836–1914	9	2	14	8
1916–1996	1	7	7	9

held on to the Senate by just one seat in 1930. If the Senate had switched in 1930 instead of two years later in 1932, this would have been merely another simultaneous switch, since the House moved from Republican to Democratic control in 1930. Surprisingly, during this whole time period there were no House-truncated switches.

Even more surprisingly, the switches in 1980 and 1986 formed a pattern unlike any in the previous history of the Congress. They involved a chamber that changed hands in rapid response to a shift in public mood, balanced by a more muted change in the other body such that party control was not altered. The shift in public mood faded, and six years later, control of the more sensitive chamber reverted to the majority party, bringing it back in line with the other house. This is, of course, what we have called a truncated pattern. It would have been notable simply because there had not been a truncated change for a hundred years, but what made it unprecedented was that the electorally sensitive chamber was the *Senate* and the insular body was the *House*. We call this novel occurrence a *Senate-truncated* pattern. It represents not just an unintended pattern but the exact opposite of what the Founders intended. It was followed in 1994 by another unintended pattern—a simultaneous shift in the partisan control of both the House and the Senate—and, of course, in 2001 by the Senate, but not the House, switching again.

The pattern of partisan change in Congress in recent decades leaves little doubt as to the inability of electoral restraints to make the Senate more insulated than the House. Only once has a switch in party control followed an expected pattern. The bulk of the switches came between 1946 and 1954, when the House and the Senate simultaneously changed control no fewer than four times. It is precisely this kind of short-term vacillation in the entire legislative branch that the constitutional provisions governing Senate elections were designed to prevent. Instead of providing continuity and restraint, the Senate was undergoing the same disruptive changes in membership and control exhibited by the lower, "popular" house. And the election of 1980 saw the responsiveness of the Senate relative to the House enter new territory. In that election, control of the Senate shifted to the Republicans, not as a delayed response to a 1978 House shift, and not simultaneously with a 1980 House shift, but as an entirely independent occurrence. For the first time, the Senate underwent an autonomous switch in partisan control.

Tenure and Turnover

Changes in majority control of the houses of Congress are the most visible and probably the most important forms of electoral sensitivity.[3] They are not, however, the only forms. In more typical elections, sensitivity is reflected in less dramatic changes in the membership. These sentiments are clearly evident in Madison's remarks in Federalist #62: "Another defect to be [rectified] by a senate lies in a want of due acquaintance with the objects and principles of legislation. It is not possible that an assembly called for the most part from pursuits of a private nature continued in appointment for a short time and led by no permanent motive to devote the intervals of public occupation to a study of the laws, the affairs, and the comprehensive interests of their country, should, if left wholly to themselves, escape a variety of important errors in the exercise of their legislative trust" (Madison et al. 1965, 379).

Six-year terms and staggered elections were intended not only to delay changes in majorities but also to provide for a Senate with fewer novice, and more experienced, members than the House. To the degree that these electoral mechanisms are functioning properly, we would expect two things: one, that the percentage of first-term members in any given session should be higher in the House than the Senate; and two, that senators' average length of service should be longer than representatives'.

The effectiveness of these electoral mechanisms in practice can be judged by comparing the proportion of new members and the average length of service in the House and the Senate. Figures 6.1 and 6.2 present this information (smoothed as a result of three-Congress averaging) for the 25th Congress (elected 1836) through the 105th Congress (ending in 1998). Turning first to the percentage of new members, the pattern for the House in the 1800s clearly supports Madison's expectations of considerable turnover. Before 1900, the proportion of new members in the House exceeded 50 percent in 11 of the 32

FIGURE 6.1. Three Election Averages of the Proportion of New Members in Congress by Chamber

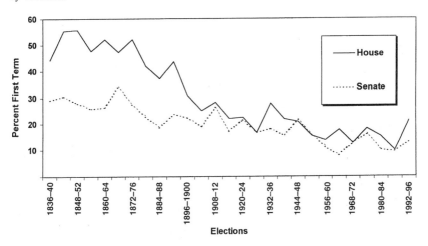

95

FIGURE 6.2. Three Election Averages of the Mean Years of Service in Congress by Chamber

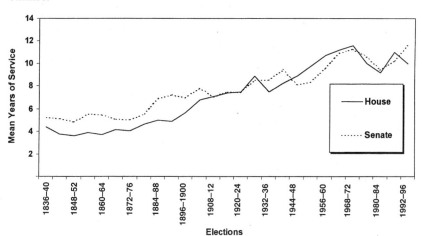

Congresses and in only two instances (the 47th and 56th Congresses) fell below one-third. Over the same period, membership turnover in the Senate was strikingly different. New members in the Senate never composed 50 percent of the body, and generally the figure was in the range of 20 to 30 percent. In some Congresses, the gap between House and Senate turnover was very large. For example, in 1842, 66.7 percent of the House membership but only 28.6 percent of the Senate membership was new.

The proportion of new membership in the House fell considerably in the twentieth century. During this period the percentage of new members never reached 50 percent and was greater than one-third in only 2 of the 49 Congresses. During the same period, the proportion of new members in the Senate was slightly lower than in the House, but the gap had been largely erased. During the second half of the twentieth century, while the proportion of new members in the Senate generally remained lower than that in the House, turnover in the two bodies had unmistakably converged.

A similar pattern can be seen with regard to the mean length of service in the House and Senate. In the 1800s, average years of service in the House fell below five in 26 of the 32 Congresses. In the Senate, during this same period, average years of service rose *above* five in 27 of the 32 Congresses. This is, of course, just what we would expect given the structural differences in House-Senate elections. But in the twentieth century, average years of service in the House rose above five in all of the 49 cases and by the end of the period was generally in the range of eight to nine. On the other hand, the mean length of Senate careers increased more modestly during this period, with the result that the average stay in the House approximated the average stay in the Senate. All told, in the most recent 49 Congresses, average length of service in the House seldom fell below 7 years and was often in excess of 10 years. In the Senate during this same period, the pattern was similar to that of the House. In fact, in 25 of the 49 most recent Congresses, mean years of service was actually *higher* in the House than in the Senate.

From the beginning of our time period till 1900, the percentage of new members in the House was always higher than the percentage of new members in the Senate, and the mean length of service of House members was always less than the mean length of service in the Senate. The intent of the Founders was realized. The election of 1900, however, produced a Congress in which, for the first time in our time period, turnover in the House was lower than that of the Senate and mean length of career in the House rose above that of the Senate. This reversal of intent was repeated in numerous other twentieth-century Congresses with regard to turnover and, especially, mean length of service.

Swing Ratio

Perhaps the most common measure of the electoral responsiveness of a body's membership is the swing ratio. It has been used to judge both the historical and comparative responsiveness of legislatures (Tufte 1973; Jacobson 1987; King and Gelman 1991; Brady and Grofman 1991; Jackman 1994; Campbell 1996). The swing ratio should be particularly useful in judging the relative insulation of the Senate from electoral forces, since it provides an election-by-election indicator of how responsive seat change is to vote change. The swing ratio is, as Niemi and Fett (1986) put it, "a summary measure that expresses the way in which institutional factors structure the translation of a given percentage of the vote into some percentage of the legislative seats" (82). It is precisely these institutional factors, namely the structural differences between House and Senate elections, that interest us here.

While the basic concept of the swing ratio is simple, it has been implemented in a variety of ways. The most important distinction is between the historical swing and the hypothetical swing. After an extensive comparison of these two forms, Niemi and Fett (1986) conclude in part that "the older, historical version of the ratio has a number of problems associated with it. . . . Fortunately an alternative, hypothetical swing ratio is available and is immune to many of these problems. As with any other measure, it is not perfect. If nothing else, it is considerably more time consuming to calculate. . . . Nonetheless, from the point of view of theory, practicality, and applicability it is a useful, and perhaps the best, operationalization of the swing ratio" (88). Following this advice, we will use the hypothetical swing ratio here to compare the House and the Senate.

The basic procedure in constructing the hypothetical swing ratio is to start with the actual election results for a given year, both the percentage of votes and the percentage of seats won, and then to project a set of hypothetical election results from this point. We have chosen to compute the hypothetical swing using the Democratic percentage of the vote, but the choice of party is arbitrary and does not affect the resulting swing ratios or interpretations. The actual computation is performed by adding one percentage point to the Democratic vote in each state for the Senate and district for the House and then recomputing the percentage of the seats that the Democratic party would win, given the additional margin. This procedure is repeated for five percentage points above and five percentage points below the actual election result, yielding a total of eleven data points for each election. These data points are then used to regress the percentage of seats on the percentage of votes, and the resulting unstandardized regression coefficient (slope) is the hypothetical swing ratio for that election. It can be interpreted as the expected change in the percentage of seats held by the Democratic party given a uniformly distributed one percentage point change in the Democratic vote.[4]

Table 6.2 reports the hypothetical swing ratios for the House and Senate for each election since 1914, the advent of mandated direct elections to the U.S. Senate. As columns 1 and 2 show, Senate elections have generally exhibited a higher swing ratio than House elections, with this difference becoming quite pronounced in recent years. Modern Senate swing ratios have been in the range of 3 to 4, while the House swing ratios have generally remained below 2. Thus, throughout most of the last few decades Senate seat change has been at least twice as sensitive to electoral vote shifts as has House seat change.[5]

The swing ratios of the House and Senate reported in columns 1 and 2 both have the percentage of seats in the elections as their dependent variable. Since all House seats are included in each election, the swing ratio for the House can be interpreted as the expected change in the percentage of Democratic seats in the House for a uniform one percent shift in the Democratic vote. The same is not the case, however, for the Senate election swing ratio, as reported in column 2. Only one-third of Senate seats are on the ballot in a given election, so the swing ratio for the contested seats is not the same as the swing ratio for the body as a whole. In a technical sense, the constitutional provision for staggered elections in the Senate can be thought of as an upper constraint on the dependent variable in the swing ratio equation. No matter how large the vote swing, the seat swing can never exceed one-third of vote swings on proportion of seats in the full body of the Senate, so we need to change the dependent variable from the proportion of the seats in the election to the proportion of the seats in the full body.

Column 3 of Table 6.2 reports the Senate swing ratios for the full Senate.

TABLE 6.2. Hypothetical Swing Ratio in the House and the Senate, 1914–96

Election	House Swing Ratio	Senate Election Swing Ratio	Senate Full-Body Swing Ratio
1914	3.18	5.45	1.84
1916	3.29	5.14	1.84
1918	2.34	4.83	1.87
1920	1.74	2.06	0.71
1922	2.64	4.23	1.51
1924	1.58	2.08	0.97
1926	1.20	3.74	1.34
1928	1.99	2.88	1.03
1930	1.97	2.51	0.90
1932	2.76	3.14	1.22
1934	2.76	2.80	1.00
1936	2.27	3.08	1.13
1938	2.66	3.27	1.17
1940	2.25	3.26	1.20
1942	1.96	2.89	1.00
1944	2.09	4.60	1.64
1946	1.95	2.48	0.94
1948	2.59	2.20	0.74
1950	2.10	3.43	1.26
1952	1.98	5.06	1.81
1954	2.11	3.44	1.34
1956	2.02	3.90	1.39
1958	2.57	3.61	1.23
1960	2.04	3.34	1.13
1962	1.71	5.04	1.86
1964	2.41	4.14	1.41
1966	1.75	2.35	0.80
1968	1.28	4.32	1.38
1970	1.29	4.21	1.39
1972	1.27	4.55	1.50
1974	2.13	4.86	1.55
1976	1.50	2.56	0.82
1978	1.45	2.97	0.98
1980	1.65	6.48	2.07
1982	1.66	4.20	1.35
1984	1.23	2.50	0.80
1986	1.02	5.00	1.60
1988	0.80	3.44	1.10
1990	1.21	2.134	0.68
1992	2.00	3.86	1.24
1994	2.18	2.47	0.79
1996	1.90	5.09	1.63

Source: Computed by authors on the basis of plus and minus 5 percent from the actual distribution.

When seat change is viewed as a proportion of the full body, we can see that the impact of vote change on the makeup of the Senate is much less dramatic than the election swing ratio (see column 2) would lead us to believe. The figures in column 3 are substantially smaller than those in column 2, but our concern is how the figures in column 3 compares to the corresponding House data in column 1.

To clarify the pattern of the relationship between the House swing ratio (column 1) and Senate full-body swing ratio (column 3), the data are presented in graphic form in Figure 6.3. In the early years of Senate elections, the full Senate swing ratio was substantially below that of the House, thus demonstrating the kind of relationship envisaged by the authors of the Constitution. Beginning in the mid-1960s, however, the House and Senate swings converged, and since the 1970s they have been often indistinguishable. Before 1964, in only two (1926 and 1962) out of twenty-six elections were Senate full-body swing ratios higher than House swing ratios. But in the sixteen elections after 1964, the Senate full-body swing ratio has been higher than the House ratio six times. The unprotected House at the end of the twentieth century is no more sensitive to swings in partisan mood than the Senate, despite the considerable constraint on Senate swing ratios produced by staggered elections.

Causes

At the broadest level, the relative insulation of the Senate can be viewed as a limited set of expected electoral patterns. As we have shown, the intended House-initiated and House-truncated patterns, once the dominant feature of Senate and House elections, have gradually disappeared, replaced by numerous simultaneous patterns and even a Senate-truncated pattern. At the level of the membership, the House's electoral structure was to yield a less veteran body, with more novices. But recently the House has equaled or even occasionally fallen below the Senate in the proportion of novice members, while House mean length of service has often exceeded that of the upper chamber. The swing ratio for the Senate, despite the relatively small proportion of its membership standing for election, now equals that of the once far more volatile House, and this volatility, when combined with relatively narrow margins of partisan control, has given us the modern Congress: two bodies that are largely indistinguishable in terms of electoral responsiveness, with the Senate being every bit as changeable as the House.

With regard to causes, the timing and the nature of the shifts evident in the data presented above suggest several prime candidates. It should not be surprising that such important changes have more than one cause. Our three different types of data point toward three different likely contributors to the electoral convergence we have documented.

The widely documented professionalization of the Congress noted by Polsby (1968) and many others cannot be separated from any discussion of the proportion of new members or the mean length of service. While the general impact of professionalization on the Congress as a whole is well appreciated, what has been less clearly apprehended is the differential impact of professionalization on the House and the Senate. Some degree of professionalization was desired and, to a modest degree, built into the Senate by the structural mechanisms we have noted here. No such mechanisms were desired for the House, as is clear from even a casual reading of Article 1. Remember that Madison's view of the House was "an assembly called for the most part from pursuits of a private nature continued in appointment for a short time and led by no permanent motive to devote intervals of public occupation to a study of the laws, the affairs, and the comprehensive interests of their country" (Federalist #62). These are, of course, precisely the characteristics of a nonprofessionalized legislative body. Inasmuch as they existed to a far greater degree in the House due to its short term and large size, the change brought by professionalization was much more profound in the House than in the Senate. In a sense, the secular trend of professionalization brought to the House what the Founders' careful use of structural mechanisms had already instilled in the Senate (for other possible unintended consequences of professionalization, see Fiorina 1996). This is the pattern we discussed above in regard to Figures 6.1 and 6.2. The advent of professionalization has both an elevating *and* a leveling effect on membership stability in the House and Senate.

Following shortly after the rise of professionalism, the change to direct popular senatorial elections in the Senate provides the next and most prominent potential cause of convergence (see Brandes Crook and Hibbing 1997). That the removal of one of the constitutional devices designed to shield the Senate from the popular mood might have reduced the insulation of the Senate is hardly unexpected. When we look to Table 6.1, we see that the sort of election patterns expected for the House and Senate dominated before 1914. After the initiation of direct elections, we find an expected pattern only once, and even this case was special in several respects.

In the modern era, by far the most widely noted change in the electoral environment of the Congress is the rapid rise of incumbency advantage in House elections in the mid-1960s (see Erikson 1971; Mayhew 1974a; Ferejohn 1977; Fiorina 1977a; Cover 1977; Born 1979; Alford and Hibbing 1981; Alford and Brady 1987; Gelman and King 1990; Jacobson 1997). A clear consequence of this rise in incumbency advantage can be seen in the swing ratios of the House and Senate (see Figure 6.3 and Table 6.2). From 1960 to 1990, swing ratios in the House dropped precipitously. As this increased incumbent safety began to move districts out of the

FIGURE 6.3. Three Election Averages of the Swing Ratio in the House and Senate, 1914–96

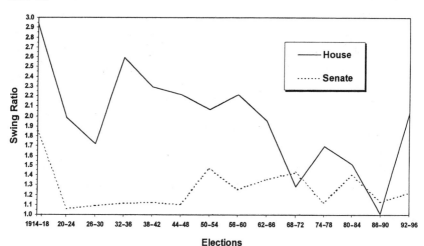

competitive range, typical vote swings proved less capable of producing comparable seat swings, thus attenuating the swing ratio. As a result, switches in partisan control of the House began to seem impossible. When a switch finally occurred in 1994, observers were shocked not that the historically insular Senate shifted at the same time as the House but that the highly insular contemporary House had switched at all. While scholars continue to debate the causes of increased incumbency advantage, too little attention has been given to the consequences. We believe one of the major consequences is the virtual elimination of the different levels of responsiveness intended for the House and the Senate.

While the move to direct Senate elections is an obvious and intuitively satisfying explanation for House-Senate convergence, the evidence here suggests it may be the least influential of the three changes, at least in its direct impact. The pattern for tenure and proportion of new members (Figures 6.1 and 6.2) is instructive. In terms of percent first-term, after large gaps between the House and Senate in the 1870s, the discrepancy diminishes to almost nothing by 1900 (well before the mandated shift to direct elections) and remains negligible thereafter. For mean length of service, the largest gaps come in the late 1880s and throughout the 1890s. By around 1900, mean tenure is practically identical in the two bodies, and after that, more often than not, House tenure is higher than Senate tenure.

Upon reflection, it is not so surprising that direct elections are only a partial cause of converging levels of electoral sensitivity. While the founders desired a stable and veteran Senate, the selection of the Senate by state legislatures had little to do with these goals. Senators chosen by the state legislatures may well have been experienced in government, but it is not at all clear that that experience would have been in the national Senate. Similarly, the changeability of the state legislatures themselves suggests that the likelihood of an individual's being reappointed at the end of a six-year term would not necessarily be enhanced by vesting this choice with those legislatures. The stable and veteran nature of the Senate was to have come from staggered elections and six-year terms, both of which have endured unchanged to the present.

In sum, before 1900 the combination of indirect elections, six-year terms, and staggered elections proved to be relatively effective in buffering the Senate from short-term changes in the popular mood. Gradually, however, the Senate and House were becoming less distinct in terms of membership turnover and seniority. The combination of rising professionalism and direct senatorial elections altered the pattern of membership turnover as well as the pattern of changes in majority control in ways feared by the Founders. Despite this substantial evidence of convergence, some evidence of Senate distinctiveness remained. In comparing House and Senate swing ratios, it is clear that up to the middle of the twentieth century the Senate was different from the House with regard to the rate at which shifts in the vote were translated into shifts in seats. While this gap appears not to have been large enough to prevent simultaneous changes in the majorities of the House and Senate on a variety of occasions, the two bodies were still not on an equal footing. The Senate never led the House or changed party control independent of the House. This pattern of relative if modest Senate insulation began to break down in about the mid-1960s.

The pattern of the House and Senate swing ratios since 1914 is worth emphasizing. Seat change in the Senate itself is only slightly more sensitive to vote change now than it was fifty years ago. The buffering of the Senate through longer terms and staggered elections continues to provide it some measure of insulation (the difference between columns 2 and 3 of Table 6.2 is instructive in this regard). Major changes in the swing ratio have been confined to House elections. The Senate changed party control autonomously in the 1980s not because the Senate of the 1980s was so much more responsive than the Senate of the 1940s or 1950s but because the House of the 1980s was so much less responsive. In fact, the extent to which convergence was driven more by the decreased responsiveness of the House than by the increased responsiveness of the Senate is a key aspect of our findings. Even though the Senate had a major insulating feature removed (indirect elections), nonconstitutional changes in the House appear to have been the more telling cause of electoral convergence.

Even so, it is important to note that electoral convergence does not imply identical electoral environments for the individuals in the two bodies. The institutional porosities of the House and Senate are now virtually equivalent, but the associated electoral environments are necessarily quite different. The election structure of the Senate is still the same highly insular system that it always was (albeit minus indirect elections). For the institutional sensitivity to be equalized under such disparate rules requires that the election-level sensitivity faced by individuals must be markedly different. The comparative election environments faced by House and Senate members are best reflected in the election swing ratios (columns 1 and 2 of Table 6.2) rather than the full-body swings. These figures show the contemporary Senate to be considerably (about a factor of three times) more sensitive to vote shifts than the House. Put another way, the House now is no more sensitive to the public mood than the Senate.

Consequences

If recent levels of electoral responsiveness prove, as we believe they will, to be more than transitory, then something of considerable consequence has occurred. The constitutional and historical electoral distinctions of the upper and lower houses, after the passage of 200 years, have faded away. We have witnessed the evolution of the lower house into a sometimes inflexible repository of stable, local interests and the associated birth of a popular upper house, functioning as a sensitive barometer of national mood (for further discussion, see Carmines and Dodd 1985). Given the considerable interdependence of the two bodies, as well as their areas of special policy responsibilities, we would expect this shift to occasion changes both at the systemic level and within the Congress itself. Our concern here is primarily with the consequences for the Senate.

It is widely recognized in the literature that the Senate has undergone considerable internal change over the last few decades. For example, more than 20 years ago Ornstein (1981) noted that changes had made "the House more like the Senate and the Senate more like the House" (366). He went on to describe in some detail a variety of dimensions on which the internal structure and functioning of the House and Senate appeared to be moving in opposite and converging directions. Using a list of House-Senate differences taken from Froman (1967) as a backdrop, Ornstein summarized the changes. We quote at length:

> The House has become *less* formal and impersonal, *less* hierarchically organized and with *more* fluid rules and procedures. The House has also become *less* able to act—much less act quickly—on policy matters. It has spread out its power and, like the Senate before it, has abandoned the notion of apprenticeship altogether. . . . More and more, the House is an ad hoc institution, without firm control over its own schedule or priorities—much like the Senate. . . . The Senate has changed, too—becoming in several respects more like the House. Since Froman wrote, the Senate has become much less leisurely . . . [;] indeed, a crushing workload and frenetic pace have changed interpersonal relations . . . and behavior. The Senate has become *more* formal and impersonal, *more* tightly organized, through its "reformed" committee system and has developed *more* rigid floor rules and proce-

> dures. . . . The Senate has tried—albeit less than successfully—to develop ways of acting *more* quickly on policy. . . . While many senators remain celebrities the rapid turnover of members—both the departure of long-time veteran powers and the influx of freshmen—have created greater anonymity among Senate ranks. (367–68)

The view from inside the Senate is apparently similar. Former Senator Daniel Evans (1988) (R-WA) used the opportunity provided by his retirement to comment on the problems he had experienced in the modern Senate: "Originally, the Senate was a complex entity that derived its unifying strength from members who devoted as much to the institution as to themselves. Today, the pressures from an overburdened agenda, an intrusive media, and a fearsomely competitive electoral process compel senators to focus more on self-preservation than on institutional integrity" (90).

While we are not arguing that the electoral changes we have described here are the sole factors responsible for these internal changes, the timing and nature of these changes strongly suggest that the converging electoral positions of the House and Senate may have played an important part in bringing about a corresponding convergence of internal characteristics. So long as the House was markedly more electorally sensitive than the Senate, its relative accessibility provided a buffer for the Senate against narrow, parochial policy demands and the attendant political conflicts. Convergence has allowed the Senate to become as appropriate a target for these demands as the House.

In the old days, shifts in the public mood registered first in the popular lower house. The Senate's more reserved, relaxed, less detailed legislative role was an appropriate legislative foil to the House only so long as the House, moving in time with the mood of the public, maintained its more rapid, rigidly organized, and highly detailed legislative mission. With the convergence of the houses, this complementary balance of roles between the upper and lower houses simply broke down. The Senate cannot serve as a body for general debate and appeal on matters of legislation and appropriation sent to it by the House if such essential and traditional House offerings are not forthcoming. The House, for its part, cannot count on the Senate to provide a detached, reflective, statesmanlike element to public policy debates.

These internal changes in the House and the Senate are consistent with and perhaps even necessary for the new policy roles of the two bodies. In a commentary on the debates regarding the televising of the Senate, Alan Ehrenhalt (1986) nicely captured both the degree to which these roles have changed and the degree to which the aura of the old days still survives:

> The debate over televising the Senate was laced with references to the difference between the two chambers, with the House serving as the impulsive voice of popular demands and the Senate as the slow, quiet voice of reason. "It is important to

the institution and to this nation," said Maryland Republican Charles McC. Mathias, Jr., "for the Senate to play the role of the saucer where the political passions of the nation are cooled." Given that context, it is worth pointing out that in recent years it was the Senate—not the House—that responded to public pressure by passing anti-busing legislation and a constitutional amendment to balance the budget. Last year, it was the Senate that adopted the bill relaxing the gun controls enacted in 1968. It is the "hot-blooded" House that has buried these popular proposals. Any or all of these initiatives may have been good ones. The point is that the modern Senate does not cool any passions. If anything, it heats them up. . . . The Senate has all the political hypersensitivity of the House if not more. (583)

And little has changed since Ehrenhalt made these observations. In the late summer of 1999, as had been the case for most of the years since 1994, when a Republican majority in Congress was installed and began to lock horns with a Democratic president, the big-ticket items of taxes and spending proved to be unusually contentious. The difference in 1999 was that budgetary surpluses had become a reality and led to discussions about whether those surpluses should be used for additional spending (Clinton's position) or to fund a tax cut of nearly $800 billion (the Republican position). The relevant point concerning this dilemma is that, in the eyes of one close observer at least, it was the leadership of the ostensibly political House that acted in the general interest of the country by signaling a statesmanlike willingness to cut a deal with the president in order to move forward (see Taylor 1999, 1921–22). Senators were the ones playing to the public by talking about politics and about waiting for a new president in eighteen months.

A similar pattern was evident a few months later when the Senate became embroiled in an unusual controversy over the confirmation of judicial nominees. Traditionally, filibusters and cloture votes have not been considered good form in deliberations over the confirmation of judges, but in the modern climate such norms have taken a beating. In September of 1999, the Republicans used a filibuster to stop Democratically preferred nominees and then Democrats used a filibuster threat to stop a nominee that President Clinton had put forward at the behest of Republican Senator Orrin Hatch, ostensibly to get Hatch to treat other Clinton nominees better (see Lewis 1999). Politics is pervading virtually every aspect of Senate activities.

An even more high-profile example of changed cameral orientations was provided by the impeachment and subsequent trial of President Clinton in 1998. While the Senate acted in perfect conformity with the wishes of the people (as expressed in countless polls) by not removing the president from office, the House, far from being the voice of the people, proceeded with impeachment even though the people did not want it. Members of the House justified their decision largely with reference to legal and historical necessities rather than momentary public opinion, thus suggesting a degree of detachment from public opinion and regard for enduring principles wholly consistent with the Founders' intentions for the Senate not the House.

The Senate can no longer be counted on for what the Framers hoped it would provide. Bicameralism is alive and well in that the House and Senate are unquestionably separate entities with important input into public policy. And the substantial differences in the size of constituencies, particularly between large-state senators and large-state representatives, can occasionally give the House and Senate different orientations to local interests and parochial concerns (see Baker 1989, 98–135; Oppenheimer 1996). But the desire for the House to have a higher level of politicization and greater sensitivity to immediate electoral concerns is no longer realized on a consistent basis.

Does the country need one house of Congress to be significantly more detached from political pressures than the other? The authors of the Constitution from the vantage point of the late eighteenth century felt the answer was a definite yes; rank-and-file citizens at the end of the twentieth century, smitten as they are with populist concepts, probably believe the more sensitivity to their concerns the better and thus answer no. Less open to subjective judgment is the belief that the houses, and particularly the Senate, may now be playing roles that they are not well designed to play.

Ornstein (1981) may have a point when he writes that the "House is inherently too unwieldy, too rigid, and too fractious to be the basic forum for national policy debate . . . [and the] . . . Senate is inherently too small and informal to be the repository of legislative expertise" (371). Ehrenhalt (1986) focuses his concern specifically on the Senate: "One can at least say for the House that it has procedural rules allowing it to function, if somewhat clumsily, in a climate of electoral obsession. The Senate has procedures that sometimes prevent it from functioning at all" (583). The danger is not necessarily that the Senate has ditched its role of coolly keeping an eye on the big picture because it now prefers the minutiae of legislative and political considerations but that its procedures, norms, structure, and size, forged as they were when the Senate was fulfilling a much different role, are not well suited for legislative micromanaging and political gamesmanship. The ability of a small number of senators to force a modification in general policy direction (see Binder and Smith 1997) is in some respects less alarming than a similar power being wielded repeatedly on the smallest of legislative details. When a body with the rules and structure of an upper house is often found to be acting like a lower house, problems will inevitably surface.

But regardless of the Senate's capacity to handle legislative details, the convergence of the electoral roles of the House and the Senate may have left the

U.S. government in an unenviable position. Madison (1987), for one, recognized the danger of having too many similarly situated entities involved in the formulation of specific policies: "It will be of little avail to the people that the laws are made by men of their own choice if the laws be so voluminous that they cannot be read, or so incoherent that they cannot be understood; if they be repealed or revised before they are promulgated, or undergo such incessant changes that no man, who knows what the law is today, can guess what it will be tomorrow" (359).

Notes

Revision of a paper previously presented at the Norman Thomas Conference on Senate Exceptionalism, Vanderbilt University, Nashville, Tennessee, October 21–23, 1999. We acknowledge the valuable assistance of Stacy Ulbig on this project.

1. Of course, Madison also saw great benefit in having each elected official represent large numbers of constituents (such as will usually be found in the Senate), thus rendering them less likely to fall under the spell of a single dominant interest (Federalist #10).
2. This covers the period from the beginning of the second party system to the present
3. Note that we are speaking only about partisan, not ideological, control.
4. Log-linear estimates have been used in previous research (see Brady and Grofman (1991), but they would be inappropriate here. These estimates have assumed a theoretical distribution centered on 50 percent of the popular vote and 50 percent of the seats. For the full-body swing in the Senate, we would expect a distribution centered on 50 percent of the vote and 17 percent of the seats. As such, the traditional log-linear model does not allow for comparable estimation of House and Senate swing ratios.
5. Hypothetical swings for the Senate in the 1970s and 1980s are quite similar to the historical swings for the same period (as reported by Pothier 1984, 92).

▪ 7 ▪

Sharing the Same Home Turf: How Senators from the Same State Compete for Geographic Electoral Support

Wendy J. Schiller

One of the unique and exceptional features of the U.S. Senate is the dual composition of the delegation that represents each state. The very fact that two senators are elected from the identical geographic constituency creates an unusual dynamic of competition and cooperation between same-state senators. Using a framework that analyzes the collective behavior of each set of senators from a state reveals that senators do not view their representational obligations in a unidimensional way. Instead, by exploring how senators construct their electoral coalitions in a state in comparison to their state colleague, I argue that Senate representation is multidimensional.

Specifically, Senate representation is composed of four intersecting dimensions: partisan, economic, geographic, and stylistic. Senators use their legislative tools to address the "interests" of their state on these four dimensions. But identifying and defining the "interests" of a state is a complex task for a senator because voters, who compose the senator's ultimate audience, may have preferences across several dimensions. For example, a voter may be a Republican, Democrat, or Independent; that same voter may be an autoworker or an accountant; that same voter may live in an urban area or the rural countryside; and that same voter may prefer a "statesman" senator over a "pork-barreler." Divisions among constituencies are not mutually exclusive; voters who live in geographic regions may have identifiable economic interests associated with living in those regions, and voters in demographic groups may have partisan or ideological views that are associated with being a member of a group. Because constituent interests can take on several forms, such as individual interest, a larger economic interest, or the interest of an organized interest group, senators use different legislative tools to formulate various types of appeals to voters.

If we assume that senators want to maximize their reelection prospects, we could argue that senators should view all the voters in the state as potential supporters. But in reality, the limited time and resources afforded to any individual senator makes strong statewide support difficult to achieve. The existence of two senators from the same state compounds the difficulty in generating statewide support because the two senators implicitly compete with each other when they try to attract the same set of constituents. When senators from the same state build similar agendas to address the same set of constituent interests, they dilute the capacity of constituents to recognize their individual records. If constituents cannot clearly contrast their two senators, it is more difficult to award credit to them, and that may ultimately weaken the reelection chances of each candidate.

Consequently, to build up the strongest possible reelection prospects, senators from the same state try to build as clear and distinct reputations as possible by selecting *different* subsets of constituent interests, opinions, and geographic areas to address in their respective legislative agendas. Elsewhere (Schiller 2000), I demonstrate that senators from the same state seek different committee assignments, attract local press coverage in different issue areas, and seek support from different interest groups and campaign contributors. In this chapter, I explore the ways that same-state senators target distinct sets of geographic areas and related demographic groups to increase electoral support.

Using Geography to Build Electoral Support

Geography plays an important role in shaping the political landscape of individual states, and navigating that landscape is a key element to winning a statewide election. When a candidate for the Senate first decides to seek office, he or she relies heavily on a home base. Clearly, the easiest base from which to pursue a Senate seat is a previously elected office, which can range from a statewide jurisdiction (e.g., governor) to a local jurisdiction (e.g., mayor) (Fenno 1996). Senate candidates who are former governors have a large advantage in that they had to build a winning coalition across the state to get elected governor in the first place. Members of Congress, however, face a more difficult task depending on the size of their state. In small states, such as North Dakota, holding a congressional seat is tantamount to holding a statewide seat and therefore brings with it all the associated advantages (Fenno 1992). But in medium- to large-population states, the challenge of expanding an electoral coalition is much greater, notably because the task of becoming well known to voters across the entire state is more difficult (Hibbing and Alford 1990; Oppenheimer 1996; Lee and Oppenheimer 1999).

The first step in building geographic support occurs when Senate candidates work to consolidate and strengthen their reputation in areas that are solidly partisan in their favor. On the basis of past history of partisan voting trends, Senate candidates will devote greater or fewer resources to particular regions in their state. For example, if a region has voted solidly Republican for fifty years, a Republican Senate candidate is not likely to devote a lot of campaign resources to that region except to ensure high turnout. Instead, the candidate will be more likely to devote resources to more competitive partisan regions or regions with a lot of independent voters.

Once the candidate is elected, the benefits of being regionally based are that the strength in that region is likely to be deep and enduring—that is, the senator is perceived as a "favorite son." The potential cost associated with basing support regionally is that constituents in other parts of the state may be less likely to perceive the senator as responsive to their needs, especially if their needs (e.g., urban versus rural) differ from those of his or her home base (see Baker 1998, 11–12). Senators work to counter the impression of being regionally focused by working to gain votes in regions that have not traditionally supported them.

State Colleagues as Obstacles to Geographic Expansion

The existence of a two-member Senate delegation presents a significant challenge to both senators in their efforts to gain favorable electoral territory in their state. For example, when one senator from the state tries to broaden his or her appeal to another part of the state that is the home base of his or her state colleague, the residents of that region may pose the question, "What can you do for us that our other senator is not already doing?" This implicit comparison is directly affected by the partisan composition of the delegation and the partisan distribution across the state. Senators from the same party and the same state essentially rely on the same core party constituency to serve as their base of reelection support. Because these two senators look similar on the partisan dimension, it is important for them to differentiate on other dimensions, including legislative and geographic, in order to establish separate identities. Therefore, they do not have the luxury of seeking geographic support in the same parts of the state. In contrast, senators from opposite parties can rely on the stark contrast of their partisanship to establish distinct identities, and they have more leeway in pursuing overlapping geographic constituencies.

Overall, senators from the same state, controlling for same or split-party delegations, try to attract as much geographic support as possible and do not readily concede territory. Even though the return may be smaller, senators will venture into typically "unfriendly" territory in a constant effort to shore up their reelection chances. An example of such behavior is that of Senator Rick

Santorum (R-PA), who was reelected to his second term in 2000. The *New York Times* aptly described his efforts during the campaign to attract votes in a region of Pennsylvania that had not typically been supportive:

> Mr. Santorum is not only working his Republican base hard but, anticipating a contest that could be decided by a few points either way, has also begun to go after the Democrats' base. Last week, Mr. Santorum held a rally in the heavily black heart of North Philadelphia, serving notice that while about 95 percent of the city's blacks usually vote Democratic, he did not intend to surrender a single black vote.
>
> One of the business leaders, Cody Anderson, praised the senator for showing up in North Philadelphia and said he was "worthy of support" because he had looked after the community's interests. "I had accepted a definition from other people of the senator," Mr. Anderson went on. "But everywhere I go recently, I've run into people who have told me of the projects he's supported—computer labs, contracts, grants."[1]

Senator Santorum clearly viewed his reelection constituency in broader terms than those of party identifiers and used a wide range of legislative tools to attract votes on other dimensions. Even a small increase in votes in an "unfriendly" region can help the senator's statewide chances for reelection.

Legislative Efforts and Electoral Success: Case Studies of Oklahoma, Ohio, and New York

In the following section, I use county-level election returns data (from 1986 to 1994) to illustrate the different constituent and geographic bases of support that senators from the same state attract. Clearly, many factors will determine a senator's electoral margins statewide, notably partisanship. Therefore, for the purposes of comparing Senate election returns for two senators from the same state in different time periods, I make the assumption that partisanship at the county level remains constant, over the short time period studied here, for the majority of the counties in a state. Of all the factors that contribute to a senator's electoral success, strong partisanship at the local level is one of the most stable and enduring. Of course, shifts in partisanship do occur, but they tend to occur over long periods of time and would not be expected to drastically change in a period of eight years.

Assuming that a minimum level of partisan strength exists in each county, the expectation is that senators from the same party will receive similar levels of support in the same regions in the state. Likewise, senators from opposite parties should receive support from voters in different regions, depending on the partisan distribution in the state. However, if senators' efforts to contrast themselves do yield benefits by attracting support from alternative constituent groups and regions in the state, then the geographic patterns of support should contradict these expectations.

To show how senators view their states in geographic terms, the delegations of Oklahoma, Ohio, and New York are examined in depth as examples of same-state senators who constructed broad geographic coalitions to secure reelection. The states of Oklahoma, Ohio, and New York were chosen as examples because they cover different regions of the country, have different internal regional configurations, and differ on partisan composition. The first case, Oklahoma, details how a Republican senator tried to attract support in a Democratic part of the state by securing targeted federal programs and funds for that region. The second case, Ohio, details how two senators from the same party can attract strikingly different levels of support in the state and how the selection of specific issues can attract crossover party votes in otherwise hostile partisan territory. The third case, New York, details how senators from opposite parties adopted representational agendas that surmounted regional and partisan divisions in the state and produced similar levels of support in common regions in the state.

Oklahoma

During the time period covered by this study, Oklahoma was represented by a split-party delegation. Senator David Boren (D) was the senior senator, and Senator Don Nickles (R) was the junior senator. Senator Boren had been a popular governor of Oklahoma before entering the Senate in 1978 and was consistently rated as the most popular elected official in the state. Senator Nickles was elected two years later, in 1980, and the landscape that he faced in building his reelection coalition in his first term presented partisan difficulty for him. The looming presence of Senator Boren as a popular state official meant that if Nickles were to build an enduring majority coalition across the state, it would necessarily have to overlap with Senator Boren's reelection constituency.

But the difficulty lay in the fact that the two men differed in their partisanship and their ideology: although Senator Boren was a conservative Democrat, the two senators were still separated by thirty-five points in their Americans for Democratic Action (ADA) ratings. Given that partisan gulf, Senator Nickles did not seek to attract crossover votes with his roll call voting record; rather, he made use of his institutional positions to appeal to voters on other dimensions. Whereas Senator Boren joined the Agriculture, Finance, and Select Intelligence Committees, Senator Nickles joined the Appropriations, Energy, and Select Indian Affairs Committees. In this way, Senator Nickles could use the partisan and ideological differences between himself and Senator Boren to establish a separate identity and at the same time expand his reelection base by addressing concrete Oklahoma interests and securing funds for particular regions in the state where he was electorally vulnerable. The strategy that Senator Nickles employed reflects the ways that senators use geographical representation as a means of overcoming or mitigating partisan disadvantages in their states.

Two newspaper articles from the *Tulsa World* detailed Senator Nickles's efforts during the 1991–92 campaign season. The first article pointed out the ideological divisions between the two senators on campaign finance reform: "The U.S. Senate approved a non-binding proposal Thursday by Senator David Boren, D-Okla., to remove tax breaks from political action committees and lobbyists and to use the revenue to fund a campaign reform package. Meanwhile, Oklahoma's other U.S. Senator, Don Nickles, helped lead a charge against Boren's plan, calling it welfare for politicians"[2]

The second newspaper article detailed Senator Nickles's efforts to attract crossover partisan votes in areas of the state by targeting economic and regional interests:

> Senator Don Nickles, R-Okla., hoping to expand his statewide voter base, last week went into the "no man's land" for Republicans. That is Little Dixie, since statehood the land of Carl Albert, Gene Stipe and other Democrats. . . . Although Nickles has won by landslides in his Senate elections, he has never carried a majority of the state's 77 counties. . . . The Ponca City Republican's strength has been in heavily populated Oklahoma and Tulsa counties, and in Canadian, Cleveland, Garfield, Kay and Payne counties. This year, there are several counties that Nickles might be able to put in to the win column at last. Thursday and Friday, however, Nickles' schedule sent him into the heart of the Democratic Party stronghold in southeastern Oklahoma. . . . He hoped he would achieve a major GOP breakthrough and carry a Little Dixie county.
>
> Because tourism and recreation are major businesses in the Little Dixie counties he visited, Nickles pointed to his work in helping to obtain improvements at McGee Creek in Atoka County and Lake Texoma in Bryan County. He noted his involvement in the establishment of the Sardis Lake Authority in the effort to build a water treatment plant to serve Pushmataha, LeFlore and Latimer counties. Nickles has also been given credit locally for a $7 million loan and grant for a gravity-flow water system to serve an estimated 3,600 residents in McCurtain County. "I have worked as hard for Little Dixie as I have the rest of the state. I would like to carry a county down here."[3]

It is clear that Senator Nickles, just like Senator Santorum mentioned earlier, perceived a benefit to reaching beyond partisan dividing lines to attract votes in counties that were traditionally Democratic.

When the results of Senator Nickles's reelection bid to a third term are

MAP 1. Oklahoma Senate Election Returns

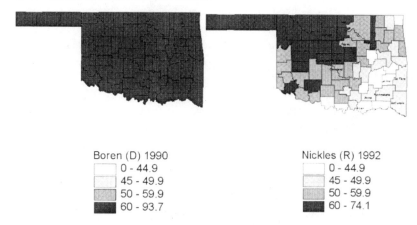

Boren (D) 1990	Nickles (R) 1992
0 - 44.9	0 - 44.9
45 - 49.9	45 - 49.9
50 - 59.9	50 - 59.9
60 - 93.7	60 - 74.1

compared to Senator Boren's reelection bid to a third term, the partisan divide in the state clearly overlaps with a geographic split in the state. Map 1 shows that the two senators had different configurations of electoral support in the state, and the counties mentioned in the above quote are identified.[4]

Senator Boren received support in almost all counties, regardless of partisan leanings, but Senator Nickles received his strongest support in the traditionally Republican western sectors of the state. The patterns in Map 1 suggest that there are limits to the extent to which split-party senators can overlap in their electoral coalitions. When one senator is overwhelmingly popular in a state, it is more difficult for the other senator to develop an equally strong statewide base. Senator Boren had previously overcome partisan disadvantages statewide when he was elected governor, and in the Senate he successfully translated and expanded that electoral coalition to attract a majority of voters in most counties. When Senator Nickles tried to do the same thing, he may have "bumped" up against the presence of Senator Boren in Democratic counties, which made the task of surmounting basic partisan opposition more difficult.

One might argue then that Senator Nickles's legislative efforts to attract more support in hostile partisan counties went unrewarded because he did not win more than 50 percent in the Little Dixie Democratic counties in eastern Oklahoma. However, Senator Nickles did receive more votes there than he had in previous elections, and Nickles fared better in the counties he specifically targeted than he did in the other Democratic counties.[5]

Ohio

In the years between 1987 and 1992, two Democratic senators, Senator John Glenn, who was elected in 1974, and Senator Howard Metzenbaum, who was

115

elected in 1976, represented Ohio. Senator Metzenbaum's home base was in Cleveland, whereas Senator Glenn was from Muskingum County in eastern central Ohio. Ohio politics has been traditionally dominated by Cleveland, which has produced most of the statewide officeholders in recent times and is a majority Democratic stronghold. One newspaper article described the trend in this way:

> Political leaders elsewhere in the state think Greater Cleveland has more than its share of statewide officeholders. . . . It's an unstated bias against Cleveland area candidates. To downstaters, they represent the worst of the worst. . . . [Candidates from Cleveland] are major contenders before they even announce for the Senate. And both are running smack into: "Oh no, not another Clevelander."
>
> Despite the grousing, the best political base is in Northeast Ohio. That's why so many candidates from here win offices. The voters in Greater Cleveland win by the numbers—those that count on Election Day.[6]

On the basis of such regional divides, both Senator Metzenbaum and Senator Glenn would be expected to base their reelection coalitions in and around the Cleveland area and expand from there into territory that was traditionally more Republican.

From early on in their Senate careers, the two senators contrasted each other: Senator Glenn was methodical, focused on issues of good government, and moderate in his ideology, while Senator Metzenbaum was more liberal and was perceived as a fighter for the consumer and the working-class Ohioan (Fenno 1990, 43–44). Their different reputations stemmed in part from their alternate legislative priorities, as illustrated in a newspaper account of their accomplishments at the end of the 101st (1991–92) Congress:

> Glenn got $11 million earmarked for universities to figure out ways to get rid of the tiny clams called Zebra mussels, the critters that are clogging water-intake valves and eating fish food in Lake Erie and other Great Lakes. . . . Mr. Checklist (as he is sometimes called) also convinced the Senate and the House that every government agency should have its own chief financial officer to watchdog spending and waste.
>
> Metzenbaum stiffened employer penalties for job-safety violations and expanded the federal government role's in research and treatment of Alzheimer's disease. A third bill seeks to protect workers' interests in cases where companies shut down "overfunded" pension plans.[7]

In addition to differences in legislative issue areas, the two senators had divergent voting records. Although their voting records were similar for most party line votes, over the six-year period from 1987 to 1992, Senator Metzenbaum had

MAP 2. Ohio Senate Election Returns

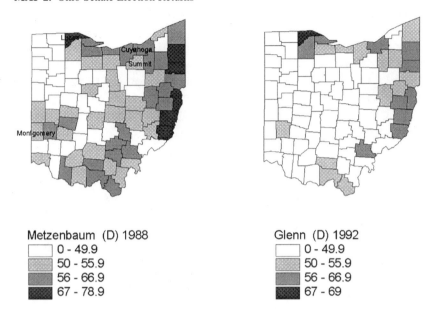

Metzenbaum (D) 1988	Glenn (D) 1992
☐ 0 - 49.9	☐ 0 - 49.9
▨ 50 - 55.9	▨ 50 - 55.9
▥ 56 - 66.9	▥ 56 - 66.9
■ 67 - 78.9	■ 67 - 69

an average ADA rating of 98, as compared with 78 for Senator Glenn, a difference of twenty percentage points.[8] In brief, both senators used their tools to sell themselves to voters in regions that were not predisposed to support them. Senator Metzenbaum used his legislative tools to establish a reputation as a senator who attended to his constituents on populist issues, whereas Senator Glenn moderated his voting record and concentrated on more national and nonpartisan policies.

Map 2 shows the distribution of votes for Senator Glenn's reelection bid to a fourth term and Senator Metzenbaum's reelection bid to a third term. In total, Senator Metzenbaum won with 57 percent of the statewide vote, compared to 51 percent for Senator Glenn. Both senators ran against strong challengers in that Senator Metzenbaum faced then Cleveland Mayor George Voinovich (who became governor and is now senator) and Senator Glenn faced Lt. Governor Mike DeWine (now senator). Both senators won a majority of the vote in the counties that contain four of the largest cities in Ohio: Akron (Summit County), Cleveland (Cuyahoga County), Toledo (Lucas County), and Dayton (Montgomery County) (see Map 2).

The pattern of support that is most striking is that Senator Metzenbaum, the more liberal Democrat, fared considerably better in central and southern Ohio than Senator Glenn, the more moderate Democrat. Metzenbaum's success in the southern and central regions of Ohio is surprising precisely because the Republican party dominates these areas of the state. Overall, Senator Metzenbaum

117

won a majority of the vote in twenty-one counties (out of a total of eighty-eight) in which Glenn failed to win a majority. Moreover, Metzenbaum won these counties by a margin greater than six percentage points, which was the difference in their margin of victory statewide. Senator Metzenbaum managed to penetrate unfriendly partisan territory in much of the southern part of the state where Glenn could not, a pattern that was attributed in part to the issues he chose to champion. Senator Metzenbaum's legislative activism appears to have been a more potent strategy for winning votes in "hostile" territory than Senator Glenn's more subtle approach.

New York

New York represents a state where both senators expanded their initial electoral bases and garnered support in similar regions of the state but did so with contrasting strategies. New York, like Ohio, tends to have a regional split between "upstate" and "downstate." Typically, upstate is considered less urban and more conservative, although it should be noted that four out of the five biggest cities in the state are "upstate." Downstate is considered more liberal and dominated by New York City. Long Island, adjacent to New York City, is often considered to have more in common with upstate than downstate. One *Buffalo News* article about Senator D'Amato's 1992 campaign, entitled "Foul Downstate Politics Defies Newton, Flows Upstream," described the difference in nonflattering terms:

> Has there ever been an uglier U.S. Senate race than Robert Abrams vs. Sen. Alfonse D'Amato? . . . It was to be brutally frank, a race with "downstate" written all over it. . . . What are nationally decried as the foul pollutants of "New York politics" are really "downstate politics" which fit in perfectly in a fabled cultural world . . . [that] the Manhattan theater people witheringly call the "bridge and tunnel crowd." In New York State, political and cultural pollution usually defies Newton and flows upstream. . . . Crucial to this, of course, is the hilariously inapt knee-jerk condescension to upstate bumpkins by those who often exemplify the worst that downstate coarseness has to offer." [9]

Assuming that this perceived variation existed between these regions of the state, the challenge for both senators would be to develop a reputation that appealed to a cross-section of voters across the state. Because Moynihan was a Democrat and D'Amato was a Republican, that meant each senator had to cross a regional divide.

Senator Moynihan was elected to the Senate in 1976, after serving as U.S. ambassador to the United Nations; he launched his campaign for Senate in the big cities of the state, primarily New York City, but also upstate in Buffalo. Senator D'Amato, on the other hand, was elected to the Senate after serving as supervisor of the town of Hempstead on Long Island, in the downstate region of the state. Both men worked to expand their original electoral coalitions beyond their initial borders. For Moynihan, the natural constituency consisted of the big cities in the state, which were traditionally more Democratic. To offset perceptions that he was a liberal, Moynihan shaped his early career around issues of foreign policy, which was his immediate prior experience and was an issue that could help attract more conservative votes. He also focused on Social Security, an issue that affected all of his constituents, regardless of geographic location. Over time, Moynihan developed a reputation as a statesman and a national policy maker in these issue areas that muted the negative impact of his partisan affiliation in areas of the state that might have been hostile to a Democrat.[10]

Senator D'Amato, on the other hand, adopted a very different agenda based on his prior experience in the world of Nassau County machine politics. Because Moynihan had been elected first, D'Amato had the task of distinguishing himself in concrete ways from his more senior colleague, something he had already begun in his first Senate campaign. In the Senate, D'Amato used his position on the Appropriations Committee to court the vote in big Democratic cities by providing funds for mass transit, such as subways and trains.[11] Securing targeted funds for regions all over the state was an effective way of expanding his reelection coalition and penetrating areas that were not favorably disposed toward a Republican. Over the course of his Senate career, Senator D'Amato became known for delivering federal dollars to his home state and acquired the nickname "Senator Pothole" for his mastery of pork barrel politics.[12] Senator D'Amato took great pride in his efforts and made them a focal point in his reelection campaigns, as noted in two recent articles about the 1998 campaign:

This time around, D'Amato is likely to face a different sort of campaign, particularly if Ferraro or Schumer is the Democratic nominee: he will be challenged on his record. D'Amato has an eager response to this: "My record? I deliver, he told me as the plane circled the Binghamton [upstate] airport. "See that down there? The runway? I got that extended twelve hundred feet. It cost seventeen million dollars. It was one of the first things I ever worked on. It took me four years to get it." (Klein 1998, 45)

"There are those who criticize me and say that I deal in small problems. They call me Sen. Pothole," D'Amato said. "But let me tell you, people's problems are not small. And the people who have problems are not small." . . . Indeed, that was the theme the state's junior senator constantly emphasized. He pointed to his involvement in obtaining funds for the Albright-Knox Art Gallery, Roswell Park Cancer Institute, Children's Hospital and Monsignor Adamski housing complex as examples of how he has "fought" for Western New York.[13]

MAP 3. New York Senate Election Returns

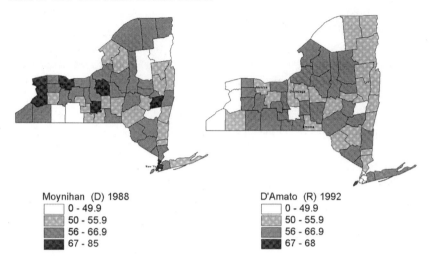

Moynihan (D) 1988
- 0 - 49.9
- 50 - 55.9
- 56 - 66.9
- 67 - 85

D'Amato (R) 1992
- 0 - 49.9
- 50 - 55.9
- 56 - 66.9
- 67 - 68

Indeed, Senator D'Amato believed that targeting legislative benefits to specific regions in the state, he could increase his electoral prospects there.

A comparison of electoral returns for Senator Moynihan's bid for a third term and Senator D'Amato's bid for a third term illustrates how both senators achieved success in securing votes across New York State (see Map 3). Overall, Senator Moynihan received 67 percent statewide, as compared with D'Amato's 49 percent statewide. Despite the larger margin of victory for Moynihan, the Democrat, the two senators both won a majority of the vote in forty-seven counties. Some of the difference in statewide vote percentage can be attributed to the fact that Moynihan won large urban cities like Buffalo (Erie County), Albany (Albany County), and New York City (New York County) while D'Amato did not. Still, D'Amato did well in the very areas upstate that he had always made a point of targeting, including the cities of Rochester (Monroe County), Binghamton (Broome County), Syracuse (Onondaga County), and surrounding areas. The relative success of both senators in common counties across the state suggests that their individual strategies of differentiation and coalition building persuaded voters to vote for both of them, even if it meant crossing partisan or geographic lines.

Unfortunately for Senator D'Amato, his 1998 reelection campaign was unsuccessful, and he was beaten by Representative Charles Schumer, a Democrat. Notably, Senator Schumer has chosen to build on his House experience by joining the Judiciary Committee, and he has also taken a seat on the Banking Committee, thereby assuming responsibility for issues that were once "owned" by Senator D'Amato. In 2000, Senator Hillary Clinton, a Democrat, replaced the retiring Senator Moynihan. The two high-profile freshman senators share many of the same issue concerns and liberal ideology, but they have taken major steps to retain contrast between them. Because Senator Clinton's geographic base during the campaign and afterwards was perceived to be similar to that of Senator Schumer, she joined committees that have little overlap with those of Senator Schumer, and she has used her early legislative agenda to target geographic regions in the state that are not already addressed by Senator Schumer's agenda.

These case studies are unequivocal in demonstrating that senators view their states in broader terms than a single dimension such as partisanship, that they recognize which geographic areas are more or less favorably inclined toward them, and that they use a range of legislative tools to construct an agenda that is designed to maximize the range and depth of their electoral base.

Geographic Patterns of Electoral Support

To show more general trends in electoral support for two senators from the same state, I constructed additional maps to show a comparison of the distribution of votes for both senators from a state for the reelection campaigns that occurred during the time period 1986–94. Maps 4 through 11 are presented to illustrate the distinctive regional coalitions that support senators from the same state. Most notably, states with same-party senators exhibit some clear divides between the two senators, despite their shared party affiliation. One such state is Oregon; during the time period of this study, Oregon was represented by two Republican senators, Senator Mark Hatfield and Senator Robert Packwood. With the exception of the issue of abortion, Senator Packwood was known to be more conservative, especially on taxes and defense issues, and more nationally focused. Senator Hatfield was known to be more liberal, especially on defense

MAP 4. Oregon Senate Election Returns

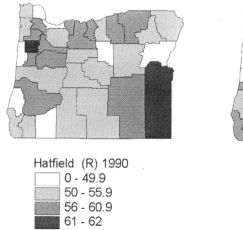

Hatfield (R) 1990
- ☐ 0 - 49.9
- 50 - 55.9
- 56 - 60.9
- 61 - 62

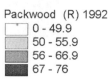

Packwood (R) 1992
- ☐ 0 - 49.9
- 50 - 55.9
- 56 - 66.9
- 67 - 76

121

MAP 5. Pennsylvania Senate Election Returns

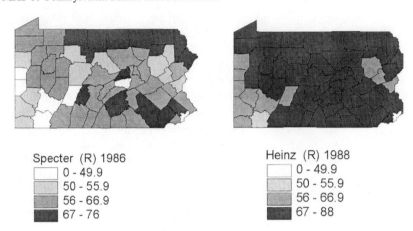

Specter (R) 1986
- ☐ 0 - 49.9
- ▨ 50 - 55.9
- ▨ 56 - 66.9
- ■ 67 - 76

Heinz (R) 1988
- ☐ 0 - 49.9
- ▨ 50 - 55.9
- ▨ 56 - 66.9
- ■ 67 - 88

issues, and more attentive to economic concerns like logging and forestry, which were dominant in the southeastern section of the state. Map 4 shows how each senator had regional strength in a different part of the state. Both senators were generally strong across the state, but Senator Packwood was more popular in the rural eastern part of the state and Senator Hatfield was more popular in the urban western part of the state.

In addition to Oregon, Pennsylvania, Michigan, Wyoming, and Nebraska provide more examples of same-party senators with different regional patterns of support for each senator (see maps 5 through 8).[14]

Pennsylvania is a good example of the ways in which senators from the same state and same party can present explicit barriers to each other in building support. Senator Specter faced difficulty in establishing a footing in western Pennsylvania, which was the home base of his delegation colleague, John Heinz. Fenno (1991b, 149–50, 165) describes how Senator Specter was eager to attract support there but could not do so without the explicit support of his senior colleague. Indeed, a newspaper who was surveyed for this chapter pointed out that the two senators were perceived as representing different regions of the state: "Heinz was considered . . . to be the senator from western Pennsylvania, while Specter was the senator from eastern Pennsylvania." Map 5 shows evidence of this division: Senator Heinz is generally stronger than Senator Specter but is especially so in the western region of the state.

In Michigan, both Democratic senators attracted the same general range of votes, but Senator Reigle attracted more votes in a greater number of counties than Senator Levin did (see Map 6). A study by Baker (1998, 11) quotes Senator Reigle explaining that Senator Levin was stronger in urban areas such as Detroit, whereas he was stronger in suburban and rural areas. In Wyoming, Senator

MAP 6. Michigan Senate Election Returns

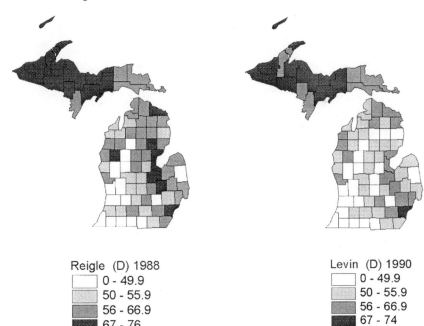

Reigle (D) 1988
- 0 - 49.9
- 50 - 55.9
- 56 - 66.9
- 67 - 76

Levin (D) 1990
- 0 - 49.9
- 50 - 55.9
- 56 - 66.9
- 67 - 74

MAP 7. Wyoming Senate Election Returns

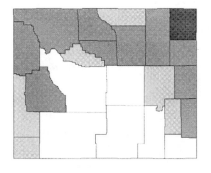

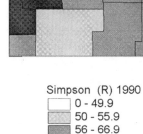

Wallop (R) 1988
- 0 - 49.9
- 50 - 55.9
- 56 - 66.9
- 67 - 72

Simpson (R) 1990
- 0 - 49.9
- 50 - 55.9
- 56 - 66.9
- 67 - 77

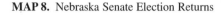

MAP 8. Nebraska Senate Election Returns

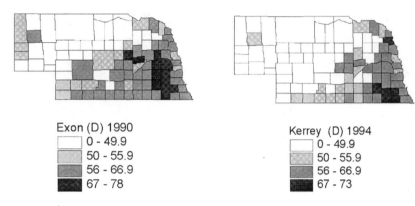

Exon (D) 1990
☐ 0 - 49.9
▨ 50 - 55.9
▨ 56 - 66.9
■ 67 - 78

Kerrey (D) 1994
☐ 0 - 49.9
▨ 50 - 55.9
▨ 56 - 66.9
■ 67 - 73

Simpson won the entire state, whereas his Republican colleague lost some southern parts of the state (see Map 7). In Nebraska, the two Democratic senators were victorious in a majority of counties, but Senator Exon won a greater portion of the central and western parts of the state (see Map 8).

In states with split-party delegations, there were more stark regional divisions, but even so, there was more overlap at the county level than we might expect. In Florida, represented by Senator Bob Graham (D) and Senator Connie Mack (R), both senators carefully constructed separate legislative agendas but overlapped to serve a major economic interest in the state (Schiller 2000). The two senators were relatively equal in popularity across the entire state, despite their contrasting party affiliations, with the exception that Senator Mack was more popular than Senator Graham in his own home base of northwest Florida. Florida is a state where both senators received close to 70 percent of the vote statewide: Senator Graham received 65.4 percent and Senator Mack received 70.5 percent. The two senators each received a majority of the vote in 66 out of 67 counties, and in 16 of those counties, the difference that separated them was less than the difference statewide (see Map 9).

Two other states that are examples of such crossover between split-party senators are Texas and South Carolina, where senators from opposite parties won a majority of votes in common counties (see Maps 10 and 11 respectively.)[15]

Taken as a whole, the geographic patterns of electoral results in states suggest that voters' choices reflect senators' efforts to divide up the representational responsibilities in a state. In the case of same-party delegations, senators do succeed in establishing strength in different sections of the state. Although the demarcation for success for a senator is winning a majority in each county, in reality Senate elections are statewide, so any percentage of votes is a benefit for senators' efforts. The maps are designed to show that in comparison to the ex-

MAP 9. Florida Senate Election Returns

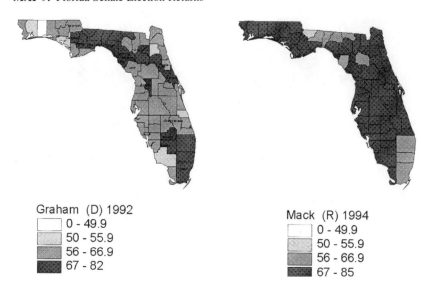

Graham (D) 1992
- 0 - 49.9
- 50 - 55.9
- 56 - 66.9
- 67 - 82

Mack (R) 1994
- 0 - 49.9
- 50 - 55.9
- 56 - 66.9
- 67 - 85

pectations of straight party voting, voters appear to incorporate other aspects of senators' records into their evaluations, as reflected in the fact that the patterns of support for same-party senators are different and the patterns of support for split-party senators frequently look similar.

MAP 10. Texas Senate Election Returns

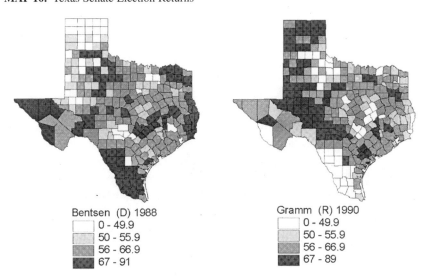

Bentsen (D) 1988
- 0 - 49.9
- 50 - 55.9
- 56 - 66.9
- 67 - 91

Gramm (R) 1990
- 0 - 49.9
- 50 - 55.9
- 56 - 66.9
- 67 - 89

125

MAP 11. South Carolina Senate Election Returns

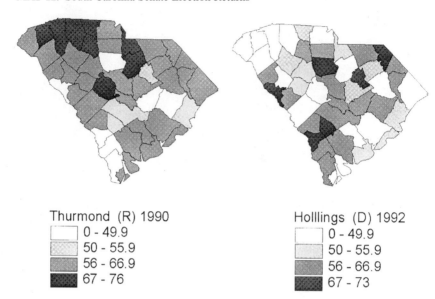

Thurmond (R) 1990
- [ ] 0 - 49.9
- 50 - 55.9
- 56 - 66.9
- 67 - 76

Holllings (D) 1992
- [ ] 0 - 49.9
- 50 - 55.9
- 56 - 66.9
- 67 - 73

Demographic Patterns of Electoral Support

To study demographic patterns of support for senators, I constructed a data set with the county-level election returns for both senators between 1986 and 1994, as well as census data on demographic variables, such as the percentages of blacks, Asians, and Hispanics; income levels; the percentages of women and the elderly; urban concentration; and the percentage of blue-collar workers, all at the county level.

Two forms of analysis were performed on these data. The first analysis was a quantitative model that predicted the difference in vote share between the two senators at the county level as a function of the above demographic variables. This demographic analysis was a modified replication of the work of Jung, Kenny, and Lott (1994), which explained the difference in vote share at the county level between senators from the same state, and the existence of split-party delegations, as a function of campaign platforms and roll call voting behavior. Although I employed a similar rationale, my analysis differed from theirs in two respects.[16] First, because I wanted to test for differences in electoral support as an indirect consequence of differences in legislative portfolios, I purposely excluded states where one of the senators was a first-time candidate. Candidates who have not yet been elected have not had a chance to use their legislative tools to forge an agenda that is subsequently evaluated by the voters. Therefore, only those states where both senators were incumbents and seeking reelection were included in the sample (N = 29).[17] Second, Jung et al. studied the 1980, 1982, and 1984 elections, but I used a different set of elections, 1986, 1988, 1990, 1992, and 1994, to see if their findings would hold for the sample of senators included in my study.

The dependent variable in my model was the difference in percent vote by county between senators from the same state, as measured by the senior senator's percent vote minus the junior senator's percent vote. The independent variables were demographic, such as the percentage of elderly in a county, the urban density of a county, the percentage of black or Hispanic residents in the county, and the per capita income in a county. The results for states with same-party delegations are displayed in Table 7.1, and the results for states with split party delegations are displayed in Table 7.2. For both types of delegations, I found that the coalitions that support senators from the same state did not include the same sectors of the population.

The results shown in Table 7.1 demonstrate that variation in income, region, and age of constituents yields different electoral results for senators from the same party. For example, in eight out of seventeen same-party delegation states, income was a significant divisor of support between the two senators. In counties with higher levels of per capita income, the senior senator won a higher percentage of the vote. In three same-party delegation states, the junior senator won a higher percentage of the vote in counties with higher levels of income. This is surprising given that income divisions usually tend to occur across parties, not within parties. Yet in this case we see evidence that the efforts of senators from the same party to reach beyond the strict party core to attract supporters from different economic levels produce payoffs.

The same patterns emerge for urban and elderly residents in counties; the evidence suggests that one senator attracts more electoral support from these groups than the other in the same county. If we look at a small state like Nebraska, both senators were popular former governors, both were Democrats, and both faced minimal opposition in their reelection campaigns. However, they had different configurations of regional and demographic support across the state. Senator Exon, the senior senator, fared better in wealthier counties, where his margin of victory was greater than that of his junior colleague, Senator Kerrey. In contrast, in counties with a larger percentage of urban residents and elderly residents, Senator Kerrey won more electoral support than Senator Exon.

In Table 7.2, we see that race tends to divide senators from split-party delegations more consistently than income does. In eight out of twelve states, the Democratic senator attracted more support from black voters; in two of those states, the Democratic senator also attracted more votes from Hispanic voters. In other words, for every increase in the percentage of black constituents, per county, the Democratic senator received a higher percentage of votes than his or her Republican colleague. The effect of income is also clear in that Republican senators got more votes in wealthier counties as compared to their Democratic Senate colleagues. For example, in Florida, where the delegation was divided, Senator Graham, a

TABLE 7.1. Predicting Differences in Share of Senate Vote by County for Incumbent Senators 1987–1994[a] Same-Party Delegations

State	Intercept	Black	Female	Old	Income	Urban	Labor	Adj. R_2
MD (24)	−50.1	−.28**	2.03**	−1.80**	−.0006**	−6.25*	−.57**	.51**
PA (67)	−13.9**	.32**		−.15	.0002**	−3.0**	.07	.25***
NJ (21)	−29.1**	.19*		.63*	.0004**	.46	−.34	.43**
MI (83)	17.5**	−.08		−.16	−.0004**	4.1**	.03	.11**
IL (102)	−2.7	−.02		.01	−.00002	.51	.01	−.05
NE (93)	−2.1	.03		−.30*	.0004**	−7.5**	.05	.12**
AL (66)	−1.1	−.12**		.32	−.0002	.29	−.008	.12**
OR (36)	−39.0**	2.1		−.30	.001**	.60	−.16	.34**
MO (115)	13.9**	−.14**		−.11	.0002	−.05	−.03	.07**
LA (64)	−33.6	.30**		−1.0**	.0005**	4.3*	−.17	.52**
IN (92)	−26.9**	.05		.26	.0004*	−.69	.15*	.12**
OH (88)	14.0**	−.01		−.11	.0002*	.41	.005	.05
MN (87)	17.6**	.46		−.50**	−.000004	−2.6*	−.21**	.42***
WY (23)	−22.0	−.53		.41	.0003	−4.5	−.04	−.04
KS (105)	10.8	−.22	.11	.16	−.0002	.85	−.02	.07**
ND (53)	15.2*	−.04		−.27**	−.0003**	−.40	.01	.11*
WV (55)	−27.9**	−.07		−.37	.002**	−7.3**	−.46**	.34***

***Statistically significant at .01, two-tailed test. **Statistically significant at .05, two-tailed test. *Statistically significant at .10, two-tailed test. [a]Senators included in vote share difference:

MD	Sarbanes (D) 88 – Mikulski (D) 92		LA	Johnston (D) 90 – Breaux (D) 92
PA	Specter (R) 86 – Heinz (R) 88		IN	Coats (R) 92 – Lugar (R) 94
NJ	Lautenberg (D) 88 – Bradley (D) 90		OH	Metzenbaum (D) 88 – Glenn (D) 90
MI	Riegle (D) 88 – Levin (D) 90		MN	Durenberger (R) 88 – Boschwitz (R) 90
IL	Dixon (D) 86 – Simon (D) 90		WY	Wallop (R) 88 – Simpson (R) 90
NE	Exon (D) 90 – Kerrey (D) 94		KS	Kassebaum (R) 90 – Dole (R) 92
AL	Heflin (D) 90 – Shelby (D) 92		ND	Burdick (D) 88 – Conrad (D) 92
OR	Hatfield (R) 90 – Packwood (R) 92		WV	Byrd (D) 88 – Rockefeller (D) 90
MO	Danforth (R) 88 – Bond (R) 92			

Democrat, was more popular among blacks and Hispanics than Senator Mack, a Republican, but Senator Mack fared better in counties with higher levels of income.

Surprisingly, the percentage of female voters did not exert a statistically or substantively important effect in any state in the sample, with the exception of Maryland and California. It appears that the percentage of female voters in counties does not systematically give one member of the delegation an advantage over the other. Being a female senator does not appear to automatically yield greater electoral support with increases in the percentage of women across counties. There were only two females senators in this sample, so any conclusion is speculative at best, but in the two states with female senators, Maryland and Kansas, neither female senator appeared to win more support from women

TABLE 7.2. Predicting Differences in Share of Senate Vote by County for Incumbent Senators 1987–1994[a] Split-Party Delegations

State	Intercept	Black	Female	Hispanic	Old	Income	Urban	Labor	Adj. R^2
NY (62)	15.6	1.24**			−.11	−.0004	4.11	−.28	.55***
TX (254)	55.9**			.07	−.02	−.002**	4.9	−.72**	.39***
IA (99	31.2	2.6**			−1.14*	−.001*	3.3	−.13	.14**
FL (67)	−8.5	.80**		.40**	.25	−.0006*	.31	−.11	.50***
KY (120)	9.8	−.64			.34	−.001*	18.1**	.11	.04*
AZ (15)	41.0**			.01	−.98*	−.0005	−7.4	−.16	.18
CA (58)	−33.8*	1.04*	1.1**	−.09	.53	.0002		.26	.24**
NC (100)	16.9	−.63**			.26	−.0004	9.6**	.65**	.46***
SD (66)	43.9	−.43**			−1.0*	−.0009	−8.4	−.34	.01
SC (46)	20.6	−.69**			−.45	.0004	3.8	.53**	.90***
NM (33)	9.5	−2.4*		.42**	−1.4**	−.0002	−6.5	−.41	.58***
OK (77)	91.2**	.26		−.80**	−.46	−.002**	1.5	−.35*	.62***

***Statistically significant at .01, two-tailed test. **Statistically significant at .05, two-tailed test. *Statistically significant at .10, two-tailed test. a Senators included in vote share difference:

NY	Moynihan (D) 88 – D'Amato (R) 92	CA	Cranston (D) 86 – Wilson (R) 88
TX	Bentsen (D) 88 – Gramm (R) 90	NC	Helms (R) 90 – Sanford (D) 92
IA	Harkin (D) 90 – Grassley (R) 92	SD	Pressler (R) 90 – Daschle (D) 92
FL	Graham (D) 92 – Mack (R) 94	SC	Thurmond (R) 90 – Hollings (D) 92
KY	McConnell (R) 90 – Ford (D) 92	NM	Bingaman (D) 88 – Domenici (R) 90
AZ	DeConcini (D) 88 – McCain (R) 92	OK	Boren (D) 90 – Nickles (R) 92

than from their male counterparts. In Maryland, Senator Paul Sarbanes was more popular among women voters than his female colleague, Senator Barbara Mikulski. In Kansas, Senator Nancy Kassebaum received slightly more support correlated with an increase in female voters than Senator Dole did, but the parameter estimate was insignificant.

The geographic and demographic data suggest that senators from the same state attract differing levels of electoral support from different configurations of constituents. It is especially remarkable that senators from the same state and the same party reap different levels of electoral support in the very same counties. Constituents respond to senators who use their legislative and political tools to differentiate themselves from their state colleagues, and same-state senators succeed in building coalitions with support from different sets of constituents.

Impact of Sharing the Same Territory on Senate Representation

Comparing the patterns of electoral support for senators from the same state indicates that senators are rewarded for responding to their constituents along

129

multiple dimensions. Senators from the same state select different subsets of interests and opinions to address in their legislative work, and they usually establish different home bases in the state. When senators from the same state do try to expand their original geographic base of support, they usually seek out regions and groups that are not already strongly supportive of their state colleague. It is more difficult to attract support from a region of the state, or specific groups within that region, if the other senator has already proven himself to be attentive to their needs. Under such circumstances, one senator has already achieved recognition and association with the region in the local press, making it more difficult for his state colleague to be given credit for also serving that region.

In this way, the search for an expanded reelection coalition leads senators from the same state to focus on different regions within the state, and hence different sets of concerns. The evidence presented in this chapter suggests that senators do not view their states in purely partisan terms and that voters do not merely respond to the partisanship of their senators when expressing their support. Senators from the same party and the same state do not fare equally well among the same groups or same regions of the state. In contrast, senators from the same state but opposite parties do often attract the same percentage of support among common groups or in common regions in the state.

Students of the Senate can benefit by rethinking the way that we define and explore Senate representation. States are truly multimember districts, and senators do not operate in a vacuum when they make choices about which issues, opinions, and regional concerns they address in the Senate. Each senator has a state colleague who presents implicit competition for constituent support but who also shares the responsibility of addressing constituent concerns. The dynamic of competition between them pushes the two senators in divergent directions, which broadens the range of constituent interests and opinions that are given voice and attention at the federal level. In sum, we are much better represented in the Senate than we commonly recognize.

Notes

1. B. Drummond Ayres, Jr., "A Republican Invades Democratic Territory," *New York Times*, May 21, 2000, A30.
2. Jim Myers, "Nickles Helps Lead Way against Boren's PAC Tax Break Proposal," *Tulsa World*, May 17, 1991, C7.
3. Rob Martindale, "Diving into Little Dixie: Nickles Tries to Give GOP at Least a Toehold," *Tulsa World*, April 26, 1992, A2.
4. I am indebted to Morris Fiorina for the helpful suggestion to compare same-state senators' geographic constituencies in this way.
5. Chuck Ervin, "Nickles Roars to Re-Election," *Tulsa World*, November 4, 1992, A1.

6. Mary Anne Sharkey, "Northeast Ohio Is Where the Senatorial Votes Are," *Plain Dealer*, May 26, 1993, 7B.

7. "Ohio's Senators Look as Busy as Candidates," *Plain Dealer*, November 4, 1990.

8. This contrast in voting records is yet another example of Uslaner's (1999b) more general finding that one senator in a same-party Senate delegation will tend to veer to the extreme of the party distribution to distinguish himself from his or her colleague.

9. Jeff Simon, "Foul Downstate Politics Defies Newton," *Buffalo News,* November 8, 1992.

10. "Re-Elect Senator Moynihan: He Delivers for the Nation and New York," *Buffalo News*, October 24, 1994.

11. "Senate Takes Right Road on Mass Transit Funds," *Buffalo News*, March 7, 1998.

12. Robert J. McCarthy, "D'Amato Points to Successes in Visit Here," *Buffalo News*, May 18, 1998.

13. McCarthy, "D'Amato Points to Successes."

14. Other same-party Senate delegations in which senators attract support from distinct regions of the state include New Jersey, Indiana, Louisiana, Alaska, and Illinois.

15. There are other split-party Senate delegations, including Iowa, Kentucky, and New Mexico, that exhibit similar patterns of overlap in regional support to those that are shown here.

16. Jung et al. (1994) assume that senators use roll call voting as their primary signaling tool to attract support from constituents. The interpretation in this chapter is that senators use a wide range of legislative tools to build their reelection coalitions and that roll call voting is just one of these tools.

17. Jung, Kenny, and Lott (1994) analyze the election returns from forty-three states. I use the same set of independent variables except that I do not include "manufacturing," "government employment," and "unemployed" because theoretically and empirically they do not add a great deal of explanatory power to the model.

· 8 ·

Winning Media Coverage in the U.S. Congress

Patrick J. Sellers

Conventional conceptions of representation often assume that a close link between legislator and constituent is empirically true and normatively desirable. If
the representative takes issue positions that match those of the district or state,
then observers conclude that representation exists (Miller and Stokes 1963;
Achen 1978; Erikson 1978) and that democratic theory holds (Pitkin 1967).

The reality of representation is considerably more complicated than this conventional wisdom suggests. Individual issues may vary in salience for members
of Congress and voters (Arnold 1990). Legislators and the public may not even
have a preference on certain policy questions. In addition, issues vary in structure. A proposed tax cut, for example, may be linked either to the greater take-
home pay that it would provide or to the spending reductions in other programs
that would be necessary to pay for the tax cut. An individual's support for the
proposal may hinge on how the proposal is presented (Iyengar and Kinder 1987;
Krosnick and Brannon 1993). Finally, constituents may be represented by an individual legislator or a collective party (Weissberg 1978). Disagreements between a legislator and her party create a tension between individual and
collective, with the constituents' preferences only partially represented.

These complexities do more than complicate the study of representation.
They also provide opportunities for politicians to manipulate the legislator-
constituent relationship for political advantage. An individual legislator works to
convince constituents that he or she shares their interests by changing the
salience of issues and restructuring them. He or she may also highlight or downplay ties to the national party, depending on the constituents' perceptions of that
party. In these agenda-setting efforts, the legislator works to focus constituents'
attention on issues where the legislator is closer than his or her opponent to their
preferences.

This chapter examines a single but crucial aspect of representation in

Congress: the interaction between party leaders and followers in structuring issues and setting the agenda. Such manipulation of agendas has been documented
descriptively in other contexts (Riker 1986). This work aims to move beyond the
art of heresthetics. It presents claims about agenda setting that are generalizable
across politicians and issues. Congressional observers have already begun to craft
generalizable claims about agenda setting inside the institution (Aldrich 1995;
Riker 1996; Rohde 1991; Sinclair 1997). The chapter focuses on efforts to set the
agenda outside Congress, particularly in the news media. I argue that congressional leaders help coordinate their followers' efforts to win media coverage of
their positions and arguments. If successful, such efforts can generate electoral
and policy benefits for the politicians, both individually and collectively.[1]

My analysis focuses on the U.S. Senate. This institution is particularly appropriate for examining the coordination of legislators' media activity. Unlike the
House of Representatives, the Senate gives party leaders few formal mechanisms for coordinating caucus efforts. The Senate leaders must therefore turn to
less formal strategies of coordination. In addition, members of the Senate regularly win more media coverage than their House counterparts. The coordination
of senators' media activities therefore has more potential for success.

The first section of this chapter discusses the obstacles to the party leaders'
and followers' promotion of their individual and collective interests in the Senate. This section also explains how and why the leaders and followers may interact to promote their individual and collective interests. In the second section,
I describe the agenda-setting strategies of Senate party leaders. The third section
documents how caucus members respond to those strategies. My evidence
emerges from a diverse collection of qualitative and quantitative data: notes
from my own work in Senator Tom Daschle's office, interviews with press secretaries of forty-one senators, and senators' press releases submitted to the Senate Press and Radio-Television Galleries.[2]

The Collective Good of Setting the Agenda

Despite the rise of candidate-centered campaigns (Jacobson 1997), contemporary members of Congress still face obstacles to winning reelection by themselves. Legislators need to produce successful policy initiatives in order to
convince constituents that they are working for their interests. But members of
Congress may not agree on the most desirable policy. Chapters 5 and 6 of this
volume document how senators' growing responsiveness to forces outside the
Senate have made it harder for the legislators to reach agreement inside the
chamber. And as Aldrich (1995) has pointed out, even shared preferences within
a caucus do not automatically produce successful legislation. Members' preferences are not always self-evident. Legislators may prefer not to publicize their

positions on certain issues, particularly controversial ones. Furthermore, no legislator has an incentive to gather this information and coordinate passage of legislation. Every member may prefer instead to free-ride on the efforts of his or her colleagues.

A caucus may begin to solve this collective action problem by creating leadership positions and assigning valuable resources to those positions. These resources provide an incentive for individual members to work to become leaders, but the caucus assigns an additional condition for obtaining the positions: advancing the collective interests of the caucus (Aldrich 1995). Leaders further these collective interests in diverse ways. In this chapter I focus on their attempts to shape the congressional agenda and news coverage of that agenda.[3]

In particular, I argue that the leaders attempt to steer debate and coverage toward issues where their own caucus is unified and the opposing caucus is divided. On each such issue, the divided caucus may be split between a more extreme position supported by party activists and a more moderate position that attracts more support from the general public. These moderate positions may be the source of agreement in the unified caucus. With such an alignment of preferences, the unified caucus can win broader public support while still creating a record of policy making and a "brand name" different from that of the opposing party (Cox and McCubbins 1993; Kieweit and McCubbins 1991). The party with greater caucus unity may also be perceived as more responsible or capable on the particular issue. This party "owns" the issue in the eyes of the general public (Petrocik 1996), while also enjoying greater unity in Congress.[4]

Thus, party leaders are most likely to focus their agenda-setting efforts on issues that meet several criteria: their own caucus is unified around a single position on the issue, the opposing caucus is not, and the general public prefers the unified party and its position. While issues meeting these criteria may be few, they offer great potential for collective partisan advantage to the party that owns them. On these owned issues, a party has often built a favorable reputation and a record of success. When promoting a message on these issues inside and outside Congress, the leader and caucus can draw on their reputation and record to make their argument more persuasive (Aldrich 1995; Cox and McCubbins 1993; Sellers 1998). A central goal in these promotional efforts is greater press coverage of the party's issues. Such coverage may generate greater public support for the party (electoral benefits), as well as greater success in inserting these issues onto the Senate legislative agenda (policy benefits).

In addition to collective benefits, these issues can also provide individual benefits to caucus members who promote them. Promoting the party message on these issues allows caucus members to draw attention to an issue and position that they personally support. In addition, they can link themselves more closely to that issue and position, helping establish a policy reputation for activity on the issue (Cook 1998). Finally, the press coverage may produce electoral benefits among constituents.

Thus, in their efforts to mobilize the caucus and promote the party message, congressional leaders may focus on the benefits of promotion that their followers might receive. To increase these benefits, a leader avoids selecting messages on issues owned by the opposing party. The follower is less likely to perceive benefits from promoting this type of message. By contrast, support for the leader's message is more likely when that message emphasizes issues that the leader's party owns and on which caucus members are unified. Here, the follower may perceive collective and individual benefits from promotion and coverage of the message. Significantly, the collective benefits are unlikely to induce the follower to promote the message: a free-riding caucus member can receive those benefits without helping promote the message. But the follower can still receive individual benefits from promoting this message (if it receives coverage). When attempting to overcome the collective action problem surrounding promotion of the party message, the leader may therefore attempt to increase these individual benefits by emphasizing issues owned by the party.

If accurate, my arguments suggest several specific patterns of behavior by leaders and followers. First, party leaders are more likely to select messages on issues owned by their party than on issues owned by the opposing party. In turn, the followers are more likely to promote the caucus message when that message uses issues owned by the party than when it targets issues owned by the opposing party. Across all these scenarios, individual concerns are more likely than collective ones to affect followers' decisions about message promotion.

The promotional efforts of followers also have important implications for the current debate between preference- and party-based theories of congressional organization (Krehbiel 1998; Aldrich and Rohde 1995). This debate has created a high, if counterfactual, standard for assessing the effects of party leadership: whether the efforts of party leaders lead legislators to behave differently than they would in the absence of such efforts. The promotional efforts of rank-and-file senators can potentially meet this standard. When a party leader organizes a promotional effort on an issue, not all caucus members may agree with the issue position making up the message. Preference-based theories would expect these disagreeing senators to ignore the party message, promoting their own position and message instead. But party-based theories would predict two possible outcomes: the disagreeing senators promote the party message despite their disagreement, or they remain silent, not wishing to undermine the party by voicing disagreement. The analysis below examines the frequency of each strategy by rank-and-file senators.

Leaders' Attempts to Persuade Followers

I first examine how party leaders in the Senate work to persuade their followers to promote the party message. My analysis focuses largely on interactions among leaders and followers in the Senate Democratic caucus, reflecting the Democratic orientation of much of the information that I collected. This material was often politically sensitive, and given my access to the Democratic leadership, it was impossible to obtain similar access to the Republicans. But given the two parties' similar incentives for coordination and promotion, the findings of my analysis are likely to apply to both Democrats and Republicans.

In the leadership strategy outlined above, leaders select messages on issues owned by their party, instead of on issues owned by the opposing party. Coverage of the former type of message is more likely to provide collective and individual benefits to caucus members, who in turn are more likely to promote the message. To examine this expectation, it is first necessary to categorize the issues facing Congress and to identify issues owned by Democrats and by Republicans. For a detailed categorization of issues, I turned to the framework developed by Baumgartner and Jones (1993).[5] Within their framework, I identified issues owned by each party—that is, issues where one caucus was unified, the opposing caucus was divided, and the general public supported the position of the unified caucus. To categorize issues by these criteria, I used Senate roll call votes from 1996, issue-specific questions from the 1996 National Election Study (NES), and Petrocik's (1996) assignments of issue ownership based on additional public opinion data.

Four issues appeared completely owned by one of the parties: health, education, and environment for the Democrats, and defense for the GOP. These four issues are not the *only* ones that the leaders are expected to promote. Instead, the four offer the greatest potential for furthering followers' collective and individual interests. The leaders therefore are most likely to promote these issues, but they may also be forced to turn to other issues.

On a number of other issues, the two parties split ownership. For example, if discussions of social welfare emphasize specific poverty programs and the provision of benefits, Democrats are more likely to be unified on the issue. But, the advantage switches to the Republicans if the discussion revolves around welfare reform. Since no party enjoys exclusive ownership of this type of issue, I expect the party leaders and followers to devote less emphasis to these issues. They are more likely to focus on issues that their party completely owns.[6]

With this categorization of issues, I turned to the actual messages selected by party leaders. I used three sources of messages. The first was a collection of all press releases submitted by legislators to the Senate press and radio television galleries from April to July of 1997. I focused here on the releases produced by the majority and minority leaders and their staff. While the total number of releases was not large (twenty-three for Daschle and forty for Lott), they nonetheless provided one measure of the two leaders' messages.

A second measure of the Democratic leader's messages was the *Daily Report,* a daily newsletter produced by the Democratic Policy Committee (DPC). I collected editions from March to July of 1997. The publication reviews recent developments in the Senate and describes upcoming floor action. It also presents substantive and rhetorical arguments from the Democratic leadership's message for the particular day and week. For example, the June 24 edition reprinted portions of a *New York Times* editorial that criticized Republican tax proposals. The *Daily Report* feature was titled "GOP Tax Tables Paint Misleading Picture of Who Benefits from House and Senate Tax Bills." In addition to frequent excerpts from newspaper editorials, the Democratic publication also uses quotes from Democratic legislators.

For a third source of messages, I turned to my notes from weekly meetings between Daschle's leadership staff and the legislative directors (LDs) of the Senate Democrats. Normally occurring on Friday afternoons, these meetings gave the leadership staff an opportunity to brief the LDs on expected developments during the upcoming weeks. Such regular meetings also allowed the leadership staff to (attempt to) persuade the LDs to support the leadership's selection of strategies and messages.[7]

I attended every LD meeting from the start of February to the end of July, a total of eighteen meetings. At each meeting I took detailed notes, particularly of the leadership staff's presentations. Again, these presentations focused on events of the upcoming week. The leadership initiated some events, while responding to or taking advantage of others. When focusing on specific legislation, the presentations were often detailed and focused on legislative maneuvering in committee or on the Senate floor. Also common to many presentations was a message component: which issues or bills the leadership planned to discuss on the Senate floor or when talking with reporters and constituents.

Research assistants and I coded the issues mentioned in all three sources, using the Baumgartner and Jones directory of issues.[8] Table 8.1 summarizes the coding. The patterns of issue emphasis were remarkably similar across the three sources of messages. The most frequently mentioned issue was macroeconomics, including the federal budget. Both leaders devoted approximately one-third of their releases to the issue (39 percent of Daschle's releases and 30 percent of Lott's). Nearly two-thirds of the *Daily Report* editions mentioned macroeconomics. And the issue arose in a message context in all eighteen LD meetings. This emphasis undoubtedly reflected both parties' efforts to steer discussions of macroeconomics and the budget toward specific topics favoring their interests. Democrats wished to discuss the federal budget in terms of specific governmental programs. On the other hand, Republicans preferred to emphasize general

TABLE 8.1. Percentage of Events That Mention Issues

	Press Releases		*Daily Report* Editions	Legislative Director Meetings
	Daschle	Lott		
Macroeconomics	39%	30%	63%	100%
Civil rights and civil liberties	13%	3%	6%	22%
Health	39%	10%	29%	61%
Agriculture	0%	0%	0%	0%
Labor and immigration	4%	8%	10%	17%
Education	22%	2%	32%	60%
Environment	13%	3%	12%	33%
Energy	4%	3%	0%	0%
Transportation	4%	0%	3%	0%
Law, crime, and family issues	0%	10%	1%	17%
Social welfare	0%	8%	9%	11%
Community development and housing	0%	0%	0%	0%
Banking, finance, and domestic commerce	22%	8%	9%	11%
Defense	4%	23%	0%	6%
Technology	4%	3%	0%	0%
Foreign trade	4%	0%	0%	0%
International affairs	0%	0%	6%	0%
Government operations	17%	15%	6%	28%
Public lands	4%	3%	0%	6%
Culture	0%	0%	0%	0%
State and local government	0%	0%	0%	0%
Total number of press releases, editions, or meetings	23	40	68	18

Note: Each column's percentages total more than 100 because an individual release, edition, or meeting may have addressed more than one issue.

revenue, spending, and deficit targets, along with innovations such as the line-item veto and the balanced budget amendment to the Constitution. While these agenda-setting goals were important, an equally plausible explanation for the frequent discussion of macroeconomics is the importance of the budget process on Capitol Hill. The budget calendar forces both parties to discuss budgetary issues throughout the year. These discussions serve both as the context for many other issues and as the most prominent battleground for conflicts between the two parties.

The minority leader and his staff gave much more emphasis to Democratic issues than to Republican ones. Many of Daschle's releases focused on health, education, and the environment (39 percent, 22 percent, and 13 percent, respectively), while devoting little attention to defense (4 percent). The editions of the *Daily Report* followed a similar pattern. Outside of macroeconomics, the three Democratic issues were the most frequently mentioned (29 percent, 32 percent, and 12 percent), while the Republican issue was not mentioned at all. Finally, the message discussions at the LD meetings frequently involved the Democratic issues (61 percent, 60 percent, and 33 percent), while rarely addressing the Republican issue (6 percent). Daschle did emphasize issues on which party ownership was divided (civil rights and civil liberties, labor and immigration, and social welfare). And he distributed releases on issues owned by neither party. In the area of government operations, for example, Daschle discussed the ongoing campaign finance investigation by the Governmental Affairs Committee. But the minority leader's attention to these areas was still less than his focus on issues clearly owned by his party.

The Democratic leader's emphasis on his party's issues contrasts with the patterns emerging from Lott's press releases. The majority leader addressed the Democratic issues much less often (10 percent, 2 percent, and 3 percent). He emphasized issues with divided ownership with similar frequency. He gave slightly more attention to government operations, specifically the campaign finance investigation. But Lott discussed defense, the issue most clearly owned by his party, in 23 percent of his releases. Overall, these percentages indicate that the two leaders focused much of their press efforts on issues owned by their respective parties. They devoted less attention to issues where ownership was divided or unclear.

Further evidence of issue ownership emerges in the extent to which each leader linked his discussion of macroeconomics to other issues. Tax cuts were central to the 1997 budget debate, particularly during the summer months. Since Republicans are often more unified than Democrats on this issue, Daschle attempted to steer the debate to more Democratic issues. Specifically, six of his nine macroeconomics releases emphasized how paying for the tax cuts would force Republicans to cut health, education, and environmental programs. The minority leader also emphasized tax cut proposals targeted to these areas, such as tax credits for college tuition. Finally, five of his releases dealing with macroeconomics contained a distributional argument that the Republican tax and budget plans would help the wealthy and hurt low- and middle-income working families.

Similar Democratic messages appeared in the *Daily Report*. Of the forty-three editions that addressed macroeconomics, twenty-one of them linked the issue to education, health, or environmental protection. And in twenty-eight of the forty-three issues mentioning macroeconomics, the DPC added the same distributional argument about the Republican tax and budget plans. The *Daily Report* discussed only macroeconomics and no other issues in only seven editions.

These attempts to link tax cuts to more Democratic issues also occurred in the LD meetings. As already mentioned, macroeconomics was a topic of every meeting. In particular, the issue of taxes was discussed at the last seven meetings, reflecting the summer debate over the tax reconciliation package. But these issues of macroeconomics and taxes were linked to Democratic issues in seventeen of the eighteen meetings. And in the last seven meetings, the discussion of taxes was always tied to the distributional argument described above.

Daschle's linkage of taxes and Democratic issues differed significantly from the message efforts of the majority leader. Lott linked these issues less frequently, discussing macroeconomics, the budget, and taxes in isolation. Thirty percent, or twelve, of the majority leader's releases emphasized macroeconomics. Most of these twelve releases emphasized how the Republicans' economic proposals would benefit all Americans: "Our goal is the total dismantling of today's tax system, replacing it with a new system that is fair, simple, uniform, and most important, a system that lowers the tax burden on working men and women" (Lott, May 5, 1997). Only five of the twelve releases addressed health, education, or the environment. When the majority leader did address a Democratic issue in a macroeconomic press release, it was either to highlight the Republican proposal for an education tax credit or to defend against Democratic attacks on Republican budget and tax proposals. The tax credit proposal represented an attempt to link taxes and education in a manner more favorable to Republicans. The proposal would purportedly make education more accessible instead of harming education as charged by the Democrats. Lott's responses to Democratic attacks marked a capitulation, however brief, to discussing taxes and macroeconomics on their terms instead of his own.

Overall, the press releases, the *Daily Report* editions, and the LD meetings consistently revealed the strategic construction of messages. Daschle and Lott tried to steer the legislative debate toward issues owned by their party: that is, issues on which their party was more likely to be unified. In the press releases each leader tried to draw attention to issues favoring his party. In the *Daily Report* and the LD meetings, Daschle worked to persuade his caucus to promote messages on issues owned by the Democrats. Even when forced to discuss macroeconomics and taxes, the minority leader tried to link those issues to health, education, and the environment. By structuring the caucus message in this manner, each leader created a message with greater potential benefits for his followers. The caucus members would therefore be more likely to help promote that message.

Followers' Promotion of the Leader's Message

The next step of the analysis assesses the effectiveness of focusing the caucus message on issues owned by the party. I expect that a follower is more likely to support the leader's message when it focuses on an issue owned by the party than when it focuses on an issue owned by the opposing party. To examine whether this behavior actually occurs, I interviewed press secretaries of U.S. senators during June and July of 1998. The analysis drew on forty-one interviews that ranged in length from ten minutes to one hour.[9] Rather than using the interviews to ask general questions about senators' press activities, I decided to focus my questions on specific issues that the Senate had recently considered. I searched for a recent Senate debate on an issue owned by Democrats and another debate on an issue owned by Republicans.

I chose the Senate debates over partial-birth abortion and a supplemental appropriations bill that occurred during May and June of 1997. Abortion has long proved a divisive issue for both parties. But in recent years, prolife advocates in the Republican party have enjoyed more success on the issue by narrowing their focus to the specific procedure commonly called partial-birth abortion.[10] Graphic descriptions and images of this procedure have helped prolife Republicans unify their party in support of banning the procedure. For similar reasons, traditionally prochoice Democrats find it harder to support the procedure.

The different levels of unity in the two parties were evident in the 1996 Senate vote to override President Bill Clinton's veto of a partial-birth abortion ban (#301). On this vote, 46 of 53 Republicans (90 percent) voted to override, while 35 of 47 Democrats (74 percent) voted to sustain the veto. Of the seven dissident or nonvoting Republicans, two were replaced by supporters of the ban in the next Congress (the time of my analysis). A nonvoting Republican later committed to support the ban. Among Democrats, one of the president's supporters (Senator David Pryor, D-AR) retired and was replaced by a conservative Republican in the next Congress. Thus, at the time of my analysis, Senate Republicans had grown even more unified behind a ban on partial-birth abortions. The Democratic caucus had grown slightly weaker in opposing that ban. The Republicans' greater unity suggests that this issue favored their party. But to meet the criteria for ownership outlined above, it is also necessary to compare the parties' positions to public opinion.

The press secretary interviews offered such evidence. Both Democratic and Republican staffers widely believed that the GOP position was more popular among the general public. Despite the divisive nature of the abortion issue, the Republicans' vivid images helped make their claims more persuasive. One Republican staffer described his confidence that his party could overcome the potential divisiveness of the abortion issue: "Abortion is the most divisive, most difficult issue here. This is because you automatically piss off half the electorate. This is particularly the case in a diverse state like [ours]. But partial birth is slightly different; we felt confident we could promote the issue. It's a more populist issue, with more general appeal" (interview, July 15, 1998). Partial-birth abortion appeared to fit the criteria outlined above for a politically advantageous issue. The Republican caucus was more unified than the Democrats, while many in both parties believed that the GOP position on the issue could win the support of the general public.

An opposite pattern of unity occurred during the debate over the supplemental appropriations bill. This legislation provided funding for a variety of emergency needs, most notably the natural disasters that had swept much of the country during the previous winter and spring. Severe winter weather, followed or accompanied by record-level flooding, devastated entire communities, particularly in the Midwest. The relief funding for these disasters gave legislative momentum to the supplemental appropriations bill, but the Republican leadership decided to attach two controversial provisions to the bill. The first would have prohibited the Census Bureau from using sampling in the 2000 census. The second created an "auto CR" (automatic continuing resolution), which would prevent the government from being shut down if Congress and the President could not agree on appropriation bills. Democrats strongly opposed both provisions because they would reduce their party's influence in the legislative process.

The congressional debate over the supplemental appropriations bill therefore became a fight over whether the two provisions should be attached. Senate Democrats were unified around their leadership's firm call for passing a "clean bill." The entire caucus opposed the sampling and auto CR provisions. Sixty percent of the Democratic senators (27 of 45) represented states that were to receive high levels of relief funding from the bill.[11] With the most disasters in their states, these twenty-seven Democrats could be expected to offer the strongest support for their leadership's strategy. But caucus members from states with less funding would not be expected to oppose that funding and the supplemental appropriations bill. These weak supporters might push less strenuously for the bill's passage, but they would oppose the sampling and auto CR provisions. This combination would still lead them to support the Democratic leadership's strategy and message.

The Republican leadership faced a more divided caucus. Senate Republicans appeared unified in support of the sampling and auto CR provisions. Fifty-eight percent of the caucus (32 of 55) represented states receiving relatively low levels of disaster funding. While these senators did not oppose the funding on the bill, they most likely did not see a pressing need for it. The senators could therefore be expected to support their leadership's strategy linking the bill to the sampling and auto CR provisions. But the remainder of the Republican caucus most likely had greater concerns about that strategy. Representing states with relatively high levels of relief funding, these senators may have felt a pressing need to approve that funding and speed it to their constituents. The attachment of the two provisions to the bill slowed the provision of relief funding. These senators were most likely less supportive of their leadership's strategy. Thus, the

Republican caucus was less unified behind their leadership than was the case among Democrats across the aisle.

Staffers from both parties believed that the Democratic position was more popular among the general public. In the interviews, Democratic press secretaries enthusiastically described how their arguments were favorably received across the country. Significantly, Republican staffers agreed with these assessments, despite their partisan incentive to downplay any Democratic success. The GOP arguments on the supplemental appropriations bill did not appear as attractive to the general public, even in states with few disasters. A Republican press secretary from one of these states described their efforts to persuade voters:

> We promoted the leadership message in [our state], but the coverage didn't reflect it. Reporters would ask [my senator] why we were adding the amendments. We would go into a long explanation of the need for the amendments. But then a reporter would ask, "Why aren't the people in the Dakotas getting help?" It was like banging your head against a wall. . . . Every night in people's living rooms, they had these images of incredible destruction in the Midwest. . . . You'd be sitting in church, and when the minister asked members to contact Congress to release the funds, everyone would turn around and look at you. (interview, July 9, 1998)

Thus, the supplemental issue appears to have been owned by the Democrats. At the start of the debate, their caucus was more unified than the GOP. And the Democratic position appeared more popular among the general public.[12]

Partial-birth abortion and the supplemental appropriations bill formed the focus of my interviews. I asked each press secretary "How much did your office work to promote a message (either the leadership's or your own) on the issue of [partial-birth abortion/the supplemental appropriations bill]?" The answers to this question provided a measure of each senator's message promotion. I coded each press secretary's response into one of four categories: no promotion (0), a small amount (1), a moderate amount (2), or a great deal (3).

I supplemented the interview data with information from two additional sources. The first was the set of senators' press releases submitted to the Senate press galleries. The second was a record of all press events (news conferences, stakeouts, etc.) held on the Senate side of the Capitol during the seven-month period (this record is compiled by the staff of the Senate radio television gallery). With this set of press releases and events, I counted the number of times that each senator promoted his or her leadership's message on partial-birth abortion and the supplemental appropriations bill. These counts went beyond the interview data in two respects. The data existed for all one hundred senators, as opposed to the forty-one offices in my interview sample. Also, the press releases and events captured the actual promotion of messages, which provided a useful check on the press secretaries' recollections of their activities a year earlier.

Partial-Birth Abortion

I analyzed these data by examining the overall levels of message promotion in each party. The Democratic and Republican caucuses in the Senate varied substantially in their promotion of their leadership's messages on partial-birth abortion and the supplemental appropriations bill. Table 8.2 documents these differences. First, Republicans appeared more active than Democrats in discussing partial-birth abortion. In the interviews, the GOP senators' average promotion on the national level was .65 (on a scale of 0 to 3). The equivalent mean for Democrats was .17, and the difference between these two averages (.48) was significant at the .05 level. Both caucuses engaged in more promotion at the state level, while the difference in their averages (.59) remained statistically significant. In the national press releases and Capitol Hill events, Republicans were still more active than Democrats (.47 and .16, respectively), although the difference was no longer statistically significant.

When explaining their press activity on partial-birth abortion, the staffers from the two parties offered contrasting reasons. The Republicans' responses focused almost exclusively on individual electoral benefits. Most notably, the partial-birth issue solidified and energized the electoral base of many senators, particularly conservatives and prolife activists. Remarkably, no Republicans supportive of the ban mentioned any policy benefits from promoting the leadership's message.

In contrast, Democrats focused on electoral and policy costs. Many Democrats viewed the issue as part of the Republicans' strategy for the next election. As one press secretary put it, "The Republicans presented the Democrats with a difficult situation. The Democrats didn't want to vote the way that they have traditionally voted, and that some traditional Democratic constituencies would want them to vote, because doing so would create perfect material for a 30-second spot" (interview, June 25, 1998). The partial-birth issue risked alienating activists in both wings of the senators' individual constituencies: prochoice women's groups and more conservative Catholic constituents. The press secretaries also lamented that the graphic pictures of partial-birth abortions proved very effective: "It's really hard to combat those horrific images that the Republicans use" (interview, July 2, 1998).

Other individual costs also discouraged the Democrats from promoting the issue. Several senators were personally torn on the issue, facing costs regardless of their decision. This tension created a strong hesitancy to discuss the issue; one press secretary said that her senator would "rather go to the dentist than have a

TABLE 8.2. Average Levels of Promotion of Leadership Message between and within Parties

| | Partial-Birth Abortion | | | | | Supplemental | | | | |
| | Press Secretary Interviews | | | Press Releases and Events | | Press Secretary Interviews | | | Press Releases and Events | |
	National Promotion	State Promotion	Number of Senators	National Promotion	Number of Senators	National Promotion	State Promotion	Number of Senators	National Promotion	Number of Senators
Overall parties										
Democrats	.17**	.28**	18	.16	45	1.61***	1.61***	18	1.38**	45
Republicans	.65	.87	23	.47	55	.09	.30	23	.42	55
Democrats										
Supporters or strong supporters of leadership message	.15*	.38**	13	.21*	33	1.75	2.08**	12	2.15***	27
Opponents or weak supporters of leadership message	0	0	4	0	8	1.33	.67	6	.22	18
Republicans										
Supporters of leadership message	.61	.78	18	.60*	43	0	.13*	15	.28*	32
Opponents of leadership message	0	0	1	0	3	.25	.63	8	.61	23

Note: The text explains each issue's classification. I classified each senator as a supporter or opponent of her leadership's message (on the supplemental, Democrats were divided into strong and weak supporters of the caucus message). For the press secretary interviews, I calculated the average level of support for the leadership message, both for each overall party and for each group within each party. The scale of message promotion ranges from 0 (no promotion) to 3 (very active promotion). For the press events and releases, I calculated the average number of events and releases in support of the leadership message, again for each overall party and for each group within each party. Then, for each pair of averages (between parties and then within each party), I calculated difference of means tests. The results of these tests are indicated in the standard manner: $*p < .1$, $**p < .05$, $***p < .01$.

conversation about the issue" (interview, July 9, 1998). Two Democratic senators faced recall efforts over the partial-birth issue, initiated by conservative voters in their state. The press secretary for one senator said that the recall effort made him decide to vote against the partial-birth ban. Finally, a Catholic church in another Democratic senator's state apparently excommunicated a woman over the partial-birth abortion issue. The press secretary for this senator mentioned that this potential for excommunication was in their minds as they approached the issue.

Partisan costs also loomed large in decisions whether to promote party messages, most notably among senators opposing their party leadership. In the interviews, only one Republican senator opposed the GOP leadership's position, but this legislator engaged in no promotional activities for or against that position.[13] In explaining this silence, the press secretary mentioned the difficulty of countering horrific images of the partial-birth procedure, but also the possible loss of Republican fundraising support for opposing the leadership.

Among Democrats, opponents of the party leadership's message and position were also silent. Their press secretaries revealed no promotional efforts either for or against the party message; there also were no press releases on partial-birth abortion from these senators. The press secretary for a southern Democrat explained the silence of her boss: "Reporters try to get him to talk when he goes against the leadership. But unless he really cares about the issue, he doesn't talk to reporters. He just votes against the leadership and is quiet about it. It's selective opposition. . . . He feels that these are his only options because they are in the minority and can't afford lots of public conflicts and debates within the party" (interview, July 10, 1998).

These partisan concerns provide more support for the partisan theories of congressional organization than for the preference-based alternatives. The latter approach suggests that legislators act according to their own preferences regardless of party ties, which suggests that this particular southern senator would have spoken out against partial-birth abortion. The legislator might have done so in a partyless chamber. But concerns about supporting his party and leader discouraged the legislator from doing so.

Finally, senators on both sides of the aisle engaged in more message promotion at the state level, which makes sense. When a senator chooses to promote his or her party's message in Washington to the national media, it may be harder for the senator to realize any individual benefits of that promotion. Many congressional activities do not receive coverage in the national media. If they do, the national coverage does not always extend to the state media. An easier way to win coverage in the state media is to promote a message to them directly. Hence, senators are more likely to realize individual benefits by promoting the leadership message to state media than to the national press outlets.

The Supplemental Appropriations Bill

An opposite pattern of promotion occurred on the supplemental appropriations bill. Democrats promoted their leadership's message much more than Republican senators advanced their party's message. In the interview data, Democrats averaged 1.61 on the national level, while the mean for Republicans was .09. The difference between the two parties narrowed slightly on the state level (1.61, .30). But on both national and state levels, the difference between the parties' averages was statistically significant. A similar pattern occurred in the press releases and events: Democratic senators were much more active than their colleagues across the aisle (1.38 and .42, respectively).

Instead of promoting the party message more actively on the state than national level, Democrats appeared equally active on both levels. The surprisingly high level of national activity may stem from how the Democratic leadership organized press activities in Washington. Daschle and his staff organized a number of media events targeting both national and state media. A Capitol Hill press conference might have mostly national reporters in the audience, but the leadership broadcast the event via satellite directly back to the media in individual reporters' states. To make the event even more compelling to both national and state media, the Democrats brought to Washington the mayors of small communities hit by disasters and citizens from those communities who had lost their homes. The local angle added by these victims made the event more compelling and immediate for the national media, while state reporters were attracted by their local citizens' activities in Washington. By structuring the events in this manner, the Democratic leadership increased the likelihood of coverage and helped caucus members realize individual benefits from promoting the leadership message on the national and state levels.

When discussing electoral benefits of the leadership's message, the press secretaries referred to both the overall Democratic party and their own individual senator. The leadership's message spelled out a clear Democratic position and helped unify the party. At the same time, the issue gave Democrats an opportunity to attack. One press secretary summarized the situation: "This was a freebie. The Republicans made a political miscalculation of the nth degree. Their actions reinforced the image that the Republicans were not in touch with the average citizen. I talked to as many reporters as possible, pushing the Democratic message: 'My God, here they go again. Didn't they learn their lesson from the government shutdown?'" (interview, June 30, 1998).

These collective electoral benefits accrued to all Democratic senators, regardless of the disasters in their states. The caucus message also provided individual electoral benefits to senators, helping them maintain or shore up political support among home state constituencies. Such efforts were particularly important for senators from states such as the Dakotas, hit hard by natural disasters.

Acknowledged a staffer from one of these states, "We knew we'd sink or swim on this issue alone" (interview, July 10, 1998).

Such home-state concerns varied across Democratic senators, as some members of the caucus represented states with few disasters and therefore little funding in the bill. As Table 8.2 indicates, these weak supporters of the Democratic leadership's message still helped promote that message, although not as vigorously as the strong supporters from hard-hit states.[14] The weak supporters engaged in these promotional efforts for several reasons. Some staffers spoke of the need to assist the devastated communities and families, even when representing states unaffected by natural disasters: "While the disasters have mainly struck the Dakotas, the bill does affect [our state] too. [Our state] gets hit by hurricanes, by tornadoes, by drought. If we don't help the Dakotas, it could be [our state] that gets hit next" (interview, June 30, 1998).

Other Democrats from low-funded states helped promote the leadership message for other reasons. The previous election of one senator had been contested by her Republican opponent. The senator participated in many leadership-sponsored activities on the supplemental appropriations bill, at least partially out of appreciation for Daschle's assistance in establishing the legality of her election. Another freshman senator had few or no disasters hit her state. But she actively promoted the leadership's message in hopes of accumulating favor with other more senior Democrats.

These explanations suggest why senators from low-funded states might help promote the leadership's message and corresponding collective benefits for the party. Instead of focusing on their state's immediate benefits from the current debate, these senators considered how their party had helped in past events or might help in future ones. These explanations are again consistent with party-based theories of congressional organization. The congressional party can help coordinate legislators' efforts across multiple issues and over time (Aldrich 1995). Rather than narrowly acting on the basis of immediate policy preferences, legislators may instead follow partisan goals in hopes of realizing future (and greater) benefits.

In contrast to the Democrats' enthusiastic embrace of their leadership's message, the Republicans were much less active on the supplemental appropriations bill. Many GOP staffers mentioned individual costs in promoting the leadership's message on these issues. Most notably, their constituents did not accept the Republican argument about the need to link the issues. Many voters believed that the Republican leadership's message and strategy were preventing relief funds from reaching disaster victims. Such concerns were most common in states with extensive natural disasters. A Republican press secretary from one of these states described their dilemma:

This was a difficult situation for us because [our state] got lots of disaster relief funds. While the burned and flooded North Dakota town got most of the coverage, the flooding was also horrible for [our state]. We were in a spot. We wanted to support the leadership, because the White House and Democrats never pass anything "clean." But the Republican strategy was ill-timed. . . . You can't tell someone whose house had fallen into the river that the funds that they're going to get are not affected by this debate. (interview, July 15, 1998)

These senators from hard-hit states were the most likely opponents of their leadership's message, since their constituents may have faced the greatest hardship from the GOP's linkage of the supplemental to the two controversial provisions. The strongest support for this strategy was likely to emerge from senators representing states with few disasters; these legislators most likely faced little constituent pressure to pass the bill quickly (without the provisions). Despite these differences, the opponents of the GOP leadership's message promoted that message more frequently than their more supportive colleagues (see table 8.2). These opponents undoubtedly faced greater home-state pressure to discuss the issue. But remarkably, these GOP senators stuck to their leadership's message, despite the temptation to desert the leadership and push for passage of a clean bill. Preference-based theories of congressional organization would predict desertion by these legislators. But instead, the GOP opponents continued to promote their party's goals, a finding that provides even more support for the party-based theories of congressional organization.

Overall, these patterns of message promotion follow my expectations outlined above. Republicans owned the issue of partial-birth abortion and engaged in more promotional activities on that issue. Democrats, on the other hand, more actively promoted their leadership's message on the supplemental appropriations bill, an issue that they owned. On both issues, senators' decisions whether to promote the caucus message hinged much more on individual costs and benefits than on collective considerations. In addition, senators in several instances failed to desert their party leadership and pursue individual home-state interests, as predicted by preference-based theories of congressional organization. Instead, these legislators based their promotional decisions on partisan considerations.

Finally, the differences between partial-birth abortion and the supplemental appropriations bill suggest a different, more transient type of issue ownership. The Democrats' advantage was made possible only by the Republicans' decision to link the sampling and auto CR provisions to the bill. That advantage began to dissipate when the bill became law. This temporary issue ownership thus depends on the parties' positions and strategies in the short term. But even a short-term partisan advantage may boost a party's legislative momentum and electoral fortunes.

Conclusion

Representation is a complicated process. Issues may vary in salience and structure, while tensions between the individual and collective make it harder for legislators to represent their constituents' interests. In this chapter I have illustrated how these complexities create opportunities for politicians to win political advantage. Such complexities and opportunities abound in the Senate. While senators often dominate press congressional press coverage, their leaders possess few formal powers for controlling the congressional agenda. They must therefore turn to less formal strategies, working to influence that agenda with media campaigns.

Leaders and followers in the Senate worked to focus the external media agenda and internal legislative agenda on issues where their party's positions were more attractive to the general public than those of their opponents. The party leaders used press releases and other venues to highlight issues owned by their party and to link discussion of other topics back to these political advantageous issues. In turn, rank-and-file members of each caucus promoted their party's message more frequently on issues owned by their party. As the temptation to free-ride posed an obstacle to collective promotion of the party message, most senators chose to promote that message when they could realize individual benefits from the effort. Another potential obstacle to collective message promotion was the temptation to defect from the leadership and promote home-state concerns. But senators largely deferred from such defection; instead, they either helped promote their leadership's message or avoided undermining it. This final pattern is consistent with party-based theories of congressional organization.

These patterns of issue ownership, message promotion, and partisan mobilization apply across legislators and issues. As such, they constitute a step toward a more generalizable theory of heresthetics and strategic political communication. A second such step investigates whether these promotional efforts are actually associated with more favorable coverage for the congressional parties. In preliminary analysis of this link (Sellers 1999), I compared the two Senate parties' promotional efforts (on the issues in Table 1) to their subsequent coverage in the *New York Times*. Both Lott and Daschle won more coverage for the leadership message if they increased the number of caucus members helping promote that message. Understandably, the size of the boost in coverage depended on the opposing party. A unified caucus promoting its own message reduced the coverage won by the opposition. But a dispersed opposition discussing diverse issues ceded the playing field, allowing a unified caucus to win greater coverage of its message.

This type of analysis can trace the transmission of party messages from their creation by congressional party leaders to their varying acceptance and promotion by individual legislators and finally to their contrasting coverage in national and local media outlets. Tracing these links can help us understand the dynamics of message promotion and partisan conflict in Congress.

Notes

A previous version of this chapter was presented at the annual meeting of the American Political Science Association, Atlanta, GA, September 2–5, 1999. The research was funded by the National Science Foundation (SBR #9870841). I wish to thank the press secretaries who contributed their time and insights to the project, and the staff of Senator Tom Daschle, the Senate press gallery, and the Senate radio television gallery. I also thank Dave Holian, Brian Schaffner, and Tiffani Allen for their excellent research assistance. Finally, this chapter has benefited immensely from the suggestions of David Canon, Tim Cook, Kathryn Firmin-Sellers, Dan Lipinski, Bruce Oppenheimer, and Phil Paolino.

1. I incorporated legislators' policy and electoral goals, to the exclusion of the goal of power (Fenno 1973). The time frame for my analysis was too short to examine legislators' attempts to expand their power by winning party or committee leadership positions. This question was part of a related project examining senators' media activities on Capitol Hill from 1979 to 1998 (Sellers and Schaffner 1999).
2. In 1997 I was an American Political Science Association Congressional Fellow in the minority leader's office. During this period I attended meetings with leadership staff and collected the press releases from the press galleries. I conducted the press secretary interviews during the summer of 1998. All quotations in this chapter, unless otherwise noted, are taken from my notes of the leadership meetings and from interviews with the press secretaries and the leadership staff. All attributions are anonymous; this was necessary to gain interview access.
3. Congressional parties are certainly not the only influences on that agenda and its coverage in the press. The president, interest groups, and external events are also important. But congressional leaders and their parties are central to the legislative process, and news coverage of Congress is likely to reflect that role.
4. My definition of issue ownership differs from the original formulation offered by Petrocik (1996). In his definition, ownership is based on public perceptions that one party possesses greater "ability to resolve a problem of concern to voters" (826). These perceptions are built from the actions of a party's constituencies and leaders: "groups support a party because it attempts to use government to alter or protect a social or economic status quo which harms or benefits them; the party promotes such policies because it draws supporters, activists, and candidates from the groups. Issue handling reputations emerge from this history" (828). In his analysis, Petrocik uses public perceptions of parties to determine ownership of issues. While including public perceptions, my definition of ownership also incorporates the actions of party elites (senators' roll call votes). If one party caucus is unified around an issue position while

the opposing caucus is not, the former party appears more capable of passing legislation to address the issue. My formulation of issue ownership is an attempt to broaden Petrocik's original definition to include elite determinants of ownership. The party elites can influence issue ownership, which in turn can affect the elites' own actions. The time period of this analysis was too short to distinguish these competing causal effects.

5. This dictionary spans 27 pages, containing 21 major categories, 169 subcategories, and multiple specific issues within each subcategory. It is available at http://weber.u. washington.edu/~ampol/agendasproject.html.

6. The split ownership of issues is partially a function of the Baumgartner and Jones (1993) issue categories. This framework performs very well for their own analysis. But in this chapter, several categories include issues owned by each party.

7. The LD meetings are only part of the Democratic leadership's attempts to distribute their interpretation of recent and upcoming events and to persuade others to accept their strategies and support their messages. On Fridays, leadership staffers also hold separate meetings with the Senate Democrats' administrative assistants, with their press secretaries, and with the minority chiefs of staff of the Senate committees. In addition, Democratic senators regularly meet on Tuesdays in caucus meetings and on Thursdays in policy luncheons (often featuring guest speakers such as a cabinet secretary, author, or economist).

8. The three sources do not cover identical periods of 1997. This difference resulted from my discovery of each source at a different time during my work in Daschle's office. For each LD meeting, I coded each issue that was mentioned as part of the leadership's message. Each mention could take a direct form: "Our message on this bill is. . . ." Or the message component could be less direct: "When you are talking with your constituents about this issue, it's more effective to emphasize. . . ." I then calculated the percentage of meetings in which each issue was mentioned. I also coded the notes for mentions of issues regardless of whether there was a message component. The resulting percentages parallel those reported below, except that issues not owned by the Democratic party receive more frequent mention. These noisier findings make sense. The Democratic leadership focuses its message efforts on issues owned by its party. But when trying to give the caucus an accurate idea of upcoming events in the Senate, the leadership must broaden its presentation and include issues owned by Republicans or by no party.

9. I actually conducted fifty-one interviews. But ten of the press secretaries had started working in their office since the previous summer, when the events of interest to my analysis occurred. I therefore was unable to use the results of these ten interviews in the current analysis. The forty-one offices that granted access were representative of the overall Senate. I interviewed eighteen Democrats and twenty-three Republicans. This sample included at least one senator from thirty-seven of the fifty states. Among the Democrats that I interviewed, the average seniority was 13.26 years; the equiva-

lent for all Senate Democrats was 13.00 years. I also calculated the average of vote ratings produced by the American Conservative Union (ACU) (where values close to 0 indicate liberal votes and values close to 100 suggest conservative votes). Democrats in the sample averaged 8.87, while the mean for the Democratic caucus was 7.45. The Republicans that I interviewed were equally representative. Their average seniority was 7.79 years, while that of the GOP caucus was 9.85. The sample of Republicans had an average ACU score of 79.21; the equivalent for all Republicans was 77.87.

10. Prochoice advocates have unsuccessfully attempted to give the procedure a less provocative name in public debate. By describing it as "dilation and extraction," the prochoice advocates attempted to remove the gruesome implication that the procedure involved the partial birth of a child. This alternative label is also more scientific in tone, thereby placing the procedure closer to accepted medical science.

11. For this ranking of the states, I first divided each state's funding from the supplemental appropriations bill by the state's number of House members. This per capita measure more accurately captures the importance of funding in each state; $500,000 is much more important in a relatively unpopulated state like North Dakota than in a populous state like California. After ranking the states by their level of per capita funding, I split them into high and low funding groups, based on the median level of funding for all states.

12. For both issues, it is potentially problematic to use staffers' retrospective perceptions as a measure of public opinion. The clear victory on each issue may have colored these recollections. But significantly, on each issue the losing party had the incentive to minimize their loss and claim that the outcome did not reflect unified public opinion. Therefore, the two parties' similar perceptions of public opinion on each issue does increase the validity of those recollections.

13. On this issue, I determined supporters and opponents of leadership positions by using the attempt to override President Bill Clinton's veto of a partial-birth abortion ban described above. If a Democrat voted to support the president's veto, I classified the legislator as a supporter of the Democratic leadership's message and position. Voting to override labeled Democrats as opponents. The reverse applied to Republicans.

14. On this issue, Democrats from high-funded states were categorized as strong supporters of their leadership's message and position, and their colleagues from low-funded states were considered weak supporters. I labeled Republicans from high-funded states as strong opponents of the GOP leadership's strategy and Republicans from low-funded states as strong supporters.

*Committees, Parties,
and Leaders in the Senate*

▪ 9 ▪

Parties and Hierarchies in Senate Committees, 1789–1946

David T. Canon and Charles Stewart III

As everyone knows, the Senate is a collegial institution, unencumbered by strict rules or a complicated internal organization. Or at least this is the Senate that modern observers of American politics know about. Especially when contrasted with the politics of the House, Senate politics have seemed so fluid for so long that most observers have concluded that these differences are inherent in the institution, and indeed in the constitutional scheme of things.

This chapter attempts a corrective for this conventional view of the Senate and therefore is an exception in a volume addressed to the topic of "Senate exceptionalism." It does so by focusing on the early development of the committee system in the Senate. In the modern Congress, the relative reliance on the committee system sets the two chambers apart—House members closely align their policy interests with their committee assignments, whereas senators are policy free agents. An institutional consequence of this difference is that the House lavishes more institutional resources on its committees than does the Senate and, conversely, that the Senate lavishes more resources on member offices than does the House. Other consequences follow as well. For instance, the other great institution of legislative organization—party—is much more evident in House committees than in the Senate. House members align more of their political ambition with improving their committee assignments than senators.

Taking this view of the contemporary Congress as a given, it is instructive to ask whether Senate committees have always played second fiddle to House committees, at least in the eyes of the legislators who populate them. Although we cannot provide a definitive answer to that question here, we can provide a glimpse of the Senate committee system during its early development. When we do, we find a Senate committee system that developed in remarkable parallel to the House system. The practice of relying exclusively on standing committees for legislative matters began in the Senate, not the House, but not by much. The Senate was slightly ahead of the House in allowing the majority party to dominate the committee assignment process, but not by much. And the Senate committee system exhibited a clear hierarchical ordering of committee value by the end of the nineteenth century, just as the House did.

In this chapter, we provide the first systematic glimpse of how the Senate committee system developed in its first century and a half, from the First Congress through the Legislative Reorganization Act of 1946. The evidence we analyze is drawn from our data set of all Senate committees assignments, standing and select. Ours is certainly not the first look at the Senate's institutional development (see Swift 1997), or even the first look at the development of its committee system (see Robinson 1954). However, our analysis is different from past research in its comprehensive sweep of history and reliance on data analysis rather than diaries, newspapers, and debates.

We have two general goals in this chapter. First, we use the data we have gathered to sketch a portrait of the partisan and individual-level underpinnings of the committee system in its earliest years. At what point did parties begin to structure the committee system? At what point did a hierarchy of committees evolve in the Senate, based on the individual calculations of senators about how to further their career and policy goals? The second aim of this chapter is to better understand the committee appointment patterns, with an eye toward identifying the factors that have influenced the distribution of power throughout the chamber.

Understanding who was appointed to Senate committees is important for many reasons. Generally, two decades of congressional scholarship have emphasized the agenda-setting power of committees in legislative action. Understanding how Senate committees were composed, assuming they were not constructed randomly, is the first step in understanding how the formal institutions of the Senate may have influenced policy making throughout its history. Specifically, although the Senate is known for its informal rules of procedure, we also know that debates over the institutional design of the nineteenth-century Senate were often heated. Weingast (1998) has argued, for instance, that the "balance rule" was designed to institutionalize a deal between northern and southern interests over the handling of slavery. If so, was that deal continued at the committee level? Several historians have noted that John C. Calhoun set off a firestorm of protest when he insisted on asserting his prerogative as president of the Senate to appoint Senate committees, under the extant rules of the day. Did Calhoun follow a different set of criteria in setting committee rosters than his predecessors? Did the rule concerning committee appointments that was instituted in response to Calhoun's move change those criteria yet again?

While it is important to establish these historical details, the greater payoff of this research is in testing various theories of legislative organization. This view of the historical study of the Senate puts us in the category of "history for hypothesis testing" (Aldrich 1997, 18). While valuing the other two approaches noted by Aldrich ("history as comparative politics" and "history as history"), we believe that general theories of legislatures can be built only with the broadest possible historical data.

While care must be exercised in making generalizations across historical eras, the great institutional and behavioral variation presented by a 150-year sweep of history present wonderful opportunities for hypothesis testing. Consider, for example, the evolution of the committee assignment process: the current method of appointment is most consistent with the requirements of the distributive theory (self-selection by high demand preference outliers), the party list method is obviously most consistent with party-based theories, and the early methods of balloting by the floor would be most likely to produce committees that were close to the median floor voters, which is consistent with a "pivotal politics" view of committees (Krehbiel 1998). While a systematic test of these theories is beyond the scope of this chapter, we will provide some suggestive evidence concerning informational and partisan theories. (See Canon and Sweet 1998 for a test of distributive theories.)

Our empirical analysis relies on a data set that we have constructed, building on the previous work by Garrison Nelson. We collected the data from the *Senate Journal,* supplemented by the various compilations of congressional debates that were published during these Congresses (*Annals of Congress, Congressional Globe,* and *Congressional Record*). For much of this exercise it was necessary to read page by page through the *Senate Journals,* since the indexing of the *Journals* and debates was often so poor and incomplete. The payoff to this strategy is evident in the number of select committees we were able to discover. Although Stubbs (1985) recorded only one select committee in the Senate before the 14th Congress (1815–16), we found 2,142. The data set attempts, as much as humanly possible, to record the comings and goings of all committee members, not only those appointed at the beginning of a Congress but those appointed in the course of a Congress as well. The result is the documentation of 30,804 standing and 11,834 select committee assignments during this period.

The remainder of our chapter is organized as follows. The first section discusses the partisan basis for the Senate committee system and presents some basic descriptive information about the partisan composition of committees from 1789 to 1946. The second section presents our data on the hierarchy of Senate committees for this same period. The third, concluding section discusses the general implications of our research for considering the topic of Senate exceptionalism.

Political Parties and Committees

Party is the primary organizing principle of the modern Congress. When and how did this principle emerge? We know that during the period covered by this chapter certain signposts can guide our initial foray into this subject. First, the literature on party emergence suggests that by the third Congress both chambers had divided into identifiable voting blocs that quickly transformed into electoral labels on the House side. The party caucus was active during the early part of this period as the device for presidential nomination, and members of the Senate, like House members, were active in nominating caucuses.

In the Senate, unlike the House, the vote for (surrogate) presiding officer was not tantamount to chamber organization, and thus it is easy to imagine that partisanship largely eluded the organization of committees. Such a view would be mistaken. Swift (1997, 67–73) notes several ways in which partisanship infected early Senate behavior on and off the floor. John Hoadley (1986, 84) finds evidence of party voting in the Senate in the 1790s, Poole and Rosenthal (1997, 36) find complete spatial separation between the Federalists and Jeffersonian Republicans by the seventh Congress (1801–2) in the Senate, and Robinson (1954, 137) reports that by the 29th Congress (1845–46) party lists were developed by the party leaders and presented to the Senate for ratification—even as the Senate rules still formally provided for balloting in the selection of committees. Behind-the-scenes negotiations within parties for committee slots were reported as early as 1806 and were common by the 1830s (McConachie [1898] 1973, 276–77).

At the same time, other factors may have undermined the operation of partisanship in the early Congress. The practice of choosing committee members by ballot clearly did not serve the interests of the majority party. Without a formal mechanism to coordinate the choice of committee slates during this period, it was impossible for parties to establish a grip on the committee system. McConachie ([1898] 1973) notes the vagaries of the balloting mechanism: "Through absence of concerted action, through a very free exercise of individual preferences, the committeeman standing second in number of votes would be elected by an aggregation of voters slightly, or it may be markedly, different from that which had conferred the chairmanship. So it would be concerning the remaining members of the committee. Thus, at the outset the ballot left larger latitude to a minority than did the House regulations" (273).

While complete records of committee balloting are not available, a few published documents and our own examination of some ballots at the National Archives reveal that while parties clearly structured voting, organized blocs of minority-party senators could cast their ballots for an agreed-upon slate of candidates, overcoming the more broadly dispersed votes of an often-unorganized majority party. Balloting sometimes produced minority-party chairs, and more

160

often minority-party members in the number two position, who were in line to become chair if it became open during the session.

We begin our look at party and the committee system by simply noting the mechanism through which committees were chosen during this period. While not a sufficient condition, a necessary condition for party control over committee assignments was that parties have some way of coordinating the assignment of members to committees. What were the rules? What was the practice?

Table 9.1 summarizes the practice of appointing standing committees from the 14th Congress, second session, to the 37th Congress (1861–62).[1] The third column reports how committees were appointed each session. Committees were appointed in two ideal-typical ways, sometimes with mixtures of the two. *Balloting* involved the Senate voting on who would serve on the committee. A *resolution* appointed members to the committee, bypassing the necessity to ballot for each committee (with responsibility for composing the committee lists delegated to the president pro tem, the vice president, or political parties, depending on the Congress). Various hybrids, which will be described in more detail below, were used between the 21st and 31st Congresses (1829–50).

The early practice of balloting for committees positions became increasingly unacceptable. McConachie ([1898] 1973) states that "[w]ith the growth of the Senate, and the increase in the number and the importance of committees, as well as with the adoption of the plan of organizing them all at the same time, the old, slow device proved irksomely tedious and time wasting" (277). It often took two or three days to complete the voting.

The first significant change came in 1823 (18th Congress), when the presiding officer was granted power to appoint committees. Three years later (in the second session of the 19th Congress), the Senate returned to balloting, but with separate votes for the chairs and other members of the committee. In many years only the most desirable committees were subjected to a ballot, with others appointed (per resolution) by either the president pro tempore or the vice president.

In the second session of the 29th Congress (1846), a critical change provided parties with much greater control over appointments. At the critical juncture, the Senate had been delaying the balloting process for days, and frustration was building. Finally after the Senate had selected six committees, Senators Sevier and Speight proposed adopting the remaining 21 committees by unanimous consent from lists presented by the two parties (*Congressional Globe,* 29-1, 66). The same practice was followed in the next Congress as Democrats filled the first three spots on each committee and then gave the list to the Whigs, who filled the last two. The only exception was the Naval and Military Committee, which had been expanded and had five Democratic slots and two Whig positions (Robinson 1954, 130).

Over the next decade, various permutations of selection mechanisms were

Table 9.1. Means of Appointing Senate Standing Committee Members and Chairs, 14th to 37th Congresses (1816–61)

Cong.	sess.	Means of Appointment	Resolution presenter	Notes
14	2	Ballot		
15	1	Resolution	Tate	
15	2	Ballot		
16	1	Ballot		
16	2	Ballot		
17	1	Ballot		
17	2	Ballot		
18	1	Resolution/ballot		Resolution provided for presiding officer to appoint committees, following balloting for five chairs.
18	2	President		
19	1	V.P.		
19	2	Ballot		Separate ballots for chairs and rest of committee members.
20	1	Ballot		
20	2	Ballot		
21	1	Finance ballot; other by V.P.		
21	2	Finance ballot; other by president		
22	1	Finance ballot; other by president		
22	2	President		
23	1	Ballot		
23	2	Ballot		
24	1	Ballot		
24	2	Ballot		
25	1	Three ballots; others by V.P.		Vice president appointed members
25	2	V.P.		
25	3	Commerce ballot; others president		
26	1	Commerce ballot; others president		
26	2	Commerce ballot; others president		
27	1	Mixed		
27	2	President pro tempore		
27	3	President pro tempore		
28	1	President pro tempore		
28	2	President pro tempore		
29	1	Ballot/motion	Sevier	Six committees filled by ballot; others by unanimous consent from party lists.
29	2	Ballot (for six chairs)/resolution	Sevier	
30	1	Resolution	Sevier	
30	2	Resolution	King	
31	1	Ballot/motion		
31	2	President pro tempore		
32	1	Resolution	Bright	
32	2	Resolution	Bright	
33	1	Resolution	Bright	
33	2	Resolution	Bright	
34	1	Ballot/motion	Cass	
34	2	Resolution	Hunter	
34	3	Resolution	Pearce	
35	1	Resolution	Allen	
35	2	Resolution	Allen	
36	1	Resolution	Bright	
36	2	Vice president		
37	1	Resolution	Fessenden	
37	2	Resolution	Collamer	
37	3	Resolution	Anthony	

used, as in the 30th (1847–48) and 31st (1849–50) Congresses, when Free Soiler John P. Hale objected to the unanimous consent of the party lists (because he was not included). He forced the Senate to select members of the Judiciary, Territories, and District of Columbia Committees by ballot (those that were of special interest to the Free Soilers), and then the other committees were selected by resolution from the party lists (McConachie [1898] 1973, 284–85). However, as of the 29th Congress (1845–46), the parties had, for the most part, taken control of the assignment process.

With the formal and informal appointment practices sketched out, what were the partisan effects? To measure and describe partisan effects over time, we rely on three measures, as follows:

1. *Relative ranking of majority and minority members.* Throughout this period, both in common practice and later codified in the rules, the rank order of the committee rosters was important because it indicated who would serve as the committee's chair in the first-ranked member's absence. One measure of majority-party dominance, therefore, is the proportion of committees in which all majority members are ranked above all minority members.

2. *Majority-party chairs.* Holding the chair of a committee during this period provided a two-pronged advantage to the majority party. Most obviously, the chair called committee meetings and generally led the legislative effort(s) of the committees. In addition, once committees began to be granted clerks, it was the chair who benefited most immediately (Fox and Hammond 1977). Therefore, a second measure of majority-party dominance is the fraction of chairs held by the majority party.

3. *Committees with a majority from the majority party.* In addition to simply holding more seats throughout the committee system, holding partisan control over a committee is an important element in majority-party control over the committee system—some would argue it is the defining element. Thus, the last measure of majority-party dominance is the proportion of committees with a majority from the majority party.

In Figure 9.1 we have graphed out each of these measures for standing and select committees. Each measure tells a slightly different story of majority-party dominance. Figure 9.1a shows that majority- and minority-party members were tightly interwoven on the committee lists until the 1850s. Until then, the majority rarely occupied all the top committee positions. In the 35th Congress (1857–58), which coincided with the first formal appearance of the Republican party in Congress (Martis 1989), this all changed. From then on, the resolution appointing committees typically listed all the majority-party members first, then

FIGURE 9.1. Measures of Majority-Party Dominance on Select and Standing Committees, 1st to 79th Congresses (1816–1946)

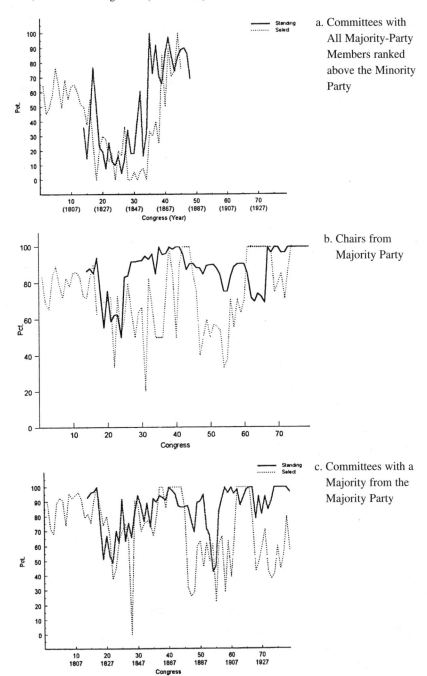

a. Committees with All Majority-Party Members ranked above the Minority Party

b. Chairs from Majority Party

c. Committees with a Majority from the Majority Party

the minority. An important amendment to this practice emerged over time, whereby the minority party was given control of certain minor committees.

Figure 9.1b documents the dominance of the majority party among the committee chairs. During the period from the 19th to the 24th Congresses (1825–36), when balloting was common, standing committee chairs frequently came from the minority party. That practice became rare in the 1830s but lasted through the 1870s. However, as the standing committee system began to blossom after Reconstruction, the frequency of minority-party chairs again increased. The practice of appointing minority-party members to the chairmanships of committees ended with the consolidation of the Senate committee system in the 67th Congress (1921–22).

Figure 9.1c shows that the number of standing committees with majority-party majorities steadily increased from the 19th Congress (1825–26) until the 1860s. From Reconstruction through the turn of the twentieth century, the majority party dominated most, though not all, committees. This parallels other time trends in Figure 9.1, particularly 9.1b, and also corresponds with anecdotal evidence provides by contemporary observers such as McConachie.

The remarks in the previous paragraphs concerned standing committees. If we look at the series for select committees in the first Congress and move toward the 14th (1815–16), we see that the standing committee series all pick up where the select committee series left off. This suggests that the transition from select to standing committees in the 14th Congress was gradual with respect to partisanship. However, moving forward, the select and standing committee series in all three panels diverge in one important respect: the minority party fared better, in general, among the select committees than among the standings. We could speculate why this is, although we have no definitive answers at this time. The standing committees were certainly more central to political success, and thus the majority party would have attended to maintaining their dominance among the standings, even at the expense of relinquishing control of the selects. At the same time, many of the select committees after the 14th Congress were created to investigate various matters within and outside the government. What this suggests is that the Senate actually facilitated, thought its select committee systems, a classic tool of the opposition. Why the majority would acquiesce to this strategy is a puzzle.

A different view of partisan practices associated with standing and select committees is provided in Figure 9.2. Here we have superimposed the time series showing the fraction of committees controlled by the majority party on top of another two sets of time series showing the fraction we would have *expected* under a null model in which committees were constituted randomly with respect to partisanship.[2] The contrasting patterns of select and standing committee partisan domination are striking. Before the 14th Congress, when the Senate did not have a standing committee system, the majority party dominated a greater fraction of committees than one would expect using the null model of random partisan assignment. Once the standing committee system was established in the 14th Congress, the partisan domination of select committee ended as a general phenomenon. From that time onward, the fraction of select committees dominated by the majority party averages out to be what one would expect if select committees were constructed randomly with respect to partisanship. For some stretches of time, such as Reconstruction and the 1920s, select committees *were* dominated by the majority party. However, there were many other times, such as the 1880s and 1890s, when *minority*-party domination of select committees was equally likely. Across the entire sweep of history, domination by the majority and minority parties in select committees balanced out.

The partisan composition of the standing committees tells a different story. Until the 29th Congress (1845–46), majority-party dominance of standing committees mirrored what we would expect if party was *not* an explicit factor in making committee appointments. This changed significantly after the 29th Congress, when the practice of appointing committees by partisan resolution became firmly established. From that point onward, there was only *one* Congress in which the fraction of committees controlled by the majority party was less than what one would predict from the null model, and in that Congress (the 53rd, 1893–94), the balance of power in the Senate was held by third-party senators.

To be clear, the Senate standing committee system before the 1946 Legislative Reorganization Act was never dominated by the majority party to the degree it is now—it was rare for the majority party to control *every* committee—or to the degree that the majority party would control a Westminster-style parliament. Still, the practice in the Senate for the past century and a half has been for the majority party to enjoy the spoils of *standing* committee assignments disproportionately more than the minority party.

What about the House? Without going into the same level of detail we have afforded the Senate, we can briefly characterize the developing partisan character of House committee compositions and contrast it with the Senate.[3] On the whole, the development of partisanship in Senate committees paralleled that of the House. During the "Era of Good Feeling" the majority party in the House also had a difficult time dominating committee memberships. However, as the second party system began to take hold in the decades preceding the Civil War, the majority party began to exert disproportionate influence on the makeup of the committees. During the Civil War the House, like the Senate, cemented the practice of having the majority party dominate the committee system—a practice that continues to this day.

One difference between the chambers occurred in the period between Reconstruction and the First World War. In the Senate we have seen that the combina-

166

FIGURE 9.2. Proportion of Senate Committees Controlled by the Majority Party, Compared to a Null Model Based on the Binomial Distribution.

a. Select Committees

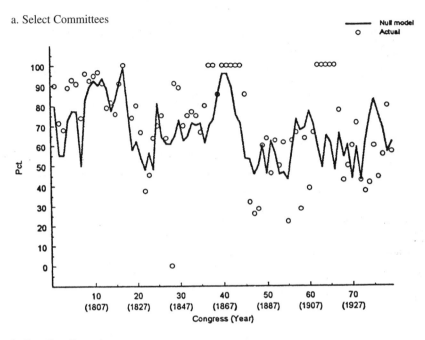

b. Standing Committees

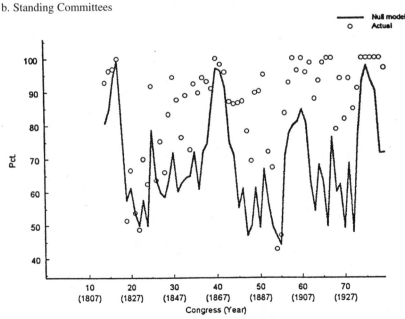

tion of a large number of committees and a small number of senators led the Senate to relax the majoritarian impulse somewhat and allow minority-party senators to chair, and sometimes hold a numerical majority on, less important committees. Such a pattern never emerged in the House. The lock on committees held by the majority party in the House was firm beginning with the Civil War and has never been relaxed.

In this section we have used some simple measures of party dominance of committee assignments to document the rise and persistence of disproportionate majority-party influence in the making of Senate committee assignments, especially in the standing committees. Thus, we must develop finer measures of important characteristics of the committee system before we can draw any firmer conclusions about the nature of partisan domination of the committee system. In the next section we develop a measure of an important characteristic of the committee system, its value hierarchy.

Committee Hierarchies in the Early Senate

A recurrent theme among modern students of Congress is the hierarchical nature of the committee systems in both chambers (Matthews 1960; Bullock and Sprague 1969; Bullock 1973, 1985; Munger 1988; Munger and Torrent 1993; Endersby and McCurdy 1996; Stewart and Groseclose 1998; Groseclose and Stewart 1999). The simplest explanation for why this hierarchy exists is functional—some committees handle business that is "more important" than other committees' business, that "must pass" in a timely fashion, or that "protects the constitutional prerogatives" of Congress. If so, then the chambers will jealously guard memberships on these committees, requiring new members to have served an apprenticeship on less important committees.

It is possible to complement this functional explanation with an explanation that derives from the individual policy, electoral, and career motivations of members of Congress. For instance, if Fenno (1973) is right and committee dynamics are fundamentally driven by the policy, election, and power goals of members, then a hierarchy of "desirable" and "undesirable" committees should emerge as well. If members tend to gravitate to electorally oriented committees early in their careers, then perforce these committees will be viewed on the whole as less desirable than policy or power committees, as we witness more members transferring off of them than transferring on. Among the policy-oriented committees, those with broader jurisdictions will dominate those with narrow jurisdictions; committees with fiscal responsibilities will dominate authorizing committees.

Finally, if a committee is responsible for producing public goods—either for the society or for the institution itself—then it will serve the collective interest of the chamber to endow that committee with features designed to heighten its desirability (Krehbiel 1991). Those features—like the ability to bring in the committee's bills under restrictive rules, larger staffs, a brighter limelight—will in turn inspire members of Congress to abandon committees that are not so well endowed in favor of service among the select few.

Regardless of one's theoretical tastes, it is easy to spin out explanations for why a legislature's committee system should contain important pyramidal features. It is harder to predict, a priori, which committees will lie at the bottom or top of the pyramid at any given historical moment. Just as difficult—if not more—is the task of the legislature itself as it figures out how to endow its committee system with a hierarchical structure that both is stable and serves the collective interests of all legislators.

The purpose of this section is to explore transfer patterns among Senate standing committees from the 1810s to the 1940s, with the goal of understanding when the hierarchical structure of the committee system emerged and what that structure looked like. We examine this subject for more than our intrinsic interest in the matter. After estimating the nature of the hierarchical structure of the Senate committee system at various points in time, we will use this information to examine the patterns of committee assignments within that hierarchy.

While some evidence of committee hierarchies has been found among the House committees in the late nineteenth century (Stewart 1992a, 1995), no research has been done on the Senate for any period before 1946. There are many reasons to believe we would not find much evidence of a standing committee hierarchy for the time period we are covering here. The relatively large number of committees per senator immediately makes a hierarchy less likely in simple mechanical terms. By the 66th Congress (1919–20) there were 75 committees representing 757 committee assignments on which the Senate's 96 members could serve—representing a ratio of nearly eight committee assignments per senator. The death of a single senator could set off a scramble for assignments involving virtually all senators. Biennial electoral turnover produced chaos. Remarking on the situation at the start of the 54th Congress (1895–96), McConachie ([1898] 1973) noted that "[f]ifteen Republicans awaited assignments in 1895. The committee list seemed somewhat shot-torn, even enfiladed, after the campaign; and the first duty was to recruit its ranks" (324).

Such conditions make a committee hierarchy difficult to maintain, but they were not the biggest obstacles facing the Senate. Probably the biggest obstacle to the development of a committee hierarchy was the relatively collegial style of senatorial life. Specific to the committee system, centralized mechanisms to allocate committee assignments only emerged over time, and at a slower pace than in the House. Before the Civil War, the sporadic use of balloting to make committee assignments surely undermined the permanence and stability of the system. We recognize now that the current hierarchy of congressional commit-tees is rooted in the property rights that representatives and senators hold in their committee assignments. With balloting, no mechanism could intervene to pro-tect the investment that a senator had made in committee service from one Con-gress to the next.

Once balloting gave way to party-initiated lists, it is difficult to know whether the resulting assignment process was more or less conducive to the development of a stable committee hierarchy. On the, one hand, the Senate abandoned ballot-ing at about the same time that the House entered a period of organizational chaos at the start of each Congress (see Stewart 1999). Allocating committee po-sitions in the antebellum Senate was contentious, to be sure, but it was much less conflict ridden than in the House, providing an opportunity for a hierarchy to emerge more quickly in the Senate. On the other hand, the identity of party leaders and the leadership structure was much more fluid in the Senate than in the House—a fluidity that continued in comparison through into the twentieth century. With a more fluid collection of individuals responsible for making com-mittee assignments in the Senate than in the House, it is quite possible that it was more difficult for the Senate than for the House to develop a hierarchical committee structure.

With these caveats properly noted, we used the "Grosewart method" to esti-mate the hierarchical structure of the Senate committee system for the pre-1946 period (Stewart and Groseclose 1998; Groseclose and Stewart 1999). Central to this method is an assumption that there are property rights in committee seats. In this context a "property right" in a committee seat means that once a seat is oc-cupied by a senator, he cannot be evicted from it against his will. In those rare cases where eviction is mandated (as when party control of the Senate changes), something akin to eminent-domain proceedings take place, where due compen-sation is provided for involuntary takings. It is in the antebellum era that this as-sumption is the most clearly problematic.

The Grosewart method differs from other attempts to estimate the pyramidal structure of the committee system through the use of transfer information. It uses an explicit choice theoretic model of the transfer process to motivate statis-tical estimation of the relative average value of serving on each committee. The coefficients produced by this technique can be interpreted substantively and have cardinal properties. In addition, because the method is embedded in an ex-plicit statistical model, we can compute standard errors of the coefficients and apply standard statistical tests.[4]

The details of the Grosewart method are provided in Stewart and Groseclose (1998) and Groseclose and Stewart (1999). For the purpose of this chapter, we need to underscore one important feature of that method: the coefficients that are estimated have cardinal properties. In other words, we can give natural meaning to a coefficient of zero, we know what a one-unit change in a coefficient means, and we can sum up coefficients to estimate the value of an individual senator's "committee portfolio." This last feature will be critical for the next section, where we use these coefficients to explain the relative value of committee *portfolios* held by individual senators, rather than doing the more traditional analysis of predicting appointment to individual committees, one committee at a time.

We performed this analysis after dividing the whole time period into three shorter eras: (1) the 14th through 48th Congresses (1815–84), (2) the 49th through 66th Congresses (1885–1920), and (3) the 67th through 79th Congresses (1921–46). This periodization breaks the analysis at the most important formal changes in the Senate committee system before the 1946 Legislative Reorganization Act (LRA). When the Senate established its standing committee system in the 14th Congress (1816), the rules provided for the appointment of committees *by session.* For most of its early history the Senate in fact took advantage of this provision, turning over an average of about 25 percent of its committee assignments between sessions before the Civil War and 15 percent afterwards (Canon and Stewart 1998, 23, fig. 5). In other words, committee turnover was about as frequent *within* Congresses as it currently is *between* Congresses. Because a committee seat acquired under a session-by-session appointment rule may be valued differently than a seat acquired under a Congress-by-Congress appointment rule, we choose to make the first major break in the analysis between the 48th and 49th Congresses (1883–86), when the Senate adopted its current rule of appointing committees for an entire Congress.

Another important formal change in the committee system occurred after the 49th Congress (1885–86). At the start of the 67th Congress (1921), the Senate abolished forty-one of its seventy-five committees, weeding out ones that had become inactive and that had existed primarily for the purpose of granting senior senators a clerk. This consolidation also may have resulted in a different appointment dynamic that shifted the relative value of committee service. Thus, we also break our analysis between the 66th and 67th Congresses. Finally, we end our analysis with the 79th Congress (1945–46), which was the last Congress before the 1946 LRA took effect.

We report the results of this estimation in Table 9.2. The earliest period is one in which the committee hierarchy—to the degree it existed—was still fairly flat and underdeveloped. The most highly ranked committees still have relatively small coefficients, suggesting a lack of consensus among senators about what constituted attractive and unattractive committees. (Alternately, the lack of very large coefficients among the top-ranked committees may be a reflection of the inability of senators to protect their positions on attractive committees in a period when assignments were often made by ballot.) Moving across the table, we see the hierarchical structure of the committee system elongate and consolidate

TABLE 9-2. Estimates of Senate Committee Service Value, 14th to 79th Congresses Using the Grosewart Method

	14th–49th Cong.			49th–66th Cong.			67th–79th Cong.	
Rank	Committee	Coeff.	Rank	Committee	Coeff.	Rank	Committee	Coeff.
1	Railroads	0.78	1	Expenditures of Public Money	4.36	1	Foreign Relations	4.51*
2	Appropriations	0.64	2	Appropriations	4.23*	2	Finance	3.60*
3	Privileges and Elections	0.54	3	Foreign Relations	3.74*	3	Appropriations	3.56*
4	Rules	0.53	4	Expends., Commerce and Labor	2.75	4	Irrigation and Reclamation	2.67*
5	Education and Labor	0.45	5	Finance	2.72*	5	Rules	2.07*
6	Military Affairs	0.44*	6	Judiciary	2.71*	6	Public Lands and Surveys	1.89*
7	Civil Service and Retrenchment	0.42	7	Banking and Currency	2.50*	7	Civil Service	1.40*
8	Commerce	0.38*	8	Commerce	2.13*	8	Judiciary	1.27*
9	Foreign Relations	0.38*	9	Naval Affairs	2.09*	9	Audit and Control	1.25*
10	Revolutionary Claims	0.27	10	Expends., Navy	1.98	10	Banking and Currency	1.04*
11	Revision of the Laws	0.27	11	Expends., Justice	1.72*	11	Enrolled Bills	1.03
12	Patents	0.25	12	Interstate Commerce	1.69*	12	Territories and Insular Possessions	0.99*
13	Library	0.25	13	Military Affairs	1.67*	13	Expends., Executive Departments	0.71
14	Naval Affairs	0.19	14	Rules	1.61*	14	Naval Affairs	0.58
15	Judiciary	0.18	15	Expends., War	1.54*	15	Agriculture and Forestry	0.52
16	District of Columbia	0.14	16	Five Civilized Tribes of Indians	1.37	16	Interstate Commerce	0.52
17	Finance	0.13	17	Expends., Interior	1.35	17	Commerce	0.46
18	Public Buildings	0.12	18	Standards, Weights, and Measures	1.35	18	Immigration	0.25
19	Indian Affairs	0.11	19	Cuban Relations	1.28*	19	Library	0.16
20	Retrenchment	0.10	20	Expends., Agriculture	1.26	20	Education and Labor	-0.04
21	Public Lands	0.09	21	Geological Survey	1.23	21	Patents	-0.06
22	Audit and Control	0.04	22	Pacific Islands and Porto Rico	1.20*	22	Privileges and Elections	-0.09
23	Post Office and Post Roads	0.01	23	Phillipines	1.02*	23	District of Columbia	-0.10
24	Enrolled Bills	-0.03	24	Transp. & Sale of Meat Products	1.01	24	Public Buildings and Grounds	-0.28
25	Claims	-0.03	25	Public Lands and Surveys	0.94*	25	Pensions	-0.31
26	Territories	-0.03	26	Disposition of Useless Papers	0.93	26	Indian Affairs	-0.44
27	Pensions	-0.13	27	Corporations Organized in D.C.	0.89	27	Claims	-0.46
28	Roads and Canals	-0.14	28	Post Office and Post Roads	0.86*	28	Military Affairs	-0.53
29	Agriculture	-0.14	29	Interoceanic Canal	0.85*	29	Printing	-0.62
30	Private Land Claims	-0.19	30	Privileges and Elections	0.85	30	Mines and Mining	-0.85
31	Improvement of the Miss. River	-0.21	31	Expends., Commerce	0.81	31	Manufactures	-0.93*
32	Mines and Mining	-0.22	32	Private Land Claims	0.75	32	Post Office and Post Roads	-0.99*
33	Printing	-0.23	33	Irrigation and Reclamation	0.70	33	Interoceanic Canal	-1.12*
34	Militia	-0.33	34	Organization ... of the Exec. Depts.	0.63			
35	Manufactures	-0.33	35	Library	0.63			

#	Committee	
36	Engrossed Bills	-0.40*
37	Pacific Railroads	-0.63
38	Transp. Routes to the Seaboard	-1.02
39	Commerce and Manufactures	-1.10*
40	Public Lands and Surveys	-2.07*
41	Investigation and Retrenchment	-3.08*

#	Committee	
36	Public Buildings and Grounds	0.62
37	Coast and Insular Survey	0.60
38	Indian Depredations	0.57
39	Canadian Relations	0.53
40	Forest Reservations	0.49
41	Audit and Control	0.43
42	Agriculture and Forestry	0.41
43	Expends., Post Office Department	0.40
44	Expends., State	0.40
45	Mississippi River Improvements	0.29
46	Fisheries	0.26
47	District of Columbia	0.21
48	Printing	0.19
49	Conservation of National Resources	0.15
50	Census	0.11
51	Immigration	0.10
52	Pensions	0.09
53	Education and Labor	0.06
54	Expends., Treasury	0.05
55	Pacific Railroads	-0.01
56	Revolutionary Claims	-0.04
57	Engrossed Bills	-0.06
58	Indian Affairs	-0.11
59	Examine the Several Branches of the Civil Service	-0.17
60	Patents	-0.19
61	Territories	-0.22
62	Epidemic Diseases	-0.24
63	Transportation Routes to the Seaboard	-0.25
64	Civil Service	-0.25
65	Public Health and National Quarantine	-0.26
66	Manufactures	-0.27
67	Mines and Mining	-0.42
68	Indian Lands	-0.72
69	Coast Defenses	-0.76
70	Railroads	-1.10*
71	Enrolled Bills	-1.28
72	Claims	-1.54*

$n = 2,560$ $n = 1,122$ $n = 607$

*$p < .10$.

TABLE 9.3. Estimates of Senate Committee Service Value, 14th to 48th Congresses, Using the Grosewart Method

	14th–29th Cong.			30th–36th Cong.	
Rank	Committee	Coeff.	Rank	Committee	Coeff.
1	Patents	0.49	1	Commerce	0.73
2	Military Affairs	0.36	2	Naval Affairs	0.59
3	Commerce	0.21	3	Judiciary	0.51
4	Roads and Canals	0.18	4	Library	0.46
5	Audit and Control	0.17	5	District of Columbia	0.41
6	Foreign Relations	0.16	6	Foreign Relations	0.40
7	Revolutionary Claims	0.15	7	Military Affairs	0.36
8	Retrenchment	0.14	8	Patents	0.32
9	Pensions	0.09	9	Post Office and Post Roads	0.25
10	Claims	0.05	10	Public Lands	0.20
11	Indian Affairs	−0.04	11	Retrenchment	0.18
12	District of Columbia	−0.05	12	Indian Affairs	0.17
13	Finance	−0.05	13	Finance	0.15
14	Agriculture	−0.10	14	Pensions	0.11
15	Private Land Claims	−0.12	15	Public Buildings	0.04
16	Manufactures	−0.19	16	Audit and Control	−0.08
17	Naval Affairs	−0.21	17	Enrolled Bills	−0.09
18	Public Lands	−0.22	18	Revolutionary Claims	−0.10
19	Public Buildings and Grounds	−0.24	19	Private Land Claims	−0.12
20	Post Office and Post Roads	−0.24	20	Territories	−0.19
21	Judiciary	−0.24	21	Printing	−0.36
22	Militia	−0.27	22	Claims	−0.38
23	Printing	−0.34	23	Agriculture	−0.69
24	Library	−0.35	24	Militia	−0.75
25	Engrossed Bills	−0.62*	25	Roads and Canals	−0.82
26	Territories	−0.84	26	Engrossed Bills	−0.87
27	Commerce and Manufactures	−1.07*	27	Manufactures	−0.95
28	Enrolled Bills	−3.24			
	$n = 905$			$n = 561$	

*$p < .10$.

TABLE 9.3. Estimates of Senate Committee Service Value, 14th to 48th Congresses, Using the Grosewart Method (*Continued*)

	30th–48th Cong.			37th–48th Cong.	
Rank	Committee	Coeff.	Rank	Committee	Coeff.
1	Judiciary	0.76*	1	Judiciary	0.95*
2	Railroads	0.75	2	Railroads	0.71
3	Naval Affairs	0.61*	3	Revolutionary Claims	0.67*
4	Appropriations	0.60	4	Military Affairs	0.63*
5	Foreign Relations	0.55*	5	Foreign Relations	0.62*
6	Privileges and Elections	0.55	6	Appropriations	0.60
7	Rules	0.52	7	Naval Affairs	0.57
8	Commerce	0.51*	8	Privileges and Elections	0.56
9	Military Affairs	0.50*	9	Rules	0.52
10	Education and Labor	0.43	10	Finance	0.50
11	Civil Service and Retrenchment	0.42	11	Civil Service and Retrenchment	0.45
12	Library	0.41	12	Education and Labor	0.43
13	Public Lands	0.34	13	Library	0.43
14	Finance	0.33	14	Public Lands	0.41
15	Revolutionary Claims	0.33	15	Public Buildings	0.40
16	Revision of the Laws	0.30	16	Commerce	0.39
17	District of Columbia	0.26	17	Revision of the Laws	0.29
18	Public Buildings	0.25	18	Enrolled Bills	0.26
19	Post Office and Post Roads	0.23	19	Post Office and Post Roads	0.21
20	Patents	0.18	20	Indian Affairs	0.17
21	Indian Affairs	0.16	21	District of Columbia	0.13
22	Retrenchment	0.16	22	Territories	0.10
23	Enrolled Bills	0.10	23	Patents	0.10
24	Territories	0.00	24	Engrossed Bills	0.05
25	Audit and Control	−0.04	25	Claims	0.04
26	Claims	−0.08	26	Audit and Control	0.00
27	Improvement of the Miss. Riv.	−0.17	27	Agriculture	−0.06
28	Agriculture	−0.20	28	Printing	−0.11
29	Printing	−0.24	29	Improvement of the Miss. River	−0.17
30	Mines and Mining	−0.25	30	Manufactures	−0.22
31	Private Land Claims	−0.26	31	Mines and Mining	−0.27
32	Pensions	−0.27	32	Private Land Claims	−0.35
33	Engrossed Bills	−0.29	3	Pensions	−0.52*
34	Manufactures	−0.44	34	Pacific Railroads	−0.71
35	Pacific Railroads	−0.69	35	Transp. Routes to the Seaboard	−1.08*
36	Militia	−0.72	36	Public Lands and Surveys	−2.05*
37	Roads and Canals	−0.82*	37	Investigation and Retrenchment	−2.99*
38	Transp. Routes to the Seaboard	−1.05*			
39	Public Lands and Surveys	−2.05*			
40	Investigation and Retrenchment	−3.04*			
	n = 1,656			*n* = 1,096	

after Reconstruction and into the twentieth century. The signs of this consolidation are the rising absolute value of the coefficients at both ends of the hierarchy.[5]

Looking a little more closely at the coefficients, we also see that the collection of attractive committees eventually expanded out beyond the core constitutional responsibilities of the Senate. In the earliest period, the clearly attractive committees were those that handled foreign relations, the army, and commercial development.[6] In the middle period, quite a few committees were added to the collection of clearly attractive committees. They included obvious "power" committees like Appropriations, Foreign Relations, and Finance but also included a few of the auditing committees (Expenditures of Public Money, Expenditures in the Justice Department, and Expenditures in the War Department) and a variety of committees that were involved in guiding America's imperialistic exploits of this period—in Cuba, Panama, the Philippines, and Puerto Rico. In the final period the collection of top committees likewise included obvious "power" committees along with some that were associated with western development (such as Irrigation and Reclamation and Public Lands).

The analysis in Table 9.2 suggests a fairly well-developed committee hierarchy after 1885 and a much weaker one before. The weakness of the hierarchy before 1885 may be either substantive or methodological. Substantively, the estimated weakness may simply be picking up the true state of affairs: the early committee system may not have been especially hierarchical, so that any attempt to wrestle it into an hierarchical form will be met with only limited success. Methodologically, we may be running afoul the problem of pooling together periods in Senate history that should be analyzed separately due to changes in political (or other) circumstances associated with committee appointments. For instance, the demise of balloting after the 29th Congress (1845–46) may have allowed a previously fluid hierarchy to solidify. If so, we might observe an especially weak hierarchy before the 29th Congress but a firmer one afterwards. Or the Civil War party realignment may have had organizational ramifications for the Senate in the same way that the House was affected (see Stewart 1999). If so, the prewar hierarchy might be quite different from the postwar hierarchy.

To address these possible problems, we further subdivided the pre-1885 time period. First, to test whether the hierarchy changed as a consequence of the demise of balloting, we broke the pre-1885 period at the 29th Congress (1845–46). Second, to examine whether the Civil War might have affected the hierarchy, we further broke the analysis at the 37th Congress (1861–62). These results are reported in table 9.3.

Breaking up the pre-1885 period into smaller subperiods does not yield dramatically different results than when we examine the period as a whole. But the results are subtly different and help to identify more precisely how the Senate

TABLE 9.4. Interperiod Rank-Order Correlation of Senate Committee Values

First Period	Second Period	Rank-Order Correlation in Committee Values
14th–29th Congresses (1815–1846)	30th–36th Congresses (1847–1860)	.23
30th–36th Congresses (1847–1860)	37th–48th Congresses (1861–1884)	.62
37th–48th Congresses (1861–1884)	49th–66th Congresses (1885–1920)	.41
49th–66th Congresses (1885–1920)	67th–79th Congresses (1921–1946)	.45

committee hierarchy eventually emerged. Some general patterns we saw in Table 9.2 persist into Table 9.3. In general, the hierarchy appears to be more elongated and consolidated in the later periods than in the earlier ones. In the earliest period, when committee balloting was common, the hierarchy was especially compressed. The only committees with value coefficients even approaching statistical significance were two burden committees—Engrossed Bills and Commerce and Manufactures. In the postballoting period (30th to 48th Congresses, 1847–84), the hierarchy was a bit more elongated and the actual ranking of committees mirrored fairly well the ranking for the next time period, the 49th to 66th Congresses (1885–1920). (The rank-order correlation between the ranking of committees in the 30th to 48th Congresses period and the 49th to 66th Congresses period is .52.)

Regardless of how we slice it, the further back in time we go, the weaker the hierarchy we observe. Once balloting ceased, a hierarchical structure slowly emerged. The hierarchy was elongated and consolidated. In addition, the hierarchies were relatively persistent from period to period, with room for evolution. This last point is illustrated in Table 9.4, where we have reported the interperiod rank-order correlation of the estimated value of committees. Except for the transition from the era of committee balloting to the period immediately before the Civil War, the interperiod correlation of the committee orderings is high.

At this point in our discussion, we can revisit briefly a point noted in the previous section—the tendency of the majority party to let the minority control a small set of committees each Congress. Anecdotal evidence suggests that these were "minor" committees. With the estimated committee values that we derived using the Grosewart method, we could test more systematically whether, within the context of each era, the minority was given control of unimportant committees.

TABLE 9.5. Probability That a Committee Will Be Dominated by the Majority Party as a Function of Grosewart Values (Probit Analysis)

	Congress						
	14–48th	14–29th	30–48th	30–36th	37–48th	49–66th	67–79th
Committee value	0.65	0.31	0.54	0.61	0.30	0.15	0.19
	(0.16)	(0.09)	(0.18)	(0.38)	(0.15)	(0.05)	(0.14)
Constant	0.77	0.55	1.09	1.09	1.16	0.99	1.50
	(0.11)	(0.18)	(0.10)	(0.13)	(0.13)	(0.19)	(0.18)
N	2,429	692	1,704	524	1,180	942	430
χ^2	15.87	10.68	9.42	2.60	4.00	8.09	1.76
Prob.(χ^2)	0.0001	.001	.002	.11	0.05	.004	.18
% majority dominated	83	71	88	85	89	88	94

We did this in a straightforward fashion. For each major period in which we estimated Grosewart values for the committees, we went back and conducted a statistical analysis, in which we predicted whether each committee would be controlled by the majority party, as a function of its committee value. We expected that Grosewart values would be a strong predictor of whether the majority party held a majority of the seats on that committee.

The analysis is reported in table 9.5. In every period but the last (67th to 79th Congresses, 1921–46), our expectations are clearly borne out. The results are the weakest in the last period, but keep in mind that this is the period when the majority enjoyed the highest rate of committee control, so there is less to explain to begin with.

The coefficients reported in Tables 9.2 and 9.3 can be used to calculate overall committee portfolio values for each senator in each Congress by simply adding up the committee value coefficients associated with each senator's committee assignments.[7] Space limitations preclude our analyzing these portfolio values in any detail or sophistication. The most important findings from such an analysis can be summarized here.[8]

Not surprisingly, veteran senators received better portfolios of committee assignments than freshmen, although the seniority gradient in overall committee assignments really only developed after party lists became the norm in the 30th Congress (1847–48). In addition to Senate service, previous House service was rewarded—senators who had previously served in the House received significantly better committee assignments than those who came directly to the Senate.

Finally, ideological moderates (compared to the whole chamber) tended to fare better than extremists, as did lawyers and college graduates.

Two patterns deserve comment because they bear on the Senate's constitutional position. First, throughout the period covered by this chapter, large-state senators received a better set of assignments than small-state senators. This is contrary to expectations that because all states were treated equally in the Senate, all senators would be as well. Second, before the Civil War, slave-state senators received better assignments than free-state senators, perhaps providing an even further check against the growing political power of the North in the population-driven House. After the Civil War, the southern advantage went away, and indeed southern senators actually became *disadvantaged* in their committee assignments, compared to northerners.

These two features of Senate committee assignments are exactly the opposite of the patterns we have found for House committee assignments, particularly before the Civil War (Stewart et al. 1995). In particular, House members from large-population states got worse assignments and slave-state members got better assignments. Why this might be is a puzzle that has yet to be addressed, but it does point out that the two chambers could maintain different committee practices along one set of criteria (such as state size and geographic location) even while maintaining a parallel track along another set of criteria (particularly partisanship). Recent work by Frances Lee and Bruce Oppenheimer (1999, chap. 5) suggests a possible answer to the puzzle. They find that small-state senators in the modern era (1946–97) seek assignments on constituency committees while large-state senators are disproportionately represented on policy and mixed committees. Given that many constituency committees appear toward the bottom of the committee hierarchy, the "better" committees, as defined by patterns of transfers, may not have been viewed as more highly desired committees by small-state senators.

Thus even though it would seem that several factors should have inhibited the development of a hierarchically structured standing committee system in the Senate, a budding hierarchy did develop before the Civil War, becoming stronger and stable over time.

Conclusion

In a volume on "Senate exceptionalism," it is tempting to suppose that everywhere we look, we will find the Senate evolving at a pace different than the House and senators behaving differently than representatives. While this often is the case, particularly in the contemporary Congress, it was not necessarily the case in the early days of the Republic. Especially when it came to the development of the committee system in the two chambers of Congress, the Senate was more like the House than it was different.

This fact is perhaps not as surprising as it might seem at first. That we even care about the Senate's role in American policy making stems from the fact that the Senate is a powerful independent policy actor. Where does that power come from? It might come from the explicitly bicameral nature of Congress, in which the Senate can veto House-passed legislation if it wants. However, the veto is a negative power, and the Senate that commands policy attention these days fills a positive policy role as often as it is a veto point.

Therefore, it seems reasonable to conclude that if the Senate had not developed its committee system in parallel with the House, we would probably be less interested in its policy role than we are. We are therefore left with an irony—the exceptional character of the Senate rests, at least in part, on the nonexceptional development of its committee system early in American history.

Notes

This chapter is a revision of a paper delivered at the Norman Thomas Conference on Senate Exceptionalism, Vanderbilt University, October 21–23, 1999. This research was made possible, in part, by NSF grant SES 93-10057 and the Relational Database on Historical Congressional Statistics. Special thanks also go to Garrison Nelson, who helped compile the Senate standing committee data set. Parts of this chapter are drawn from Canon and Sweet (1998) and Canon and Stewart (1998).

1. The appointment of select committees followed the same general rule as the appointment of standing committees. Before the 14th Congress, the Senate rules called for the appointment of Senate select committees by ballot. The condition of the *Annals of Congress* and Senate *Journal* make it impossible to know what fraction of select committees were actually appointed by ballot and what fraction were in fact appointed by the presiding officer or suggested by a list provided by the motion maker.

2. We developed the null model borrowing from Stewart et al. 1995. Assume that in the appointment of a single committee, the Senate picks N members from the Senate, the fraction of 2 of which belongs to the majority party. If members are drawn independently, then the number of members who come from the Speaker's party across all committees follows the binomial distribution

$$f(x) = \binom{n}{x} \theta^x (1-\theta)^{n-x}, \ x = 0, 1, 2, \ldots n$$

where

$$\binom{n}{x} = \frac{n!}{x!(n-x)!}$$

For instance, if the committee had three members ($N = 3$) and the majority party consisted of 60 percent of the Senate ($2 = .60$), then the expected fraction of the time that the majority would pick no one from its party would be 6.4 percent; it would pick one member 28.8 percent of the time, two members 43.2 percent of the time, and all three members of the majority party 21.6 percent of the time. Thus, three-member committees should have a majority from the chamber majority party 65.8 percent (43.2 percent plus 21.6 percent) of the time.

To simulate random selection, we considered each committee appointed in each Congress. Taking the size of the chamber majority and the number of members on that committee as fixed, we calculated the fraction of time that such a select committee should have a majority chosen from the chamber majority. We then averaged all these values across all committees in a Congress to produce the null model predictions graphed in the figure.

3. The comments in this paragraph are based on our performing a similar sort of analysis for House committees as we have performed here for the Senate committees.

4. We have omitted standard errors from the tables that report the Senate committee rankings in order to save space. Standard errors appeared in the original draft of this chapter and are available from us upon request.

5. Another sign of the consolidation of the committee hierarchy is the decline in the size of the standard errors, which are not reported here.

6. Here, we are defining "clearly attractive" committees to be those with positive coefficients that are statistically significant at the 10 percent level.

7. The logic and statistical justification behind this are presented in Stewart and Groseclose (1998).

8. The multivariate analysis on which these remarks are based was contained in the original draft of this chapter and is available from us upon request.

· 10 ·

Analyzing Institutional Change: Bill Introduction in the Nineteenth-Century Senate

Joseph Cooper and Elizabeth Rybicki

In the nineteenth century, procedure with respect to the introduction of bills underwent a profound transformation in both the House and the Senate. Over many decades bill introduction evolved from a process in which bills were introduced by committees into one in which bills were introduced by individual members. This chapter examines the evolution of bill introduction in the Senate during the nineteenth century and asks two related sets of questions. First, how did procedures for bill introduction evolve in the nineteenth-century Senate, and what similarities and differences exist between Senate experience and House experience? Second, why did procedures change in the Senate, and what explains the similarities and differences in the experience of the two bodies?

Though the topic of bill introduction may appear mundane, the procedures for introducing bills are an integral part of the overall system by which each house processes its workload. They thus affect and are affected by other components of the system—the role of committees in receiving and preparing business for floor consideration, the manner in which the access of business to the floor is regulated, and the processes of debate and amendment on the floor. As a consequence, an analysis of the evolution of methods of bill introduction in the Senate, as compared to the House, provides a lever for identifying and analyzing enduring aspects of similarity and difference in the character of these two bodies. Equally important, it provides a lever for assessing frameworks commonly applied to explain legislative change. Thus, after tracing the evolution of bill introduction in the Senate and comparing it to the House, we shall use this experience to assess the power of three approaches to explaining legislative change that are prominent in the scholarly literature—those based on party, self-interest, and context. This analysis, in turn, will allow us to draw some conclusions regarding the distinctive character of the Senate as a political institution and the need to blend approaches in analyzing change.

However, before we begin a caveat must be stated. Though the overall direction and final result of evolution in the Senate and House are the same for public and private bills, the process by which private bills evolve from committee bills to member bills varies substantially from that of public bills in both bodies. Moreover, in the case of private bills, as in the case of public bills, Senate evolution differs in some significant ways from evolution in the House. We shall therefore focus our analysis on public bills both because we cannot give both types of bills the extended treatment they require and because arguably public bills are the more important ones. As necessary and appropriate, however, we shall also provide some basic information on the evolution of private bills both in our tables and in notes to the text.

The Evolution of Bill Introduction in the Senate

We divide our analysis of the evolution of bill introduction into three periods. The first is the period from 1789 to 1825. This is the period of the rise and decline of the first party system and the emergence of standing committee systems in both bodies (Cooper 1970; Canon and Stewart 2001). The second is the period from 1825 to 1861. This is the period of the rise and decline of the second party system and the period in which the Senate replaces the House as the premier legislative institution (Swift 1997). The third, and last, is the period from 1861 to 1897. This is the period of the third party system, and it is the period in which many of the key institutional features of the modern Congress from the Rules Committee to unanimous consent agreements became important components of the decision-making process (Binder 1997; Gamm and Smith 2000).

The Early Decades: 1789–1825

The original procedures for introducing bills in the House and Senate were quite different than they are today. They were based on a very pristine view of the needs of representative government and reflected very different conceptions of what constituted proper or legitimate methods of lawmaking. The prevailing notion during the first decade of government under the Constitution was that the principles of policy should be settled by the legislature as a whole before business was sent to smaller committees. The rationale for this belief, rediscovered by modern rational-choice theory, was that prior arrangement by smaller committees would prejudice results and in so doing impair both the capacity for deliberation and the ability of majorities to identify and fulfill their desires. Concomitantly, the belief that the whole, not the parts, should control policy was also seen to require that bills be introduced only with the permission of the whole and preferably after the principles of action were clear and acceptable to the whole. In the Senate, and even more in the House, bills were seen as "inchoate law" and therefore not properly introducible solely on the authority of an individual member or committee (Harlow 1917; Cooper 1970).

The impact of these beliefs is clearly evident in the rules and practices of the first several Congresses. Business was initiated through the introduction of subjects in the form of resolutions, petitions, and messages, and in important areas of policy, subjects so introduced were first discussed on the floor and/or Committee of the Whole before being referred to a select committee in the Senate or to a select or one of a small number of standing committees in the House. In addition, the rules of both houses stipulated that bills could be introduced only with the permission of the whole and that motions to do so must lay over for a day. The House rule, moreover, was more stringent with respect to introduction by members than the Senate rule. It required that motions made by members for leave to bring in a bill, even when approved, had to be sent to a smaller committee to frame and bring in the actual bill (Swanstrom 1985; Cooper and Young 1989).

The control of the whole over the initial consideration of important business, however, began to erode even before 1801 and could not long be sustained. This was particularly true in the Senate, whose small size made it less inclined to differentiate the committee of the whole from the floor as the proper place to deliberate on the principles of action and less hesitant to rely directly on smaller committees. The rate at which proceedings on the floor or in committee of the whole with respect to important subjects were transformed into mere conduits for reference to smaller committees thus differed in the two bodies as did the development of standing committees. Nonetheless, by Madison's first term as president (1809–13), what had long been true in minor areas of business had become the prevailing practice in major areas as well. In both houses important subjects were generally referred first to smaller committees with no or only pro forma consideration by the membership as a whole. Equally important, the triumph of smaller committees as agents of first reference was closely accompanied by the triumph of standing committees over select committees as the form of smaller committee relied upon by each house for the initial consideration of business. In both houses by 1817 committees that were standing either by rule or continuing appointment dominated select committees in the receipt of business from the chamber. Last, but not least, in both houses by 1817, such committees by rule or resolution were given the power to bring in bills at their own discretion on all subjects referred to them. As in the case of reference, reluctance to grant bill power to smaller committees was from the beginning largely restricted to major business and less strong in the Senate than the House. Nonetheless, it eroded in both as the initial consideration of important subjects by the chamber as a whole became a formality and as standing committees became the preferred locus or site for considering them. An unavoidable and associated consequence was to undermine the original rationale for withholding bill power from smaller committees. What the triumph of a standing committee system signaled was a profound change in conceptions of the proper nature of the law-making process. Traditional norms that prized members as generalists and regarded committees with suspicion were replaced by new norms that prized members as specialists and encouraged deference to standing committees. Providing them with discretionary bill power thus increasingly appeared to be the most reasonable and efficient way to legislate, and in the House became common practice several years before being formally added to the rules (Cooper 1970; Cooper and Young 1989; Canon and Stewart 2001).

Given the rules and practices of both houses in these decades, committee bills were the dominant vehicle for framing and advancing public legislation both before and after the rise of the standing committee system.[1] In the House virtually all public bills were committee bills. As noted, the rules made member bills exceedingly cumbersome, and there were very few instances of attempts by members to challenge or transform existing procedure. However, as first reference to smaller committees expanded, referrals to them increasingly began to take the form of resolutions instructing them to inquire into the expediency of acting in a certain manner, not resolutions instructing them on the content of what they were to report, as was typically the case when the desirability of action was first decided in committee of the whole. Moreover, such resolutions became more detailed as the standing committees emerged, enlarged their control over the first reference of subjects, and gained discretionary bill power (Cooper 1970; Cooper and Young 1989). In the Senate committee bills also were the primary means relied upon for introducing public legislation and, as in the House, resolutions referring important subjects to smaller committees for inquiry became more prevalent with the passage of time and more detailed once a standing committee system had emerged and gained discretion to introduce bills on all subjects referred to them. However, in contrast to the House, Senate rules made member bills a viable option. Member public bills were thus present from the start and constituted a sizeable proportion of the public bills introduced in the Senate both before and after the Senate in 1816 amended its rules so as to establish twelve standing committees and give all standing committees bill power (see Table 10.1). Nonetheless, the restrictions in the rule governing bill introduction were operative. On occasion, especially in the first few decades, members were challenged on the floor when they sought permission to introduce a bill or to waive the requirement for a day's notice (Swanstrom 1985).

TABLE 10.1. Senate Bill Introduction 1789–1823

Congress	Total Bills	% of Bills That Are Public	Member Bills as % of Total Bills	Member Bills as % of Public Bills
1st (1789–91)	23	100	17	17
2nd (1791–93)	27	85	26	30
3rd (1793–95)	44	79	34	37
4th (1795–97)	31	87	35	30
12th (1811–13)	106	79	26	30
17th (1821–23)	160	55	28	41

The Senate, however, did lag the House in elaborating and refining its rules to smooth the conduct of business more generally. In 1811 the House began the process of turning the previous-question rule into an effective method of cloture, and in 1822 it adopted a general germaneness rule in place of the limited germaneness provision in its original rules. It also began in 1812 to define an order of business in its rules that it further extended in 1822, while also adopting a two-thirds suspension rule to protect the ability of its rules to regulate access to the floor (Tieffer 1989; Binder 1997). In contrast, the Senate eliminated its previous-question rule, did not adopt a general germaneness rule, and declined to write the rudimentary order business that it followed in practice into its rules. However, it did change its rules to give precedence to the unfinished business (McConachie [1898] 1973).

The Growth of Member Bills, 1825–61

In this period, member public bills become predominant in both Houses.[2] In the Senate the percentage of such bills at first increased steadily from the levels attained in the 1820s, then fell back briefly in the mid-1840s, and then resumed its upward climb. As a result, by the mid-1850s, 70 percent of public legislation was introduced by members, not committees. In the House, interest in member bills intensified in the late 1820s and 1830s and led to two important rules changes. In 1837 the House reformulated its original bill introduction rule so as to give members the power to introduce bills on their own initiative once the permission of the House had been secured and to protect the authority of standing committees to receive such bills. In 1838 a second rules change provided additional time in the order of business for members to introduce bills (Cooper and Young 1989). Once these changes occurred, the percentage of member public bills sharply increased. The end result was that by 1861 the level of reliance on member public bills matched that of the Senate—71 percent, despite a far slower start (see Table 10.2).

TABLE 10.2. The Increase in Member Bills, 1831–61

	House			Senate		
Congress	Total Bills	% of Bills Thaty Are Public	Member Bills as % of Public Bills	Total Bills	% of Bills That Are Public	Member Bills as % of Public Bills
22nd (1831–33)	762	62	0	342	47	41
25th (1837–39)	—	—	—	713	45	53
27th (1841–43)	829	41	13	468	47	67
29th (1845–47)	—	—	—	455	45	46
31st (1849–51)	494	46	42	484	64	62
32nd (1851–53)	368	65	52	647	48	62
34th (1855–57)	—	—	—	646	55	70
36th (1859–61)	1,020	48	71	—	—	—

However, such convergence was limited to bill introduction. The House continued to outpace the Senate in elaborating its rules regarding the conduct of business. During this period the previous-question rule was perfected as an instrument of cloture on the floor, an hour rule was adopted limiting speeches on the floor and in the Committee of the Whole, and a five-minute rule was passed limiting debate on amendments in the Committee of the Whole. In addition, the House continued to elaborate its order of business, regulating the times at which different classes of business could be reached and limiting opportunities for substantive debate on procedural matters, including the introduction and reference of bills (Cooper and Young 1989; Binder 1997). The Senate did far less in all these regards. Though the filibuster became a problem for the first time in its history, attempts to institute a previous-question rule and an hour rule were withdrawn before a vote in the early 1840s, and renewed support for a previous-question rule was stymied in the early 1850s. Similarly, attempts to limit debate on motions to proceed to consider and to allow amendments to be tabled without affecting the underlying bill were voted down in the early 1850s (Binder 1997; Binder and Smith 1997). Nor did the Senate rethink its position on germaneness, despite the problems that lack of control over debate and amendment were beginning to cause. The Senate did finally incorporate an order of business in its rules, but a less detailed one than prevailed in the House. It also sought to prioritize access to the floor when multiple special orders authorizing bills to be considered on a particular day created conflicts (McConachie [1898] 1973). However, the less restrictive procedures of the Senate and the lack of any stringent limitations on debate and amendment preserved ready and flexible access to the floor for all members as well as their ability to use such access to pursue and protect their own agendas.

As a consequence, the power of the individual member remained strong in the

Senate. The power of the standing committees did increase, since they constituted the prime locus for policy leadership, and the chairs of the important committees were, in the absence of a Speaker and any party apparatus past a caucus system for choosing committees, the prime party leaders in the Senate (Gamm and Smith 2002). However, committee power and party power were checked by the role and prerogatives of the individual member. Indeed, soon after the Senate in the mid-1840s established the current system of choosing committee members by party lists, seniority norms strengthened and became difficult to challenge (Kravitz 1974). Overall, the Senate remained a body that worked by mutual consent with substantial regard for the power of the individual member. It therefore relied by necessity on the forbearance and courtesy of individual senators to conduct and advance its business. In contrast, in the House the increased elaboration of the rules, both by regulating access to the floor and by limiting debate, served to enhance the power of committees and, to a lesser degree the Speaker, at the expense of the ordinary member. The new prerogatives members gained in bill introduction did little to stabilize or extend their influence. The power of committees was protected by the rule that redefined the bill introduction procedure, by related rule changes in 1837 and 1838 that barred debate on the introduction of member bills and resolutions, and, in a body of several hundred members, by the confinement of member bill introduction to limited hours during certain days. Nor was the enhanced power of committees accompanied by increased strength in seniority norms as was true in the Senate. Rather, seniority considerations were clearly subordinated to the needs of party and the Speaker (Price 1977). As a result, by the 1850s the individual member in the House had far less status and power than his predecessors in the 1790s or even the 1820s. Nonetheless, the individual member was still far from a captive of the Speaker or powerful committee chairs. Under the rules members still had the power to discuss the reference of bills and resolutions, to move resolutions that addressed policy issues on the floor, to speak freely and at length in committee of the whole, and to obstruct action through a variety of dilatory tactics and motions. Equally important, the agenda powers of the Speaker and committee chairs were minimal. As a result, they often had to depend on mechanisms, such as suspension and unanimous consent, whose difficulty in implementation preserved the power and independence of the individual member (Cooper and Young 1989; King 1997; Binder 1997).

The Triumph of Member Bills: 1861–97

In the decades that followed 1861, reliance on member bills in areas of public legislation continued to expand, with the result that by the 1880s virtually all such bills were member bills in both the House and the Senate (see Table 10.3).[3] Equally important were the changes in procedure that were associated with the

TABLE 10.3. The Increase in Member Bills 1861–1893

	House			Senate		
Congress	Total Bills	% of Bills Thaty Are Public	Member Bills as % of Public Bills	Total Bills	% of Bills That Are Public	Member Bills as % of Public Bills
37th (1861–63)	792	77	60	578	84	83
40th (1867–69)	—	—	—	980	72	89
42nd (1871–73)	4,052	54	89	1,652	67	93
45th (1877–79)	—	—	—	1,865	54	93
47th (1881–83)	7685	31	93	2,509	54	91
52nd (1891–93)	10,623	26	97	—	—	—

Note: Figures for the 45th, 47th, and 52nd Congresses are based on a sample of 10% of bills.

triumph of member bills. In the House the 1880 rules changes removed the historic requirements for permission and one day's notice but also totally barred debate on the referral of bills. In fact, of course, the requirements for permission and notice had long been mere formalities, and opportunities for debate when bills were referred had been limited for several decades. In the 1890 rules changes introduction and reference were taken off the floor, a practice that has continued to this day. Whatever the gains in efficiency, this step foreclosed the opportunity to challenge or propose alternatives to the Speaker's decisions and for all practical purposes made reference entirely subject to his interpretations of the rules and precedents of the House (Cooper and Young 1989).

In the Senate, procedural change was far less sweeping. The 1877 rules sought to bar the consideration of bills until referred and reported but nonetheless allowed them to be objected to and placed directly on a calendar. The 1884 rules eliminated the requirements for permission and one day's notice. As in the House, such changes brought the rules into conformity with what had long been governing practice. In contrast to the House, however, the 1884 rules nonetheless provided that the introduction of a bill, if objected to, had to be postponed for a day. More important, they did not alter the historic provisions in the rules that required bills to be introduced and referred on the floor and permitted referrals to be debated. Nor did the late-nineteenth-century Senate follow the example set by the House with respect to standing committee jurisdictions. The House defined them in the rules from the very beginning and in 1880 made reference in line with these jurisdictions mandatory. In the Senate standing committee jurisdictions were not formally defined but entirely controlled by precedent. Reference thus continued to be subject to the discretion of the Senate as a whole. As a result, the ability of Senators to object to the reference of bills and place them directly on the calendar, to debate and add instructions to referral motions, to propose reference to a select committee, and to influence which of the more than forty standing committees that existed in the early 1890s received a bill were preserved (Riddick 1941, 1980).

The changes in House procedure with respect to the introduction and reference of bills were in accord with the centralization of power in the Speaker that occurred after 1870 and especially after 1880. By 1890 the Speaker controlled access to the floor. He had gained absolute power over recognition in the decades that followed the end of the Civil War and chaired a Rules Committee of five, which between 1880 and 1890 had developed from a select committee with narrow jurisdiction over House rules to a standing committee with privileged access to the floor and the power to bring forward special orders that could set the time and terms of debate on legislation. In addition, the Speaker could rely on his appointees on the fourteen other committees that had been granted privilege on certain bills, nine of these grants dating only from 1880, to block the calendar whenever he desired. All this signaled that the House had given up on its long and unsuccessful quest to apportion access to the floor in a fair and objective manner through a prescribed order of business and was no longer willing to make do with suspension and unanimous consent, which had been the traditional default mechanisms. Rather, it now opted to give the Speaker control over the agenda in the interests of advancing the majority-party program. Similarly, by 1890 the majority party had closed off the remaining opportunities that the rules provided for minority obstruction. Given the development of the previous question as a cloture mechanism for floor debate, the main opportunities for obstruction after 1860 pertained to dilatory tactics in the Committee of the Whole and on the floor, including the disappearing quorum. However, the Rules Committee provided a mechanism for controlling general debate in the Committee of the Whole, and rules changes in 1890 gave the majority control of proceedings in Committee of the Whole and gave the Speaker authority to disregard dilatory motions and to count all members present in determining a quorum on the floor (Alexander 1916; Cooper and Young 1989; Binder 1997).

It is thus not surprising that the same changes in 1890 that codified the powers of the Rules Committee and eliminated the remaining sources of obstruction also took introduction and reference off the floor, to the further advantage of the Speaker and the committee chairs. This change merely capped a century of development in which the individual member's ability to influence the terms of reference or to discharge committees simply evaporated as rules changes increasingly limited the ability of members to gain access to the floor at any point in the order of business if the Speaker did not favor them with recognition. The individual member in the House had long been disadvantaged by the weakness of seniority norms as constraints on the Speaker's power to appoint the standing committees as well as by the manner in which the large number of standing committees and the large size of the House combined to relegate many members to committees of little importance. The growth in the Speaker's control over the floor and the agenda, combined with high levels of party voting and an active caucus, provided even more powerful sources of constraint. The power of members thus declined to a far lower ebb than in 1860. Members began to complain from 1880 on that they had been reduced to ciphers. Indeed, though usually ignored, this is one of the main complaints of Wilson's (1885) classic work on the Congress of the 1880s. By 1890 their position had not improved but worsened because of the Speaker's heightened control over all aspects of the legislative process. Thus, what changed between 1880 and 1890 was that of their two masters, committee chairs and Speaker, the latter gained dominance over the former and even greater power over the individual member because of the manner in which increases in the Speaker's power as party leader, due to heightened party unity, and increases in his formal powers, due to rules changes, reinforced one another (Cooper and Brady 1981a; Cooper and Young 1989).

In the Senate as well, the end of the story is congruent with the course of its development in the nineteenth century. In the decades that followed the Civil War the Senate also took several steps to enhance its ability to conduct its business in a manner that was both efficient and responsive to majority will. By 1884 it had limited debate on a number of procedural motions, imposed a germaneness requirement on amendments to appropriations bills, allowed amendments to be tabled without damage to the underlying bill, and established a special time period for bringing minor business to the floor with debate limited to five minutes per speaker. Most important of all, it had created a new rule (IX) under which appropriation bills and other forms of major business could be brought to the floor by nondebatable, privileged motions without regard to their position on the calendar (Riddick 1980). It is also true that by 1890, prompted by both heightened party unity and the press of business, more powerful party caucuses and newly emergent party steering committees provided a stronger organizational foundation for centralized leadership than had existed in the past. By 1897 a clique of majority party leaders, whose power was based on their control of the party apparatus and the key standing committees, began to lead the Senate in a far more oligarchical manner than had ever been the case before 1890 and would ever again be true after 1910 (Rothman 1966; Smith and Gamm 2001).

Nonetheless, the Senate resisted rules changes that would alter its fundamental character as a body that worked on the basis of mutual consent and forbearance, even as the strength of party began to rise in the 1880s and 1890s. Despite the heightened partisan atmosphere and substantial dissatisfaction over the filibuster, major efforts to impose some form of cloture failed once again in the 1890s. Nor did the rules that were adopted to make the conduct of business more efficient threaten the power of individual senators in any major way. The various limitations on procedural motions, the germaneness restrictions, and the expanded ability to table amendments were not powerful or extensive enough to have any substantial effect in limiting debate or determining outcomes. The period set aside for handling minor business with debate severely limited was restricted to roughly an hour and the limitation itself was subject to objection by any individual senator. The new and more flexible procedure for bringing major business to the floor under Rule IX appears to have been of some consequence for a brief period, but reliance on it eroded and it declined in significance for a variety of reasons—the need to compete with the unfinished business which was called at the very same time as motions under the rule, the precedence that special orders retained over such motions, conflicting rulings on the implementation of the rule, and most important of all, inability to end debate once a bill was brought to the floor. Finally, no matter what the procedures and limitations prescribed in the rules, unanimous consent requests could be and were used to disrupt the orderly consideration of business or to escape the limitations of a rule (McKee 1891; Gilfry 1909; Watkins and Riddick 1964).

In sum, the nineteenth-century Senate, like the House, failed to solve the problem of establishing a system for conducting its business that was both prescribed and effective. Before 1860, it worked largely through unanimous consent, and it continued to work this way after 1860 (McConachie [1898] 1973). The lack of viable cloture procedure ruled out all other alternatives, despite the difficulties that unanimous consent involved. As a result, the Senate's ultimate answer to regulating the conduct of its business was quite different than the House's. It chose to perfect unanimous consent, not to impose cloture and a Rules Committee. It thus began after 1860 to develop and extend unanimous consent from a motion made by senators haphazardly to promote their immediate needs into a mechanism for forging collective agreements to fix a day certain to consider a bill and/or limit debate. By the 1870s such agreements were frequent, but the Senate's regard for the rights of the individual member still led it to tolerate for decades the disorder that the informal status of such agreements bred. Finally, in 1914, under circumstances and pressures very different than those that had formerly prevailed, it transformed them into formal agreements of the Senate that the presiding officer could enforce (Gamm and Smith 2000). Similarly, though majority-party leaders took control of the Senate by 1897, their power was based on the leverage they secured from the heightened degree of party unity; their dominance of the party apparatus and the strategic use of the caucus, party steering committee, and party Committee on Committees that high party cohesion permitted; and their own positions as chairs of the most important Senate standing committees. In short, their power was rooted informally in the party structure and was not reinforced formally to anywhere near the same degree as the Speaker's power in the House. Leadership thus was exercised far more than in the House at the sufferance of the members and with much less power or control over fellow partisans or the minority. It is thus not surprising that in the Senate oligarchic party rule never sought to cripple the filibuster, accepted the seniority rights members enjoyed under the full-fledged seniority system that had emerged in the Senate by the 1870s, could be challenged and frustrated on occasion by its own partisans, and simply disappeared without any rules revolt once the majority party developed a dissident wing early in the next century (Brady and Epstein 1997; Smith and Gamm 2001). Nor is it surprising, given the Senate's willingness to live with disorder in its formal system rather than impair the rights of members and the need for party leaders to respect these rights as well, that bill introduction and reference remained on the floor in the 1890s and thereafter, and were not affected by the rise or decline of party rule.

Conclusions

Important similarities and differences characterize the evolution of bill introduction in the House and the Senate. Both bodies over the course of the century transformed the introduction of public legislation from a process in which committees played the dominant role to one in which introduction became a hallmark of member prerogative and activity. However, the pace of change varied substantially, with the Senate far ahead of the House until the 1850s. Nor was the pace of change the only important difference. Whereas the transition to member bills climaxed in the House in 1890 by taking introduction and reference off the floor, this was not true in the Senate. At the end of the century Senate rules provided for the introduction and reference of bills on the floor, and they continue to do so today.[4] Last, but not least, the broad dynamics of change in the two houses were very different. In the House the transition to member bills was part of a century-long transition in which changes in rules and practice regarding the standing committees, access to the floor, and debate and amendment on the floor served to consolidate power in the standing committees and ultimately in party leaders at the expense of the individual member. In contrast, though the evolution of bill introduction in the Senate was also accompanied by changes in its rules and practices, the Senate continually took pains to limit the monopoly power of committees, to preserve the access of members to the floor, and to protect freedom of debate and amendment on the floor. As a result, senators were not subject to the same bad bargain House members had to endure—the receipt of discretion to introduce bills at the cost of loss of power to the standing committees and party leaders over the fate of those bills.

Explaining Change

Three broad approaches have been relied upon in the literature to explain institutional change in Congress. The first is reductionist and emphasizes explanation at the individual level in terms of member self-interest. It argues that institutions are human constructs and hence that explanation should focus on the egoistic and atomized preferences of the individuals who compose them. In short, the guiding premise is that institutional structures and processes are best explained at the micro level of analysis in terms of the manner in which the self-interested motivations of individual actors combine to produce and change them. The second focuses on the dynamics of collective action and emphasizes the role of party and the collective interests of party members. This approach proceeds at a mezo or intermediate level of analysis and declines to view institutional analysis in anarchic or atomistic terms. It rather chooses to highlight the cooperative and organizational dimensions of action and sees legislative structure and process as responsive to and explainable in terms of the role of party. Parties, as the most stable, inclusive, and comprehensive groups that form within a legislature, are seen to provide the prime basis for collective action. Although the "glue" that holds parties together is subject to varying interpretations, what is agreed upon is that parties, working through elected leaders and internal coordinating mechanisms, provide the means for solving collective action problems in legislatures because of their ability to mobilize political support, to control and exploit the leverage inherent in the formal structures of decision making, and to take responsibility for leading and directing the decision-making process. A third, and in many respects the most traditional approach, focuses on broader contextual factors. This approach does not deny that legislatures are human constructs or the importance of organization in structuring action. What it argues, however, is that human choices and patterns of cooperative action are shaped and constrained by broader contextual forces, and thus that the key to explanation lies in understanding the impact of these forces on both individual choice and collective action. In short, the guiding premise is that structure and process are best explained at macro levels of analysis.

Given these three perspectives, let us assess their ability to explain the evolution of bill introduction in the Senate and the similarities and differences that exist with respect to the House.

Party

It has become quite common in the study of Congress in recent decades to see party as a determinant of structure and structural change (Schickler 2000). As with all three perspectives, however, the power or force of party as a determinant can be and has been conceived in varying ways. Some conceive its cohesion and organizational capabilities in terms of the shared interest members have in promoting their reelections and controlling positions of power in the legislature. Others see its power and impact as derived from the shared policy orientations and preferences that unite members ideologically and induce them to act cooperatively to gain desired policy objectives. In reality, the two reinforce each other, though most authors explicitly or implicitly frame their analysis in terms of one or the other (Smith 2000; Cooper and Young 2002). However, in the case of bill introduction, party as a determinant, no matter how framed, fails to explain either the evolution of bill introduction in the Senate or similarities and differences with the House.

If we turn first to a general examination of the relationship between party strength and bill evolution, the patterns of variation are highly distinctive in both houses. This can be seen simply by averaging the party vote score by decades.[5] In the Senate the mean party vote by decade from 1799 to 1829 fell from 64.3 percent to 46.3 percent. Yet the proportion of member bills increased to 40 percent of the total (see Table 10.1). In the two decades from 1829 to 1849 the mean party vote by decade rose from 46.3 percent to 68.6 percent but then fell in the decade of the 1850s to 51.6 percent. Yet during these three decades member bills increased fairly steadily to the 70 percent level. Results in the House were similar, though levels of party voting were almost invariably higher. There were no member bills in the House until the late 1830s, but the character of variation in the mean party vote by decade was similar to that in the Senate. The mean party vote by decade fell from 70.3 percent in the decade between 1799 to 1809 to 44.2 percent in the decade between 1819 and 1829. It then rose to 69.5 percent from 1829 to 1839 and to 76.6 percent from 1839 to 1849 and fell again to 52.7 percent in the 1850s. Yet once the rules were changed to facilitate member bills in 1837–38, the increase in these bills as a percentage of public bills was rapid and highly linear (see Table 10.2).

It is thus difficult to see party as determinant of the evolution of bill introduction in any general or overall sense. But a more limited argument can still be made: that after the rise of the second party system, minority members, confronted with committees led and controlled by the majority party, seized on member bills as a way of attracting attention to their legislation and increasing its chances of passage. Our data, though limited to the Senate, do indicate that the great preponderance of committee public bills were majority bills in the 1830s, 1840s, and thereafter. Still, there is good reason to be dubious of the claim that the growth of member bills was driven by minority members. Member bills could be expected to be referred to a standing committee once introduced in any event, and detailed resolutions of inquiry provided a ready alternative to a member bill. Our data sustain such skepticism. In 9 of the 10 Senates between 1831 and 1873 that we have examined, minority members introduced a lower proportion or about the same proportion of member bills as their proportion in the Senate. The single exception is the 27th Senate (1841–43).[6] Similarly, though it is true that the success rate of minority member bills relative to minority committee bills did increase in the 1840s and 1850s, so too did the success rate of majority member bills relative to majority committee bills. Nor were the increases in the relative success of minority or majority member public bills in this period consistent with the increases in the overall percentage of public bills introduced by members.[7] In sum, then, our data provide only slim and isolated support for the minority-party thesis.

We can conclude that party has little, if any, explanatory power when it comes to the evolution of member bills in either the House or the Senate. Nor is this surprising. Even aside from the differences that now exist between those scholars who find party to be an important determinant of structural change and those who do not, the fact remains that the current debate centers on aspects of structure and process that directly and immediately pertain to the role and impact of party (Schickler and Rich 1997; Aldrich and Rohde 2000). Yet many aspects of structure and process are not so directly and immediately related; rather, they concern more general problems of time, workload, and division of labor to which structural arrangements must also respond (Polsby 1968; Cooper 1977). Indeed, a good argument can be made that most institutional change over time in Congress has concerned these aspects of structure and process. Nor should such changes be dismissed because their political effects are cumulative and indirect. Over time they too can have important consequences for agenda control. The rise of the standing committee system from 1789 to 1821 and the evolution of its control over the reference and retention of bills during the remainder of the nineteenth century provide a good illustration. Our findings on bill introduction provide another.

Self-Interest

As in the case of party, self-interest, defined in individualistic terms, is a familiar and popular perspective for deriving explanations of institutional change in Congress, and one that is subject to different forms of framing (Evans 1999). Those who adopt this perspective typically equate self-interest with member self-interest. But they approach explanation in different ways, depending on how they operationalize the concept of self-interest: that is, depending on which self-interested motive or combination of motives they emphasize as the driving force for members. Inspired by Richard Fenno's (1973) classic formulation, the three types of motives they rely upon are reelection, power within the legislature, and policy goals. The latter, however, is usually framed in a more restrictive manner than Fenno originally suggested when he defined this motivation as the desire for "good public policy" 1973, p. 1). It rather is understood in distributional terms, and often in a very narrow or parochial manner, as befits an individualized emphasis on self-interest.

Given this, if we seek to explain the evolution of bill introduction in terms of member self-interest, two broad approaches exist in the current literature. One is internally oriented and emphasizes the desire of members to change legislative procedures both to increase their personal power and to serve the policy interests of their constituents. In this approach the desire for reelection is not denied but remains implicit, and limited attention is given to the span of constituency interests members seek to serve or to different modes or forms of distributional politics. Current attempts to explain changing patterns of committee jurisdiction in terms of the entrepreneurial activities of members provide a good example (King 1997). A second is externally oriented and emphasizes the desire for reelection. This approach to explanation has been extremely influential among students of Congress and was originally tied to the narrowest form of distributional politics. As developed by Mayhew (1974) and Fiorina (1977), an integral corollary of a careerist approach to Congress was an emphasis on the delivery of particularistic benefits to constituents as the primary means of winning elections. As a consequence, credit seeking, advertising, and position taking were identified as the three prime strategies for members to follow to win reelection. In recent years, in response to the growth of both partisanship and plebiscitary democracy in the United States, the approach has been broadened to recognize the importance of issues whose span or reach is national and to highlight modes or types of politics that are conflictual or "zero sum game" instead of "divide the pie" in character (Fiorina 2001). Such change is compatible with an approach focused on reelection as well as with the strategies of credit seeking, advertising, and position taking originally proposed for gaining reelection. All that is required is to redirect the thrust of these strategies by enhancing the importance of position taking and casting advertising and credit seeking as forms of "spin."

Both types of self-interest approaches to explaining the evolution of bill introduction merit examination, but both start with some serious disadvantages. On its face, an explanation premised on the desire of members to gain power and policy advantage within the Congress does not appear promising. Over time the increasing number of member bills did not contribute to the power of members. Rather, in combination with the tightening of opportunities for debate in introducing and referring bills that was associated with the transition to member bills, it circumscribed the power of members in the Senate and seriously undermined it in the House. Moreover, even if assessment is limited to the short run, as is appropriate for processes of change that are highly incremental, problems remain. The authority to introduce bills at one's own discretion is not a preeminent source of personal power within a legislative body in a separation-of-powers framework, and especially not when functional alternatives, such as res-olution of inquiry, exist and standing committees receive the bills once intro-duced in any event. Nonetheless, it can be and has been argued that the growth of member bills was motivated by the desire of individual members to gain added leverage vis-à-vis the standing committees in passing pet pieces of legis-lation (Damon 1971). Similarly, careerist explanation, based on the desire for re-election, has to be reformulated into a far broader notion of pursuing a career to have any resonance in the nineteenth century. In the nineteenth century, mem-bers in the House and the Senate did not desire or expect to spend most of their careers in Congress. They were not avid seekers of reelection. In the House, members often chose not to run for reelection, and in the Senate, resignations before the end of one's term were common (Ripley 1969b; Price 1977; Brady, Buckley and Rivers 1999). However, if members did not pursue careers in Con-gress, they did pursue careers in politics. They sought to use service in Congress as a pathway to state and national offices of a variety of types. If, then, we define careerism in terms of the pursuit of a political career, not merely a legislative ca-reer, the external form of careerist explanation remains applicable. It can be and indeed has been argued that the increase in the number of member bills was tied to the desire of members to publicize themselves for their own personal and po-litical gain (Alexander 1916).

If we turn now to assessing the merits of these two forms of explanation based on self-interest, some support can be found for the claim that member bills were prompted by the desire of members to gain leverage over the commit-tees. But it is quite limited. A good test of this claim is to compare rates of pas-sage. Though our data are restricted to the Senate, the gap between the percentage of member bills that passed and the percentage of committee bills that passed does narrow in three of the four Senates that we examined for the pe-riod between 1845 and 1857. However, the proportion of public bills introduced by individual senators was quite substantial by the 1840s, did not fluctuate in line with the narrowing of the gap in favor of member bills, and continued to ex-pand after the 1860s, when the gap again widened in favor of committee bills.[8] Equally important, a division of member bills into constituency topic and na-tional topic bills, on the basis of whether a bill does or does not confer a highly disproportionate benefit on a particular state, adds considerable insight. In terms of this distinction, such narrowing that did occur was due far more to an increase in the success rates of member constituency topic bills relative to committee constituency topic bills than to an increase in the success rates of member na-tional topic bills relative to committee national topic bills.[9] Hence, if the desire of members to gain more power internally was a factor, it was more closely tied to external incentives than internal incentives.

All this brings us to the more substantial argument for the power of self-

TABLE 10.4. Public Bills by Type and Agent

Congress	% Member-Introduced Public Bills with Constituency Topic (% with National Topic)	% Constituency-Topic Bills Introduced by Members (% by Committees)	% National-Topic Bills Introduced by Members (% by Committees)
12th (1811–13)	32 (68)	42 (58)	26 (69)
17th (1821–23)	53 (47)	46 (54)	36 (64)
22nd (1831–33)	56 (44)	49 (51)	33 (67)
25th (1837–39)	39 (61)	59 (41)	50 (49)
27th (1841–43)	44 (56)	78 (22)	60 (40)
29th (1845–47)	55 (45)	63 (37)	35 (65)
31st (1849–51)	47 (43)	73 (27)	60 (40)
32nd (1851–53)	62 (38)	70 (30)	52 (48)
34th (1855–57)	64 (36)	82 (18)	56 (44)
37th (1861–63)	17 (83)	81 (19)	83 (17)
40th (1867–69)	35 (65)	91 (8)	89 (11)
42nd (1871–73)	48 (52)	97 (3)	91 (9)

Note: Constituent topic bills include the following: road and harbor repair or construction, railroad construction, incorporation, establishment of collection and judicial districts, compensation of judges and other public officials, the time and place for holding district court, Indian removal, restoration of civil liberties, settlement of private land claims, and grants of lands or the right-of-way through public lands. Percentages do not always equal 100 because in some cases the record does not indicate whether the bill was introduced by a committee or a member or introduced by some other means.

interest in explaining the evolution of bill introduction—the desire of members to advance their careers by using member bills to publicize themselves. Here again, a distinction between constituency topic and national topic bills is useful. In the case of the Senate, if we look at the percentage of member bills that were constituency topic as opposed to national topic in the 10 Senates we examined, the overall average from the 12th Congress (1811–13) through the 34th Congress (1855–57) is 50.3 percent. In short, despite some variation in individual Congresses, member bills were roughly equally divided between constituency topic and national topic bills in the period in which member bills became predominant. Nonetheless, if we look at the percentage of constituency topic bills that were member bills, it is clear that members, not committees, were the driving force in the growth of constituency topic bills to a far greater degree than with respect to national topic bills (see Table 10.4).

Nor is this the only evidence that can be mobilized in support of explanation based on self-interest. If we distinguish senators from states with three or fewer representatives in the House from senators from states with four or more, some striking differences emerge. Small-state senators in the ten Senates we examined

TABLE 10.5. Public Member Bills: Small-State and Large-State Comparisons

(Years)	% of Small-State Member Bills with Constituency Topic (% with National Topic)	% of Large-State Member Bills with Constituency Topic (% with National Topic	% of Small-State Senators in Senate (% of Large-State Senators)	% of Constituent-Topic Member Bills That Were Introduced by Small-State Senators (% by Large-State Senators)	% of National Topic Member Bills That Were Introduced by Small-State Senators (% by Large-State Senators)
12th (1811–13)	60 (40)	25 (75)	28 (72)	38 (62)	12 (88)
17th (1821–23)	88 (12)	25 (75)	33 (67)	74 (26)	12 (88)
22nd (1831–33)	65 (35)	35 (65)	33 (67)	81 (19)	55 (45)
25th (1837–39)	59 (41)	18 (82)	31 (69)	76 (22)	33 (66)
27th (1841–43)	57 (43)	28 (72)	27 (73)	70 (30)	41 (59)
29th (1845–47)	78 (22)	50 (50)	24 (76)	26 (74)	9 (91)
31st (1849–51)	42 (58)	52 (48)	29 (71)	40 (60)	50 (50)
32nd (1851–53)	79 (21)	49 (51)	18 (62)	55 (45)	23 (77)
34th (1855–57)	72 (28)	59 (41)	29 (71)	41 (59)	28 (72)
37th (1861–63)	22 (78)	13 (87)	44 (56)	59 (41)	43 (57)
40th (1867–69)	44 (56)	26 (74)	39 (61)	61 (39)	42 (58)
42nd (1871–73)	48 (52)	48 (52)	35 (65)	40 (60)	40 (60)

Note: Constituent topic bills include the following: road and harbor repair or construction, railroad construction, incorporation, establishment of collection and judicial districts, compensation of judges and other public officials, the time and place for holding district court, Indian removal, restoration of civil liberties, settlement of private land claims, and grants of lands or the right-of-way through public lands. Percentages do not always equal 100 because in some cases the record does not indicate whether the bill was introduced by a committee or a member or introduced by some other means.

were far more inclined than large-state senators to introduce constituency topic bills than national topic bills. So much so that although they accounted for roughly only a third of the Senate in our ten Senates, they nonetheless were the driving force for constituency topic bills in these Senates, especially from the 1820s to the 1840s (see Table 10.5). This fact is in accord with recent evidence regarding the greater particularistic inclinations of small-state senators and provides added testimony to the power of the distributional incentives that fueled member bills (Lee and Oppenheimer 1999). We do not have the same breadth of data for the House. But the evidence we do have that is comparable makes an even stronger case for the role of self-interest in propelling member bills than in the Senate. In the House, as reliance on member bills gained momentum, the percentage of member bills that were constituency topic rose from 42 percent in the 27th Congress (1841–43), shortly after the rules changes of 1837–38, to 70 percent in the 31st Congress (1849–51) and 73 percent in the 32nd Congress (1851–53) (Cooper and Young 1989).

Clearly, then, member self-interest played an important role in the transition from committee bills to member bills in both the House and Senate. Nonetheless, it is far from the whole story. In and of itself, an explanation of the transition from committee to member bills based purely on self-interest cannot explain the long process of evolution that was required in both houses or the differences in the pace and results of change in the two bodies. Nor can it explain why, especially in the Senate, national topic bills, along with constituent topic bills, played a major role in the growth of member bills or why national topic bills figured so prominently as a proportion of member bills introduced by large-state senators (see Tables 10.4 and 10.5). In the former regard, the rough balance between national topic bills and constituency topic bills is attributable not only to the activities of large-state senators but also to the activities of small-state senators, who did not at all confine themselves to constituency topic bills. In the latter regard, it is arguable, of course, that in the case of both large- and small-state senators, the introduction of national topic bills is attributable simply to self-serving position taking and that the disparities that existed were due to the greater demands for posturing in states that were larger and more complex politically. But that is to assume that the Websters, Clays, Calhouns, Bentons, and Sewards of the second party system were nothing but mere position takers. It is to assume that they had no serious and deeply felt policy convictions on issues, such as slavery, the tariff, bank, and national expansion and development, that crossed constituencies, divided the nation, and defined the major points of conflict in the politics of the period. Without disregarding the need for all politicians to do some posturing, such a claim exaggerates the case for position taking far beyond its merits.

We can conclude, then, that whatever its strengths, member self-interest is not sufficient unto itself to explain the evolution of bill development in the Senate or the differences in House and Senate experience. To point out its limits, however, is not to dismiss the power of self-interest as an explanatory mechanism. It is only to affirm that its effects are highly conditioned and thus that it does not provide a sufficient or adequate basis for explaining bill introduction or any other aspect of structural change in Congress.

Context

The contextual approach focuses on determinants or factors at more comprehensive or generalized levels of analysis than those that focus on particular organizational components or the self-regarding drives that ostensibly control human choice (Polsby 1968; Cooper and Brady 1981b). As a consequence, this approach is even more open to framing and in need of specification than the other approaches. In the case of Congress, as in the case of all institutions, multiple contexts can be identified and they exist as circles within circles. Hence, what is regarded as contextual is not definitively identifiable in terms of some firm or absolute distinction between the internal and the external. Rather, it can be seen to include systemic features of institutional structure, norms, and linkage as well as factors that are clearly outside the boundaries of the institution. The precise boundaries of the contextual are thus subject to the purposes of the researcher, the test being the value or worth of the explanatory results. What must be true of a contextual approach, however, is that explanation does not treat what is identified as contextual as a constant or given, with little role in explanation, but rather as a critical source of explanatory power. For our purposes, we shall regard context as the institutional setting within which decision making occurs and see it as molded or shaped by two key ingredients—the formal linkages that tie the House and Senate to the electoral and executive components of their immediate political environments and the sum of broad and diffused institutional attributes, such as size, workload, conceptions of legitimacy, behavioral norms, and established modes of procedure and practice, that together define and constitute the internal working environment.

Our notion of context thus involves the intersection between the broader political environment and the internal institutional environment. It assumes that the processes of institutional change are never governed by motivations in the abstract but that choices are made in a historical context that influences conceptions of self-interest, regulates the interplay between self-regarding and other-regarding motivation, and limits options (Simon 1985). It further assumes that there are both stable and dynamic aspects to context so that forms of linkage and organizational attributes operate both to transmit and energize the forces of change and to direct and restrain them (Cooper 1981).

How well, then, does a contextual approach help explain the evolution of bill introduction in the Senate and similarities and differences with the House? The answer is "quite a lot," though not in isolation from assumptions about motivation at the individual level. That the Senate, like the House, in the first decades of government under the Constitution required the permission of the chamber to introduce bills and relied primarily on committees bills is attributable to prevailing conceptions of law making. It is equally true that the differences, as well as the similarities, in Senate and House practice with respect to bill introduction during our first period are attributable to contextual factors. As noted earlier, even in the early Congresses the small, almost intimate, size of the Senate prompted less restrictive practices in referring subjects to committees and a very broad and simple bill introduction rule. What should be added now is that the effects of size were powerfully reinforced by the high regard senators had for their status as senators and the habits of mutual deference that flowed from such regard (Swife 1997).[10] As a result, Senate practice involved member bills from the very start. Similarly, the fact that member bills in the Senate grew to substantial proportions by 1825 is also explainable in contextual terms. When attachment to the pristine representative ideals of the early Congresses, based on generalist norms, eroded and resulted in a discretionary grant of bill power to standing committees, the looseness in the original Senate rule could and did serve as a vehicle for a sizeable expansion in member bills. In the House, the greater size of the body from the start, combined with a more limited sense of entitlement on the part of members, led to a complex and constraining rule, one that made member bills highly impractical and placed emphasis on the introduction of bills through committees. In the House, then, in contrast to the Senate, when the original ideals that had led to this rule atrophied and a standing committee system arose whose units were granted bill power, the bill introduction rule still barred member bills for all practical purposes. House members thus relied far more than senators on the functional equivalent of member bills—detailed resolutions of inquiry referring legislative subjects to committees.

Similarly, context holds the key to explaining the growth and rise to predominance of member bills during the period from 1825 to 1860. In the Senate this development is tied to the transformation of the Senate into the nation's leading political institution during these years (Swift 1997; Riker 1955; Mayhew 2000). This transformation, in turn, is tied to all the elements of context identified earlier. In terms of linkages, change in the character and impacts of its ties to the electorate profoundly altered the role and power of the Senate. The extension of suffrage, the rise of state party organizations and the canvass, and the continuing erosion of the doctrine of instruction all combined to tie senators closer to the electorates in the states and in so doing transformed the Senate into a body whose members began to act as policy initiators and leaders instead of mere critics of and checks on House and executive proposals. These tendencies were powerfully reinforced by the uneven growth of population in the North and South and the different methods of electing the House and Senate. By 1820 northern control of the House was established and unchallengeable. In the Senate, however, the principle of representation by states rendered the North and the South equal. Given that the key issues of the day were sectionally defined, this made the Senate the arbiter of national policy issues both with respect to key substantive issues such as the tariff, economic development, and slavery and with regard to the systemic issue of preserving the balance between North and South as new states came into the Union (Kromkowski 1999).

Nonetheless, the aspects of context that relate to institutional attributes were also of importance. The Senate's closer ties to the electorate and its enhanced strategic position led not only to an increase in its activism and power but also to a profound change in the way in which it conceived its duties and responsibilities, in the values and norms that defined it as an institution. No longer did the Senate conceive of itself as an American House of Lords; rather, it conceived itself as the unit in the national political system best fitted to represent the nation and exercise policy leadership in the public interest (Swift 1997). Equally important, the ability of the Senate to fulfill its new sense of mission as leader and arbiter of the policy process was greatly facilitated and enhanced by its size and lax procedures.[11] These allowed the Senate to become the center of national policy debates, which in turn made it the focal point of national attention. Thus, its role as the preeminent unit in the national political system was confirmed and strengthened. It is no accident that the leading American politicians in this period were senators, such as Clay, Webster, Calhoun, Douglas, and Benton, rather than House members or even, with some exceptions, presidents. Nor is it an accident that the main pathway to the Cabinet and to presidential nomination was through the Senate, not the House or state office.[12]

In such a context, member public bills understandably flourished in the Senate. They were fed by a sense of the Senate's mission, by policy commitments, by constituency concerns, and by career ambitions. Such bills were easy to introduce under Senate rules and were readily acceptable. Indeed, permission to introduce them had long been transformed into a mere formality, not a means of ensuring policy control by the whole body. Moreover, they provided more effective methods of both promoting oneself and advancing one's policy objectives than detailed resolutions of inquiry, and they had strategic advantages when action was stalled due to House inaction or when there was objection to a House bill. In contrast, development was slower in the House and more attributable to constituency bills. Yet the results by 1860 were similar in both houses. This was due, in part, to the fact that by the 1830s the expanded size and workload of the House had made resolutions of inquiry a highly inefficient mechanism for allowing members to introduce business.[13] However, it was tied as much, if not more, to the change in representative ideals. Once the House, like the Senate, abandoned the view that the whole should control policy decision making and bill introduction by smaller committees, the transition to member bills was inevitable. If discretionary committee bills were legitimate, so too were discretionary member bills, with the result that the original rule appeared increasingly as an anachronism. If there were differences in the rate of development, then, it was simply that the Senate had a broader range of incentives and a more favorable institutional setting.

Finally, context does much to explain the end of the story in both the nineteenth-century Senate and House. In the Senate and House the tipping point with respect to member bills in public areas of legislation had been reached by 1860, and there was little, if any, incentive to reverse the momentum in this direction.[14] The direct tie between senators and constituents grew even stronger as state party organization gained increasing importance and as the canvass as a method of selecting senators grew even more dominant. In a politics that continued to be sectionally defined and was more highly structured by state party organizations led by senators, the power and prestige of the Senate as an institution continued to grow. The Senate thus extended its position as the preeminent national political institution, which created an ever more favorable climate for member bills (Riker 1955; Rothman 1964). Similarly, in the House there were no incentives for halting the momentum in favor of member bills. The constituency linkages and growing size and workload of the House, as well as the declining power of the individual member, barred any reversal of the trend.[15]

The prime difference between the House and Senate was rather one of the preservation of member rights on the floor with respect to the introduction and reference of bills. As noted, Senate-House differences in this regard fit in with the march to centralized power in the House and the Senate's continuing desire to preserve and protect the prerogatives of its members. Thus, as far as bill introduction was concerned, institutional setting had more to do with the differences in procedural results than the force of party, which increased in strength in both houses. In the Senate it was its norms in combination with its size that determined the outcome. By 1890 the size of the Senate had grown to eighty-eight, two and a half times its size in 1803, but still fifty-four members fewer than the size of the House in that year. Thus, it was not of such proportions as to preclude or muzzle introduction and reference on the floor, with the result that the ability of members to block or control reference could be preserved. In contrast, the size of the House, 332 members by 1889, severely limited the feasibility of allowing members to use floor introduction and reference for strategic purposes, and House rules, which had long for all practical purposes barred debate when bills were introduced, in 1880 barred it on reference as well. Hence, though reference on the floor still involved some advantages for the individual member, their weight in 1890 was insufficient to block taking introduction and reference off the floor. In a House that had for many decades steadily reduced the power of the individual member and now was willing to make its Speaker a czar in the interests of ensuring majority party control, efficiency needs easily trumped preserving rights that had been reduced to a pale shadow of their original selves (Cooper and Young 1989).

Conclusions

In sum, then, in explaining the evolution of bill introduction in the nineteenth-century Senate and the similarities and differences in House and Senate experience, an emphasis on context provides indispensable elements of explanatory power. Nonetheless, if a self-interest approach is inadequate, so too is a contextual approach. Thus, our emphasis on institutional setting only explains the choices that were made when it is blended with assumptions about motivation. Such assumptions are open to the researcher, and we have assumed that they pertain to broad policy issues as well as career interests. Still, it is no accident that self-interest in the form of career aspirations cannot be denied an explanatory role, even if it is an incomplete one. In contrast, the force of party does not contribute much to explanation. It should nonetheless not be dismissed because it does not work here. Rather, two things may be concluded. The first is that since party does have explanatory power in other areas (e.g., limitation of debate and amendment in the House), there is no single approach to explanation—no magic formula or algorithm that can be universally applied (Remington and Smith 1998; Evans 1999). Second, when a form of explanation based on party does work, it, like self-interest, does so within contextual determinants and parameters (Binder 1997; Smith and Gamm 2001). In short, the force of party may be seen as a form of collective motivation, whether rooted in career or policy goals, and as a motivational factor it needs to be blended with institutional and environmental forces to explain its impacts or effects. The explanation of institutional change thus always involves blending facets of context and motivation, and in differing ways depending on the aspect of structure or process that is involved. In other words, it requires strategies that enable explanation to integrate micro, mezzo, and macro approaches or perspectives, rather than being confined to a single one, and to do so in ways appropriate to the topic or object of explanation.

Continuing Problems

We cannot end this chapter without noting that the answers we have supplied, as helpful and clarifying as we believe them to be, still raise difficult and larger issues. If context and motivation must be blended in explaining institutional change, such blending must not subordinate one to the other. Neither a rigid notion of the role of context that treats motivation as a junior partner because it is ostensibly controlled by context nor a pristine view of motivation that treats context as a junior partner because it exists only as a set parameters around the forces that truly determine decision making is adequate. On the one hand, context influences the very definition of interest and the balance between different types of motivation rather than simply constraining preordained conceptions of values and interests. On the other hand, motivation is rooted in the human psyche. It is not the prisoner of context but, as all of human history demonstrates, something with leeway to battle and to change existing patterns of thought, behavior, and institutional structure. Only the explanatory schemes that we cling to so as to be freed from uncertainty—in a sense, our own intellectual weaknesses—induce us to ignore these complexities and seek simple deterministic ways of confronting a highly contingent reality. Blending thus means doing more than treating choices as necessary results once conditions are determined or treating conditions as broad parameters that define the playing field but do not affect the game or the players. Yet at present we have only begun to confront the problems of blending context and motivation in a fashion that escapes the limits of any single approach, whether framed in terms of individual self-interest, the role of party, or the role of contextual factors (Satz and Ferejohn 1994; Scharpf 1997; Strahan 2002).

Similarly, the fact that there is no simple, all-purpose approach or formula to explaining institutional change also creates difficult issues. If context and motivation must be blended, the character of the blend must also vary in different areas and be sensitive to the specific components that have explanatory power in those areas. Yet how then to escape reducing all explanation to the particular and idiosyncratic, how then to preserve generalizability? To put the point another way, how can contingency be combined with explanatory power? The answer may well be that political scientists cannot expect absolute and simple generalizability any more than quantum physicists can; we too can expect only bounded generalizability in relation to established conditions. If so, it is not generalizability that is destined for the dustbin of intellectual history but only explanation that takes certainty and simplicity as its hallmarks. Contingency does not mean that general classes of conditions and determinants cannot be established and related or that empirical evidence is irrelevant (Schickler 2001). Still, somehow we must learn to traverse the twilight zone between assumptions of simplicity and determinism and those of particularism and chaos. As yet, unfortunately, it remains a journey many refuse to embark on, while those who do must be guided more by conviction and instinct than by a ready and serviceable compass. That, however, is the mark of any truly challenging voyage of discovery.

Notes

This chapter was originally a paper prepared for delivery at Norman Thomas Conference on Senate Exceptionalism, Vanderbilt University, October 21–23, 1999.

1. Committee bills were even more dominant in areas of private legislation. In the Senate they constituted 86 percent of private bills in the 12th Congress (1811–13) and 88 percent of private bills in the 17th Congress (1821–23). In the House there were few, if any, member bills, public or private, in this period. See Cooper and Young (1989, n. 3).

2. In private areas of business, committee bills continued to dominate in both House and Senate. In the House the percentage of committee private bills fell only from 98 percent in the 27th Congress 1841–43) to 84 percent in the 36th Congress (1859–61). The Senate pattern was more erratic. The percentage of committee private bills fell from 77 percent in the 22nd Congress (1831–33) to 53 percent in the 27th Congress (1841–43) but then rose to 82 percent in the 29th Congress (1845–47) and 87 percent in the 34th Congress (1855–57). In short, committee bills dominated private legislation in both bodies before 1860, and in the Senate such bills were as prevalent in the late 1850s as in the early 1820s. As a result, with all bills taken into consideration, and given the greater proportion of private bills, member bills constituted only somewhat more than 40 percent of all bills in the late 1850s in both houses.

3. In the period after 1860, practice changed quickly and decisively with respect to private bills as well. By the 42nd Congress (1871–73), 73 percent of private bills were member bills in the House and 82 percent in the Senate. By the 47th Congress (1881–83), 99 percent of private bills were member bills in the House and 97 percent in the Senate. As a consequence, the overall total changed as well, even though the proportion of private to public bills increased substantially from 1860 to 1890 in both houses. Thus, by the 47th Congress (1881–83), 97 percent of all bills were public bills in the House and 94 percent in the Senate.

4. However, in recent decades the Senate has provided a mechanism by which members can introduce bills at any time the Senate is in session by filing them at the desk. This was done first by special orders and then by rule (Tieffer 1989; Riddick and Fruman 1992). In 1946 the Senate also finally adopted the House practice of defining mandatory standing committee jurisdictions in the rules; this has enhanced the authority of the presiding officer over reference (Riddick 1980; Maltzman 1997).

5. The party vote data are provided by Garry Young and measure the percentage of roll call votes in which a majority of one party votes against a majority of the other party.

6. In the 27th Senate (1841–43), the 44.2 percent of the Senate who were in the minority introduced 55 percent of member bills. In the 29th Senate (1845–47), the 41.4 percent of the Senate who were in the minority introduced 44 percent of member bills. These were the only two Senates of the ten Senates we examined in which minority members did not introduce substantially fewer member bills than their proportion in the Senate.

7. In the 25th Senate (1839–37) the percentage of minority member bills passed to the percentage of minority committee bills passed was 50 percent to 55 percent, and in the 27th Senate it was 44 percent to 75 percent. In contrast, in the 29th Senate (1845–47), 31st Senate (1849–51), 32nd Senate (1851–53), and 34th Senate (1855–57), the comparable figures were 43 percent to 37 percent, 38 percent to 35 percent, 33 percent to 29 percent, and 44 percent to 43 percent. Majority member bills did not reverse the situation in their favor as did minority member bills. But they moved in the same direction and appear to have done so somewhat earlier. The percentage of majority

member bills passed to majority committee bills passed in the 25th Senate was 49 percent to 66 percent, and in the 27th Senate it was 56 percent to 64 percent. In the 29th, 31st, 32nd, and 34th Senates the gap varied between 6 percent and 11 percent in favor of committee bills—about the same-size gap that prevailed in the 27th Senate. Finally, neither of these trends was consistent with the increasing percentage of member bills overall. The proportion of member bills of all public bills fell from 67 percent to 46 percent between the 27th and 29th Senates, just as minority member bills were gaining the upper hand relative to minority committee bills. Moreover, when the overall percentage of member public bills had increased to 62 percent in the 32nd Senate and 70 percent in the 34th Senate, the relative advantage of minority member bills declined somewhat rather than increased. Similarly, the ups and downs in the overall percentage of member bills did not correlate with the pace of improvement in the passage of majority member bills relative to majority committee bills. Once the gap between majority member bills and majority committee bills had been cut in half between the 25th and 27th Senates, it remained stable until the 1860s.

8. In the 27th Senate (1841–43), the percentage of member bills passed to committee bills passed was 49 percent to 65 percent, and this relationship was typical of the situation in the 1830s. In the four subsequent Senates, the percentage of member bills passed to committee bills passed was 33 percent to 31 percent in the 29th Senate (1845–47), 28 percent to 50 percent in the 31st Senate (1849–51), 38 percent to 47 percent in the 32nd Senate, and 42 percent to 50 percent in the 34th Senate (1855–57). Yet the percentage of public bills that were member introduced was 67 percent in the 27th Senate, 45 percent in the 29th Senate, 62 percent in the 31st Senate, 62 percent in the 32nd Senate, and 70 percent in the 34th Senate. Moreover, by the 37th Senate (1861–63), the percentage of member bills passed to committee bills passed dropped to 36 percent to 72 percent, and the gap remained of this size into the 1880s as the percentage of committee public bills continued to dwindle.

9. In the 22nd Senate (1831–33), 25th Senate (1837–39), and 27th Senate (1841–43), the average gap between the percentage of member constituency topic bills that passed and the percentage of committee constituency topic bills that passed was the same as the average gap between the number of member national topic bills that passed and committee national topic bills that passed—23 percent in each case in favor of committee bills. In the 29th Senate (1845–47), 31st Senate (1849–51), 32nd Senate (1851–53, and 34th Senate (1855–57), the average gap between member constituency topic bills and committee constituency topic bills that passed was reduced to 1 percent in favor of committee bills, whereas the average gap between member national topic bills that passed and committee national topic bills that passed was 18 percent in favor of committee bills. As was true generally, the gaps with respect to both types of bills widened to higher levels in favor of committees after 1860.

10. The size of the Senate in 1789 was 26. Two decades later, in 1809, it had grown only to 32. In the next two decades, its size increased to 46 by 1819 and 48 by 1829, but it

remained only about a fourth the size of the House, which increased from 65 in 1789 to 142 in 1809, 186 in 1819, and 215 in 1829 (Martis 1989).

11. The size of the Senate grew only from 48 in 1829 to 52 in 1839 but then grew to 62 by 1849. By 1859 it had increased somewhat more to 68. Nonetheless, it remained as small as the House had been at its inception in 1789 (Martis 1989).

12. In the years between 1801 and 1817, only 22 percent of permanent (not temporary appointees) Cabinet members had prior Senate service. In the years between 1837 and 1853, 40 percent had served in the Senate. As for pathways to the presidency, Senators were prominent contenders for presidential office even before 1825, though they were more often in the Federalist party than the Jeffersonian and were more often losers than winners. However, their prevalence and importance as presidential contenders increased after 1825. From the election of 1828 through the election of 1860, there was not an election in which one of the prime contenders had not served in the Senate, and in some elections it was true of the runner-up as well. Moreover, ex-senators were often the winners—Jackson, Van Buren, Harrison, Pierce, and Buchanan.

13. The size of the House increased from 187 in the 17th Congress (1821–23) to 242 in the 25th Congress (1837–39), the Congress in which the rules were changed to permit and facilitate member bills. Thereafter, however, it declined slightly and stood at 238 in the 36th Congress (1859–61) (Martis 1989). The number of public bills introduced was 139 in the 17th Congress (1821–23), 338 in the 27th (1841–43), and 491 in the 36th Congress (1859–61). This upward trend, however, was irregular and not consistent. The total number of bills, public and private, was typically more than twice this number, but the House had a separate track for private bills (Cooper and Young 1989).

14. The Senate did not attain its prewar size of 68 until the 40th Congress (1867–69). Thereafter, it increased to 76 in the 45th Congress (1877–79) and 88 in the 51st Congress (1889–91). As for workload, the number of public bills increased from 357 in the 34th (1855–57) to 1,154 in the 47th (1881–83). The tipping point for private member bills was not reached until the early 1870s, when private member bills as a percentage of all private bills rose to 82 percent in the 42nd Congress (1871–73) as compared with 46 percent in the 40th (1867–69). Why this occurred so quickly is not clear. Though the number of private bills expanded from 277 to 564 between the 40th and 42nd Congresses and to 1,355 by the 47th Congress, the example provided by the dominance of member bills in public areas was probably as important a factor as the growth in private business.

15. The House did not fully attain its prewar size until the 41st Congress (1869–71), when it numbered 243. Thereafter, it increased to 293 in the 45th Congress (1877–79) and 332 in the 51st Congress (1889–91). As for workload increases, the number of public bills increased from 491 in the 36th Congress (1859–61) to 2,398 in the 47th Congress (1881–83) to 2,812 in the 52nd (1891–93). Increases in private legislation were even more explosive. The number of private bills rose from 529 in the 36th Congress to 2,207 in the 42nd (1871–73), 2,398 in the 47th, and 2,812 in the 52nd. In line with

these increases, the percentage of private member bills rose from 16 percent in the 36th Congress to 73 percent in the 42nd Congress and 99 percent in the 47th Congress. In the case of the House, the expansion in private business arguably played a greater role in changing practice than in the Senate. We may note that even in the 42nd Congress the percentage of private member bills in the House was less than in the Senate (73 percent to 82 percent) but that thereafter it accelerated faster and passed the Senate by the 47th Congress (1881–83)—99 percent to 89 percent.

· 11 ·

Emergence of Senate Party Leadership

Gerald Gamm and Steven S. Smith

The long-standing individualism and informality of Senate proceedings has limited scholarly interest in the development of Senate party leadership and organization. "No one is *the* Senator," Woodrow Wilson wrote in 1885. "No one may speak for his party as well as for himself; no one exercises the special trust of acknowledged leadership" (213). In the 1970s, Jones (1976) suggested that Wilson's description fit the modern Senate as well, insisting that "strong substance-oriented policy leadership by party leaders is neither possible nor desirable in the United States Senate" (19–20). The rules of the Senate, it is commonly observed, protect the rights of senators to debate and offer proposals on the floor of the Senate and grant few special privileges to its presiding officer or the majority party's floor leader. Consequently, neither the Senate's party leadership nor its formal rules have generated much scholarship.

Yet a century has produced quite visible changes in the role of Senate party leaders. During a typical three-day period in the late 1890s (May 25–27, 1896), Nelson Aldrich (R-RI), who was regarded as the leader of the Senate's majority party, did not make a single motion or speech. No other senator assumed the responsibility to direct the flow of legislative business that week. In a similar period in the 1990s (May 23–25, 1994), Senate Majority Leader George Mitchell (D-ME) made thirty-five motions or unanimous-consent requests (excluding motions to reconsider and requests to end a quorum call), addressed the Senate six times to explain the order of business or a similar purpose, made speeches on two subjects, and offered four amendments, resolutions, or cloture motions. Such a presence on the floor does not necessarily qualify Mitchell as a substance-oriented policy leader, to use Jones's standard, but it does represent a significant change in the responsibilities and strategies of party leadership since the 1890s.

Existing studies of the development of Senate party organization and leadership suffer from multiple purposes. Rothman (1966), the most influential study, focuses on the emergence of highly centralized parties in the 1890s—what Rothman regards as the starting point of modern, disciplined Senate party organization. In contrast, Brady, Brody, and Epstein (1989) and Brady and Epstein (1997) argue that the emergence of strong committee chairs in the 1910s represented a decisive break with the older, centralized pattern of Senate organization described by Rothman. Meanwhile, neither Rothman nor Brady et al. examine the development of floor leadership in the 1910s and 1920s. Other scholars, such as Munk (1974), Baker and Davidson (1991), Riddick (1971), and Ripley (1969a, 1969b), emphasize the creation of formal leadership posts after the first decade of the twentieth century but give little attention to earlier innovations.

Explanations of Senate party development are fragmented and varied. Rothman (1966) argues that the development of strong state parties and political careers was essential to Senate party development, while Brady et al. (1989) contend that noncareerists, affected by changes in electoral coalitions, bred party centralization in the 1890s. Munk (1974) asserts that the new floor leader's post was the product of President Wilson's need for a lieutenant to push his program through a divided, filibuster-prone Senate. Finally, Baker and Davidson (1991) argue that the Senate's long-standing reliance on "baronial committee chairmen" ended in the 1910s and necessitated the creation of new leadership positions to coordinate the work of the Senate (1–2).

These disparate observations and inferences do not provide a basis for understanding the place of parties and leaders in the development of the Senate. Like their counterparts in other contexts, Senate parties and leaders help solve the problems of collective action for the membership (Calvert 1987; Frohlich, Oppenheimer, and Young 1971; Rohde and Shepsle 1987). Senators require means to coordinate activities such as setting the agenda, drafting legislation, and mobilizing majorities. Our theory is that the changing structure and tasks of Senate parties will reflect the evolving collective action problems confronted by senators.

Unlike the House, where changes in formal rules are common as majorities seek to adjust procedure and structure to their needs, the Senate seldom experiences changes in its rules. The possibility of a filibuster has long meant that an inconvenienced Senate majority cannot impose rules changes that might disadvantage the minority (Burdette 1940; Binder and Smith 1997; Binder 1997). Generally, adjustments by the majority party must be made some other way. This certainly has been true in recent decades (Smith and Flathman 1989). As we argue in this chapter, adjustments to changing conditions often took the form of new leadership structures and strategies in the decades just before and after the turn of the twentieth century.

Our task is to explain major innovations in Senate party development. This is a large task that we can only begin in this chapter. In the next section, we outline a general perspective on the emergence of new party organs and leaders as solutions to collective action problems, and outline testable hypotheses. We move to a description of the emergence of Senate party organs and leaders. We then turn to a closer look at evidence bearing on the competing hypotheses. Unfortunately, with the small number of events to be explained and the large number of factors at play, formal statistical analysis is not very helpful. Nevertheless, some possibilities can be eliminated. On the basis of the evidence at hand, we conclude that variation in competition between the parties—not careerism, policy distance, or workload—best accounts for the most important organizational innovations in the Democratic and Republican parties of the Senate.

Collective Action and Party Leadership

Our working hypothesis is that the changing structure of Senate parties and the shifting strategies of party leaders reflect the evolving collective action problems experienced by senators. These problems emerge from the inability of senators to achieve their individual goals by individual action alone. Senators with common policy, career, or electoral goals must coordinate their activities in creating institutions, setting the legislative agenda, drafting legislation, and mobilizing majorities. At times, the strategies may entail changes in party rules, organization, or leadership. At other times, a change in the choices made by an incumbent party leader is all that is required. Of course, a majority party may seek changes in chamber rules to improve its circumstances, but a Senate majority party's ability to manipulate the rules is limited by inherited rules—above all, the absence of a general rule limiting debate. As senators' goals vary, or as conditions affecting their ability to achieve these goals change, so do the collective policy and electoral problems confronting Senate parties.

The difficulty of changing chamber rules in response to evolving collective action problems distinguishes the Senate from the House. As recent literature has emphasized (Binder 1997; Binder and Smith 1997; Dion 1997), House majorities have frequently modified their chamber's rules to address procedural and organizational problems. In the House, a minority disadvantaged by the change is unable to block the change. But Senate minorities, particularly minority parties, can block the adoption of new rules by filibustering. Even the threat of a filibuster by a small minority can stall a rules change because of the inconvenience and disruption caused by a filibuster. One consequence of this difference between the chambers is evident in the length of their standing rules: the rules of the House are more than three times as long as those of the Senate. Another consequence is that senators must look to other ways to adjust to evolving collective action problems, such as modifying the practices of their party organizations.

Members of a party that coordinates efforts in pursuit of collective goals are advantaged over members of a party that does not, so there is an incentive to

214

create and maintain the means for such coordination. Interparty competition over elections, public policy, and power encourages collective efforts in the pursuit of party goals. As one party moves to better solve collective action problems, competitive pressures are created for the other party to do so as well.

Even when coordinated party activity is valued, senators still may not be willing or able to organize their activities. Serious obstacles to coordinated party activity exist. Like all public goods, party goals tend to be pursued inefficiently. Because no single senator has much of an effect on the achievement of the collective policy or electoral fortunes of a party, senators tend to contribute less to their achievement than is in their interest. Furthermore, someone, a single senator or a group of senators, must be motivated to assume responsibility to coordinate party activities. Someone must see some benefit—a selective benefit that is acquired only if one accepts coordination responsibility—from devoting time and resources to the pursuit of collective goals. When the duties of coordination are onerous, the selective benefit for leaders must be substantial. And even if party organization and leadership are created to pursue party goals, rank-and-file senators must be concerned about holding leaders accountable, which entails time and effort. These obstacles to collective action—the free-rider problem, the leadership-motivation problem, and the accountability problem—imply that party organization and leadership are not free of cost. Only at times when senators recognize that the benefits of collective action outweigh the costs imposed on them do innovations in party organization and leadership occur.

In the Senate, as elsewhere, parties emerged as a product of electoral competition and the desire to influence congressional policy choices (Aldrich 1995). But many of the organizational features of modern Senate parties—floor leaders, whips, party committees—did not emerge until the late nineteenth or early twentieth century. We seek to test the proposition that these features emerged as a product of a particular collective action problem of the two parties: interparty competition for control of the Senate. Specifically, we test the proposition that parity or near-parity in the strength of the Senate parties stimulates the parties to enhance their organizational effectiveness through innovation.

Relative party strength has figured centrally in explanations of changes in House rules, especially those rules that shape the parliamentary rights of minorities (Binder 1997; Dion 1997). As observers have noted, a small-majority party cannot afford to lose the votes of even a few members without losing majority control over legislative outcomes. Moreover, with a small-majority party, a change of a few seats reverses majority control of the chamber. Consequently, small margins enhance the incentive to maximize the effectiveness of the party efforts—to retain control for the majority party and to gain control for the minority party. At the same time, strong majorities, where strength is a function of both cohesion and size, are more likely than weak majorities to suppress minority rights in the House (Binder 1997). But the lack of variance in minority (or minority-party) rights in the Senate, in contrast to the House, has limited scholarly interest in the effect of party competitiveness for organizational change in the upper chamber.

Party competition is not the only possible explanation for party development in the Senate. In fact, existing scholarship on the Senate emphasizes other factors. This previous work suggests that innovations in party organization have resulted from electoral or policy objectives of senators and their parties. Scholars have identified four such sources of change.

First, *senatorial careerism* has played contrasting roles in theories of Senate party development. Rothman (1966) argues that the centralization of Senate parties in the late nineteenth century resulted from the increasing number of senators who regarded Senate service as a career and who owed their advancement to state party organizations. Yet Ripley (1969b) insists that, until the 1880s, careerism slowed the elaboration of Senate party organization and central leadership posts because career-minded senators, unlike representatives, were unwilling to tolerate strong central leaders. And Brady and colleagues (Brady et al. 1989; Brady and Epstein 1997) assert that it was the dominance of "noncareerists" in the Senate that facilitated the centralization of power in the late nineteenth century.

Second, *policy distance between the parties* has been emphasized by many analysts of congressional party development. The policy or spatial perspective is made explicit in Cooper and Brady (1981a) and is developed further by Sinclair (1983, 1995), Rohde (1990), Smith and Deering (1990), Brady (1988), Brady et al. (1989), and Brady and Epstein (1997); the thesis has been most explicitly detailed in Aldrich and Rohde (1997, 1998). Now labeled the "conditional party government" thesis, the perspective holds that congressional parties are policy coalitions of varying degrees of cohesiveness and polarization. When intraparty cohesiveness is high and interparty distance is great, legislators are eager to license strong central leaders to do their bidding for them, knowing that leaders will act in a manner consistent with their interests while coordinating the activity of fellow (and like-minded) partisans. The thesis holds that declining cohesiveness and polarization reduce legislators' willingness to tolerate strong party leaders and increase the independence of standing committees in policy making.

Third, *workload* has been cited as a foundation for organizational innovation. McConachie (1898, 313–21) observed how the Senate's increasing workload compelled adjustments in procedure and practice during the late nineteenth century. It is reasonable to expect that parties would make adjustments of their own. Indeed, Baker and Davidson (1991) argue that the independent power of committee chairs eroded sharply in the 1910s, when the

Senate reorganized its affairs to respond to World War I and to an increasingly powerful president. According to them, the new positions of party leadership emerged because new conditions "necessitated a coordinated Senate leadership quite beyond the capacity of individual committee chairmen" (2).[1] A war effort, domestic emergencies, a large policy agenda, or even new forms of press coverage may create new demands for coordination, particularly from within the majority party, which is likely to be blamed by outsiders if the Senate fails to act on desired legislation.

Finally, many scholars contend that institutional change is often timed with the *influx of new members* (Aldrich and Rohde 1997; Davidson and Oleszek 1977; Evans and Oleszek 1997b; Fenno 1997). New members, according to this perspective, have no vested interested in existing institutional arrangements and may even perceive a mandate to change the way their chamber and party operate. Because a large freshman class may or may not be timed with increasing parity in the relative strength of the parties, its effect on the incidence of organizational innovation warrants direct examination.

Analytical Approach and Data

The timing of responses to evolving collective action problems is complicated. At times, parties may make adjustments in anticipation of changing conditions. Through the early twentieth century, the lag between fall elections, state legislative sessions, and the start of a new Congress—with an entire session of the old Congress filling the intervening 13 months between November elections and the usual beginning of the new Congress in December of the following year—allowed many adjustments before the new Congress met.[2] At other times, perhaps where a collective action problem is more incremental or a solution not readily implemented, an adjustment may be made long after initial signs of a problem are visible. Furthermore, collective action problems are not always solved and certainly are not solved efficiently, so we do not expect a one-to-one correspondence between indicators of the severity of possible collective action problems and party solutions. Recurring collective action problems may not generate a cascade of solutions: a preexisting party innovation may provide a sufficient solution to many future problems. The deck is stacked against finding strong relationships between simple indicators of collective action problems and party innovations.

We pursue two strategies in attempting to identify the strength of the relationships between collective action problems and party innovations. First, we examine innovations in Senate parties in the nineteenth and early twentieth centuries. Because many of these developments have not been adequately documented in previous studies, this discussion provides essential background for what becomes our dependent variable. As part of our discussion, we describe how contemporaries explained these innovations—noting that, in most cases, they emphasized the relatively close strength of the two parties. Second, we examine time series for measures of relative party strength, careerism, party polarization, workload, and the number of freshmen on party innovations during the period between the Civil War, when the modern two-party system stabilized, and the early 1930s, when the basic organizational features of modern Senate parties were in place. While the evidence is limited and a multivariate analysis is ruled out by the nature of the data, relative party strength appears to be the best available explanation for innovation in Senate party organizations in the late nineteenth and early twentieth centuries.

Our dependent variable is major innovation in Senate party organization. We identified innovations by searching newspapers for stories about the selection of leaders, meetings of caucuses, and other important party activities for the period 1829–1946.[3] The resulting archive of news stories was our principal source of qualitative data for identifying developments in Senate organization. To uncover changes in party practice as well as organization, we also studied the *Congressional Globe* and the *Congressional Record,* reviewing Senate floor action for the last week of May in every fourth year between 1858 and 1938 inclusive. Whenever unusual floor activity during that week suggested that examining earlier or later weeks would clarify what was happening on the floor, we did so. We noted which senators offered motions, spoke on behalf of their parties, opened and closed sessions, publicly sought to fix or announce the schedule of the Senate, and performed other regular functions. Also, we identified senators who performed certain ceremonial tasks for the Senate, such as making the routine motions at the start of each Congress. From this qualitative material, we identify three major periods of party innovation in the Senate and observe connections to interparty competition.

In addition, we explore the relationship between the emergence of new party organs and interparty competition, senatorial careerism, the influx of freshmen, polarization, and increases in workload, as suggested by existing accounts. Trends in quantitative indicators for the factors are reported. The small number of cases (Congresses) in this study and the even smaller number of Congresses with innovations precludes useful multivariate estimates, but direct inspection of time series allows reasonable inferences about the importance of the factors.

Party Innovations

The modern position of floor leader emerged slowly, over the last decades of the nineteenth century and the first decades of the twentieth century. Table 11.1 lists the caucus chairmen and elected leaders of the two Senate parties. (No accurate

TABLE 11.1. Senate Caucus Chairmen and Elected Floor Leaders

Republican Caucus Chairmen (1857–1944) and Elected Floor Leaders (1913–2000)

John P. Hale (NH), term ended December 1862
Henry Anthony (RI), December 1862–September 1884
John Sherman (OH), September 1884–December 1885
George Edmunds (VT), December 1885–November 1891
John Sherman (OH), December 1891–March 1897
William Allison (IA), March 1897–August 1908
Eugene Hale (ME), December 1908–March 1911
Shelby Cullom (IL), April 1911–March 1913
Jacob Gallinger (NH), March 1913–August 1918
Henry Cabot Lodge (MA), August 1918–November 1924
Charles Curtis (KS), November 1924–March 1929
James Watson (IN), March 1929–March 1933
Charles McNary (OR), March 1933–February 1944
Wallace White (ME), January 1945–January 1949
Kenneth Wherry (NE), January 1949–November 1951
Styles Bridges (NH), January 1952–January 1953
Robert Taft (OH), January–July 1953
William Knowland (CA), August 1953–January 1959
Everett Dirksen (IL), January 1959–September 1969
Hugh Scott (PA), September 1969–January 1977
Howard Baker (TN), January 1977–January 1985
Robert Dole (KS), January 1985–June 1996
Trent Lott (MS), term began June 1996

Democratic Caucus Chairmen (1873–2000) and Elected Floor Leaders (1899–2000)

John W. Stevenson (KY), term ended March 1877
William Wallace (PA), March 1877–March 1881
George Pendleton (OH), March 1881–March 1885
James Beck (KY), March 1885–May 1890
Arthur P. Gorman (MD), May 1890–April 1898
David Turpie (IN), April 1898–March 1899
James K. Jones (AR), December 1899–March 1903
Arthur P. Gorman (MD), March 1903–June 1906
Joseph Blackburn (KY), June 1906–March 1907
Charles Culberson (TX), December 1907–December 1909
Hernando Money (MS), December 1909–March 1911
Thomas S. Martin (VA), April 1911–March 1913
John Kern (IN), March 1913–March 1917
Thomas S. Martin (VA), March 1917–November 1919
Oscar Underwood (AL), April 1920–February 1923
Joseph Robinson (AR), December 1923–July 1937
Alben Barkley (KY), July 1937–January 1949
Scott Lucas (IL), January 1949–January 1951

(Continued)

TABLE 11.1. Senate Caucus Chairmen and Elected Floor Leaders *(Continued)*

Democratic Caucus Chairmen (1873–2000) and Elected Floor Leaders (1899–2000)

Ernest McFarland (AZ), January 1951–January 1953
Lyndon B. Johnson (TX), January 1953–January 1961
Mike Mansfield (MT), January 1961–January 1977
Robert Byrd (WV), January 1977–January 1989
George Mitchell (ME), January 1989–January 1995
Tom Daschle (SD), term began January 1995

Note: No accurate list of nineteenth- and early twentieth-century caucus leaders has previously existed. The most re-liable sources of information on congressional leadership—records of the Senate, the Senate Historical Office, and the Congressional Research Service; *History, Rules, and Precedents of the Senate Republican Conference, 105th Con-gress* (1997); the 1998 Web site of the Senate majority leader; the *Biographical Directory of the United States Con-gress, 1774–1989* (1989); Riddick's 1971 study; Byrd's (1993) volume of historical statistics and tables—all rely on incomplete and inaccurate lists of caucus leaders. Caucus chairmen and party leaders are not identified in the *Sen-ate Journal,* in the *Congressional Record,* or in older accounts of congressional debates and proceedings.

To compile this list, we searched for contemporary accounts of caucus meetings for each Congress since the 1820s. For the period 1857–1945, entries were based on accounts of Democratic and Republican caucus meetings published in various newspapers, including the *Baltimore Sun,* the *New York Times,* the *Washington Evening Star,* the *Washington Post,* and the *New York Evening Post.* Post-1945 entries were based on Riddick (1971), Byrd (1993), and Vincent et al. (1996).

Caucus minutes themselves do not survive from the nineteenth century. Riddick (1971, 3), who as parliamentar-ian of the Senate gained access to the caucus minutes, reported that surviving Democratic minutes begin in 1903 and surviving Republican minutes begin in 1911. (These minutes have recently been published.) Thus, Riddick (1971) reported two lists of Senate Democratic and Republican leaders for the period since 1893. His first list, which in-cluded pre-1903 Democrats and pre-1911 Republicans, was fragmentary and based on unidentified, "unofficial," sources, while his second list was "determined from the caucus minutes of the two major parties" (6–8). Munk (1974), who compiled a somewhat different list than Riddick, noted, like Riddick, that the "identities, titles, and terms of service" of leaders in the 1890s and 1900s were "difficult to define with certainty" (25). Of his two lists, only Riddick's second list—the list of Democrats since 1903 and of Republicans since 1911—appears to be accurate. Though Riddick placed greater confidence in this second list, various publications have subsequently republished the two Riddick lists as a single, authoritative list of Senate leaders. The *Biographical Directory of the United States Con-gress, 1774–1989* (1989) changed its biographies to reflect the data in Riddick's two lists, while tables in Byrd (1993) and Vincent et al. (1996) directly reproduce those data.

We find that newspaper accounts of caucus meetings correctly reported every event that Riddick cited from the caucus minutes; indeed, newspaper stories sometimes quoted language directly from the caucus proceedings. Given the accuracy of newspaper accounts for the later years in which caucus minutes survive, we regard earlier newspa-per accounts as faithful records of earlier caucus meetings. We have located accounts of the election (and, in most cases, biennial reelection) of each leader in this table as well as accompanying references to the death or retirement of the preceding leader. On the basis of this new and large body of data, we have made few revisions to the entries that appear in Riddick's second list—and these few revisions reflect reports of caucus meetings that appear not to have been available to Riddick. However, we have thoroughly revised and expanded the list of pre-1903 Democratic leaders and pre-1911 Republican leaders. Drawing on an unpublished draft of this chapter (including this table), the Senate Historical Office updated its records, its Web site, and the *Biographical Directory* in early 2000.

list of nineteenth- and early-twentieth-century caucus chairmen has previously existed.) Before the 1890s, neither party elected its leader. Leadership existed, to be sure, but it was leadership that senators assumed because of their ability and their activity, not because of their election to an official party position.

Neither Nelson Aldrich (R-RI) nor Arthur Pue Gorman (D-MD)—the Republican and Democratic senators who, in the 1890s, assumed primary responsibility for setting their parties' agendas, shaping legislative strategies, and building coalitions—was elected specifically to be his party's leader. Gorman served as Democratic caucus chairman, while Aldrich was a member of his party's steering committee; these were significant positions, but Gorman and Aldrich's stature as leaders initially existed independent of these offices. Apart from creating regular steering committees in the early 1890s, the two men exercised their leadership within preexisting institutions—though through his aggressive leadership Gorman transformed expectations for the role of Democratic caucus chairman.

The most significant innovations in Senate party organization occurred in three main stages. Although some isolated changes occurred at other times—such as the creation of an ad hoc Republican steering committee in the 1860s or the popular practice, beginning with Gorman's resignation in the late 1890s, of referring to the Democratic caucus chairman as "party leader"— in only three eras were significant changes clustered together. First, in 1875–79, the Democratic caucus began relying on the two caucus committees that had earlier been established by the Republican caucus—a committee on committees and an ad hoc steering committee—and Democrats established the precedent that Senate officers would change with a shift in party control. Second, in 1892–93, both caucuses created regular steering committees, granting these committees broad powers to set agendas and shape legislation. Third, in 1913–15, the two party caucuses recognized the formal positions of majority and minority leaders and established the positions of whips.

Background: The Antebellum Senate

Partisanship, dormant since the days of the old party battles between Federalists and Republicans, reemerged in the Senate in the 1820s. The divide between the supporters of Andrew Jackson and his opponents, which would soon fracture a harmonious Republican party into Democrats and Whigs, was the foundation of modern Senate party organization. Through the 1820s and early 1830s, Jackson Republicans and anti-Jackson Republicans had shared leadership of the Senate's major committees. That practice ended in December 1833, when the Senate's anti-Jackson majority voted to elect committees by ballot—rather than permitting the president pro tempore, Hugh L. White (Jacksonian, Tenn.), to appoint committees—and then proceeded to elect anti-Jackson senators to the chairman-ships of most major committees. Anti-Jackson ("Coalition") senators, who in the preceding Congress had chaired 2 of the Senate's 12 leading committees, now chaired 8.[4] "The composition of the committees on the subjects of principal anx-iety, the finance, public lands, judiciary, naval affairs, &c.," the *Daily Albany Argus* observed, "exhibit the perfect drill of the Coalition."[5] Establishment of partisan control of the standing committees in 1833 marked a watershed in Sen-ate development.

The *New York Evening Post* sharply criticized the decision to elect rather than appoint committees in 1833. "What the opposition feared was that the minority of the Senate might have too great a strength in the committees," the *Post* stated. "That they could not be appointed by a more moderate and impartial man than Mr. White will be and has been acknowledged, but it was not likely that he would select and pack them to suit the designs of the opposition party."[6] The change in the rules, the *Post* added, was "made from reasons of temporary polit-ical expediency."[7] As one observer noted at the end of the balloting, "The for-mation of the Committees in the Senate shows the relative strength of parties in that body."[8] In 1833, this was a dramatic innovation, protested vigorously by the minority Jackson loyalists. Three years later, however, when Jackson Democrats gained control of the Senate, they followed the precedent and took control of eleven of the twelve leading committees. "The Whigs of that body have been cast into utter darkness," the *Columbian Centinel* reported in December 1836. "Not one of them has been placed at the head of a Committee of any conse-quence."[9] Parties—not impartiality—now organized the Senate.

Party control of the committee system emerged at a time when partisan fac-tions in the Senate were tightly balanced. In December 1833, when the 23rd Congress convened, a majority of senators identified with the anti-Jackson coalition. That majority was new, small, and tenuous. Anti-Jackson senators held twenty-six seats, Jacksonians held twenty, and Nullifiers held two. "I pre-dict that a few months only will pass before the administration will count a de-cided majority in the senate," a correspondent for the *Albany Argus* wrote in December 1833. "The Coalition cannot continue to act together."[10] Two years later, at the start of the 24th Congress in December 1835, the "Coalition" held twenty-four seats, exactly half of the seats in the chamber; Jackson Democrats held twenty-two seats. Between December 1835 and December 1836—with the admission of Arkansas and the resignation of several anti-Jackson senators in states now controlled by Democrats—a slender anti-Jackson plurality be-came a solid Democratic majority. It was in this era, when control of the chamber was fiercely contested and often in doubt, that committee chairman-ships became partisan positions.

But these crucial party decisions were not enforced by party organizations.

Considerations of personal popularity could override partisan loyalties in assigning members to committees and electing chairmen. Senators continued to be ranked on committees without regard to partisanship. And the entire process of committee assignments in the late 1830s and early 1840s was generally delegated to the presiding officer. If they existed at all, party caucuses exerted minimal influence on the organization of Senate committees until the middle 1840s.

Senate caucuses assumed full control of the standing committees in December 1845, when senators rejected a resolution that would have given the power of appointment to Vice President George M. Dallas. At a time when the two parties were again closely balanced, four Democrats voted with the Whig minority to force the election of committees by ballot (Hatfield 1997, 156). That decision, more than any other single event, created the modern party caucus. "The members of the Senate in the majority have been in private meeting the greater part of the day, in their legislative chamber. The business before them was of great importance," the *New York Evening Post* reported on December 8, 1845. "In consequence of the vote on Thursday refusing to suspend the rule which requires the appointment of the standing committees to be made by ballot in open session, it became a matter of consequence and even of necessity with the members of both parties to come to some explicit understanding between themselves, before the balloting came on, in order to ensure unity of action."[11] Senate Democrats and Whigs both met in caucuses that week. Within a few days, establishing another lasting precedent, members of the Senate adopted committee lists by unanimous consent—with senators ranked on these prearranged lists according to party (McConachie 1898, 282–83, 325–26).

Committee assignments, which had been complicated in the 1830s by partisan divisions, themselves laid the groundwork for new partisan institutions. With the caucus now responsible for assembling committee lists, senators increased the coordination capacity of the caucus. In December 1847, the Democratic caucus created its first committee on committees, charging it to recommend committee assignments to the full caucus.[12] Because of its ability to coordinate the caucus's decision and floor strategy, the committee on committees quickly became a powerful organ of the party. The Democratic committee on committees in 1849 recommended that the caucus remove Thomas Hart Benton (D-MO) from the Foreign Relations Committee, which he chaired, questioning his party loyalty and doubting his sympathy for the South.[13] The caucus deposed Benton from the committee chairmanship, though not from the committee. Ten years later, in December 1859, the newly organized Republican caucus established its own committee on committees (McConachie 1898, 341).

Caucus Committees and Senate Officers, 44th–46th Congresses

March 1875	Postwar Democratic Committee on Committees
January 1876	Democratic Ad Hoc Steering Committee
March 1879	Partisan and caucus control of Senate officers

The post–Civil War Senate was a chaotic place. Senators would frequently use the floor to set the Senate's agenda, as senator after senator explained why one bill deserved precedence over another. On January 8, 1868, for example, John Sherman (R-OH), Lyman Trumbull (R-IL), and Oliver Morton (R-IN)—three Republicans—debated the next day's order of business. Sherman took the floor to suggest an agenda for the next day, Trumbull responded by asserting that the next day's business did not need to be decided in advance; Sherman replied that he believed setting the agenda in advance would be helpful; then Morton entered the debate to state that he agreed with Sherman on this matter (*Congressional Record,* January 8, 1868, 384). Such debates occurred regularly.

As the Senate's workload grew, the order of business assumed increasing importance. Senators who could bring discipline to the Senate agenda could ensure that bills that they favored gained priority over other bills. Recognizing the advantages in solving this collective action problem, senators began regularly to discuss the Senate agenda in caucus meetings (Rothman 1966, 17–18, 30). Gathered in each caucus, though, was a large and diverse set of senators, who themselves could rarely reach agreement.

In the middle 1870s, a few years after Republicans had begun relying on ad hoc steering committees to coordinate caucus business, Democrats named their first ad hoc steering committee and established their committee on committees. The creation of these caucus committees coincided with growing Democratic strength. After the 43d Congress (1873–75), when Democrats held just nineteen of seventy-four seats, the Democratic contingent increased rapidly in size—to twenty-eight seats in the 44th Congress (1875–77) and to thirty-five in the 45th Congress (1877–79). In March 1879, when the 46th Congress convened, Democrats held their first Senate majority since the outbreak of the Civil War. The resurgence of the Democratic party altered the partisan balance in the Senate and appears to have motivated party innovations.

In January 1876, Senate Democrats named their first ad hoc steering committee. Struggling to articulate a position on states' rights when white Democrats were "redeeming" southern governments, Democratic senators charged the ad hoc committee with recommending a response to Republican demands for federal intervention. Most members of the caucus appear to have believed that adopting a militant, pro-Redemption position on the Senate floor—the approach favored by House Democrats—would jeopardize their party's prospects for picking up additional seats in the North. Creating the ad hoc committee was "an easy way of getting rid of the troublesome subject," the *New York Times* suggested. "A prominent Democratic Senator said to-day that they were not going to have any of the foolishness in the Senate that had been seen in the House, and would not give an opportunity for the opposition to lead off any of their indiscreet members into unguarded expressions upon which political capital could be manufactured."[14] Plainly, the electoral consequences of a divisive issue were involved in this party move; at the same caucus meeting, Democrats discussed plans to name members to a bicameral campaign committee. In their decision to create the Ad Hoc Steering Committee, Democrats were balancing an important policy goal of many members against the collective electoral interests of the party.

One year earlier, the caucus had reestablished its committee on committees— which had not existed since the secession crisis—and asked the committee to meet with its Republican counterpart. "The object was to insist that in view of the increased representation of the democracy in the Senate they should be entitled to additional representation on important committees," the *Washington Star* explained in March 1875.[15] In reporting the organization of this new committee, the *New York Times* also emphasized the viability of the Senate Democratic party. "The Democrats think their increased membership entitles them to more places on the committees," the *Times* stated, and they had instructed their caucus committee "to submit a claim to that effect to the majority."[16]

In 1879, when Democrats finally gained control of the Senate for the first time in two decades, they established a new precedent by replacing the Senate's secretary, clerk, and other officers, arguing that these officers and their patronage properly belonged to the majority party. Henry Anthony (R-RI), chairman of the Republican caucus, objected to the action. "This was the first time in the history of the Senate that such sweeping changes had been proposed," he argued. "Heretofore the principal offices of the Senate had been exempt from the reprisals of victorious partisans, and changes in the political character of the membership of the body wrought no material changes in its offices."[17] Four years later, when Republicans were again a majority, they followed the Democratic example.

Even as Democrats extended the partisan principle to the Senate officers, they retained Isaac Bassett, the assistant doorkeeper and a Republican, in his office (*Congressional Record,* April 24, 1879, 799–800; February 11, 1896, 1588). That decision, and the accompanying decision to create a Democratic post of "acting assistant doorkeeper," established two Senate officers responsible to and chosen by one of the two Senate parties. In 1896, Sherman and Gorman, chairmen of the Republican and Democratic caucuses, offered resolutions on the floor of the Senate to transform these two appointed positions, nominally chosen since 1879 by the sergeant-at-arms, into elected positions (*Congressional Record,* February 11, 1896, 1588). The Senate renamed these two "assistant doorkeeper" positions in June 1929 and began referring to these officers as "party secretaries" (*Congressional Record,* June 18, 1929, 3058).

Steering Committees, 52d–53d Congresses

December 1892   Regular Republican Steering Committee
December 1892   Regular Democratic Steering Committee

Taken together, the innovations of the middle and late 1870s reflected a choice by the Democratic caucus to establish new party-based institutions to structure Senate business. But steering committees remained ad hoc, irregular committees until the 1890s, created sporadically by caucuses to address immediate problems. Newspaper reports do not support Rothman's (1966, 30, 48) assertion that steering committees had begun to be appointed on a regular basis in the middle 1880s. Sometimes, as in May and June 1886 or in July and September 1890, a caucus would attempt to agree on an agenda without creating an ad hoc steering committee, but consensus remained elusive.[18] When the Republican caucus failed, after two separate meetings, to settle the order of business in February 1887, they finally decided to appoint another ad hoc steering committee. "Republican Senators made two more attempts to-day to agree in caucus upon what they should do for the rest of the session, and with the usual result—a wrangle and a flat failure," the *New York Times* reported. "The Senators talked for a long time, but the longer they talked the further away they drifted from an agreement, and so they finally gave it up and went home to dinner. A committee will try to arrange an order of business for the present month to be submitted to the caucus, and the Senators will probably meet for another fruitless discussion some time next week."[19]

Until the early 1890s, these ad hoc committees could offer little leadership to the caucus or the chamber: they were temporary and they were not easily controlled by an ambitious senator. Caucus chairmen in this era rarely sat on the committees themselves and frequently changed the composition of the ad hoc committees (Rothman 1966, 48–49). Their very legitimacy was often questioned by members of the other caucus and nearly as often by dissident members of the steering committee's own caucus. As late as December 1892, Republican senators criticized a Democratic steering committee, describing its activities as "pernicious."[20]

But the criticism was meant to deflect attention from the Republican caucus's own decision to establish a more regular steering committee. In the last weeks of 1892, as Republicans realized that they were on the verge of losing control of the Senate, they created a steering committee to assist the party in its state-by-state battle to save Senate seats and to organize the Senate's legislative agenda for maximum partisan advantage. Senate Republicans met "to devise a scheme to aid Western Republicans in their efforts to capture the Legislatures of several States," the *New York Times* reported. "They will not give up their control of the Senate without a determined fight."[21] Sherman, Republican caucus chairman, appointed five members to the new steering committee that December.[22]

The steering committee was still in existence a month later, exercising the power to convene meetings of the Republican caucus "to arrange the plan of legislation for the remainder of the session."[23] After the winter of 1892–93, the Republican steering committee was appointed with regularity, and it enjoyed great authority in setting the caucus's agenda. When William Allison (R-IA) convened a meeting of the Steering Committee in January 1895, the *New York Times* explained that "the whole situation so far as the Senate is concerned will be discussed, and a programme of action on the part of the minority will be considered."[24]

The Democratic caucus, which had also anticipated a battle for control of Congress, created its own steering committee in December 1892. This was the Steering Committee condemned—and emulated—by Republicans. "The next Senate will represent the will of the people and not the questionable and designing methods of those politicians who have in the past made a specialty of throttling public opinion," the partisan *Washington Post* stated that month. "There has been organized a Senatorial committee, headed by Hon. Arthur Pue Gorman, of Maryland. Speaking for the Democracy, Senator Gorman gives every assurance that the rights of his party will be vigorously contended for, and that the Republican plot to reverse the will of the people will surely be thwarted."[25]

In March 1893, at the start of the next Congress, Democratic senators authorized Gorman to appoint "a committee of seven to formulate a plan of reorganization" for the Senate.[26] The committee, which assumed the functions of a committee on committees, appears to have remained in existence throughout the life of the Congress as an ongoing steering committee. Once the functions of a steering committee were merged with those of a committee on committees, the Democratic caucus continued to rely on this single caucus committee, called the Democratic steering committee, after they returned to the minority in 1895. The practice continued into future decades. The Democratic caucus chairman, who had routinely served as chairman of his caucus's committee on committees (Rothman 1966, 36, 63; Haynes 1938, 483), chaired this omnibus steering committee.[27] Republicans, in contrast, maintained a committee on committees distinct from their steering committee.

Both the Democratic and Republican steering committees emerged in the winter of 1892–93, at a time when party control was fiercely contested. Significantly, both caucuses charged their respective committees not only to manage their party's legislative program but to intervene in state-level elections for senators. These regular steering committees were the products of a particular crisis, established to balance electoral needs with legislative needs. Once created, though, steering committees persisted even after the immediate crisis had passed.

By the middle 1890s, party leaders like Aldrich and Gorman were using steering committees to direct party policy and strategy. Committee memberships stabilized, and the steering committees assumed a strong role in managing the Senate's business. Gorman chaired the Democratic steering committee in the 1890s, and Aldrich, Allison, and their closest allies gained firm control of the Republican steering committee through the 1890s and 1900s (Rothman 1966, 49).[28] In 1907, when the Democratic caucus considered electing the steering committee rather than authorizing Charles Culberson (D-TX) to appoint its members, the *Washington Star* noted that the steering committee constituted the foundation of party leadership. There is no justification for "making Mr. Culberson a nonentity as to the party's committee dispositions and steering program," the *Star* argued. "In the very nature of things he should have a large voice in choosing his lieutenants and directing the courses to be taken. Otherwise he might be, probably would be, reduced to the terms of a mere executor."[29]

Allison and Aldrich's reliance on the Republican steering committee is noteworthy. Rather than calling more caucus meetings or assuming floor leadership responsibilities himself, Allison created a permanent party committee. Allison named the committee himself, and he, Aldrich, and their allies used the committee to manage the Senate business. "The Republican steering committee consists of nine members," the *New York Times* noted in March 1905, "and the five bosses control the steering committee."[30] Agenda-setting power was thus centralized in the steering committee, but it remained far less centralized than it had become in the speakership of the House or would yet become in the modern Senate. His control of the steering committee helped legitimate Aldrich's unelected leadership in the 1890s and 1900s. "Arranging the legislative schedule in detail week by week, the committee extended the party leaders' authority unimpaired from the caucus to the chamber," Rothman (1966) argues. "Senators knew that they had to consult the committee before attempting to raise even minor matters" (58–59). When the new Senate office building was dedicated in 1909, no one wondered why the Caucus Room was the structure's grandest space.

Floor Leaders and Whips, 63d–64th Congresses

March 1913	Designated majority leader
March 1913	Designated Republican minority leader
May 1913	Democratic whip
December 1915	Republican whip

Until the late nineteenth century, the caucus chairmanship was a largely ceremonial position. According to Rothman (1966, 16), Anthony named the members of the Republican committee on committees but did not sit on the committee himself or attempt to influence the committee in any way. Sherman was unable even to secure his own committee preferences. In March 1885, on the day that new committee assignments were announced, Sherman rose on the floor of the Senate to declare—"in tones," according to the *New York Times,* "in which anger was scarcely suppressed"[31]—that he refused to accept reappointment to the Finance Committee. The *Times* and the *Washington Post* reported that Sherman's anger resulted both from the ideological composition of the committee and the committee on committees' decision not to offer him the chairmanship. Sherman's position as chairman of his party's caucus appears to have mattered little in the battle to shape committees. "Neither the caucus nor the caucus committee," the *Post* stated, "seems to have seen its way clear to make the change desired by the Senator from Ohio."[32]

Though the caucus chairmanship itself carried no unusual responsibility for managing the Senate's business, various senators in the 1890s were beginning to assume roles as informal party leaders. The most important of these leaders were Gorman and Aldrich, who not only worked to discipline their own parties but cooperated together to expedite the Senate's business. Aldrich and Gorman did their work quietly. They oversaw the business of their respective steering committees, and they regularly took senators aside for discussions on the floor, in committee rooms, and in cloakrooms. Gorman did not "manifest any strong qualities as a floor leader," the *New York Times* noted in his 1906 obituary. "His success was entirely in the skillful arrangement of deals."[33] Aldrich, whose mastery of financial and tariff legislation laid the groundwork for his leadership, helped manage the Senate's affairs for more than two decades. "In all matters political or parliamentary Aldrich is easily the leader of the Republicans in the Senate," the *Baltimore Sun* observed in 1901. "He knows when to 'bluff,' when to bully, when to flatter and when to anger. The man who is lacking in alertness he bluffs, the timid man he bullies, the vain man he flatters and the man whose judgment is overturned when angry he torments and taunts until he loses his temper and is put at fault."[34] As Thompson (1906) argued five years later, "Aldrich is a chess player with men" (32).

The precedents established by Aldrich and Gorman proved enduring. Gorman left the Senate in 1899, one year after resigning the Democratic caucus chairmanship, because of his opposition to the Spanish-American War. Since he, unlike Aldrich, had emerged as an active party manager while holding his caucus's chairmanship, Senate observers not only commented on the need for a new Democratic leader but expected the new Democratic caucus chairman to fill that role. Newspaper after newspaper devoted lengthy stories to Gorman's decision to resign as caucus chairman and to speculation over his successor. These stories, in 1898 and 1899, represented the first news accounts to regard the caucus chairman as the elected leader of one of the Senate parties.[35] As the *Washington Post* noted in 1899, "The Democrats recognized the leadership of Senator Jones, of Arkansas, by making him their caucus chairman."[36] After 1899, the Democratic caucus chairman was regularly described as the "minority leader" of the Senate; by the middle 1900s, observers began referring to him as a "floor leader." Republicans continued to regard the roles of party leader and caucus chairman as entirely distinct. They did not regard their caucus chairman as their presumptive party leader.

With the transformation of the Democratic caucus chairman into the party's Senate leader, the old norm of unanimous, nonconflictual elections for caucus chairman—long observed by both parties—began to erode in the Democratic caucus. The first open contest for Democratic leader occurred in 1911. When John Kern (D-IN) was elected Democratic caucus chairman in 1913, he was chosen by a divided caucus. "In the interest of party harmony," the incumbent caucus chairman, Thomas S. Martin (D-VA), withdrew his name as a candidate for reelection, ensuring Kern's unanimous election.[37] Describing the election, the *New York Times* noted matter-of-factly that "this makes Mr. Kern the Democratic floor leader in the Senate."[38] Kern, the first Democratic leader since 1895 to preside over a majority party, was the first Senate leader consistently referred to as "majority leader."

Kern's success at managing the floor and controlling the party's agenda strengthened preexisting expectations that the Democratic caucus chairman should be his party's leader. Under Kern's leadership, the Senate frequently recessed at the end of the day rather than adjourn while a major bill was before the Senate. The maneuver saved time and limited senators to two speeches during the unadjourned legislative day. To keep routine legislation flowing through the Senate while a major bill was under consideration, Kern called up legislation on the Calendar at a convenient time—typically late in the day when senators' interest in the major bill waned, as modern Senate floor leaders do. Kern also asked for frequent quorum calls, in part because Democratic absenteeism was a serious problem (Oleszek 1991, 31–32). On roll call votes, Kern instituted a practice of noting which of his colleagues were unavoidably absent on Senate business, perhaps to protect the reputations of his colleagues but also to increase pressure on absent colleagues who had no good excuse to be missing. Still, Kern was often not visible on the floor, especially in his second Congress as majority leader.

In the wake of the retirements of Aldrich and Eugene Hale (R-ME) in 1911 and the loss of majority status in 1913, Republicans could no longer ignore the Democratic example. Jacob Gallinger (R-NH), elected caucus chairman in 1913, was regularly described not only as Republican caucus chairman but as the party's "floor leader."[39] And the practice continued after Gallinger's death. "Senator Henry Cabot Lodge of Massachusetts today was elected chairman of the republican conference of the Senate without opposition," the *Washington Star* reported in 1918. "This means that Senator Lodge is the republican leader of the Senate."[40] By 1921, when the *Times* reported that Lodge had been "re-elected floor leader,"[41] the designation was firmly established. Through the middle 1940s—when Republicans formally created the separate positions of conference chairman and floor leader—their conference chairman assumed full responsibility for floor leadership.[42]

The development of caucus chairmen into floor leaders can be measured in the number of motions to adjourn or recess offered by each leader. In the 59th Congress (1905–7), Allison, the Republican caucus chairman, offered a total of 15 such motions (*Congressional Record* index), indicating the very limited personal direction he provided in floor sessions. By contrast, Kern offered 172 and Lodge offered 92 in their first full Congresses as majority leader. Also in 1913, the modern practice originated of having the majority and minority caucus chairmen serve as the committee to notify the president that the Senate had convened.

The drilling-ground of party leadership in the Senate, the caucus reached its apogee under Kern. As Kern and Gallinger established their roles as floor leaders, they worked closely with their caucuses. Kern, as majority leader, established agendas directly in caucus, rather than working through his steering committee (Oleszek 1991, 28–30). And Gallinger, who assumed leadership of a minority party, appears not even to have appointed a Republican steering committee.[43] When Republicans regained their majority in 1919, Lodge "resuscitated" the steering committee but used it ineffectively (Widenor 1991, 53–54). The personal power of floor leaders in the 1910s made the collective management of steering committees increasingly anachronistic (Haynes 1938, 484–86). In later years, when Democratic and Republican leaders expanded their role on the floor and assumed greater personal responsibility, they consulted less often with their caucuses. Having created modern party leadership in the Senate, the steering committee and the caucus dwindled in significance as managers of the Senate's business.

The caucus's principal importance in the modern Senate was reduced to the task of electing the party's leaders at the start of a Congress. In the nineteenth century, the Republican and Democratic caucuses had elected only chairmen and secretaries.[44] Democrats created a new office, the whip, in May 1913.[45] The suggestion to establish the whip was made in the midst of a caucus meeting as Democrats expressed their concern about the number of members who were planning to travel out of town. "Realizing how slender is their majority the democrats were practically unanimous in the demand that no chances be taken," the *Star* reported, and they quickly embraced the plan to choose a party whip "when plans were discussed for keeping members in line and getting them to the Senate when important votes were to be taken."[46] The Republicans established the position of whip in December 1915, at the start of the 64th Congress (Oleszek 1971, 959).[47]

Floor leaders and whips emerged at a time when Democratic senators controlled the chamber for the first time in nearly twenty years—and controlled it with few votes to spare. When Democrats assumed control of the 63d Congress (1913–15), they held fifty-one of ninety-six seats. Not since the 1890s had a Senate majority been so small. "The next Congress will show a top-heavy democratic majority in the House, but a very light one in the Senate," the *Washington Evening Star* commented in November 1912. "Whatever passes the Senate must poll every democratic vote in the chamber."[48] One month later, in another editorial, the *Star* anticipated the institutional innovations that would quickly distinguish the 63d Congress—noting that the close balance between the two parties in the upcoming Congress made party leadership an urgent problem. "The democrats are confronted by two things, both worthy of consideration: (1) Their majority will be uncomfortably slender, and (2) the opposition will be ably led," the *Star* noted. "If, therefore, they fail to provide for their best leadership, either in committee work, or in the general debate in the chamber, they will be heavily handicapped."[49]

The creation of designated floor leadership positions in the middle 1910s set the stage for the modern pattern of active management. As Republican whip under Lodge, Charles Curtis (R-KS) actively managed the routine business of the Senate. After Lodge's death in 1924, Curtis continued to develop his role as floor manager in his new position as majority leader. Curtis was the first Republican leader since the Civil War who was chosen without regard to seniority. He and Joseph Robinson (D-AR), who became Democratic leader in 1923, were also the first full-time managers of the Senate floor. Even more than Kern or Lodge, Curtis handled the routine management duties personally—managing the call of the Calendar, noting the absence of a quorum, recessing or adjourning the Senate. Robinson, as minority leader in the 1920s and majority leader in the 1930s, was also a vigorous presence in the Senate chamber. He and Charles McNary (R-OR), who became Republican leader in 1933, worked closely together, concentrating the powers of floor management in their own hands and leaving little responsibility to their caucuses, steering committees, and whips (Bacon 1991; Neal 1991). In abandoning the transitional style of behind-the-scenes management that characterized the Senate from the 1890s through the early 1920s, Senate parties embraced a style of personal management that clarified responsibility within the party for floor strategies and spokesmanship.

A Quantitative Overview

We have identified three periods of innovation in party organization, with the timing of specific developments somewhat different for the two parties. Contemporary accounts support our hypothesis that interparty competition played a role in motivating the innovations. But we noted at the start that several other explanations have been offered: senatorial careerism, the influx of freshmen, polarization, and increases in workload. The question remaining is whether the effect of interparty competition can be confirmed with more systematic quantitative evidence. The appropriate approach would be to estimate the contribution of each factor in a multivariate model. Unfortunately, the small number of Congresses included in the scope of this study undermines the value of multivariate estimates. Instead, we report time series for indicators of the factors and, by inspection, rule out several possibilities.

Our measures are as follows:

1. Interparty competition is measured by a variable called *relative party strength.* Party strength reflects a party's size and cohesiveness. For each Congress, party size is expressed as a percentage of all senators; cohesiveness is the Rice index of cohesion (Binder 1997). Relative party strength is the absolute difference in the strength of the two parties.

2. *Party polarization* is measured as the difference in means between the parties on senators' first-dimension D-NOMINATE scores (Poole and Rosenthal 1997).

3. We measure careerism by determining the Congresses in which each senator was a member of the Senate and calculating, for each Congress, the mean number of Congresses of previous Senate service; we call this variable *mean service.*

4. A related measure is the *number of freshmen,* defined as the number of members serving in their first Congress. Congresses of service for each senator are identified by using the corrected ICPSR identification codes for individual senators, as included in the NOMINATE data sets made available by Keith Poole (Poole and Rosenthal 1997).

5. Senate *workload* is measured on the principal component shared by several

FIGURE 11.1. Party Innovations (Marked with Vertical Lines) and Trends in Relative Party Strength, Party Sizes, Number of Freshmen, Mean Years of Service, and Workload (in Standardized Scores)

a. Party Polarization and Difference in Party Strength

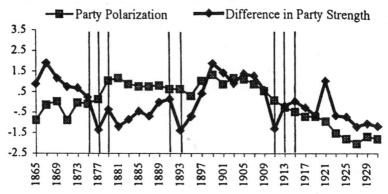

b. Number of Freshmen and Mean Years of Service

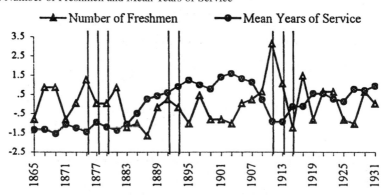

c. Workload and Difference in Party Strength

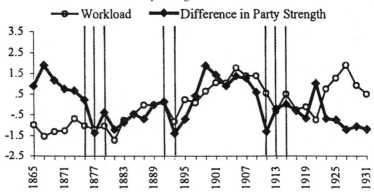

indicators of workload: number of Senate public bills introduced, number of Senate roll call votes, number of Senate bills passed, number of laws enacted, and number of days in session. (Binder 1997 uses a similar approach.)

In Figures 11.1a–c we show scores for each of these variables, standardizing the scores to facilitate comparisons. Figure 11.1a shows that there is little relationship between party polarization and innovations. Figure 11.1b shows that the number of freshmen and the mean years of service are sometimes relatively low and sometimes relatively high in Congresses with party innovations. Figure 11.1c demonstrates that workload is not related to party innovations—it is not distinctively high or low, or rising or falling, at times of party innovations. As Figures 1a and 1c show, small differences in party strength (when the parties are of nearly equal strength) appear to be related to the timing of party innovations. This relationship is far from perfect. Still, innovations do appear when small differences, or closing differences, in party strength are present.

Discussion

Party innovations are the product of collective action problems, which, we tentatively argue, are especially acute in periods of near-parity in party strength. When elections resulted in evenly matched Senate parties, party innovation often took place; rarely did significant party innovations occur at other times. This pattern of party innovation has little to do with party polarization, which reached a peak late in the 1890s and early 1900s. Careerism, too, does not seem to be related to innovations, although our period gives us a limited perspective on the wider range of careerism that would be visible if the early nineteenth century was taken into account. Variation in workload does not appear to underpin party innovation.

Although our inferences must be tentative, the most viable inference is that Senate majority parties innovate at moments of weakness. This observation leads us to be suspicious of explanations that have sometimes been said to underlie party development. The Cooper-Brady argument that party polarization drives party centralization, developed as a model of House leadership, does not transfer to the development of Senate party institutions. Careerism, connected by Rothman to the emergence of strong state parties and centralization, does not seem to be timed with party innovation either. And the more generic organizational argument that workload generates a need for coordination mechanisms does not appear to account for the timing of party innovations during this period.

The close connection between centralization within the House majority party and the centralization of the policy-making process in that chamber is not duplicated in the Senate. A Senate majority party, whatever its internal cohesiveness and centralization, usually cannot overcome minority party obstruction to pro-posals that redistribute parliamentary advantages. If sufficiently cohesive, it may rely on central party leaders to set party strategy, but it generally does not for-mally empower the central leaders to do things that they could not otherwise do. In fact, most important developments in Senate party organization and leader-ship structure occurred at times other than peak intraparty cohesiveness, inter-party polarization, and one-party numerical dominance. Senate parties elaborated party organization or created new leadership posts in periods of ma-jority weakness, internal division, and close partisan divisions within the cham-ber. These innovations generally occurred off the floor and beyond the rules, within the extralegal institution of the party caucus.

Institutional context is critical to the process of legislative party develop-ment. The preservation of individual and minority rights on the Senate floor has had significant implications for party development. First, the difficulty of pass-ing party proposals on the floor greatly limits the potential policy value of a highly centralized leadership apparatus within a Senate party. And, second, most procedural strategies must be pursued by informal means and, to the extent they are transferred to the floor, with the acquiescence of a substantial number of mi-nority-party members. Partisan considerations, in short, have been crucial to the development of the Senate.

Notes

We are grateful to Paul Beatton, Jason Kassel, Brian Roraff, and Dan Stevens for their su-perb research assistance and to Sarah Binder and Eric Lawrence for the use of data they have collected for other projects. We are also grateful to Richard Baker, Jo Anne Mc-Cormick Quatannens, Donald Ritchie, and Wendy Wolff, in the Senate Historical Office, and Stanley Bach, in the Congressional Research Service. Gamm thanks the Woodrow Wilson Center for its support. Smith thanks the Dirksen Congressional Center for its support.

1. This perspective stands in sharp contrast to Brady and Epstein's (1997) assertion that the 1910s were a period "in which the House and Senate became more committee- and less party-oriented and leadership style changed from command to bargaining" (33).

2. Although senators often met for a special session in March, this session was gener-ally brief.

3. As part of that search, we consulted handwritten, paper indexes to the *Washington Star* (located in Washington's Martin Luther King, Jr., Public Library) and the *Balti-more Sun* (located in Baltimore's Enoch Pratt Public Library) as well as the pub-lished indexes to the *New York Times*. Since the indexes did not cover the entire period—the *Sun* index began in 1891, the *Star* index began in 1906 (though an ac-companying, fragmentary index includes some entries in 1889), and the quality of

the *New York Times* index varied enormously over this period—we also read accounts of the opening weeks of each new session of Congress in the three indexed newspapers as well as in the *Washington Post,* the *New York Evening Post,* the *New York Herald,* the *Boston Daily Advertiser,* the *Columbian Centinel,* the *Albany Argus,* and the *Albany Evening Journal.*

4. The Senate established its standing committee system in 1816, when it created eleven committees (Gamm and Shepsle 1989, 53–54). One of the original committees, Commerce and Manufactures, was divided into two committees in 1825. These are the twelve committees that we examine.

5. *Daily Albany Argus,* December 21, 1833, 2.

6. *New York Evening Post,* December 12, 1833, 2.

7. Ibid.

8. *Columbian Centinel,* December 28, 1833, 1.

9. *Columbian Centinel,* December 21, 1836, 1.

10. *Daily Albany Argus,* December 21, 1833, 2.

11. *New York Evening Post,* December 8, 1845, 2.

12. "From the South," *New York Evening Post,* December 11, 1847, 3.

13. *New York Herald,* December 20, 1849, 3. See also *New York Evening Post,* December 19, 1849, 3.

14. "Democratic Senators in Caucus," *New York Times,* January 28, 1876, 1. See also "Congressional Topics," *New York Times,* January 27, 1876, 1.

15. "Senate Caucuses," *Washington Star,* March 6, 1875, 1. See also "The Democratic Caucus," *New York Times,* March 7, 1875, 1; "Democratic Senators in Caucus," 1.

16. "The Democratic Caucus," 1.

17. "The Senate Reorganized," *New York Times,* March 25, 1879.

18. "Quarreling in Caucus," *New York Times,* May 28, 1886; "Another Republican Caucus with Meagre Results," *New York Times,* June 2, 1886; *New York Times,* July 29, 1890, 1; *New York Times,* September 12, 1890, 1.

19. "A Fruitful Caucus," *New York Times,* February 6, 1887.

20. "Doubtful Senate Seats," *New York Times,* December 16, 1892.

21. "They Want a 'Steering Committee,'" *New York Times,* December 15, 1892, 5; "Doubtful Senate Seats."

22. "The Republican 'Steerers,'" *New York Times,* December 21, 1892, 5.

23. "Republicans in Caucus," *New York Times,* January 17, 1893, 2.

24. "To Agree upon a Policy," *New York Times,* January 7, 1895, 1.

25. "The Senate Is Safe," *Washington Post,* December 19, 1892, 4.

26. "Democrats in Caucus," *New York Times,* March 8, 1893.

27. Ibid.; "Closure in the Senate," *New York Times,* December 5, 1894; "The Next Senate," *Baltimore Sun,* March 8, 1895; "The Senate Committees," *New York Times,* March 22, 1897; "Posts for Minority," *Baltimore Sun,* December 15, 1901; "Some Opposition to Gorman," *Baltimore Sun,* March 6, 1903; "Democratic Caucus," *Washington Star,* March 6, 1903; "Gorman Still Leader," *Baltimore Sun,* December 9, 1905.

28. "To Agree upon a Policy"; "Preparing to Adjourn1.

29. "The Minority in Congress," *Washington Star,* December 4, 1907.

30.. "'The Big Five' Who Run the U.S. Senate," *New York Times,* March 19, 1905.

31. "Mr. Sherman Declines to Serve," *New York Times,* March 14, 1885.

32. "The Republican Senate Caucus," *Washington Post,* March 12, 1885.

33. "Gorman Dies Suddenly; Was Seemingly Better," *New York Times,* June 5, 1906.

34. "Aldrich as a Leader," *Baltimore Sun,* December 29, 1901.

35. "Mr. Gorman Resigns," *Baltimore Sun,* April 30, 1898; "Turpie Succeeds Gorman," *New York Times,* April 30, 1898; "Democratic Senators Caucus," *Washington Star,* April 30, 1898; "Mr. Gorman Retires," *Washington Post,* April 30, 1898; "Why Mr. Gorman Was Not Chosen," *Baltimore Sun,* May 4, 1898; "Will Succeed Mr. Gorman," *Baltimore Sun,* February 2, 1899.

36. "Both Parties in Caucus," *Washington Post,* December 6, 1899.

37. "Martin Drops Out," *Washington Star,* February 28, 1913.

38. "Radicals Control Senate," *New York Times,* March 6, 1913.

39. Ibid.; "Dean of Senators, J. H. Gallinger, Dies," *New York Times,* August 18, 1918.

40. "Republicans Name Lodge as Leader," *Washington Star,* August 24, 1918.

41. "Re-Elect Senate Leaders," *New York Times,* March 6, 1921.

42. "Senate Republicans Pick Temporary Slate of Leaders," *Washington Star,* January 18, 1944; "GOP Senators Vest Leadership in Three Men," *Washington Star,* March 15, 1944; "Republicans in Senate Decide to Continue 3-Man Leadership," *Washington Star,* December 24, 1944.

43. "Gallinger Heads Party," *Washington Star,* March 5, 1913.

44. See, for example, "Senatorial Caucuses," *Washington Star,* March 5, 1885; "Notes from Washington," *New York Times,* March 6, 1885; *New York Times,* December 4, 1887, 2; *Washington Post,* December 4, 1887, 2; "A Democratic Caucus," *Washington Star,* March 7, 1889; "First Day in Congress," *New York Times,* December 8, 1891; *New York Times,* December 9, 1891, 2; "Democrats in Caucus," *New York Times,* March 8, 1893; "Republican Senate Caucus," *New York Times,* December 9, 1896; "The Senate Organization," *New York Times,* March 7, 1897; "Only Talk in Caucus," *Washington Post,* March 7, 1897; "Both Parties in Caucus," *Washington Post,* December 6, 1899; "Democratic Caucus," *Washington Star,* March 6, 1903; "Republican Senators Hold a Brief Caucus," *Washington Post,* December 6, 1905; "Senate Dozen Win," *Washington Post,* April 5, 1911; "Gallinger Heads Party," *Washington Star,* March 5, 1913.

45. "Senator J. Ham. Lewis Elected Party Whip," *Washington Star,* May 28, 1913.

46. Ibid.

47. "Senate Republicans Perfect Organization," *Washington Star,* December 6, 1915.

48. "Mr. Gorman and Mr. Martin," *Washington Star,* November 12, 1912.

49. "The Senate Democrats," *Washington Star,* December 20, 1912.

*The Senate as a
Policymaking Institution*

· 12 ·

The "60-Vote Senate": Strategies, Process, and Outcomes

Barbara Sinclair

Whether from Jimmy Stewart's *Mr. Smith Goes to Washington,* the great civil rights battles of the 1960s, or yesterday evening's news, Americans, if they know anything about the Senate, know of the filibuster. Both glorified and reviled, the Senate filibuster has been the subject of much commentary, written and oral, and some excellent analyses have recently appeared (Binder and Smith 1997). Yet there is still much that we do not know about the impact on the legislative process and on legislative outcomes of extended debate and related Senate floor rules.

The Senate has always operated under rules that vest enormous power in each individual senator. In holding the floor and in proposing amendments, senators face fewer constraints than the members of any other legislature in the world. Yet senators have not always exploited the possibilities inherent in the rules to the same extent and in the same way. In this chapter, I explore when and how senators use their prerogatives under Senate rules and how that has changed in recent decades; I then examine the effect of the strategic use of the Senate's rules on the legislative process in the chamber and on legislative outcomes.

Senate Rules and Senate Exceptionalism

The claim that the Senate is a unique legislative chamber rests on the Senate's highly permissive rules concerning floor debate and amending activity. Senators can hold the floor as long as they like so long as cloture is not invoked, a procedure that requires a supermajority. Senators can offer as many amendments as they wish to almost any bill, and usually those amendments need not even be germane.

241

The best evidence indicates that these rules have their origins not in the designs of the Framers or the considered judgment of the Senate giants of the nineteenth century but in decisions not made (Binder 1997; Binder and Smith 1997). With its small membership and workload, the early Senate had no need for formal restrictions on debate to get its work done. Early senators appear to have assumed that after due floor consideration a final vote would be taken and that a simple majority would decide the outcome, and this was, in fact, what occurred (Binder and Smith 1997, 50–51). The lack of restrictions in rules became a problem when the political and institutional context changed, but by that time inherited rules usually made it possible for a minority of senators with a vested interest in the permissive rules to block change.

The Senate has nevertheless several times altered its debate rules, and the circumstances of its doing so are illuminating. The most important change came in 1917 when the Senate adopted Rule 22, which, for the first time, provided for a way to cut off debate over the objections of some senators. When "a small group of willful men" blocked President Wilson's proposal to arm American merchant ships in 1917, Wilson managed to focus intense public attention on the Senate's debate rules, and public opinion forced the body to agree to a procedure for cutting off debate. Even so, the cloture procedure instituted was cumbersome. Sixteen senators had to file a petition requesting a vote to end debate on the matter at issue; two days after the filing, a vote would be taken, and if two-thirds of those present and voting supported the cloture motion, debate would be limited to one hour per senator.

The rule has been changed several times since. Most importantly, in 1975 the threshold for cutting off debate on legislation was reduced to three-fifths of the total membership (usually sixty), though stopping debate on a proposal to change Senate rules still requires a two-thirds vote.

The Senate has sometimes agreed to statutory debate and amendment germaneness limitations. Most significantly, the Budget Act of 1974, which instituted the modern budget process, limits debate and amendments to budget resolutions and reconciliation bills. Shielding these budget measures from possible filibusters and nongermane amendments occasioned little controversy in the Senate (see Binder and Smith 1997, 192–93).

Permissive Rules and Activist Behavior

Although still permissive by most standards, Senate rules have actually been tightened somewhat over time. Yet as Table 12.1 shows, the use of extended debate and of cloture has increased enormously over the post–World War II period. To be sure, the data must be regarded with some caution (see Beth 1995; also Sinclair 1997, 47–49). When lengthy debate becomes a filibuster is, in part, a

TABLE 12.1. The Increase in Filibusters and Cloture Votes, 1951–94

Years	Congresses	Filibusters per Congress	Cloture Votes per Congress	Successful Cloture Votes per Congress
1951–60	82–86th	1.0	.4	0
1961–70	87–91st	4.6	5.2	.8
1971–80	92–96th	11.2	22.4	8.6
1981–86	97–99th	16.7	23.0	10.0
1987–92	100–102nd	26.7	39.0	15.3
1993–94	103th	30	42	14
1995–96	104th	25	50	9
1997–98	105th	29	53	18

Sources: Cloture votes from "A Look at the Senate Filibuster," DSG Special Report, June 13, 1994, No. 103-28, Appendix B (compiled by Congressional Research Service).
Successful cloture votes from Ornstein, Mann, and Malbin (1994, 16.2).
Data for 103rd Congress from Richard S. Beth, "Cloture in the Senate, 103rd Congress," memorandum, Congressional Research Service, June 23, 1995.
Data for the 104th and 105th Congresses from the Congressional Quarterly Almanacs (1995–98).

matter of judgment. Furthermore, as I show below, filibusters have changed their form in recent years, and threats to filibuster have become much more frequent than actual talkfests on the floor. As a consequence, cloture is sometimes sought before any overt evidence of a filibuster manifests itself on the floor. Nevertheless, experts and participants agree that the frequency of obstructionism has increased, as Table 12.1 indicates.[1] In the 1950s, filibusters were rare; they increased during the 1960 and again during the 1970s. By the late 1980s and the 1990s, they had become routine, occurring at a rate of more then one a month—considerably more if only the time the Senate was in session was counted. Cloture votes increased in tandem, and more than one cloture vote per issue is now the norm. Cloture votes are, however, increasingly less likely to be successful: in the early to mid-1980s, 43 percent of cloture votes got the requisite sixty votes to cut off debate; in the late 1980s and early 1990s, 39 percent did; in the period 1993–1998, only 28 percent did.

The character of the measures subject to filibusters also changed over this period. During the 1950s and 1960s, civil rights was most often at issue, just as it had been since the late 1930s (Binder and Smith 1997, 85). In the late 1960s, with the major civil right legislation successfully enacted, the targets of filibusters began to broaden: in late 1970, for example, opponents of a protectionist trade bill and supporters of a compromise welfare reform bill ganged up to filibuster a social security bill to which the trade provisions and a weaker version of welfare reform had been added (*CQ Almanac* 1970, 1030). In the same year, William Proxmire and several other senators filibustered the conference report of the Department of Transportation appropriations bill because conferees had ignored the Senate's vote in opposition to the supersonic transport plane. Furthermore, as these examples show, filibusters were no longer a tool only of conservatives. The modest success of cloture reformers in 1975 after many years of failure almost certainly is at least partly attributable to these changes. The new use of the filibuster was goring the ox of a broader range of senators.

During the same period, another change in how the Senate's permissive rules worked in practice occurred. Although senators have always had wide discretion in the offering of amendments on the floor of the Senate, during the 1950s most were quite restrained in attempting to alter committee-reported legislation on the floor (Sinclair 1989). Most senators offered few amendments, in a small range of issue areas, most often confining their amending activity to bills reported from committees on which they served. In the late 1960s, senators' behavior began to change, and, by the 1970s, senators were offering a great many more amendments to a wider range of issues and not confining their targets to bills from committees on which they served. Committees found themselves more frequently challenged on the floor, legislation was less likely to be perfunctorily approved without change on the floor, and the Senate floor became a much more active decision-making arena.

Rules, Incentives, and Political Context: Why Behavior Changed

Senate rules, then, have always been permissive, but the extent to which senators have taken advantage of them and exploited their potential has changed over time. How can we account for the change in senators' behavior? If we assume that senators are purposive actors, a change in behavior should be explainable by a change in the political context that alters senators' best strategies for advancing their electoral and policy goals. The altered political context offers new opportunities or imposes new or different constraints and thereby changes the incentives for senators to exploit the rules.

As I have argued at length elsewhere, first a change in Senate membership and then a broad change in the political environment did change senators' incentives and so changed their behavior and thereby the Senate (Sinclair 1989; see also Loomis 1988; Foley 1980; Oppenheimer 1985; Rohde, Ornstein, and Peabody 1985). The Senate of the 1950s and before was a clubby, inward-looking body in which senators seldom exploited their great powers (Matthews 1960). Influence was decentralized but relatively unequally distributed and centered in strong committees and their senior leaders, who were most often conservatives, frequently southern Democrats. The Senate's institutional structure and the political environment rewarded restraint (see Sinclair 1989; Huitt 1965).

The lack of staff, for example, made it harder for new senators to participate intelligently right away; so serving an apprenticeship prevented a new member from making a fool of himself early in his career. It also made specialization the only really feasible course for attaining influence. The majority of senators, especially the southern Democrats, faced no imminent reelection peril so long as they were free to reflect their constituents' views in their votes and were capable of providing the projects their constituents desired. The system of reciprocity, which dictated that senators do constituency-related favors for one another whenever possible, served them well. The seniority system, bolstered by norms of apprenticeship, specialization, and intercommittee reciprocity, assured members of considerable independent influence in their area of jurisdiction if they stayed in the Senate long enough and did not make that dependent on their voting behavior. For the generally moderate to conservative Senate membership, the parochial and limited legislation that such a system produced was quite satisfactory. The Senate of the 1950s was an institution well designed for its generally conservative members to further their goals.

The 1958 elections brought into the Senate a big class of new senators with different policy goals and reelection needs. Mostly northern Democrats, they were activist liberals, and most had been elected in highly competitive contests, in many cases having defeated incumbents. Both their policy goals and their reelection needs dictated a more activist style; these senators simply could not afford to wait to make their mark. Subsequent elections brought in more and more such members, and in the 1960s the political environment began a major transformation. A host of new issues rose to prominence, politics became more highly charged, the interest group community exploded in size and became more diverse, and the media—especially television— became a much bigger player in politics.

This new environment offered alluring new opportunities to senators. The myriad interest groups needed champions and spokesmen, and the media needed credible sources to represent issue positions and provide commentary. Because of the small size and prestige of the Senate, senators fit the bill. The opportunity for senators to become significant players on a broader stage, with possible policy, power, reelection, or higher-office payoffs, was there, but to take advantage of the opportunity senators needed to change their behavior and their institution.

From the mid-1960s through the mid-1970s, senators did just that. The number of positions on good committees and the number of subcommittee leadership positions were expanded and distributed much more broadly. Staff too was greatly expanded and made available to junior as well as senior senators. Senators were now able to involve themselves in a much broader range of issues, and they did so. Senators became much more active on the Senate floor, offering more amendments and to a wider range of bills. Senators exploited extended debate to a much greater extent, and the frequency of filibusters shot up. The media became an increasingly important arena for participation and a significant resource for senators in the pursuit of their electoral and policy goals.

By the mid-1970s the individualist Senate had emerged. The Senate had become a body in which every member regardless of seniority considered himself entitled to participate on any issue that interested him for either constituency or policy reasons. Senators took for granted that they—and their colleagues—would regularly exploit the powers that the Senate rules gave them. Senators became increasingly outwardly oriented, focusing on their links with interest groups, policy communities, and the media more than on their ties to one another.

By the late 1980s, another major change in senators' behavior became manifest. Senators were increasingly voting along partisan lines. In the late 1960s and early 1970s, only about a third of Senate roll call votes pitted a majority of Democrats against a majority of Republicans. By the 1990s, from half to two-thirds of roll calls were such party votes. The frequency with which senators voted with their partisan colleagues on party votes increased significantly as well. By the 1990s a typical party vote saw well over 80 percent of the Democrats voting together on one side against well over 80 percent of the Republicans on the other.

The greater partisanship grew out of a number of important changes in the political context that altered the character of the political parties. Most importantly, partisan realignment in the South led to conservative southern Democrats' being replaced by even more conservative southern Republicans. As a result, the congressional Democratic party became more homogeneously liberal and the Republican party more conservative. Outside the South as well, Republican candidates and activists were becoming more ideologically conservative, and so were new Republican senators.

The Strategic Use of Senate Rules

From the late 1930s to the late 1960s, when filibustering was strongly associated with civil rights, filibusters were aimed primarily at killing legislation. This was also the era of powerful committee chairmen leading quite autonomous committees; nongermane amendments were most famously used by leaders to circumvent recalcitrant committees. Thus, Majority Leader Lyndon Johnson offered the 1960 civil rights bill as a nongermane amendment on the floor to a bill aiding an impacted school district in Missouri; the Judiciary Committee chaired by Senator James Eastland of Mississippi, an unrelenting foe of civil rights, refused to report such legislation.

With the growth of Senate individualism and senators' increasing exploitation of their prerogatives under Senate rules, the uses to which senators put their powers multiplied. Killing legislation continued to be the aim in many cases, but filibustering also came to be used almost routinely to extract concessions on legislation. Senators as individuals increasingly employed nongermane amendments to pursue their personal agendas, often forcing votes on their issues over and over during a Congress. Also on the rise has been extended-debate–based obstructionism that appears aimed at killing or weakening legislation but actually is a form of position taking—intended to make a statement about a senator's stance and its intensity. Targeting one measure in order to extract concessions on another, sometimes known as hostage taking, has become increasingly frequent. With the growth of partisan polarization, the minorities making use of Senate prerogatives are more often organized partisan ones. In the 1990s especially, exploiting Senate prerogatives to attempt to seize agenda control from the majority party has become a key minority-party strategy.

Certainly since the development of the individualist Senate, senators as individuals have used extended debate, directly and indirectly, to try to kill legislation that they strongly oppose, and they continue to do so today. Sometimes constituency interest is the basis of the opposition. In 1978, for example, Senator Mike Gravel of Alaska obstructed, delayed, and finally managed to kill the Alaska lands bill, which Alaskans believed put too much of their state off limits to development. In 1989, Senators Helms, Hollings, and Ford of the tobacco-growing states of North and South Carolina and Kentucky took turns over three days in an effort to keep a permanent airline smoking ban from coming to a vote. In the 1990s Nevada's senators repeatedly filibustered legislation establishing a nuclear waste dump in their state.

Ideology often fuels such efforts. Liberal Senators Howard Metzenbaum and James Abourezk took on their own party leadership and a president of their own party when, in 1977, they filibustered President Carter's energy plan over natural gas deregulation (*CQ Almanac* 1977, 737–39). Lacking the votes to prevent cloture, they "filibustered by amendment": they had filed hundreds of amendments before cloture was invoked and now proceeded to call them up one by one and insist on votes. By also objecting to usually routine unanimous-consent requests (to dispense with the reading of an amendment, for example) and by insisting on quorum calls at every opportunity, they delayed action for nine days and provoked Majority Leader Byrd into using heavy-handed parliamentary tactics to end the delay. (Postcloture rules were later altered to curtail this strategy.) During 1981 and 1982, Republican Senator Lowell Weiker waged a protracted fight against antibusing language, delaying passage of the Department of Justice authorization bill for over eight months. In 1990, the Bush administration and the key committee leaders in the House and Senate had worked out a deal on Bush's education initiative, but conservative Republicans Coats, Helms, and Grassley refused to assent to the bill's being called up and thereby killed it. Both

247

ideology and constituency interest seem to have motivated the notorious gas tax filibuster that Senators Helms and East of North Carolina waged in late 1982. With Christmas quickly approaching, Helms and East held their increasingly annoyed Senate colleagues in Washington as they filibustered the conference report of a broadly supported bill providing transportation funds and raising the gas tax.

In 1998, Dianne Feinstein killed what she argued was an overly broad anti-cloning bill when she objected to unanimous consent to proceed and then won the vote on the motion 54 to 42. This appears to be that unusual case where a filibuster—actually the threat of a filibuster—by a few individuals succeeded in its purpose not by wearing out the opposition or running out the clock but by changing minds. Backed up by an effective informational campaign waged by medical research and disease advocacy groups, Feinstein persuaded a number of her colleagues that the bill would stymie important medical research.

Given the size of the support coalition, the opponents in some of these cases and in many others presumably realized that their chances of success were minuscule; in such cases, their effort, it seems reasonable to conclude, was really position taking. Thus when in 1997 Senator Ted Kennedy continued to oppose a compromise Food and Drug Administration reform bill that many of his liberal Democratic colleagues had agreed to, one can assume that, rather than actually expecting to kill the legislation, he was sending his allies in the relevant policy community a signal that he still had very serious reservations about the legislation and perhaps was attempting to stimulate some press attention. A similar conclusion applies when, in 1998, Senator Phil Gramm and several other conservative Republicans stalled the conference report on the agriculture research-food stamps bill over the provision restoring legal aliens' eligibility for food stamps.

Throughout this period, sizable partisan groupings have used extended debate to try to kill legislation they vehemently opposed—often with success. Republicans killed labor law revision and campaign finance reform in the 95th Congress (1977–78). In a peculiar twist, Majority Leader George Mitchell led Democrats in killing Bush's capital gains tax cut in the 101st Congress; most Democrats, but not enough to constitute a majority of the Senate, opposed Bush's proposal, so the majority party used the filibuster. In the 103rd Congress, the minority Republicans used actual and threatened filibusters to deprive Clinton and the majority Democrats of numerous policy successes; Clinton's economic stimulus package, campaign finance and lobbying reform bills, and bills revamping the Superfund program, revising clean drinking water regulations, overhauling outdated telecommunications law, and applying federal labor laws to Congress were among the casualties. In the 104th and 105th Congresses, minority Democrats used extended debate to kill a number of Republican priorities, including ambitious regulatory overhaul legislation and a far-reaching property rights bill.

Senators often do not believe that they can kill legislation or do not even want to but use their prerogatives to extract concessions from the bill's supporters. Both organized partisan groupings and individuals have found this an effective strategy. For example, Republicans during the first two years of the Carter administration forced Democrats to water down the Humphrey-Hawkins full-employment bill and to impose major restrictions in legislation reauthorizing the Legal Services Corporation. In 1989 and 1990, Republicans compelled Majority Leader Mitchell and the Democrats to negotiate with the administration and congressional Republicans in order to get a clean air act passed in the Senate. In the 103rd Congress, Republicans extracted concessions on a number of major Democratic bills—voter registration legislation ("motor voter") and the national service program, for example. Then in the 104th Congress Democrats used the same strategy to force concessions on product liability legislation, the Freedom to Farm bill, and telecommunications legislation, among others.

Characteristic of the individualistic Senate is individual members using their prerogatives to extract concessions on legislation. In 1980 an Alaska Lands Bill finally passed, but only after Alaska's senators induced bill supporters to weaken their legislation considerably. In 1982, the Senate—and then the House—accepted an amendment concerning state veto power in return for William Proxmire's agreeing not to carry out his threat to filibuster a compromise nuclear waste bill. During the same Congress, Howard Metzenbaum extracted a series of concessions on a rewrite of the western water law both at the initial floor stage and at the conference stage. In June of 1999, Phil Gramm blocked passage of a broadly supported bill allowing the disabled to keep their Medicaid and Medicare benefits when they took paid jobs until supporters agreed to drop the funding mechanism that he disliked.[2]

Senators' use of nongermane amendments to pursue their personal agendas is also characteristic of the individualistic Senate. The strategy is probably most closely associated in the public mind with Senator Jesse Helms, who, since the 1970s, has forced innumerable votes in every Congress on hot button issues such as abortion, pornography, and school prayer. In the late 1980s, for example, he enormously complicated the legislative process on a big education bill by offering an amendment barring so-called "dial-a-porn" services. On the other end of the ideological spectrum, Paul Wellstone has become adept at the same strategy. In spring of 1999, for example, Wellstone, a strong opponent of the 1996 welfare reform legislation, offered and forced to a roll call vote an amendment to the defense authorization bill requiring the Department of Health and Human Services to report on former welfare recipients' ability to achieve self-sufficiency—a nongermane amendment that he had offered to other bills before.

Holding up one matter in order to extract concessions on another, sometimes known as hostage taking, though once a tactic seldom used, has become increasingly frequent in recent years. In the mid-1980s, for example, farm state Democrats held up the nomination of Ed Meese as attorney general in order to extract from Majority Leader Bob Dole a promise to schedule agricultural aid legislation. Two more recent examples illustrate how complicated such strategic maneuvering has become. In 1995, Jesse Helms, chairman of the Senate Foreign Relations Committee, sponsored a State Department reorganization bill that the Clinton administration and many Democrats opposed. Helms brought the legislation to the floor, but after two attempts as imposing cloture failed, Majority Leader Dole stopped floor consideration. Frustrated, Helms began bottling up ambassador nominations, the START II treaty, and the Chemical Weapons Convention. Democrats responded by blocking action on a flag desecration constitutional amendment and a Cuba sanctions bill, both Helms's priorities. Negotiations and concessions eventually unstuck the impasse, though only the Cuba sanctions bill actually became law. In the summer of 1996, Majority Leader Dole allegedly sought to stack the Senate conference delegation on the Kennedy-Kassebaum health insurance reform bill with supporters of medical savings accounts (MSAs), which Republicans favored but a Senate majority had rejected on a floor vote. Senator Kennedy, a strong opponent of MSAs, threatened to filibuster the naming of conferees until an acceptable compromise on MSAs was reached. In response, Senator Don Nickles objected to the naming of conferees on the minimum-wage bill until conferees on the Kennedy-Kassebaum bill had been appointed. Again, negotiations eventually led to a resolution.

Most visible in recent years have been senators holding hostage nominations in order to extract concessions on other matters from the administration. To be sure, senators use their powers to block nominations they oppose, even if a Senate majority clearly supports the nomination. Thus, cloture votes showed a sizable majority for the confirmation of Henry Foster as Surgeon General, but lacking the sixty votes to cut off debate, the nomination died. James Hormel, an open homosexual nominated by President Clinton as ambassador to Luxembourg, almost certainly commanded well over majority support, but opposition from extreme conservatives led Majority Leader Lott to refuse to bring it to the floor. Increasingly often, however, senators block nominees they do not oppose in order to gain a bargaining chip vis-à-vis the administration. The nomination of William Holbrook as ambassador to the United Nations in 1999 was held up over matters having nothing to do with him. Senator Grassley wanted the administration to respond to his concerns about the treatment of a State Department whistleblower; Senators McConnell and Lott hoped to extract from the president a promise to appoint their candidate to the Federal Elections Commission. Senator Orrin Hatch, chairman of the Judiciary Committee, held up most judicial nominees during the first half of 1999 in order to force the president to appoint his choice, a person strongly opposed by environmentalists, to the bench. Even members of the president's own party occasionally use the strategy. In fall of 1997, for example, Senator Ron Wyden wanted the Pentagon to reopen an investigation into a military transport plane crash that had killed a constituent. Finding the Pentagon's responsiveness to his request unsatisfactory, Wyden put a hold on the nomination of Gen. Henry Shelton to become chairman of the Joint Chiefs of Staff. That got the Pentagon's attention; Wyden's problem was quickly resolved and Shelton's nomination was released (*Roll Call*, September 29, 1997).

With the growth of partisan polarization, exploiting Senate prerogatives to attempt to seize agenda control from the majority party has become a key minority-party strategy. In the 101st Congress, minority Republicans tried to force a capital gains tax cut onto the legislative agenda but were prevented from getting an up or down vote by the majority-party leadership's use of extended debate. Lowering the capital gains tax was a top Bush priority, one that most congressional Republicans strongly supported and many but not all congressional Democrats strongly opposed. Having failed to include a capital gains tax cut in the bill that the Finance Committee reported, Republicans attempted to add it as an amendment on the floor. The bill at issue was, however, a reconciliation bill and thus was protected from filibusters. In addition, under the Byrd rule the Republican amendment would require the waiver of a point of order, and Republicans lacked the sixty votes necessary to win that waiver. Majority Leader George Mitchell made it clear that they would not get that vote without the sixty votes and that he would filibuster any other bill to which they attempted to add the tax cut. Republicans nevertheless offered the capital gains tax cut as an amendment to a bill to aid Poland. Democrats under Mitchell's lead threatened to filibuster the amendment, and the bill was stymied. After two failed cloture votes, Republicans gave up.

The model of this partisan strategy at its most effective is the Democrats' successful drive to raise the minimum wage in 1996. After their enormous electoral victory in 1994, congressional Republicans totally dominated agenda setting (McSweeney and Owens 1998). President Clinton advocated raising the minimum wage in his 1996 State of the Union address; but despite the proposal's popularity with the American public, strong Republican opposition was expected to ensure that the proposal would be dead on arrival in Congress. Majority Republicans would not even allow consideration of the legislation.

To force the issue onto the agenda, Senate Democrats decided to offer the minimum-wage increase as an amendment to every piece of legislation the majority leader brought to the floor. Lacking the votes to kill the minimum wage or impose cloture on legislation that he did want to pass, Majority Leader Dole was forced to pull bill after bill off the floor, prompting news stories of Senate grid-lock. House and Senate Democrats, the White House, and organized labor all worked to keep the issue in the news and to put pressure on moderate Republicans. Public approval of a minimum wage increase went up to 85 percent. With an election approaching, Senate and House Republicans capitulated, and both chambers passed legislation raising the minimum wage.

The combination of a elaborate and sophisticated public relations campaign and a carefully planned and orchestrated procedural strategy now characterizes such minority-party efforts. Ideally the minority party would like to enact legislation and garner credit with the public for having done so. However, since it is the minority in an increasingly polarized legislature, actually passing legislation is often an unrealistic goal. If the PR campaign is successful, the minority party will at least have increased the visibility of an issue that benefits it, reinforced the party's identification with the popular issue, and made the majority party pay a price in bad publicity for blocking the legislation. Democratic efforts on campaign finance reform and tobacco in the 105th Congress did not produce legislation, but they did take a toll on the Republican party's image.

Majority leaders have responded by attempting to impose cloture and the attendant germaneness requirements early in the process. They have "filled the amendment tree" to block minority-party amendments. That is, using the majority leader's prerogative of first recognition, the majority leader offers amendments in all the parliamentarily permissible slots and thus cuts off the possibility of any other amendments. Lott's use of these strategies angered Democrats, who claimed he was trying to run the Senate like the House (see, e.g., *Congressional Record*, July 26, 1999, S9192 passim). However, as the Democrats showed, a persistent Senate minority can always get a vote on its issues. Majority attempts to block such votes not only eventually fail but also tend to entail costs to the majority in terms of significant legislative problems and bad press.

Legislative Routines and Their Impact on the Legislative Process in the Individualist, Partisan Senate

Given the extent to which senators now exploit their prerogatives, how does the Senate manage to legislate at all? As Table 12.2 shows, major legislation is now very frequently subject to some sort of extended-debate–related problem discernible from the public record. ("Holds" and threats to filibuster, as well as actual extended-debate–related delay on the floor, were coded affirmative.) In recent Congresses, about half of major measures ran into a filibuster-related problem in the Senate. The definition of *major* used here—those measures listed by *Congressional Quarterly* in its lists of major legislation plus those measures on which key votes occurred, again according to *CQ*—yields 40 to 60 measures

TABLE 12.2. The Increasing Frequency of Extended-Debate–Related Problems (% of "Filibusterable" Major Measures Subject to Extended Debate)

Congress	Years	Filibuster Problem
91st	1969–70	10
95th	1977–78	22
97th	1977–78	24
101st	1981–82	30
103rd	1989–90	51
104th	1993–94	52
105th	1995–96	53

per Congress. Thus, while truly minor legislation is excluded, the listing is not restricted to only the most contentious and highly salient issues. So if much of the Congress's important workload is at risk, how does the Senate operate?

Since the 1950s, the Senate has done most of its work through unanimous consent agreements (UCAs). By unanimous consent, senators agree to bring a bill to the floor, perhaps to place some limits on the amendments that may be offered or the length of debate on specific amendments, and then maybe to set a time for the final vote. Some UCAs are highly elaborate and set out agreements on the entire floor consideration of a bill. Robert Byrd as majority leader was famous for negotiating extraordinarily complex UCAs before a bill was even brought to the floor. The only systematic analysis to date suggests that even under Byrd a series of partial agreements was more frequent than one comprehensive agreement (Evans and Oleszek 1999). That is certainly the usual procedure today. As a highly knowledgeable participant explained: "Usually you have a UCA only to bring something to the floor, and then maybe you have another one that will deal with a couple of important amendments, and then perhaps a little later, one that will start limiting amendments to some extent, and then perhaps one that specifies when a vote will take place. So it's done through a series of steps, each of which sort of leaves less and less leeway."

The party leaders oversee the negotiation of unanimous-consent agreements and are deeply involved in the more contentious cases. The majority- and the minority-party secretaries of the Senate now are the most important staffers involved and serve as clearinghouses and as a point of continuous contact between the parties. When the majority leader, after consultation with the relevant committee chairman, decides he wants to schedule a bill, he may leave the negotiation of the agreement to the committee chairman, or he may take the lead role himself. The more complex the political situation and the more important to the party the legislation at issue, the more likely the majority leader is to take the lead. In either case, the majority-party secretary will be consulted to ascertain which senators have indicated that they want to be consulted before the bill is scheduled. If a fellow party member has expressed opposition to the bill's being brought to the floor, negotiations may be necessary to take care of his concerns. When the majority has an agreement it can support, the majority party secretary will convey it to the minority party secretary in writing, who will give it to the minority leader and the relevant ranking minority member. The minority secretary will also call any senators on the minority side who have asked to be notified and will find out their concerns. Eventually the minority will respond with a written counteroffer and convey it to the majority through the secretaries. This process may go through several rounds. The leaders will also sometimes negotiate face to face. If and when they reach a tentative agreement, both parties put out a recorded message on their "hot line" to all Senate offices. The message lays out the terms of the agreement and asks senators who have objections to call their leader within a specified period of time. If there are objections, they have to be taken care of. When every senator is prepared to assent to the unanimous-consent agreement, the majority leader takes it to the floor and makes the request.

The two party secretaries maintain the lists of "holds." "A hold," as one knowledgeable participant explained, "is a letter to your leader telling him which of the many powers that you have as a senator you intend to use on a given issue." A typical such letter, addressed to then Majority Leader Trent Lott and copied to the majority secretary, reads, "Dear Trent: I will object to any time agreement or unanimous consent request with respect to consideration of any legislation or amendment that involves _____, as I wish to be accorded my full rights as a Member of the Senate to offer amendments, debate and consider such legislation or amendment. My thanks and kindest personal regards." Each party secretary maintains a list of the "holds" placed by senators of his or her party. The party secretaries confer every morning and tell each other about any new holds on legislation or nominations. They do not, however, reveal the names of their members that have placed the holds.

The hold system is an informal practice, not a matter of Senate rules, and its history is murky. It may well have begun as simply a way of making sure senators were notified before matters of special interest to them were scheduled. Senators might want to be sure that they were not otherwise committed, that they were prepared for floor debate or ready to offer an amendment. Senators still ask to be informed before something of particular interest to them is scheduled; unless they are committee or subcommittee leaders on the issue or otherwise known players, they cannot count on being consulted unless they make such a request. These requests are sometimes called "consults" and are sometimes just lumped under "holds." However, most "holds" are threats to object to a unanimous-consent agreement, and in a body that conducts most of its business through UCAs, that is in effect, as a leadership staffer said, "a threat to filibuster."

Visible filibusters are now just the tip of the iceberg. The Senate's permissive rules have much more effect on the legislative process through filibuster threats than through actual filibusters. "Classic" filibusters, with the Senate in session all night, senators sleeping on cots off the Senate floor, and filibusterers making interminable speeches on the floor, no longer occur. Holds are the "lazy man's filibuster," a staffer complained. Placed sometimes by staff on their own initiative and sometimes at the instigation of lobbyists, "holds" require little effort on the part of senators, the staffer continued, yet they enormously complicate the legislative process and not infrequently kill or severely weaken worthy legislation. Given the secrecy surrounding holds, no data on their frequency exist. However, interview evidence suggests that they are common. One senior aide's claim that "there are holds on virtually everything" may be an exaggeration, but the complaints and frustration expressed by so many senators and aides indicates that holds are an everyday fact of life in the contemporary Senate.

Since holds are nowhere specified in Senate rules, why do Senate leaders condone and, in fact, maintain the hold system? "It's to the majority leader's advantage to have holds because it gives him information," a knowledgeable observer explained. "He's always trying to negotiate unanimous-consent agreements, and he needs to know if there are pockets of problems, and holds do that." An expert concluded succinctly, "The only way you could get rid of 'holds' would be to change the rules of the Senate drastically."

Critics often argue that leaders should be tougher and "call the bluff" of members more often. The threat to filibuster supposedly inherent in "holds" would, in many cases, prove to be empty rhetoric if put to the test, such critics claim. In fact, "holds" are not automatic vetoes. A "hold" cannot kill an appropriations bill, for example, and in deciding how seriously to take a "hold" on less vital legislation, the leader weighs the reputation of the senator placing the "hold." "Some people are taken more seriously because it's just assumed they're willing to back it up," a leadership aide explained. When senators place "holds" that their leader cannot honor, he will attempt to at least provide a face-saving way out for his member. Thus, when President Clinton named James Hormel ambassador to Luxembourg by recess appointment, James Inhofe, one of the Republican senators most opposed to his appointment, very publicly put a "hold" on all administration nominations. This was an untenable hold, most participants and observers agreed, because "there will be people who will want appointments because it covers everything supposedly. So people will start pressuring him." Before he brought up any nominations, Lott extracted a letter from the administration essentially reiterating current policy on recess appointments but providing Inhofe with cover. Inhofe declared victory in a press release and lifted his blanket hold.

Although holds are certainly not absolute, the time pressure under which the Senate operates gives them considerable bit. As a staffer explained, "Holds are

255

effective because the majority leader has a finite amount of time. If there are going to be cloture votes and the like, it can take days to ram something through this place. You can't do it on every bill. You can only do it on a selected few bills." Senators want floor time used productively. In making a choice of which bills to bring to the floor, the majority leader must consider how much time the bill will take and what the likelihood of successful passage is. As a result, senators who want their bills to receive floor consideration are under tremendous pressure to negotiate with those who have "holds" on them. "Things that aren't a top priority for the majority leader, he wants you to work it out," a senior staffer explained. "If you go to him and say you want something brought to the floor, he'll say, 'You work it out. You find out who has holds on it. You work out whatever problems they have, and I'll schedule it when you've worked it out.'"

Thus, often simply to get to the floor, a measure must command a substantial supermajority. When time is especially tight—before a recess and at the end of a session—a single objection can kill legislation.

If a majority is willing to pay the price in time and inconvenience, a single senator or a handful cannot stop a majority from bringing a measure to the floor and passing it. Forty-one senators can. With senators as individuals and collectively so willing to use their prerogatives aggressively, anything contentious must command sixty votes in order to pass. "We've developed what I call the 60-vote Senate," a longtime participant said. "We have a lot of cloture votes, but not a lot of successful cloture votes," he continued. "So long as the minority sticks together and has [40-plus] votes, they can prevent that."

The Impact on Legislative Outcomes

What, then, is the impact of the Senate's rules and how they have been used over the past several decades on legislative outcomes? Reliable answers can only come from systematic analyses. Here I begin that task by examining enactments in selected Congresses from the late 1960s to the late 1990s. The effect of extended debate on the content of legislation is almost certainly greater than its effect on whether the legislation passes and is very much worthy of study. The first step, however, is to assess the impact on the more easily measured variable of enactment.

The least ambiguous indicator of outcome is whether a legislative measure was enacted, and that is my dependent variable here. Since legislation varies so much in significance, examining all legislation would be unlikely to yield much enlightenment. My data are restricted to major legislation as defined by Congressional Quarterly's list of major legislation, augmented by those measures on which there were key votes, again according to Congressional Quarterly.[3] This yields a list of measures considered major by expert contemporary observers.

TABLE 12.3. The Decreasing Rate of Enactment 1969–98

Congress	Years	# of Major Measures	% Enacted
91st	1969–70	49	82
95th	1977–78	57	70
97th	1981–82	50	68
101st	1989–90	52	64
103rd	1993–94	54	65
104th	1995–96	56	52
105th	1997–98	40	50
Total		358	65

Included are constitutional amendments, which require a two-thirds vote in each chamber but no presidential signature, and budget resolutions, which require simple majorities in each chamber and no presidential signature. The great bulk are ordinary bills. In each case, when a measure successfully completes the process, it is coded as enacted.

This list of measures can reasonably be interpreted as the active congressional agenda. In addition to significance, CQ seems to require that the measures be ones on which some congressional action is expected. Thus, clearly the list cannot be interpreted as the broader national policy agenda, and it certainly exhibits selection bias toward measures with a reasonable chance of enactment.

The data set consists of the following Congresses: the 91st (1969–70), the first Congress of the Nixon presidency; the 95th (1977–78), the first Congress of the Carter presidency; the 97th (1981–82), the first Congress of the Reagan presidency; the 101st (1989–90), the first Congress of the Bush presidency; the 103rd (1993–94), the first Congress of the Clinton presidency; the 104th (1995–96), which was the first Congress in forty years in which Republicans controlled the House; and the 105th (1997–98).

Of the 358 measures in the data set, 64.5 percent were enacted; 35.5 percent—just over a third—failed (see Table 12.3). The proportion of the congressional agenda of major measures enacted declined over time from 82 percent in 1969–70 to about half in the 104th and 105th Congresses (1995–98). This decline was not the result of an increase in the size of the agenda. In fact, the lowest proportion enacted occurred when the agenda was smallest—the 105th Congress.

The proportion of major legislation enacted declined over the same period that senators increased their exploitation of the Senate's permissive rules. Is there a relationship? By examining the frequency of measures surviving the various stages of the legislative process, we can begin to answer that question.

TABLE 12.4. Attrition in the Legislative Process

Legislative Action	House	Both or President	Senate
Total CQ major measures		358[a]	
Reported by committee	306 (86%)		298 (83%)
Passed by chamber (of those reported)	282 (79%)		246 (69%)
Passed by chamber (though not reported)	23 (6%)		28 (8%)
Total passed by chamber	305 (85%)		274 (77%)
Passed by both chambers		261 (73%)	
Got to the president or his signature not required		248 (69%)	
President did not veto		215 (60%)	
Veto overridden		5 (1%)	
Postveto compromise		11 (3%)	
Became Law (or equivalent)		231 (65%)	

a. All percentages are percent of 358.

As Table 12.4 shows, of the 358 measures, 86 percent were reported by a House committee and 83 percent by a Senate committee.[4] These substantial figures confirm that CQ picks measures on which action is expected and that in most but certainly not all instances some legislative action does, in fact, occur. Even for these measures, the first stage—getting out of committee—is the single greatest barrier; but there is little difference in measures' likelihood of surviving committee in the two chambers. Most but not all measures reported by a House committee subsequently passed on the House floor (79 percent of 358) as did a small number of measures (6 percent) never reported by a House committee. Altogether, 85 percent of the 358 measures passed the House. The likelihood of a measure passing on the Senate floor was, however, considerably lower: 69 percent of the 358 were reported from a Senate committee *and* passed on the Senate floor, and another 8 percent passed although they were never reported. Altogether, 77 percent of the 358 measures passed the Senate—significantly lower than the rate for the House. Of course, measures need to pass both houses, and 261 (73 percent) of the 358 did. In the end, 231 of 358 measures or 65 percent were enacted.

These figures suggest that, at least for the Congresses in this study, once a measure emerged from committee, the Senate floor proved to be the single greatest obstacle and the place that the greatest attrition occurred.

Does the increasing frequency with which measures encounter extended-debate–related problems explain this pattern? Filibuster problems do, in fact, depress a measure's chances of surviving the legislative process; of those measures that did not encounter such a problem, either because senators chose not to use their prerogatives or because the measure enjoyed statutory protection, 74

TABLE 12.5. Where Measures Failed

What Happened ?	91st, 95th, 97th		103rd, 104th, 105th	
	N of Failed Measures	% of Failed Measures	*N* of Failed Measures	% of Failed Measures
Passed by neither House nor Senate	16	38	21	31
Passed by House but not by Senate	12	29	24	35
Passed by Senate but not by House	8	19	2	3
Passed by House and Senate	6	14	19	28
Total number of measures that failed	42		68	

percent were enacted; in contrast, only 54 percent of those that did experience a filibuster problem became law.[5] Since filibusters and filibuster threats are by no means always intended to kill legislation, those figures suggest a considerable effect.

As I have demonstrated elsewhere, the character of the committee process—particularly whether it is partisan—is related to the likelihood of floor passage; the relationship is considerably stronger in the Senate than in the House; and committee partisanship is still more strongly related to the likelihood of final enactment (see Sinclair 1999).[6] Thus, increasing partisanship has also contributed to the decline in enactments and particularly by reducing a measure's chances of surviving the Senate. Filibuster problems are more likely to occur on partisan legislation, and when a measure both is partisan at the committee level and encounters a filibuster problem, its chances of enactment are significantly decreased. Fewer than half (46 percent) of such measures were successfully enacted in contrast to 80 percent of the measures that were neither partisan nor experienced an extended-debate–related problem and 57 percent that had one but not both of these characteristics.

The Senate, then, has become a major choke point in the legislative process. As table 12.5 shows, in the earlier Congresses under study (the 91st, 95th, and 97th), legislation was a bit more likely to pass the House and not the Senate than vice versa, but the difference was not substantial. During the 1990s Congresses in the data set (103rd, 104th, and 105th), not only did much more legislation fail enactment, but that which did was much more likely to be stopped in the Senate than in the House. The combination of senators increasingly exploiting their prerogatives under Senate rules with high partisanship has contributed significantly to the declining rate of enactment.

What evaluative conclusions can be drawn from this? Legislative accomplishment cannot be equated with the number or the percentage of major measures enacted. Whatever one's notions of good public policy, one will find bills killed in the Senate whose fate one bemoans and others for which one applauds the result if not the means by which it came about. Furthermore, the Senate does still function as a legislature; it passes essential legislation such as appropriations bills, though sometimes with difficulty.

Yet the combination of partisanship and individualism does make the legislative process in the Senate fragile and subject to breakdown. Given Senate rules and current expectations about how they may be used, any one senator can cause trouble, and an organized partisan minority can prevent a majority from working its will. In such a body, passing legislation is harder and blocking action easier than in a majoritarian body; minorities command enormous bargaining leverage, especially when time is tight, and intensity counts for more in the legislative process. The "60-vote Senate" poses a significant barrier to the enactment of legislation and to policy change. The existence of a second powerful and independent legislative chamber has always contributed to the status quo bias of the American political system; the ways in which that unique chamber has evolved in recent decades have amplified that effect.

Finally, what conclusions can we draw about studying and understanding the Senate? Most democratic legislatures are majoritarian bodies, and almost all of our theories about legislatures posit such legislative rules. Empirical congressional scholarship has focused heavily on the House of Representatives. Sometimes scholars talk as if theories and generalizations drawn from these two bodies of work apply to all legislative bodies, including the U.S. Senate. My analysis, I believe, makes it clear that this is an untenable assumption. Because of the Senate's uniquely permissive rules, the opportunities and constraints facing individual senators and Senate leaders are different from those facing the members and leaders of a majoritarian legislature, and consequently their behavior may well be different. While we cannot simply assume that generalizations generated from work on the House apply to the Senate, the existence of two such different legislative bodies as the House and the Senate offers great opportunities to scholars to test hypotheses, especially about the relative importance of external political context factors and internal institutional factors as determinants of member behavior, legislative process, and outcomes. To date, we have made insufficient use of this "natural experiment."

Notes

1. Sources are given in the note to Table 12.1. The DSG publication relies on data supplied by Congressional Research Service experts; these experts' judgments about what constitutes a filibuster are not limited to instances in which cloture was sought. For the 103rd through the 105th Congresses, a measure of instances in which cloture was sought is used as the basis of the "filibuster" estimate. One can argue that this

overestimates because in some cases cloture was sought for reasons other than a fear of extended debate (a test vote or to impose germaneness); however, one can also argue that it underestimates because those cases in which cloture was not sought—perhaps because it was known to be out of reach—are not counted. For an estimate based on a different methodology, see Table 12.2.

2. *Washington Post,* June 17, 1999.

3. For this analysis, I excluded key vote measures on which controversy was confined to the amendment on which the key vote occurred and the underlying legislation was not controversial unless the amendment carried either the president's or the majority-party leadership's agenda.

4. In a few cases, the reports were without recommendation or negative.

5. Measures that did not get far enough to encounter the prospects of a filibuster problem are coded as missing data on the filibuster variable.

6. This relationship holds when control of the presidency and Congress is divided but not in the 103rd Congress, when it is unified.

· 13 ·

How Senators Decide: An Exploration

C. Lawrence Evans

In June 1999, the Senate moved toward a cloture vote on legislation to set quotas on the quantity of steel imported into the United States. Domestic steel producers and organized labor supported the initiative, while a coalition of free traders and farm groups (concerned about foreign retaliation against their own products) was staunchly opposed. A top aide to a Senate Democrat summarized how his boss made up his mind on the vote:

> He has a free trade orientation to start with. . . . There's only limited steel in [the state], but the steelworkers have broadened to represent other workers. We received calls from state unions on this. . . . Every vote is a combination of an intellectual attitude, some mix of state interests, an interest group analysis. . . . Our trade staff prepared a detailed pro-con memo for [the senator]. We met with him and worked through it. The initial recommendation was, "This will pass anyway, so vote for it."

As the floor vote neared, however, the Clinton administration stepped up its lobbying effort against the bill. The staffer continued: "The vote was getting closer, and it was no longer a throwaway. So we took a closer look. A few days before the vote, we gave him another memo, updating him. . . . There was a follow-up meeting on the day of the vote. He ended up voting against cloture."

Contrast this fairly systematic approach to decision making with the process used by another Democrat on the same legislation. An aide recalled,

> _____ was giving a speech at [a union gathering.] The guy who was going to introduce him walked over and said, "It would be great if I could announce that you are supporting the steel imports bill." _____ said, "Sure, go ahead." . . . He

decided right then. An important labor issue and a significant party constituency versus some abstract principle of free trade? That's a no-brainer. Politics ruled.

The staffer explained that his boss typically makes rapid decisions about upcoming roll call votes and policy issues in general. Not surprisingly, the office relies on verbal communications far more than written memos. "We don't spend a lot of time agonizing about the pros and cons of an issue. Look at the politics, whether there's a state interest, then decide. We don't hem and haw."

As these two vignettes suggest, the process of roll call decision making in the U.S. Senate varies. It varies by senator, by issue, and also over time. And senators' voting decisions are shaped by a wide range of forces—from constituent opinion and organized interests to Senate party leaders and the administration. The central premise of this chapter is that the voting decisions of senators can provide a useful window for examining a number of important questions about behavior, deliberation, and representation in the Senate. How do senators actually make decisions about the myriad of policy issues they confront? How much weight do they place on their own attitudes and core political values, the agendas of advocacy groups, and other factors? How common is conflict among these touchstones, and what strategies are used to resolve such conflict? In the modern Congress, decision making in both the House and Senate is often highly partisan, especially on the floor. But what are the policy consequences of Senate partisanship? Majority-party leaders in the chamber lack many of the procedural prerogatives and other resources used by their House counterparts. What role do party leaders play in the roll call decisions of rank-and-file senators? What tactics do they use to shape legislative outcomes? How effective are these tactics? The purpose of this chapter is to explore how senators make decisions about the positions to take and roll calls to cast on major legislation considered by the full chamber. In the first section, I overview the research and provide background about information gathering and roll call voting in the contemporary Senate. The second section is a description of the cues or touchstones that senators use to make roll call choices. For purposes of illustration, I analyze the impact of these factors on roll call behavior for three measures considered on the Senate floor in summer 1999. I close with a brief conclusion that touches on the theme of Senate exceptionalism, the role of parties, and the quality of congressional deliberation.

Information Gathering in the Senate

The existing literature has taught us a lot about the correlates of floor decision making, especially the relationship between specific roll call decisions and various constituency characteristics (Uslaner 1999b). Other research explores the number and substantive meaning of the various issue dimensions that structure roll call behavior (Poole and Rosenthal 1997; see also Londregan 1999). Recent work also analyzes the strategic timing of position taking in the Senate (Box-Steffensmeier, Arnold, and Zorn 1997). Still, roll call data can only take us so far toward understanding legislative decision making. Such decisions, Richard Fenno (1986) emphasizes, are conditioned by a sequence of considerations and contextual factors that play out over time. For instance, political scientists agree that party line voting became increasingly common in the 1990s. But there is considerable scholarly disagreement about the causes of these divisions. Some scholars (Rohde 1991; Aldrich and Rohde 1997–98; Cox and McCubbins 1993; Sinclair 1995) emphasize the procedural prerogatives and other resources used by party leaders to influence rank-and-file lawmakers. Another view (Brady and Volden 1998; Krehbiel 1998) is that party line voting arises from the different policy preferences of Republican and Democratic members. It is difficult to evaluate these competing hypotheses with roll call data alone. Over two decades ago, in *Congressmen's Voting Decisions,* John Kingdon (1973, 1989) explained why: "Party voting may be a function of some constituency factor, coalition support of different kinds, sanctions employed by legislative leaders, administration pressure, cue-giving within the Congress, ideological similarity among fellow party members, and other possible factors, or various combinations of them" (11). As a result, scholarly efforts to evaluate the impact of party leaders, constituents, and other factors on congressional voting can benefit from systematic research about the *process* through which roll call decisions are made. In his landmark study, Kingdon provided useful guidance for conducting such research. As a generation of congressional scholars and students will recall, he relied on semistructured interviews with members of the House about specific roll call choices. The unit of analysis was the decision of an individual lawmaker on a particular vote, allowing Kingdon to evaluate the considerable issue- and member-specific variance that existed in legislative behavior. Kingdon asked his respondents a series of questions about the factors shaping their voting decisions; constituent preferences, the role of interest groups and party leaders, and so on. The result was a significant and unique contribution to our understanding of congressional behavior. Unfortunately, it would be highly difficult, if not impossible, to replicate Kingdon's research design in the contemporary Congress, especially for the Senate. Members are much busier now than they were during 1969, when Kingdon conducted his fieldwork. The time of an incumbent U.S. senator is a particularly rare commodity. In addition, relative to their 1960s counterparts, current members of Congress operate within a hostile public and media environment. They tend to be wary of outside analysts—even political scientists. Still, a number of scholars have usefully relied on interviews with knowledgeable staff for information about member attitudes, strategies, and behavior (Bullock 1976; Whiteman 1995). Hall's (1996) award-winning study of committee and floor participation demonstrates the potential value of using staff as informants about member motivations. And Salisbury and Shepsle (1981) persuasively argue that congressional offices are best conceptualized as "enterprises" and that the proper unit of analysis for congressional research is the office rather than the member. This chapter is part of broader research in which I rely on interviews with top aides to thirty-six senators, equally divided by party, to explore how roll call decisions are made on a sample of 20 major issues considered by the full chamber during the 106th Congress (1999–2000). The sample of senators is broadly representative within each party, and the issues were among the most salient matters considered by the Senate during the period. The staff members I spoke with were mostly chiefs of staff and legislative directors, and they tended to be highly informed about legislative deliberations within their offices. As in the Kingdon study, the unit of analysis here is the decision rather than the office or the issue.[1]

Office Resources and Information Search

We do not know very much about the nuts and bolts of roll call decision making in the modern Senate. Much of our understanding about congressional voting derives from Kingdon's (1973) classic study, which focused on the House of almost three decades ago. His analysis emphasized an elaborate system of cue taking among lawmakers, with voting decisions occasionally being made on the floor. After arriving in the House chamber, members typically touched base with like-minded colleagues among the bill managers or on the committee of jurisdiction. Or a member might secure advice from one of the party whips, who typically stood by the door. Lawmakers often spoke with members of their state delegations.

Kingdon's compelling portrait of House roll call voting remains a staple of the scholarly literature about Congress, and it rightly has influenced a generation of student readers. But the way contemporary U.S. senators make roll call decisions diverges from his portrayal in certain ways. For one, current senators are far more extensively staffed on the major issues of the day. Kingdon found that House members rated staff as having a major or determinative impact on just 9 percent of the roll call decisions in his sample. This low percentage may partially arise from a disinclination among members to attribute significant influence to their staff employees. But it also reflects the limited role played by congressional aides during the period when Kingdon studied the House. In the late 1960s, the typical House office employed less than ten staffers, and only a fraction of that number were devoted to legislative duties (Fox and Hammond 1977). In both chambers, the number of personal staffers increased markedly in the 1970s. By the early 1990s, Senate offices employed an average of forty staff persons, with the precise number varying by state population. Certain small-state senators employed fewer than 30 staffers; members from the largest states controlled as many as seventy (Joint Committee 1993, 1380).

Within individual Senate offices, there typically is an elaborate division of labor, with five to ten legislative aides assigned duties in specific policy areas. Consider the personal office of James Jeffords (a Republican member before switching to independent status in 2001), who represented the relatively low-population state of Vermont. His deputy chief of staff handled foreign affairs. The legislative director (LD) was responsible for transportation and energy. Five legislative assistants (LAs) covered issue portfolios such as judiciary/banking and agriculture/environment. In addition to personal office aides, the large number of committee leadership posts in the Senate provides many members with additional staff resources. As chair of the Committee on Health, Education, Labor, and Pensions during the 106th Congress, Jeffords controlled another twenty professional staffers.[2] As a result, the typical office enterprise in the contemporary Senate has the internal expertise necessary to advise the member on almost any major issue that comes up. In almost all of the offices under focus in this study, legislative staff communicate directly with the senator before the vast majority of roll calls. These contacts can take the form of written memos, verbal briefings, telephone conversations, or some combination of these modes of communication. The following are brief descriptions of how three senators typically prepare for floor votes:

> On every vote, _____ gets briefed on paper and face to face. We have a system with a form. The sheet includes the name of the bill, the amendment, who's sponsoring the amendment, what they are saying. You go over the basics pro and con, who has been contacted, and what they are saying, and then you make a recommendation. There's a space on the form for views from the state. That has to be filled in. If there's lead time, say five minutes before the vote, the LA goes in, hands him the sheet, and talks him through the information it contains.

> It's almost a Socratic method. [My boss] consumes enormous quantities of information, and that gets hard on staff. He likes to talk, mull things through. If possible, he gets a memo the night before a vote, ideally the week before if we can do it. He calls in before every vote from the cloakroom—before every vote without fail. I monitor the floor whenever the Senate is in session. A vote starts and I get a call. Always. [He asks], "Is it easy or hard?" . . . We use a code. We talk in terms of the senator and not the vote. It's too easy to get screwed up with tabling motions, budget points of order. So if it's a Leahy motion or amendment, I tell him, "Go with Leahy," or "Go against Leahy."

It's like basketball—a moving, freewheeling game. No memos. We have a Monday morning staff meeting to go through the markups and big votes for the week. It's all oral. We talk it through—saves thousands of man-hours. During the week, if there's a bill up, a couple votes, he'll ask, "What's cooking?" and we'll make a recommendation. Ninety percent of the time you can say, "This is where he'll be."

A full analysis of the divergent approaches to information gathering employed by senators is beyond the scope of this chapter. But the way senators use their staff resources appears to reflect in part a member's professional background before election to the chamber. More concretely, senators who are former House members tend to run less hierarchical, more free-flowing offices, with more direct access among LAs to the member. The former House members in my sample also are particularly likely to rely on the advice of colleagues in making roll call judgments. In short, they are more likely to exhibit a decision-making style that scholars associate with the House. In addition to the broad differences across offices in decision-making styles, there is considerable variance within individual offices by issue. The most significant factors here are the importance of an issue to a senator, whether the member is on the committee of jurisdiction, and how much advance notice an office has about a roll call.

My informants emphasized that advance warning is particularly important. Consider floor action on the GOP tax bill in July 1999. The goals and policy agendas of most senators were evoked by the roll calls on the measure, and there was advance notification about most of the amendments. One moderate Democrat began preparing for the roll calls weeks in advance. His chief of staff described how the process began. "He pulled us in yesterday on the tax bills and said, 'I need to sort this out, do some reading.' We put Bill Bradley on his call list. We got some CRS [Congressional Research Service] products for him to look at. I gave him a 3 by 5 card with a list of senators to talk to. He'll talk to Roth and Rockefeller."

I spoke with the staffer a few weeks later, around the time the tax votes occurred. He continued to emphasize the depth of the search process: "_____ asked for point papers on the surplus, data about historical trends. He was trying to find out for himself if the surplus was real. . . . I pulled in an article by a Stanford economist, and he read it. We scheduled hours of quiet time for him in his hideaway office. He talked to people at CBO and OMB. He talked to Jack Lew."

In contrast, some votes occur with little or no advance warning, and senators must scramble to gather the information necessary to cast a politically nuanced vote. Surprise votes often occur on amendments offered to budget resolutions, appropriations, and reconciliation measures. But the absence of a general germaneness provision in Senate rules also makes surprise amendments possible on nonbudgetary legislation. Senate staff often refer to sequences of surprise amendments and motions as "voteramas." Under these conditions, senators usually look toward low-investment informational cues, such as the party or ideology of an amendment's sponsor or the votes of like-minded colleagues.

Staff emphasize the pitfalls of information gathering during voteramas. Remarked the chief of staff to one conservative Republican, "When there's 20 amendments up on the floor and no one really knows them, that's when bad screw-ups occur. Your boss has to be smart. If Wellstone's on it, we're going to be skeptical. If Roberts is a yes, [my boss] is probably for that. If it's Bob Kerrey, maybe. John Chafee? Ugh. It's the sponsor and the issue." According to an aide to a southern Democrat, "We had 300 plus votes last session, but 45 came in one sitting [with] just a few minutes of debate on each amendment. Bang and vote, bang and vote." I asked him how he staffed the senator under such conditions. "I keep the floor on [the television monitor]. I send lots of e-mails out. On tax bills, having the amendments available on-line helps a lot. In other cases, less so, because it's not fast enough."

Not surprisingly, the amendment votes cast during voteramas are disproportionately party line. Caught by surprise, members tend to play it safe and stick with their fellow partisans. On tax and budget bills, for instance, one office in my sample routinely provided the senator with a list of pending amendments, with the understanding that he would vote for all GOP-sponsored proposals and against all amendments offered by Democrats—unless a proposal was highlighted in yellow. During the 106th Congress, the amendments offered during voteramas often were party message proposals, reinforcing the tendency to use "party of the sponsor" as the key voting criterion.

Recent innovations in information technology have facilitated the flow of information into Senate offices, even during voteramas. Before the mid-1990s, it could be difficult to get the text of surprise amendments. In the minutes leading up to a vote, legislative staff would have to scramble to the floor in search of amendment language. By the early 1990s, the two parties were providing television feeds that scrolled down the language of bills and amendments as the full Senate took them up. Beginning in the late 1990s, this process went on-line. With a fifteen-minute lag, Senate offices can now download the text of bills and amendments, as well as the accompanying debate. Some staff comment that this material is difficult to interpret and of limited practical value. But others describe the innovation as a potentially valuable source of information when unexpected amendments and motions come up on the floor.

Another important innovation for diffusing information about the floor agenda is the proliferation of partisan e-mail listservs. For instance, LDs in Democratic offices communicate with each other and the leadership on a daily basis about upcoming floor issues and other party matters. The LAs responsible for particular issue areas are similarly linked by e-mail. During Senate consideration of managed health care reform in summer 1999, staff to the Democratic Policy Committee regularly provided Democratic health LAs with arguments, fact sheets, and related information via e-mail. Similar electronic linkages exist between offices on the GOP side. Within each party, the press secretaries in member offices are similarly wired to each other and to the leadership message operation.

The bottom line? In the contemporary Senate, individual offices are inundated with information about pressing policy issues and roll call votes. Much of this information is political, tactical, and partisan. It is exactly the kind of strategic intelligence that Kingdon argued legislators need to cast an informed floor vote. But the practical exigencies of information gathering reflect the administrative, technological, and increasingly partisan context of the modern Senate. Consider the comments of a longtime Senate chief of staff who also has House experience.

> In the House, everyone sort of finds people they respect—a stable of colleagues who are respected on an issue. So you'd go to Andy Jacobs on social security. You'd go to Lee Hamilton on foreign affairs. A member would noodle onto the floor, turn to Lee, and ask, "What should I do on Kosovo?" Senators check in with people too [before a vote], but the whole floor situation here is less dynamic. These guys have big staffs . . . plenty of people to brief them before they get down to the floor.

The aide emphasized the informational resources of individual senators: "Members of the House are more often specialists, more likely to need their colleagues' help on a regular basis. Senators [in contrast] are orbital universes unto themselves."

Roll Call Touchstones

As mentioned, Salisbury and Shepsle (1981) argued that legislative scholars should adopt a perspective of "congressman as enterprise." That is, we should analyze the behavior of offices rather than attempt to unravel the complex web of influence between lawmakers and their employees. Senate staff do influence the viewpoints, tactics, and decisions of their principals. But senators also hire employees who share their core values. They hire staff with the expectation that these individuals will help them develop agendas and proposals in new areas. Thus, Senate staff primarily should be viewed as resources for members.

In his study of the 1960s House, Kingdon (1973) found that lawmakers generally did not view staff as significant factors in their decision making. But in the Senate offices I have examined, the member speaks to a staffer or receives a relevant memo before almost every roll call. I asked how often the member casts a vote without such input. Typical answers included "almost never," "less than 1 percent of the time," and "less than 10 times a year." Indeed, certain senators require that a knowledgeable aide be physically present in the corridor off the floor immediately before any roll call. Otherwise, "you're in serious trouble."

Such responses may reflect self-aggrandizement by staff, just as an analogous inclination may explain why Kingdon's respondents may have downplayed the role of staff in their roll call decisions. But I systematically followed up with concrete questions about the precise nature of staff input on particular votes—"Who talked to the senator?" "When did he/she receive the memo?" and so on. On the basis of these interviews, it is apparent that legislative staff have some input into the vast majority of roll call decisions made in the chamber. As a result of the extensive role of staff, and because of the difficulties of unraveling influence between members and their aides, I adopt the Salisbury and Shepsle perspective of "senator as enterprise." One implication—when I explore the factors considered by Senate offices on roll call decisions, staff input is left off the list.[3]

Senators cast hundreds of roll calls per year. Many of these votes are similar to previous roll calls or so clearly evoke a member's personal, constituency, or partisan interests that the decision is straightforward. Other votes present the member with new issues, or the relationship between the various alternatives and the lawmaker's electoral, policy, and other goals is unclear. And major votes can present senators with tradeoffs among different goals.

An aim of this research is to chart the processes through which senators make voting decisions under conditions of uncertainty or significant cross-pressure. For purposes of illustration, we can explore the factors relevant to vote choice on three issues considered during summer 1999: extension of the Northeastern Dairy Compact, the Y2K liability bill, and managed health care reform. For the dairy measure, the focus is on the August vote to invoke cloture and thus bring debate to a close. On Y2K, the emphasis is on the June vote on initial Senate passage. For managed care, my focus is on the final passage vote in July but also the more controversial amendments considered on the floor at that time. Table 13.1 provides summary data about the impact of six touchstones on member decision making for the three items. By *touchstone,* I am referring to a factor—a political actor or consideration—that plays some role in a member's decision calculus on a roll call. Six touchstones are mentioned in Table 13.1: general constituent interest, organized advocacy groups, the relevant party leadership, other senators, the administration, and a senator's core attitudes and policy views. On most roll calls, all of these factors are incorporated (to some extent) into the decision-making process. However, a factor's degree of importance will vary from member to member, from issue to issue, and over time. From the interviews, I

TABLE 13.1. Numbers of Roll Call Decisions on Three Issues (Dairy Compact, Y2K Liability, and Managed Care Reform Legislation) for which Touchstones Were of Major, Moderate, or Minor Importance

Touchstone Importance	General Constituent Interest	Advocacy Groups	Party Leadership	Other Senators	Administration	Core Attitudes and Political Views
Major	7	26	9	14	0	18
Moderate	6	7	6	9	2	6
Minor	23	3	21	13	34	12

Source: Interviews with Senate staff.

was able to code whether each touchstone was of major, moderate, or minor importance to a voting decision.[4]

General Constituent Interest

For the three pieces of legislation, Table 13.1 indicates that general constituency interest was a major factor in seven of the roll call decisions, a moderate factor in seven, and a minor factor (or less) in twenty-two. In his study of roll call voting, Kingdon defined "constituency" factors to include business interests and other organized elites, as well as mass opinion. My focus is more on ordinary citizens—the perceived mood of voters in the state. But also included here are the activities of opinion leaders and advocacy coalitions if their impact clearly took the form of grassroots mobilization. Interestingly, participants in the process emphasize that senators also consider potential shifts in constituent views and concerns when making roll call choices.[5] In the wake of the school shootings at Columbine High School, a number of GOP offices mentioned that their senators were attentive to the volatility of constituent opinion on gun issues during consideration of juvenile justice legislation in spring 1999. Similar calculations were mentioned on managed health care issues a few months later.

As Kingdon and others have observed, members of Congress use a wide range of indicators to gauge constituent opinion. Mail and telephone contacts are regularly mentioned as information sources, and these contacts are counted, tabulated, and interpreted with interest. Of course, such communications are highly sensitive to high-intensity constituent concerns and, increasingly, to sophisticated grassroots mobilization techniques aimed at stimulating—or simulating—constituent contacts with their representatives. An increasingly proportion of these contacts take the form of e-mail.

Table 13.2 summarizes the mail and telephone calls received by one office

TABLE 13.2. Count of Mail and Telephone Calls in a Sample Senate Office (Week of June 21–25, 1999)

Subject	Number of Contacts	At the End of Week
1. Anti PBS Air "It's Elementary"/Anti Gays	942	Mostly Monday
2. Anti Steel Imports	825	Decrease
3. Pro HR 1422/SS COLA based on CPI-E (PC)	735	Increase
4. Pro Notch Victims/Social Security (PC)	615	Steady
5. Miscellaneous	595	Steady
6. Pro S. 303/Networks on Satellites	385	Increase
7. Anti S. 254/Anti Gun Control (PC)	300	Steady
8. Anti Know Your Customer Banking	155	Increase
9. Anti New Gun Control Legislation	155	Steady
10. Anti CAFÉ Standards	145	Increase
11. Anti HR 45/Nuclear Waste Transportation	120	Steady
12. Pro Adult Education Funding	95	Decrease
13. Pro Bankruptcy Reform Act	40	Steady
14. Anti 602P/E-Mail Tax for USPS (hoax)	35	Steady
15. Anti Flag Burning	35	Mostly Friday
16. Pro Flag Burning	30	Steady
17. Pro Strengthen Social Security	30	Steady
18. Pro Civil Asset Forfeiture Reform	25	Steady
19. Pro Stronger Gun Control	20	Decrease
20. Anti S. 622/Hate Crimes Prevention Act	15	Steady
Mail Totals for the Week of June 21–25, 1999	Instate 4,681 Outstate 175 TOTAL 4,856	
Previous Week's Total (June 14–18)	TOTAL 5,899	

(from a medium-sized state) during a week in June 1999. As is typical, the legislative agenda for the period is only partially represented among the issues mentioned in these contacts. Indeed, of the measures considered on the floor in the surrounding weeks, only the steel import quota legislation was a top-20 mail item—and that was on the list because of an organized letter-writing campaign coordinated by the steelworkers. Managed health care reform, which would create gridlock on the floor the following week, did not even make the top-20 list.

Most citizens simply do not articulate strong preferences about the vast majority of roll call choices that senators confront on the floor—even for major items on the Senate agenda. Still, perceptions about current and potential constituent viewpoints can be a significant factor in roll call decision making. During 1999, the Y2K legislation, which dealt with technical issues of legal liability, was perceived as all but invisible to the average voter. General constituent attitudes likewise were not seen as a major factor on the dairy compact issue, with certain exceptions. The dairy vote was viewed as critical to dairy producers in a small number of northeastern states and in the upper Midwest. In these areas, the issue generated substantial media coverage, which in turn created a degree of attentiveness that reached beyond the organized dairy community.

However, of the three issues addressed in Table 13.1, general constituent interest was most significant for managed health care reform. Mass opinion was viewed as a major factor in half of the offices sampled for the issue. The quantity of mail generated by the matter was less than most offices expected, and the general public did not closely follow the legislative debate about legal liability and medical necessity. But labor and business groups ran television commercials in a number of states at the time of Senate floor action. And both parties viewed managed care votes as potential fodder for future Senate campaigns.

I asked one Republican chief of staff about constituent interest in the managed care bill. He immediately ticked off statistics about the number of uninsured citizens in his state, the number enrolled in Medicaid and Medicare, and the number served by HMOs. During floor action on the measure, the office received just 200 e-mails and phone calls about managed care, and "most of these people didn't know what they were talking about. It was straight out of someone's press release." But the office closely monitored coverage of the debate in home-state newspapers. "We did a lot of public relations, radio, and press releases. . . . These issues tend to poll Democrat." After the leading newspaper in the state editorialized in favor of the Republican plan, the staffer judged the outcome "a big victory for us because we fought them to a draw." On managed care, then, perceptions about current and potential public opinion on the matter were a factor in roll call decision making, even though the average voter was unfamiliar with the details of the legislative debate. Interestingly, the level of public interest in managed care reform varied from state to state, depending on the degree to which HMOs had penetrated local markets for health insurance.

Organized Advocacy Groups

The second column of Table 13.1 captures the importance of interest groups in roll call decision making on the three items. Kingdon's (1978) definition of "interest group" was relatively broad. Among other actors, it included "lobbying organizations, identifiable but unorganized sets of people, and even such social classifications as 'middle-class taxpayers'" (146). I adopt a somewhat narrower definition here to help distinguish this touchstone from general constituent interest. By organized advocacy group, I mean exactly that—an organized collectivity of individuals, typically with some lobbying presence in the state or in Washington.

As indicated in Table 13.1, the Senate offices under focus here generally perceived organized groups as a more significant touchstone than mass opinion. Advocacy groups were viewed as a major factor in over 70 percent of the voting decisions; the analogous figure for general constituency interest was less than 20 percent. Indeed, organized groups were a significant factor on all three measures, although there were major differences across states on the dairy vote.

Of course, there also are important links between constituent opinion and the activities of interest groups. Groups located in the state receive by far the most attention from an office. Dairy producers were a major factor on the dairy compact vote. But the decision making of senators was mostly driven by the interests of dairy farmers in their own states, and the industry was divided by region on the compact extension. Senate staff regularly comment that national lobbying organizations are given limited weight in a member's decision calculus unless they also have a presence in the state. And the more effective lobbyists usually bring officials or group members from the home state with them when they meet with a senator. A number of offices generally do not allow lobbyists in to see the member unless constituents accompany them.

Modern advocacy groups seek to influence roll call decisions via a range of tactics, including grassroots mobilization efforts. Such tactics further complicate the distinction between constituent interest and organized groups as roll call touchstones. On managed health care, for instance, the American Medical Association ran television ads in eleven states supporting reform. During floor action, the organization flew in planeloads of doctors from these states to help lobby wavering senators. Business and insurance groups also ran national advertising campaigns, again targeting pivotal votes. The AFL-CIO spent $500,000 on ads that aired in eight key states.

One example—Illinois Republican Peter Fitzgerald was widely viewed as a swing voter on a number of managed care issues. The week of floor action, the AFL-CIO spent $40,000 on radio ads in Chicago alone. The advertisements encouraged listeners to call the freshman and ask, "Which side are you on?"[6] The same week, representatives of fifteen large companies with a major Illinois presence (e.g., Caterpillar, John Deere, and UPS) met with Fitzgerald in Washington. The American Medical Association, which is based in Chicago, also ran ads in the city urging listeners to telephone Fitzgerald's office. The freshman Republican eventually voted with the Democrats against final passage.[7] Thus, interest groups matter, and their influence is often channeled through the folks back home.

Party Leaders

The extended party leadership (floor leaders, whips, deputy whips, and policy committee chairs) was a major factor on nine of the decisions in Table 13.1, of moderate importance on six, and a minor factor on twenty-one. Here the differences across issues are particularly striking, in part because the three items were selected to illustrate different levels of partisan disagreement. All of the staff I spoke with agreed that the leadership had played no role in member decisions on the dairy compact. The lead backers of the proposal did work with Majority Leader Trent Lott to bring the matter to a vote. But beyond procedure and timing, the leadership was inactive.

Party leaders were more of a factor on the Y2K bill. The chief of staff to a Republican senator explained why: "[On Y2K], the party was involved up and down the line. Look at the top of the Standard and Poors 500 and you see Silicon Valley and High Tech. Members have figured out where the wealth is. . . . The Democrats are captives of the plaintiff's bar, and this bill forces them to choose between their long-time constituency and the new money in the High Tech community—people who are just getting active in politics. . . . The vote is an easy one for us and we welcome the Democrats' distress."

Lott and Majority Whip Don Nickles (R-OK) were integrally involved in mobilizing support for the legislation and moving it to the top of the floor agenda. Democratic leaders also were active, attempting to hold their fellow partisans in line against the measure—at least until the Clinton administration's initial opposition began to falter. At that point, Democratic leaders backed off.

The two party leaderships were a significant touchstone on managed health care reform. On both sides of the aisle, the initiative was viewed as a significant "party message" issue. A nascent centrist coalition was quickly countered by Democratic leaders interested in sharpening their party's public message on managed care issues and distinguishing it from the Republican stance. When Republican John Chafee attempted to push a centrist alternative, GOP leaders persuaded party moderates to ignore his effort. Recalled one Republican aide, "This one came up over two years. It was like two armies marching out of the mountains, across the river. They saw each other and each knew where the other one was. There were virtually no surprises." Within both parties, the leadership spearheaded the public relations effort on managed care. During chamber action, both parties had informal war rooms set up near the floor, manned by senators and staff who were available for talk shows and interviews. The Democrats referred to their operation as the "Intensive Communications Unit."

On the GOP side, a leadership-appointed task force chaired by Nickles drafted the Republican plan. Democrats countered with strategically crafted amendments aimed at confronting Republicans with politically difficult votes. One popular proposal—offered by Charles Robb (D-VA)—would have allowed women to designate a gynecologist or obstetrician as their primary care provider and would have given doctors and patients the right to determine the duration of hospitalization after a mastectomy. To minimize floor defections on such amendments, members of the GOP task force surveyed their fellow partisans about the likely Democratic proposals. A Republican staffer recalled: "There was something like 16 questions—all the Democrat amendments—and they asked for yes, no, or undecided on each. The sheet asked what your problems were on the Democrat amendments."

Republican leaders used the survey results, along with other materials, to help draft narrower alternatives in the same topic areas as the Democratic amendments. The aim was in part to provide Republicans with political cover. For example, Republicans responded to the Robb amendment with an alternative offered by Olympia Snowe (R-ME) that just included the mastectomy language. Most Republicans voted against the Robb amendment and for the Snowe proposal. A number of Republican senators did vote with the Democrats on certain of the amendments. But the GOP leadership ensured that these defections were sufficiently spread out that Republican proposals still carried the day. Overall, staff from both parties described the GOP whipping process on managed care as highly effective.

Other Senators

As Table 13.1 indicates, other senators were a major touchstone in fourteen of the thirty-six decisions concerning the dairy, Y2K, and managed care initiatives. By "other senators," I am referring to significant contacts with—or consideration of—other members who are not part of the extended leadership. In the interviews, for instance, I asked if the relevant senator sought out the advice of a colleague about the vote under focus and also whether the member was directly lobbied on the matter by another senator. Thus, in addition to cue taking for informational purposes, this touchstone encompasses a range of member-to-member contacts that might affect the voting calculus. Also included are contacts made at the staff level if they were conducted at the instruction of the member—"Call Rockefeller's office and get his take on this"—or if such staff contacts were significantly above and beyond the routine interactions that occur between LAs with similar issue responsibilities.

The nature of the member-to-member contacts varied somewhat across issues. For the dairy vote, the contacts typically were at the member level. Extending the dairy compact was a major political challenge for Vermont Senators Patrick Leahy and James Jeffords and certain other northeastern colleagues. A number of midwestern senators, led by Herb Kohl (D-WI) and Rod Grams (R-MN), were adamantly in opposition. On both sides of the fight, the lead senators compiled lists of members who were solidly in their camp, solidly against, or to some degree undecided. As the LD to one cross-pressured Democrat recalled, "We knew this fight was coming up. The Ag LA talked to the dairy folks in [the state] and asked if they cared who won. Half said, 'No, stay out.' The others said, 'Support Leahy because we may want our own compact down the line.' That's the clearest direction we got." The staffer emphasized that the member-to-member lobbying was central to her boss's decision: "_____ was heavily personally lobbied by Feingold and Leahy, and they're both buddies. Each side said that [dairy interests in the state] were with them. _____ had to tell these friends either, one, 'I'm with you' or, two, 'I'd like to, but my state dairy people say no.' . . . In the end, we thought we had a more credible explanation [by] going with the Northeast." The chief of staff to another Democrat commented: "Kohl and Leahy personally lobbied this one furiously. [My boss] talked to Leahy three or four times here and on the phone and more times on the floor. Leahy's chief of staff called and pitched it to me as a favor, not on substance." By all accounts, Senator Jeffords was similarly promoting the interests of his Vermont constituents among Republicans. For most offices, the parochial interests of home state dairy producers and the firms they supplied were the pivotal factors in the vote. But the member-to-member lobbying also mattered.

In contrast, the member-to-member contacts on Y2K and managed care were more informational, rooted in the substantive and strategic complexities of these issues. On Y2K, a number of GOP senators spoke with Robert Bennett (R-UT), chair of a special committee dealing with Y2K issues, and with Commerce Committee chair John McCain (R-AZ), who was lead sponsor of the measure. A number of Democrats sought advice from Chris Dodd (D-CT), John Kerry (D-MA), and Ernest Hollings (D-SC), all of whom were active in the debate. On managed care, GOP senators relied on the leadership of Bill Frist (R-TN) because of his background as a heart and lung surgeon and his general expertise in the area of health policy. Frist also was on the GOP task force for managed care. The task force divided the Republican Conference into zones, with a task force member assigned to work with colleagues from that area. The member-to-member contact on managed care was substantive, political, and extensive.

In short, other colleagues can be an important touchstone in the roll call decisions of senators. Most often, senators turn for advice to policy experts who share their core values and political goals. These contacts usually are not last-minute exchanges on the floor immediately before a vote is cast. Instead, they tend to occur earlier in the decision-making process.

Administration

The Clinton administration was not viewed as a significant factor in roll call decision making on the three bills. Indeed, the administration was judged as a minor consideration across the board, except for the cases of two Democrats on the Y2K measure. On dairy, the administration was opposed to the compact extension, but regional and member-to-member considerations dominated Senate decision making. On Y2K, the administration's position shifted from early opposition to support for a compromise alternative. The preliminary opposition did help keep certain Democrats in line, but this constraint vanished as Clinton's position on the issue evolved.

Interestingly, none of the offices I interviewed about managed care perceived the administration as a major factor, even though the original "Patient's Bill of Rights" was drafted by an administration-appointed commission. Administration officials also spoke on a number of occasions at Democratic caucus meetings about the measure. But Senate Democrats primarily viewed Edward Kennedy (D-MA), (then) Minority Leader Tom Daschle (D-SD), and other Democratic leaders as the key party actors on managed care reform. A number of offices mentioned the impeachment experience as a reason for Daschle's policymaking prominence and the limited deference afforded the Clinton administration.[8] Especially in the 106th Congress, the impact of the president on Senate policy making mostly originated in the power to propose and the administration's influence over the national political agenda.

Core Attitudes and Political Views

In contrast to the other touchstones referenced in Table 13.1, the senator's core attitudes and political views was a touchstone that I did not ask specific questions about with regard to impact on voting decisions. But it was clear from the interviews that, on certain issues, a member approached a roll call choice by consciously relating the matter to his or her ideology and/or prior voting record. Asked about their boss's vote on the steel import quota measure, for instance, a number of staff immediately responded, "That was easy, he's a free trader" or "That's a quota bill and we're against quotas."

Clearly, we need to be careful in gauging the importance of a senator's political philosophy or record to a roll call decision. Such considerations are less visible and concrete than are the other touchstones. Moreover, there may be a natural tendency for Senate staff, who are highly political people, to exaggerate the philosophical underpinnings of their boss's decisions. Still, the linkages between a member's underlying attitudes and roll call choice surfaced repeatedly in my interviews. And a member's prior voting record can be a useful informational touchstone when there is uncertainty about a vote. Such linkages also have consequences for the deliberative character of roll call decision making.

As a result, I attempted to balance the potential importance of this touchstone with the obvious measurement problems by looking for spontaneous references to underlying political attitudes and their connections to vote choice. That is, I waited for respondents to mention such considerations and then made a judgment call about whether the touchstone was of moderate or major importance.

Again, these data should be interpreted with care, but there is substantial variance by issue, and the differences make good intuitive sense.

The dairy compact, for instance, was a classic parochial fight, and this last touchstone was of limited relevance. On Y2K, a number of Republicans viewed the issue in terms of their overall stances on liability and tort reform. Certain Democrats mentioned that their bosses regarded the proposal as an "access to justice" issue—above and beyond any political inclination to satisfy the trial lawyers. Not surprisingly, core attitudes and political views were a pervasive factor in the decisions about managed care reform. The issue had been on the agenda for three years; it tapped into ideological divisions between Republicans and Democrats; and senators routinely had been asked to explain their positions before and after the 1998 elections. Constituent, group, and party factors mattered a great deal on managed care. But core attitudes and political views also played a significant role.

Conclusion

The analysis in this chapter illustrates how legislators make decisions on major issues in the contemporary Senate. And my emphasis on the *processes* through which senators decide provides useful perspective on a number of theoretical and empirical questions of interest to legislative scholars. Briefly consider the differences between member decision making in the Senate and the House; the ongoing controversy about party power in Congress; and recent generalizations about the decline of deliberation in the modern Senate.

First, the main contours of roll call decision making have not changed fundamentally since the first publication of Kingdon's book in 1973, and important continuities also exist in the process of member decision making across the two chambers. In the contemporary Senate and House, legislators must repeatedly take positions and cast votes on complex issues subject to significant uncertainty and binding time constraints. Constituency imperatives—including mass opinion and interests groups with an important constituency presence—are central to decision making in both chambers. Similarly, the emphasis that the two political parties now place on formulating and publicizing a coherent party "message" shapes how senators and House members alike make up their mind on certain key issues such as managed care reform.

However, the analysis in this chapter also suggests important differences in member decision making across the two chambers. For one, compared to the House leadership, Senate party leaders often lack the formal powers necessary to control the floor agenda. As a result, the choice context on the floor is far less predictable in the Senate relative to the House, complicating the decision-making process for individual senators. Moreover, senators represent larger, more diverse constituencies than is the case for House members and thus typically confront a broader range of interests and pressures when deciding how to vote. However, Senators also have greater access to personal staff resources than do their House counterparts. The enhanced informational capacities of the typical Senate office enterprise help make decision making within the chamber more manageable—and also contribute to the hyperindividualism that characterizes the modern Senate.

As mentioned at the beginning of this chapter, a number of scholars have argued that party leaders in Congress do not regularly exert a significant and independent impact on legislative outcomes. Instead, congressional policy making is largely driven by the preferences of pivotal lawmakers—for instance, the median voter on the House floor or the senator providing the 60th vote on a cloture motion. Another view is that party leaders and party organizations can matter a great deal. The conditional party government perspective, for example, posits that when the majority caucus is relatively united about policy, rank-and-file lawmakers will empower their centralized party leadership, granting them the tools necessary to shift outcomes toward the preferences of the majority caucus (Aldrich and Rohde 1997–98).

The analysis in this chapter suggests that Senate party leaders do influence the legislative process under certain conditions. They help structure the choices that members confront on the floor. And they also shape the processes through which individual lawmakers decide how to vote. On managed care, for instance, some preliminary efforts were made on both sides of the aisle to forge a centrist coalition between the Republican and Democratic party stances. But leaders in both parties convinced wavering moderates that their political goals would be better served by staying loyal to the relevant party position. Each party sought to sharpen its public image on health care issues and distinguish its message from that of the other side. There was minimal arm-twisting. Rather, the emphasis was on convincing pivotal members that it was critical to present a unified partisan front to the voters and interested advocacy groups. During the 106th Congress, the legislative impact of party in the Senate typically took this form.

Under what conditions does party matter? The conditional party government approach emphasizes unity among members of the majority caucus. Clearly, there was the possibility of preference cohesion among Senate Republicans on managed care, tax reduction, and other issues considered on the floor during the 106th Congress. But the real impact of party was on the *process of preference formation*. Thus, we need to look beyond conceptualizations of a preexisting distribution of preferences to determine the conditions under which party matters in the Senate. And isolating such conditions requires that we closely examine the processes through which senators make up their mind on major issues and roll calls.

Finally, serious questions have been raised by scholars, legislators, and media analysts about the quality of deliberation in the contemporary Senate. A few years ago, Senator Robert Byrd (D-WV) even remarked that "the Senate's role as a deliberative body should be to endeavor to help the people hear all sides so that consensus may form; yet, as an institution the Senate is more and more ceasing to perform that deliberative function. It is not the Senate that I once knew. The Senate has lost its soul."[9] Byrd argued that members are spread too thinly, lack the time necessary to make informed judgments, focus too much on message and sound bites, and lean too heavily on staff.

If we are to evaluate the quality of Senate deliberation, though, we need to move beyond broad generalizations and consider up close how members actually make decisions on major issues. What are meaningful and realistic criteria for gauging deliberation in the modern Senate? To what extent do senators receive the information necessary to cast an informed vote? For that matter, precisely what constitutes an informed vote? To what extent do members consider different sides of an issue and competing evidence? Is the information gathering and analysis that occurs within a Senate office a form of deliberation? Is member-to-member contact and dialogue a necessary condition for a decision to be deliberative? Answering these questions is beyond the scope of this chapter. But sustained observation of the processes through which senators make choices on major policy issues can help us evaluate the deliberative capacity of this fascinating institution.

Notes

1. For each of the twenty issues included in the broader study, data were gathered from twelve Senate offices, equally divided by party. Thus, the total number of observations (roll call decisions) to be analyzed in the project is 240. In devising the sample of offices, I primarily relied on personal contacts. Thus, the selection process here diverges from the random design used by Kingdon (1973, 1978, 1989). For each office, my primary goal was to secure access to the staff person closest to the senator on the issues under study. In addition, it was critical that the relevant aides speak with me as candidly as possible about the decision-making process used on these issues. Selecting the sample randomly would have produced little access and even less candor. As a result, I constructed the sample in a piecemeal fashion via personal contacts who could vouch for my trustworthiness. Still, the sample constitutes a fairly large proportion of the entire membership. As mentioned, it is equally divided by party. Within each partisan cohort, efforts were made to keep the sample broadly representative by ideology and region. I also looked for a mix of junior and senior members. For reasons of access and candor, I promised in writing to all of the respondents that none of the remarks they made to me would be traceable to them or their bosses. Thus, the interviews were conducted on a

not-for-attribution basis. I took extensive notes during each conversation and then typed them up. In deciding what questions to ask the staff informants, I mostly worked off Kingdon's interview protocol. Indeed, I found that his core questions still work remarkably well. A preliminary questionnaire was developed and pretested with two Senate chiefs of staff that I knew and trusted. I spoke with them at length about question wording, topics to address, the likelihood of candid responses, and so on and made certain adjustments in question wording and order to reflect their concerns. In addition, at various points during the 106th Congress, top aides in ten of the thirty-six offices included in my sample met two or more times with groups of my students in Williamsburg, Virginia, at the College of William and Mary and spoke with them informally about the relevant senator's approach to the major issues on the legislative agenda. These sessions enhanced the level of rapport during my subsequent interviews with the staffers in Washington and also turned up interesting information about the Senate and member decision making.

2. *Congressional Staff Directory,* Spring 1999, 74.

3. In the revised editions of his book, Kingdon (1978, 1989) suggests that the "member as enterprise" approach is appropriate for analyzing decision making within the modern Congress, in part because of the proliferation of personal office staff.

4. When a touchstone is rated as a major consideration for a senator on a vote, it is likely that the factor also had some influence on the decision. So if the lobbying of party leaders is perceived as important on an issue, most probably the leadership influenced member behavior. But generalizations about influence should be based in part on linkages between the *preferences* of interested actors and the relevant legislative outcome. Such data were gathered as part of my broader project. But our focus in this chapter is on factors *considered* in the decision making process. Such consideration may or may not directly translate into influence.

5. For a conceptual discussion of the importance of potential publics in congressional decision making, consult Arnold (1990).

6. Robert A. Davis, "Hard to Get a Firm Grip on Fitzgerald," *Chicago Sun-Times,* July 15, 1999, 39.

7. Ibid.

8. Daschle also had a long track record as a policy expert on health care issues that predated his tenure as Democratic leader.

9. Hearing before the Joint Committee on the Organization of Congress, 103rd Congress, 1st sess., February 2, 1993, S. Hrg. 103-36, 5.

282

· 14 ·

Representational Power and Distributive Politics: Senate Influence on Federal Transportation Spending

Frances E. Lee

Bias in congressional spending is one topic that interests the general public almost as much as political scientists. The vast academic literature on distributive politics is mirrored by the hundreds of stories on the topic that the news media publish each year. As Krehbiel (1991) has observed, news stories about pork barrel politics are, "if not a dime a dozen, at least cheap" (263). A Nexis search for the term *pork barrel* in news articles from the past year produced more than 200 hits. The *NBC Nightly News* has a recurrent segment entitled "The Fleecing of America," devoted to embarrassing members of Congress and other governmental officials who procure funding for inefficient or undeserving government projects. There is even a nonpartisan Washington, D.C., think tank, the Citizens against Government Waste, that is single-mindedly dedicated to unearthing pork barrel spending and exposing the members of Congress responsible for it in an annual, widely disseminated publication, the *Congressional Pig Book Summary.*

Academic and popular press treatments of the subject generally differ in one key respect. Popular exposés of pork barrel spending focus on the individual lawmakers involved, typically suggesting that they, through lack of virtue or public spirit, neglect the common good in their self-serving pursuit of reelection. Political scientists, by contrast, take little interest in the failings of individual members of Congress and focus instead on institutional explanations for patterns in congressional spending, particularly on the features identified by Ferejohn (1974), "geographic representation, majority rule, and the committee system" (252).

Although the political science literature on distributive politics is extensive and diverse, these three institutional characteristics remain the usual suspects in all political scientists' studies. Within this list, the principal culprit behind biases in distributive policy making—that is, behind excessive and inequitably distributed spending on particularized benefits—is geographic representation. Members of Congress are elected by and responsible to geographic districts, not the whole nation. This simple fact creates a collective action problem in federal policy making: constituents in these geographic constituencies benefit from federal programs and projects, even when they are inefficient from a national perspective, because the costs of funding them are distributed broadly across the nation while the benefits are concentrated in particular localities. In seeking reelection, members of Congress thus provide these particularized benefits to their constituents.

The internal organization of Congress adds to this picture. Congressional committees confer jurisdiction and influence over policy areas to small groups of members, leading many scholars to argue that they advantage their members in obtaining particularized benefits for constituents. Given members' ability to select their own committee assignments, some have contended that congressional committees, in turn, are composed of members who have a stake in the relevant policies, making committees unrepresentative of the larger chamber. Similarly, membership in the majority party increases members' influence, enhancing their ability to procure local benefits relative to members of the minority party. Finally, the electoral interests of incumbents play a role: several scholars have theorized that electorally vulnerable members have greater incentives than others to seek particularized benefits as a (relatively) noncontroversial strategy to win friends without creating enemies. In sum, these fundamental characteristics of American governing institutions are the key players in the academic account of distributive politics.

There are, however, some curious omissions in the literature on distributive policy making. Despite their interest in institutional explanations for policy outcomes, political scientists concerned with distributive politics have tended to overlook one prominent institution: the Senate. Most studies of distributive politics in Congress have focused exclusively on the House. This neglect of the Senate is difficult to explain because the theories advanced in the literature clearly apply to the Senate as well as to the House. Senators, like House members, are elected by and responsible to geographic constituencies. Like House members, many senators perceive that procuring and protecting particularized benefits for their constituents serves their reelection interests. Committee membership and majority-party status enhance senators' influence over policy making just as they enhance House members'. Speaking broadly, the Senate as an institution has as much power over distributive policy as the House.

Even those studies of distributive politics that have examined the Senate's role have failed to take into account that body's most distinctive institutional characteristic, its basis of apportionment. The Senate is the only legislature in the United States to which the courts have not applied the principle of "one person, one vote," and by comparison to this standard, it is the most malapportioned national legislature in the democratic world (Lijphart 1984, 174). If we expect that a geographic area's representation on particular congressional committees or by representatives of the majority party will affect the amount of federal dollars it receives, then we should also take into account its number of representatives in the Congress as a whole. Put differently, Senate apportionment distributes representational power in a peculiar way—conferring enhanced representation on states with small populations—and, to the extent that representational power affects federal distributive policy, small states will receive additional federal dollars. Indeed, recent studies have shown pervasive small-state advantages across federal distributive programs: small states consistently receive more federal dollars per capita than large states, even after controlling for differences in state need for federal funds. These studies, however, have not assessed the importance of Senate apportionment relative to the other political variables that shape distributive policy.

The purpose of this chapter is to assess the importance of Senate apportionment relative to the other variables that are thought to influence distributive politics: committee, party, electoral, and apportionment. To do this, I conduct multivariate regression analyses of federal spending for some of the largest distributive programs, grants-in-aid to states for surface transportation. Of the four variables, Senate apportionment—the one that has received the least amount of attention in the literature—has the strongest and most consistent effect on distributive policy. One of the most exceptional characteristics of the U.S. Senate turns out to be an exceptionally important variable for understanding the politics of distributing federal funds.

Institutional Sources of Political Benefits

For purposes of this study, *political benefits* (Rundquist 1980, xiii) in federal distributive policy making refers to the projects and outlays that members of Congress are able to direct to their constituencies in excess of what that their constituents would receive without their representation. In other words, political benefits are the distributive bonuses that constituents gain through the influence of their congressional representatives. As discussed above, these bonuses can have several possible sources: constituencies may gain advantages in distributive politics through their representatives' committee assignments, majority-party status, electorally motivated pork seeking and, in the case of overrepresented states, their enhanced Senate representation.

Committee Assignments

While once almost an article of faith in congressional studies, the idea that committees enable members of Congress to obtain particularized benefits for their districts has become controversial during the past decade. The conventional wisdom held that members of Congress use their prerogatives and influence as committee members to gain special benefits for their constituents. Committees, after all, possess a number of negative and positive powers over the congressional agenda that limit the opportunities of the full chambers to revise their work and circumvent their authority. Expressed in its most comprehensive form by Weingast and Marshall (1988), the distributive perspective on congressional committees envisions the entire committee system as an institutional mechanism enabling members of Congress to capture gains from trade.

More recently, Gilligan and Krehbiel (1990) have challenged this view of the congressional committee system, arguing that committees are designed to advance the legislature's collective goals by providing specialized information to the chamber, not to furnish distributive benefits to their members. This informational perspective on committees emphasizes the expertise that committee members develop and the many ways that Congress keeps committees in check. As evidence for this perspective, Krehbiel (1991, 151–91) demonstrates that the House generally accords fewer procedural protections to committees with jurisdictions over highly particularistic programs than it grants to other committees.

Empirical work testing the distributive perspective on committees has yielded mixed results. There are, in fact, at least as many studies showing that committee members obtain few or no additional benefits for their constituents from the programs within their committee jurisdictions (Anagnoson 1980, 1982; Chernick 1979; Gist and Hill 1984; Hird 1991; Hooton 1997; Levitt and Poterba 1999; Ray 1980a, 1980b; Rundquist and Griffith 1976; Rundquist 1978) as there are studies finding that they do (Alvarez and Saving 1997; Anderson and Tollison 1991; Arnold 1979; Carsey and Rundquist 1999; Ferejohn 1974; Goss 1972; Gryski 1991; Plott 1968; Strom 1975). At minimum, these mixed results indicate that the role of congressional committees in distributive politics can easily be overstated. Committees are clearly not free to propose any sort of funding distribution to the floor but are constrained by the preferences of majorities within their respective chambers.

Partisan Representation

Although distributive issues very rarely involve a high level of partisan conflict, a number of scholars have recently pointed to the role of parties in shaping federal distributive policy. Emphasizing the ability of parties to advance the collective interests of their members, these scholars argue that parties assist their members in electoral politics by directing federal funds toward their constituencies. Levitt and Snyder (1995), for example, show that distributive programs initiated during periods of solid Democratic control of Congress exhibited a bias toward districts containing Democratic voters, while programs instituted while the Senate was controlled by the Republican party did not.

Electoral Incentives

All members of Congress are not equally motivated to seek particularized benefits for their constituents. First, vulnerable members of Congress have enhanced incentives to seek the electoral benefits that these activities afford. As Fiorina (1989, 48) and others have observed, constituency service and obtaining particularized benefits are relatively noncontroversial activities and are unlikely to divide voters, thus providing electoral benefits with few electoral costs. Although this hypothesis has not been tested with Senate data, Stein and Bickers (1994) have shown that the districts represented by members of Congress who were elected by narrow margins receive more new grant awards than other districts.

Second, incumbents' incentives to seek particularized benefits are conditioned by their need to offer a consistent presentation of self to their constituents. Sellers (1997) shows that members of Congress who run for office by emphasizing budget cutting and fiscal discipline do not benefit electorally from procuring particularized benefits, while more fiscally liberal members do.

Senate Apportionment

Despite the lack of scholarly attention it has received, Senate apportionment greatly affects the amount of representational power that geographic areas have in Congress. Thinking in per capita terms, the residents of Wyoming, the least populous state, have sixty times as much congressional representation as the residents of California. This fact is likely to shape federal distributive policy for three reasons.

First, the distribution of representational power in the Senate will incline that body to prefer to distribute funds in ways that are disproportionately favorable to small states. The Senate is an egalitarian, individualistic body that grants few special prerogatives even to its leaders. Because of its collegial legislative process (Smith 1989), at a basic level every senator is the equal of every other. At the same time, every state has equal representation in the Senate. To the extent that federal spending reflects this equality of power, then, the Senate will tend to distribute funds equally to states. Given the vast differences in state population, however, an equal distribution of funds across states means that the less populous states will receive dramatically more federal funds per capita than populous states. Although the House has different spending priorities than the Senate as a result of its different basis of apportionment, it will not neutralize the effect of Senate apportionment on distributive policy outcomes. Instead, the House's basis of apportionment leads it to prefer population-based distributions of federal funds, not distributions that are disproportionately favorable to large states. When the two bodies go to conference on distributive policies, then, even a simple split of the difference between the House's preference for a population-based funding distribution and the Senate's preference for greater state equality results in distributions of funds that are skewed toward small states.

Second, the Senate's apportionment scheme affects individual senators' representational strategies. Senators representing small states have more incentive to pursue particularized benefits than those representing large states because any given federal outlay or project will affect a greater proportion of a senator's constituents in a small state than in a large state (Atlas et al. 1995, 625). As a consequence, any given particularized benefit will do more to enhance a small-state senator's statewide visibility and credit-claiming opportunities than the same benefit would provide for a large-state senator. This fact makes a Washington style of pursuing particularized benefits more attractive to small-state senators (Lee and Oppenheimer 1999, 123–27). Data on committee assignments reveal that small-state senators are overrepresented (given their presence in the chamber) on constituency committees while large-state senators are overrepresented on policy committees (Lee and Oppenheimer 1999, 127–33). If small-state senators do, in fact, work harder to procure particularized benefits for their constituents, then small states will have additional advantages in federal distributive policy beyond those resulting from their equal Senate representation.

Third, Senate apportionment shapes the incentives of coalition leaders as they build support for distributive programs in the Senate. Because a state's need for federal funds correlates closely with population, the great variation in state size means that some states have far greater needs for federal funds than others. As a result, even though all senators' votes are of equal value to coalition builders, they are not of equal "price." Coalition builders can include benefits for small states at a lower cost to program budgets than comparable benefits for more populous states, making small-state senators more attractive as coalition members than large-state senators. Senate distributive policies will thus tend to reflect small-state senators' preferences more closely than their large-state colleagues' (Lee 2000).

Assessing the Variables

The goal of this chapter is to assess Senate apportionment relative to the other political variables that scholars have identified as influences on federal distributive policy—committee assignments, partisan representation, and electoral incentives. It is not likely, after all, that all of these variables will have equally strong and consistent effects on distributive patterns. For a start, the effect of committee assignments on distributive policy will be contingent on the degree of autonomy that the chambers grant to committees. As Smith (1989) argues, "Committee power is observable and important only when the policy preferences of a committee and the chamber differ" (170). At the same time, however, "committees are nothing but agents of their parent chambers" (168). Given this subordinate status, committees can obtain legislation disproportionately favorable to their own members only when the chambers permit it. No doubt, committee members enjoy a variety of informational advantages that assist them in shepherding their legislation on the floor. In the contemporary Congress, however, committees do not enjoy the protections afforded by the norms of comity and reciprocity characteristic of the Congress of the 1950s. As a consequence, committee members seeking to garner disproportionate benefits now need to rely on procedural protections that restrict the ability of nonmembers to amend or alter their work. Few procedural protections are available to Senate committees because of the absence of restrictive rules. In the House, moreover, committees with jurisdiction over distributive programs—such as Agriculture, Public Works, and Interior—receive fewer procedural protections than other committees. In light of these considerable constraints, committee membership is unlikely to yield as many distributive advantages as previous researchers have often assumed.

Generally speaking, the role of political parties in distributive politics has not received the attention it deserves, especially compared to the level of scholarly interest in the effects of congressional committees. This is not surprising, considering that many of the most influential early studies of distributive politics were conducted in the mid-1970s, when party unity in Congress had fallen to some of its lowest levels in history. By the late 1980s, however, party unity had increased to highs unprecedented in the postwar era and has since remained at high levels (Rohde 1991). Given this change in context, it is only reasonable to suppose that party plays a more important role in distributive policy making today than in the 1960s, the 1970s, or even the 1980s. At times, however, control of Congress is divided between the parties, making it difficult for even highly unified majority parties in either chamber to direct funds disproportionately toward their members' constituents. After all, a Republican-controlled Senate can check a Democratic-controlled House that attempts to direct funds disproportionately to Democratic-leaning states. As a result, partisanship will have less effect on distributive politics during periods of low party unity or divided control of Congress.

Electoral vulnerability, by comparison, is likely to be a more important variable for understanding the behavior of individual members of Congress than for understanding distributive policy at an aggregate level. Vulnerable incumbents constitute only a small percentage of members of Congress. As Jacobson (1993) writes, "Only a small and diminishing minority of contests involve a high-quality challenger with the financial resources for a full-scale campaign" (125). Indeed, the 1998 congressional elections saw the largest number of safe seats since 1958. Because of the paucity of competitive races for Congress, only a relatively small number of incumbents will have this extra incentive to seek particularized benefits. As a factor for understanding distributive patterns, then, electoral vulnerability will probably be less important than other variables.

Despite the lack of scholarly interest in the subject, Senate apportionment is likely to have an influence on federal distributive policy that is equal to, if not greater than, that of each of the three other variables. The small-state advantage is, after all, a structural feature of the Senate. The effects of committee and party, by contrast, are contingent on other factors: the willingness of the chambers to grant committees autonomy, the strength and unity of parties in cooperating to advance their members' interests, and whether partisan control of Congress is divided. In addition, unlike the committee power hypothesis, the hypothesis that Senate apportionment will affect distributive policy does not require one to make antimajoritarian assumptions. As Krehbiel (1991) argues, the committee power theory of distributive politics assumes that a "committee gains at the expense of a majority" by "exercis[ing] its parliamentary rights to get a majority to do what is not in the majority's interest with respect to a single issue" (76). Senate apportionment requires no such assumption because most (31) states are overrepresented in the Senate. Distributional schemes that direct disproportionate benefits to small states will thus garner broad support in the chamber as a whole; if a committee reports such a bill to the Senate floor, a large majority of senators will be likely to support it.

Finally, Senate apportionment is likely to have a more consistent and pervasive effect on distributive policy than committee and partisan representation because of its stability over time. The partisan and committee representation of districts and states is always changing, while federal distributive policy exhibits a great deal of inertia. A district might be represented by a Democrat who is not on the Transportation and Infrastructure Committee in the 104th Congress, for example, and then by a Republican who is on the committee in the 105th Congress. But because the 104th Congress passed a major six-year reauthorization of highway programs, its policy choices will shape federal transportation spending through 2004, thus rendering that district no advantage in highway spending despite its representation on the committee in the 105th Congress by a member of the majority party. As a consequence of dynamics like these, federal distributive policy will not keep pace with changing committee and party representation even if these variables do in fact have a strong effect when policies are made. Senate apportionment, however, is a constant. Whenever Congress funds, authorizes, or reauthorizes programs, small states enjoy advantages from Senate apportionment.

Measuring the Sources of Political Benefits

To ascertain the effects of these variables on distributive policy, I conducted multivariate regression analyses of federal outlays to states for surface transportation programs between 1983 and 1997.[1] These programs provide funding for construction, maintenance, and repair of interstate, primary, and secondary highways, bridges, pedestrian walkways, and bicycle paths; mass transit; and research and demonstration projects for improving transportation. Taken together, surface transportation programs represent one of the federal government's greatest domestic policy commitments and consistently account for at least 20 percent of all the federal government's grants-in-aid to state and local governments.[2]

Surface transportation programs provide a good test for the effects of these variables for three reasons. First, these programs are highly distributive in character and thus relatively uncomplicated by ideological or other nondistributive issues. As such, they are programs that legislators perceive as requiring them to "stand up and be counted on geographic allocations" (Arnold 1990, 135). Second, Congress has resolutely maintained its authority over geographic distribution in these programs. Funds for these programs are distributed by congressional statutes that apportion the funds by formulas and delegate little authority over allocation to the executive branch. As a result, distributive patterns in these programs can easily be attributed to congressional action. Third, demand for transportation funds is great across all areas of the country, in contrast to other programs such as water projects and urban development. Every state has roads, highways, and bridges and thus has members of Congress who take an interest in the distribution of transportation dollars. If there are great differences in states' ability to procure these funds, these are more likely to reflect differences in their congressional influence than in their demand for funds (see Rich 1989).

Focusing on a single policy area has some additional advantages. Many researchers have studied distributive politics with highly aggregated data on federal expenditures (see Alvarez and Saving 1997; Levitt and Poterba 1999). This approach presents a serious conceptual problem, however, because it is very difficult to include meaningful controls for geographic areas' need for funds when expenditures for so many programs are grouped together. The study of distributive politics is aimed at uncovering how political power shapes the geographic distribution of funds separate from considerations of need or merit. As Anagnoson (1980) and Hird (1991) argue, models not including adequate measures of need are misspecified, often in ways that overstate the importance of political variables. Examination of federal outlays in a single policy area makes it much easier to include appropriate and meaningful measures of need.

Studying a single set of related programs not only enables the use of better control variables but also allows for better measurement of the political variables of interest. Political variables will have an effect only at the time when Congress makes allocational decisions. In the case of transportation programs, Congress makes these decisions when it reauthorizes the programs, usually in single multiyear authorizations that revise funding formulas and identify demonstration projects. As discussed above, a state's committee and partisan representation changes over time; similarly, its members of Congress are sometimes electorally vulnerable, sometimes not. By looking at a set of related programs that Congress considers all at once, one can measure political variables at the appropriate times: that is, when the programs are authorized. If, on the other hand, one analyzes federal spending across many programs at once, the relevant political variables cannot be accurately measured because it is not possible to identify appropriate times to take the measurements.

Congress reauthorized surface transportation programs on four occasions during the period studied: in 1982, 1985, 1987, and 1991.[3] On each of these occasions, Congress considered and adjusted the funding formulas that determine the amount of federal funds that each state receives for surface transportation programs. Thus, the committee, party, electoral, apportionment, and need variables were each measured for the years when Congress passed reauthorizing legislation. Outlays were grouped into the four periods affected by each of these reauthorizations. I then estimated four OLS regression models ($N = 50$) to measure the sources of political influence on states' per capita allocations for surface transportation.[4]

Variables Included

To test for the effect of committee representation on distributive policy, I included five variables in the models. First, I included two variables measuring states' representation on the committees with jurisdiction over surface transportation programs at the time that those programs were reauthorized: (1) the number of their senators on the Environment and Public Works Committee and (2) the percentage of their House delegation on the Public Works and Transportation Committee. Second, I included two variables measuring states' representation on the Appropriations Committees: (1) the average percentage of the state's House delegation on the Appropriations Committee and (2) the number of years a state was represented on Senate Appropriations during the period.[5] These variables were added to the model—even though the formulas in the authorizing legislation determine the allocation of the overwhelming majority of transportation funds—because Appropriations Committee members often earmark special projects in transportation appropriation bills. Throughout the period these projects perennially sparked turf battles between the members of Public Works and Appropriations, and on many occasions appropriators succeeded in writing them into legislation. Third, I included a dummy variable indicating whether a state was represented by a committee leader in the House or Senate.[6] If committee members had advantages in obtaining transportation funds, the coefficients for these variables would be positive and statistically significant.

Two variables accounted for the role of political parties in distributive politics: (1) the percentage of each state's House delegation affiliated with the majority party and (2) the state's number of majority-party senators. To the extent that members of the majority party had an advantage in procuring particularized benefits, these variables would have a positive effect on per capita outlays for surface transportation.

Next, three variables measured how electoral incentives affect distributive patterns. First, electoral vulnerability might enhance members' incentives to seek particularized benefits. To test for this effect, I included two variables: (1) the percentage of the state's House delegation elected by margins of less than 10 percentage points in the congressional elections immediately preceding the surface transportation reauthorization and (2) the number of a state's senators elected by margins of less than ten percentage points over the preceding six-year Senate electoral cycle. If electoral vulnerability affected incentives in the expected way, the coefficients for these variables would be positive and statistically significant. Second, constituency ideology might condition members' incentives to seek particularized benefits. Members of Congress who represent fiscally conservative states would not be able to gain much electoral mileage from procuring particularized benefits. As a rough indicator of state ideology, I used the presidential vote in the election immediately preceding the surface transportation reauthorization. If a state's ideological conservatism reduced members' incentives to seek particularized benefits, this variable would have a negative effect on per capita outlays.

The effect of Senate apportionment on distributive policy was modeled using the reciprocal of state population (1/state population in millions). This transformation was needed to reflect the nonlinear relationship between state population and per capita outlays (see also Lee 1998, 47). Because populous states receive such large sums in absolute terms, relatively small cuts in their shares could finance large per capita increases for the smallest states. A single per capita dollar cut in California's allocation could finance, for example, a $66 per capita increase in Wyoming's allocation. Because of the very different absolute sums involved in large and small states, the effect of state population on Senate outcomes was expected to follow the Phillips curve.[7] Under this functional form, the effect of state population on per capita outlays was greatest for the smallest states, but the slope of the line flattened out at the higher values of state population.

Finally, the models included several variables measuring state need for federal surface transportation dollars. Lobbyists for sparsely populated states often contend that those states have to build and maintain a larger amount of highway miles on a per capita basis than other states, thus placing a greater burden on their taxpayers. To account for this difference in need for highway funds, I included two variables: (1) number of interstate highway miles per capita and (2) total number of primary and secondary highway miles per capita.[8] Second, to account for differences in state need for mass transit funds, I used a variable for the percentage of state population in metropolitan areas. To the extent that need determined how much states receive for transportation funds, these variables would bear a positive relationship to state per capita outlays.

Findings

Table 14.1 displays the unstandardized and standardized coefficients obtained for each of the four regression models. These findings reveal that both need considerations and political influence shape federal distributive policy. Taken as a group, the need variables explain more of the variation in per capita outlays for transportation than the political variables. States' representational advantages in distributive politics do matter. Senate apportionment had a strong, statistically significant effect on outlays for every time period. Committee leadership, electoral incentives, and partisan representation each had statistically significant effects on distributive policy under the most recent authorization, 1992–97, but not for the other time periods examined. For each time period, the regression model explains a substantial amount of the variation in per capita outlays, with adjusted R^2 statistics ranging from .74 to .85.

Of the need variables, per capita interstate mileage has the greatest effect on transportation outlays. This is not surprising because the federal government assumes a greater degree of responsibility for interstate highways than for any other transportation program. Congress evidently takes into account the different burdens taxpayers bear in building and maintaining their states' interstate highways: states with more interstate mileage per resident receive considerably higher per capita outlays for transportation. The coefficient for this variable is large and statistically significant ($p < .01$) for each of the time periods examined.

TABLE 14.1. Federal Per Capita Outlays to States for Surface Transportation Regressed on Representation Variables, Controlling for State Need (N = 50)

	1992-1997 B Beta (*t* value)	1988-1991 B Beta (*t* value)	1985-1987 B Beta (*t* value)	1983-1984 B Beta (*t* value)
Senate Representation				
Reciprocal of	207.03***	253.60***	126.67***	55.39**
state population	.35	.68	.41	.30
(in millions)	(3.24)	(4.02)	(3.25)	(2.07)
Committee Representation				
Number of senators	-94.73	-85.04	-54.50	-6.77
on Environment	-.15	-.19	-.14	-.01
and Public Works	(-2.24)	(-2.08)	(-1.90)	(-.34)
Percentage of state	.53	2.28*	1.05	.86
delegation on	.03	.14	.05	.09
House Public Works	(.45)	(1.41)	(.58)	(1.08)
Number of years the state	2.29	17.72	4.63	6.82
is represented on Senate	.01	.09	.03	.07
Appropriations	(.11)	(1.12)	(.47)	(1.08)
Average percentage of	-.02	-.97	-.91	.15
state delegation on	-.00	-.05	-.05	.01
House Appropriations	(-.01)	(-.46)	(-.65)	(.15)
Represented by a	92.22*	-2.26	8.56	26.60
committee leader	.10	-.00	-.02	.07
in House or Senate	(1.51)	(.05)	(.24)	(.93)
Partisan Representation				
Percentage of state's	2.40***	.14	-.17	.08
House delegation	.20	.02	-.03	.02
in majority party	(2.47)	(.16)	(-.31)	(.24)
Number of in	65.45**	24.84	9.82	-8.13
senators in	.12	.09	.04	-.05
majority party	(2.19)	(1.08)	(.54)	(-.59)
Electoral Incentives				
Percentage of state's	4.58***	1.05	1.00	.57
House members	.29	.08	.09	.11
who are marginal	(4.18)	(.81)	(1.05)	(1.29)

(Continued)

295

TABLE 14.1. Federal Per Capita Outlays to States for Surface Transportation Regressed on Representation Variables, Controlling for State Need (N = 50) *(Continued)*

	1992-1997 B Beta (t-value)	1988-1991 B Beta (t-value)	1985-1987 B Beta (t-value)	1983-1984 B Beta (t-value)
Number of state's	-17.76	2.13	2.10	3.14
senators who	-.04	.04	-.01	.02
are marginal	(-.64)	(.42)	(.10)	(.23)
Statewide vote for the GOP	-13.40***	-4.92*	-2.30	-2.01*
in presidential election	-.24	-.14	-.08	-.13
preceding reauthorization (%)	(-3.82)	(1.52)	(-.83)	(-1.62)
Need Measures				
Percentage of state's	2.68**	4.01***	2.85***	1.53***
population in	.19	.44	.38	.33
metropolitan areas	(1.83)	(2.88)	(3.50)	(3.01)
Per capita interstate	661822.41***	342980.94***	340124.00***	211540.79***
highway miles	.91	.72	.85	.94
in the state	(7.02)	(5.32)	(7.81)	(8.55)
Per capita primary	-10786.31	-2822.57	-1983.60	323.95
and secondary highway	-.19	-.07	-.06	.02
miles in the state	(-1.84)	(-.54)	(-.50)	(.13)
Constant	749.78+++	115.87	55.97	46.00
	(2.79)	(.44)	(.29)	(.54)
F	19.62+++	10.58+++	14.79+++	16.82+++
Adj. R^2	.85	.74	.80	.82
Mean of dependent variable	$591.57	$369.42	$279.75	$174.02

* $p < .10$; ** $p < .05$; *** $p < .01$ (one-tailed tests).
+ $p < .10$; ++ $p < .05$; +++ $p < .01$ (two-tailed tests).

State need for mass transit funds also plays a role, with the variable for percentage of state's population in metropolitan areas consistently taking a positive coefficient that is statistically significant ($p < .05$) in all of the time periods. One of the need variables, per capita primary and secondary miles, does not perform as expected. Contrary to theory, the coefficients for this variable consistently have negative values. On the whole, however, the results for the need variables show what one would expect: that Congress clearly does consider differences in state need for funds when making distributive policy.

Turning to the political variables, representation on the committees of jurisdiction has little effect on the amount of funds states receive for transportation. Congressional committee leaders procured additional funds for their states only during the most recent time period ($p < .01$). States represented by committee leaders were not measurably advantaged in distributive politics during the other three authorization periods.

Only one of the committee membership variables in one of the models, percentage of the state's delegation on House Public Works, has a statistically significant effect ($p < .10$) in the expected direction. Interestingly, 1987 was the only year during the period when the House considered either a surface transportation reauthorization or a transportation appropriations bill under a closed rule.[9] As such, this was the only year when the House gave up the opportunity to alter the Public Works Committee's proposal on the floor, thus granting the committee more autonomy than usual. Arguing in favor of the rule on the House floor, Congressman William F. Clinger (R-PA), member of the Public Works Committee, pointed out that "the record will show that that the Committee on Public Works has almost without exception brought bills to the floor with open rules." On this occasion, he contended that "exceptional circumstances" made the closed rule necessary because the highway reauthorization would expire in less than two months, and delay would mean that "vital projects will not be constructed this year" (*Congressional Record,* Wednesday, January 21, 1987, H284). Despite such arguments, the closed rule was controversial (see Starobin 1987), with members complaining about the restrictions it would impose on their ability to amend the funding formula or the special projects included in the bill, among other concerns. Indeed, the data suggest that the constituents of House committee members did receive more benefits under transportation programs than other members of the chamber over the four-year period following the 1987 reauthorization.

Generally speaking, however, members of the Public Works and Appropriations Committees were unable to procure disproportionate benefits for their constituents in transportation programs. Committee members may have been better able than other members of Congress to claim credit for special transportation projects in their districts—such as the Bud Shuster Highway, a 53-mile stretch of I-99 in Altoona, Pennsylvania—but as a group they did not succeed in skewing the overall distribution of federal surface transportation funds to their constituents' benefit. The variable for representation on the House Public Works Committee has the expected positive coefficient for all four time periods but is statistically significant only for the 1988–91 period. The variable for representation on the Senate Environment and Public Works Committee, however, always has a negative coefficient. Membership on the House and Senate Appropriations Committee has no statistically significant effect on transportation outlays, with the coefficients tending to be positive for the Senate representation variable and negative for the House representation variable. Taken as a whole, these data provide little support for the distributive theory of congressional committee organization.[10]

The results for the partisan representation variables support the proposition that majority parties in Congress advance their members' electoral interests by helping them obtain particularized benefits for their constituents in only one of the four time periods. The partisan representation variables usually have positive coefficients, however. Clearly, divided control of Congress makes it more difficult for majority parties in either chamber to disproportionately advantage their members. Control of Congress was divided for two of the transportation reauthorizations examined: in both 1982 and 1985 the House was controlled by the Democratic party while the Senate was controlled by the Republican party. Perhaps it is not merely coincidental, then, that party representation does not affect distributive patterns during these two time periods. In 1985 the House and Senate had such difficulty reaching agreement on how to distribute transportation funds that they eventually dropped all controversial provisions—including all the special projects that House members and senators wanted—and approved a very short bill that did nothing more than authorize federal monies for preexisting transportation projects and programs. In 1991, by contrast, a highly unified Democratic party that controlled both chambers of Congress reauthorized surface transportation programs. Federal transportation spending during the following period (1992–97) also bore a pronounced partisan imprint, with states represented by Democrats in Congress receiving considerably higher per capita outlays than states represented by Republicans ($p < .05$).

The results also lend some support to the proposition that differences in members' electoral incentives shape the geographic distribution of federal funds. Fiorina (1989) and Stein and Bickers (1995) argue that vulnerable members of Congress are likely to work harder than others at procuring particularized benefits as a relatively easy, noncontroversial way to improve their image with constituents. The variable for percentage of the states' House delegation elected by margins of less than ten percentage points always has a positive coefficient and is statistically significant ($p < .01$) for one of the time periods. Senators, however, do not appear to respond to electoral vulnerability in this way. The coefficient for states' number of marginal senators is always negative. In addition, the data provide some support for the hypothesis that state ideological context shapes members' incentives to seek particularized benefits. For every time period, the variable for statewide percentage of the vote cast for the Republican party's presidential candidate has a negative coefficient and is statistically significant for 1992–97 ($p < .01$), 1983–84 ($p < .10$), and 1988–91 ($p < .10$), suggesting that members of Congress representing more ideologically conservative states perceive fewer electoral payoffs from directing federal spending to their constituents.

298

Of the political variables in the models, Senate apportionment has the strongest and most consistent effect on distributive policy. In every time period examined, states that were overrepresented in the Senate by reference to the one-person, one-vote standard received higher per capita outlays for transportation than underrepresented states. Even after controlling for differences in state need for transportation funds and a large number of other political variables, the coefficient for the Senate representation variable is positive and statistically significant ($p < .01$) for all the models. Comparing the standardized coefficients for the political variables reveals that in every one of the time periods Senate apportionment has a greater effect on per capita transportation outlays than any other political variable included. Senate apportionment clearly represents a key variable for understanding federal distributive policy making; in the case of surface transportation programs, in fact, it is more important than any of the other variables—committee membership, party representation, and electoral incentives—that scholars have identified as political influences on distributive policy in the United States.

Conclusion

More than a quarter century ago, Ferejohn (1974) identified three sources of bias in distributive policy making—geographic representation, majority rule, and the committee system. Since then, a massive literature has developed on the topic. That literature, however, has generally ignored a unique characteristic of the Senate—its remarkable scheme of representation—and its important effect on distributive policy making. In this chapter, all these potential sources of bias in federal spending—committee, party, electoral, and apportionment—were integrated in a single model to determine which had the greatest influence on federal policy making.

First, I found that committee representation is generally not important in explaining the distribution of federal surface transportation funds. These generally negative findings point to the important constraints on congressional committees considering distributive programs. In general, the House keeps the Public Works Committee on a short leash, considering most of the bills it reports under open rules. And in the Senate, of course, there is no such thing as a closed rule. That Congress imposes such restrictions on the committees overseeing transportation programs is not surprising. Most members of Congress care about transportation projects because, unlike water projects or farm subsidies, all areas of the country can benefit from transportation spending. They are thus unwilling to concede influence over this policy area to the committee members and give them free rein to procure special benefits at their expense.

As a result of these restrictions on committee autonomy, "Successful committee members influence others not by wielding formal authority or by engaging in command-and-control tactics. Rather, they persuade" (Krehbiel 1991, 256). In building broad chamber support for their proposals, Public Works Committee members provide special benefits to the districts of members not on the committee (for a systematic treatment of this subject, see Evans 1994). During consideration of the 1998 transportation reauthorization, Public Works Committee Chair Bud Shuster (R-PA) continued this practice of building support for his committee's bills by asking his committee staff to contact all members of Congress to ask them if they would like to submit requests for special projects in their districts. The need for committee members to build support for transportation programs in this way prevents them from obtaining disproportionate benefits for their own constituents.

Second, the results show that, in general, party and individual electoral incentives do not measurably influence distributive policy making. The one exception among these variables was the statewide vote for the Republican party in the preceding presidential election. Consistent with Seller's (1997) findings, members of Congress representing more ideologically conservative states consistently procured fewer additional dollars for their states in transportation programs than senators representing more liberal states. The House and Senate partisan representation variables, as well as the House electoral incentives variable, did affect states' per capita outlays for surface transportation in the most recent time period, however. This particular finding corroborates the recent work of Stein and Bickers (1995) and Levitt and Snyder (1995).

Finally, these findings demonstrate that, to gain a complete understanding of distributive policy making, it is essential to take the Senate and its peculiar apportionment scheme into account. Senate apportionment confers representational advantages on small states that lead the Senate to prefer allocations of federal funds disproportionately favorable to them. The findings presented here show that Senate apportionment leaves a deeper and more consistent imprint on distributive policy than other sources of states' representational advantage. This is not surprising when one considers that, unlike the advantages that states gain from their representatives' party affiliations and electoral incentives, Senate apportionment is a constant. States' partisan representation and the electoral interests of their representatives vary over time—advantaging some states and then others—but small states are always advantaged by Senate apportionment.

Notes

Thanks to Rory Austin, Jim Garand, Emery Lee, Wendy Schiller, Steve Smith, and Bob Stein for helpful comments on earlier drafts of this chapter.

1. The data are drawn from a program-level data set, the U.S. Domestic Assistance Programs Database, compiled by Stein and Bickers (1995, 153–60). Programs related to surface transportation were identified by first isolating all the programs administered by the Department of Transportation and then excluding all those programs that are not reauthorized as part of the regular highway/mass transit authorizations (e.g., air travel, Coast Guard).

2. This figure was calculated with data from the U.S. Bureau of the Census's *1998 Statistical Abstract of the United States.*

3. Transportation Assistance Act of 1982 (PL 97-424), Interstate and Defense Highways Funds Apportionment (PL 99-104), Surface Transportation and Uniform Relocation Assistance Act of 1987 (PL 100-17), and Intermodal Surface Transportation Efficiency Act of 1991 (PL 102-240), respectively.

4. Annual transportation outlays for each state during the authorization period were summed and then divided by the state's total population at the time Congress reauthorized the programs.

5. Unlike authorizations, appropriations are made annually. For this reason, it is necessary to take into account the composition of the committees over the entire authorization period. For the Senate, I used the number of years that the state was represented on the Appropriations Committee. For the House, I used the average percentage of the House delegation on Appropriations across the years in the authorization period.

6. Committee leadership was defined as chairing the full Public Works Committee or the subcommittee with jurisdiction over surface transportation or serving as the ranking minority member on the full committee.

7. For a discussion and illustration of this functional form, see Brown (1991, 130).

8. Data are from the U.S. Bureau of the Census's *Statistical Abstract of the United States,* various years.

9. On all the other occasions between 1982 and 1997, the House considered committee reports of surface transportation reauthorizations under open rules; transportation appropriations bills between 1982 and 1996 were considered under either open rules or special rules specifying some restrictions on amendments. No other closed rules were granted.

10. The inclusion of variables for representation on the House and Senate subcommittees with jurisdiction over surface transportation programs yielded no statistically significant coefficients either. *F* tests revealed that these subcommittee variables did not explain enough variation in states' per capita outlays to warrant inclusion in any of the models, so they have been excluded for the sake of simplicity.

Lessons from Impeachment

· 15 ·

Examining Senate Individualism versus Senate Folkways in the Aftermath of the Clinton Impeachment

Ross K. Baker

Few facts are in dispute as to the events that led up to the impeachment of President Bill Clinton by the U.S. House of Representatives on December 19, 1998, and his acquittal by the U.S. Senate on February 12, 1999. The concern of this chapter is less with the outcomes of the impeachment and trial than it is with the very different ways that these processes were played out in the House and in the Senate.

I hypothesize that the role of one of the Senate folkways identified almost forty years ago by Donald R. Matthews (1960)—institutional patriotism, considered by many scholars to be obsolete or little venerated in the modern Senate—played an important role in the decision of the Senate to conduct a formal trial rather than opt for censure or an abbreviated inquiry. I suggest that it has never entirely disappeared but has existed in an attenuated state and was rejuvenated by the unique circumstances surrounding the impeachment trial of President Bill Clinton.

The Background of the Impeachment of Bill Clinton

The impeachment grew out of an intimate encounter that took place in a Little Rock, Arkansas, hotel room in 1991 between then Governor Clinton and a young state employee named Paula Corbin. After Clinton became president, Ms. Corbin, who later married and was known now as Paula Corbin Jones, sued the president for sexual harassment under federal civil rights statutes.

Although the case would later be dismissed by federal Judge Susan Weber Wright because Mrs. Jones could produce no evidence that she had actually suffered any damage to her career from her apparent refusal to submit to

Governor's Clinton's sexual overtures, she was permitted to introduce evidence that the man who was now sitting in the White House had a history of making sexual advances on women. To strengthen her case, her lawyers attempted to track down such women and call them as witnesses against the president. At roughly the same time, the former Solicitor General of the United States, Kenneth Starr, was appointed under the 1978 Independent Counsel Act to investigate certain investments that had been made by Clinton and his wife Hillary in the Whitewater real estate development in Arkansas when he was governor.

Lawyers for Paula Jones learned of an intimate relationship that Clinton had been having since 1995 with a young White House intern named Monica Lewinsky who had left her White House job in April 1996 for a post in the Department of Defense. While at the Pentagon, Lewinsky was befriended by a woman named Linda Tripp, in whom she confided her relationship with the president. Tripp began secretly recording her conversations with Lewinsky. Such evidence of Clinton's involvement with another woman would obviously be of great value to Jones in her suit against the president. Unhappy about the loss of her access to the president and dissatisfied with the Pentagon, Lewinsky asked the president to find her a more suitable job in New York. To this end, the president enlisted the help of his close friend, an influential lawyer and former civil rights leader named Vernon Jordan.

On December 17, 1997, the president informed Lewinsky that she would be called as a witness in the Paula Jones case. Shortly thereafter, on January 12, 1998, Linda Tripp turned over the tapes of her conversations with Lewinsky to Independent Counsel Kenneth Starr, who quickly requested of Attorney-General Janet Reno and a panel of federal judges that he be permitted to widen the scope of his inquiry to include the president's relationship with Lewinsky. The very next day the president gave evidence to Paula Jones's lawyers in a deposition. In this deposition, Clinton denied a sexual relationship with Lewinsky.

When newspapers broke the story of the president's alleged relationship with Lewinsky on January 21, 1998, the president emphatically denied it. Starr's decision to pursue an inquiry was based on his belief that Clinton had concealed his relationship with other women in order to protect himself in the Jones case. When Paula Jones's case against Clinton was dismissed on April 1, 1998, it appeared that the president was out of trouble. Starr, however, had convened a grand jury in the District of Columbia to deal with the accusations surrounding Clinton's relationship with Monica Lewinsky and the possibility that he had lied about it to avoid having it exposed in the Jones case.

The president appeared before that grand jury on August 19, 1998, and admitted to an "inappropriate relationship" with Monica Lewinsky but denied having had sexual relations. Independent Counsel Starr continued to conduct an investigation for the purpose of recommending to the House of Representatives whether they should initiate impeachment proceedings against the president. On September 9, 1998, Starr's report was presented to the House. On October 8, the House, by a 257-to-176 vote, authorized the Judiciary Committee to conduct a formal investigation into whether there were grounds for impeachment. It was the last vote the House would take on this matter that was even remotely bipartisan.

After a stormy set of Judiciary Committee hearings in which all twenty-one Republicans voted to recommend impeachment to the whole House and all sixteen Democrats voted against, the House itself, on December 19, voted largely along party lines to impeach the president on two counts. The first accused Clinton of perjury before Starr's grand jury for denying a sexual relationship with Monica Lewinsky. The second charge alleged that Clinton had engaged in obstruction of justice in trying to buy Lewinsky's silence by concealing gifts that he had given her and by attempting to find her a more prestigious job than one she had at the Pentagon.

On January 7, 1999, the trial of the president opened in the Senate, with the case against the president being presented by members of the House Judiciary Committee, known in the language of impeachment as "managers." The president was defended by his personal attorneys and lawyers from the White House legal staff.

After five weeks of testimony, the Senate acquitted President Clinton. With a constitutional minimum of two-thirds or sixty-seven needed for conviction, the president was found not guilty on both counts. Neither count gained so much as a simple majority. On perjury he was acquitted by 55–45, and on obstruction the vote was 50–50. Between the time the House voted to authorize an impeachment inquiry on October 8 and the day that they impeached Clinton on December 19, a congressional election took place that reduced the Republican majority in the House to a mere six seats, and House Speaker Newt Gingrich resigned. The 55–45 Republican majority in the Senate in place since the 1996 elections remained the same. Accordingly, both House and Senate had Republican majorities, but very narrow ones. The core of the Republican majority in the House was the remnant of the seventy-three conservative Republicans elected in 1994 who harbored a deep personal dislike for President Clinton. House Democrats, for the most part, saw impeachment as a vendetta against a popular president and his policies. The setting was not a favorable one for bipartisan action.

The House: The Ascendancy of Partisanship

Was it totally out of the question that the House of Representatives might conduct a nonpartisan impeachment? The most likely answer is that only a heroic effort on the part of the leaders of Republican majority and an equally herculean restraint on the part of the Democratic minority might have produced a less fractious process. But it is important to recognize that even before the impeachment process began, relations between Democrats and Republicans were in tatters. After the House Judiciary Committee had taken its final party line vote amidst much partisan posturing, a staff member of a Judiciary Committee Democrat was asked whether the contentiousness of the hearings was such that Democrats and Republicans might not now be on speaking terms. She laughed and said, "They weren't speaking to each other before the hearings."

It is difficult to put a date of origin on the most precipitous phase of the House's slide into bitter partisanship, but it probably went into its steepest decline when Democratic Speaker Jim Wright was forced from office in 1989, largely as the result of charges of impropriety unearthed and publicized relentlessly by Rep. Newt Gingrich of Georgia, then the second-ranking Republican in the House. When asked, at a press conference, how Wright felt about Gingrich, he replied, "I feel the same way a fire hydrant feels toward a dog" (Barry 1989, 632).

But many Republicans felt the same way during the forty unbroken years of Democratic dominance in the House. "Time and again, the internal politics of the House . . . [proved] a source of deep frustration for the Republicans who often [could] neither legislate nor score political points" (Connelly and Pitney 1994, 91). The Republicans felt so oppressed that in a floor speech in 1990, Minority Leader Bob Michel likened the conduct of the Democrats to that of dictatorial measures taken by the Communist party in the Soviet Union. Democratic attitudes toward the Republicans were summed up in Jim Wright's final address to the House before stepping down in 1989. He charged the Republicans with "mindless cannibalism." Bob Michel accused the Democrats of turning the House into a "den of iniquity."

Relations between the parties, if anything, became worse after the 1994 Republican takeover. Taking a cue from what the Republicans had done to them, the Democrats engaged in stalling tactics to frustrate the "Contract with America," the legislative program that had served as a platform for House Republicans in the 1994 election.

Newt Gingrich, the author of the contract, assumed the speakership and asserted the powers of the office more aggressively than any Speaker in modern times.[1] One of his boldest moves was to ignore the presumption of seniority in choosing committee chairs and to hand-pick more junior members to head major committees. Among these Gingrich choices was Rep. Henry J. Hyde of Illinois to be chairman of the Judiciary Committee.

Toxic Turf: The Judiciary Committee

Rep. Hyde, a widely respected member, was perhaps best known for his authorship of the 1993 Hyde Amendment that denied Medicaid payment for abortions except in limited circumstances. Despite his emphatic stand on abortion, Hyde was generally well liked by Democrats and Republicans alike. But the membership of the committee consisted mostly of those who either sought out the committee or were placed there by their party leaders to do battle on the most contentious and least negotiable issues of the day: abortion, gun control, immigration, and school prayer.

A rough measure of just how polarized a committee this was on the eve of impeachment may be seen in the ratings posted by the most socially liberal and socially conservative interest groups, the Americans for Democratic Action (ADA) and the Christian Coalition, respectively.[2] Based on their roll-call voting records for 1996, the ADA's average rating for the committee's ten most senior Democrats was 89.5 out of a possible 100; the Christian Coalition's score for them was 1.5 out of the same 100. On the Republican side, the ten most senior Judiciary Committee Republicans had a Christian Coalition score of 85.1 out of 100; the same ten averaged an ADA score of 6.5 (Barone and Ujifusa 1997).

In 1974, the House Judiciary Committee had been given the responsibility for conducting the impeachment investigation and hearings into the conduct of President Nixon. The 1974 committee, however, was a very different body from the 1998 version. It contained a number of Republican members who kept an open mind about the possibility of impeaching a Republican president and made the vote on articles of impeachment in the Judiciary Committee bipartisan.

In contrast, the 1998 Judiciary Committee was composed largely of the most zealous members of each party. "Greater party cohesion resulted in part from the disappearance of the cross-pressured faction in each party [and] made it more difficult to reach compromises across the aisle" (Fleischer and Bond 2000, 192). Through a combination of retirements, redistricting, defeats, and switching parties, the period of the 1994 congressional elections witnessed a dramatic reduction in the number of moderate (mostly Sunbelt) Democrats in the House. The number of moderate Republicans, who mostly hailed from the Northeast and Midwest, also declined. Of the 73 freshman Republicans elected in 1994, the overwhelming number were very conservative (McDonald 1999, 8–10).

Within their own party caucuses in the House, conservative Democrats and liberal Republicans became an endangered species and not very popular with their more doctrinaire colleagues. So although "party leaders over the years [had] damned apostates in their ranks, . . . they [had] also depended upon some of them to act as bridges to the opposition. Members in the middle served as messengers, informants, agents of negotiation and brokers of compromise" (McDonald 1999, 9–10).

The House Judiciary Committee was the very distillation of the parent body: die-hard conservatives and passionate liberals. Gingrich considered the possibility of giving jurisdiction to a select committee of House members rather than to the starkly partisan Judiciary Committee and asked Rep. James E. Rogan (R-CA) to study the impeachment process and make recommendations on which would be best way to handle it. Rogan reported that "regular order" should be observed and that Judiciary take jurisdiction (Baker et al. 1999, 6)

While the decision to reject a select committee to hear the impeachment made it a certainty that the issue would be debated in the highly partisan forum of the Judiciary Committee, it is by no means certain that the creation of such a committee would have averted a highly polarized debate given the overall partisan complexion of the House and the depth of feeling that prevailed.

The Senate Prelude: The Bipartisan Imperative

On the Saturday that the House voted to impeach the president, members of the Judiciary Committee led by Chairman Henry Hyde walked across the House side of the Capitol, under the dome, and into the north end of the Capitol that is the territory of the Senate and presented the article of impeachment to the secretary of the Senate. It was the first time since the impeachment trial of President Andrew Johnson in 1868 that House members had made such a trek.

It was assumed from the very start of the impeachment process that it was unlikely that the constitutionally required two-thirds of the U.S. Senate (sixty-seven votes if all senators were present) would vote to convict Clinton and turn him out of office. If all forty-five Democrats stuck with Clinton, the Republicans, with fifty-five members, would fall well short of the two-thirds majority.

The mathematics alone seemed to state eloquently that the outcome in the Senate would be an acquittal of the president. But how that outcome was arrived at became, for the 100 members of the Senate, more critical than the result itself. For the Senate to arrive at an almost-certain acquittal only after a harsh and bloody struggle was a prospect deeply troubling to many senators. While calls for bipartisanship had been heard in the House before the impeachment was taken up, they were uttered more with hopefulness than with conviction.

On the Senate side, the commitment to a bipartisan process—whatever the eventual outcome—was far more widespread and intense, and the tone was set early on by the leadership. The leader of the Republican majority in the Senate, Trent Lott of Mississippi, "wanted to escape the tar of partisanship. 'We could have rolled [Minority Leader Tom] Daschle,' the majority leader [said], but it would have hurt the overall atmosphere. For the sake of the Senate's reputation, both men decided to keep things relatively cordial" (Baker et al. 1999, 9).

Institutional Patriotism Revisited

The maintenance of the reputation of the Senate, especially in the aftermath of the harsh partisanship in the House, appears to have played a major role in the outcome of the trial of the president. This was the case even though the norm identified by Donald R. Matthews (1960) forty years ago as "institutional patriotism" (101–102) has been viewed by scholars in recent years as a declining constraint on senators' behavior.

With specific reference to the influence of how the strictures of institutional loyalty impinge on the actions of House members, Richard F. Fenno (1978) dismissed the norm as "a pleasant Capitol Hill hypocrisy." He saw little vitality in the principle that "members are supposed to value the House as an institution and do nothing to diminish its prestige or demean its members" (167).

While not wholly abandoning the force of the norm on the U.S. Senate, Barbara Sinclair, in 1989, significantly redefined it as it applied to the upper chamber. Reverting to Matthews's original term *institutional patriotism,* she argued, "To the extent that the institutional patriotism norm dictates that senators focus their energy and attention inward on the Senate, and to the extent that it requires a 'total' 'emotional commitment to Senate ways' and bars 'using the Senate for purposes of self-advertisement and advancement,' the norm is defunct" (100).

Likewise, she wrote that "if [institutional patriotism] implies an unwillingness to criticize the institution, then that aspect of the norm is also dead" (100). She conceded that a residual form of institutional patriotism might still exist in the Senate insofar as senators refrained from the kind of lacerating institution bashing found in the House. Senators gave voice to lamentations about the Senate based on a concern that it had changed for the worse, but Sinclair concluded, paraphrasing Matthews, that "no longer are senators . . . fiercely protective of, and highly patriotic in regard to the Senate" (100).

What took place in the Senate when the articles of impeachment were delivered on December 19 was, of course, without modern parallel. Accordingly, the events leading up to and including the trial may be of such rarity that they can spoken of as exceptional. Nonetheless, the protection of the reputation of the institution, especially in light of the widespread condemnation of the House, seems to have inspired in senators something akin to institutional patriotism. It might more accurately be described as institutional preservation and, by extension, self-preservation, but whatever name we attach to it, there was a rallying to the institutional colors distinctively different from the *sauve qui peut* attitude that has been the more typical attitude when Congress has been under attack. In this instance the reputation of the U.S. Senate and the interests of the famously individualistic senators became, at least for a time, congruent.

For the Senate to fall into acrimonious partisan disarray as the House had done would have damaged members of a body who thought well of themselves and who seemed to have a stake in the reputation of the Senate that was larger than that of the average House member. These sentiments came through strongly in my interviews with nine U.S. senators between March 9 and June 24, 1999:

Thad Cochran (R-MS), Wayne Allard (R-CO), Phil Gramm (R-TX), Michael Crapo (R-ID), Jack Reed (D-RI), Paul Sarbanes (D-MD), Chris Dodd (D-CT), Robert Torrucelli (D-NJ), and Chuck Hagel (R-NE). Eight of the nine senators had previously served in the House of Representatives.

The remainder of this chapter is devoted to an examination of the effort to keep the Senate's part of the impeachment/trial process bipartisan. I will also ask a number of questions and venture some tentative answers based on the interviews. The questions are these:

1. What were the major efforts to ensure bipartisan action in the Senate?
2. What role did the norm of institutional patriotism play in the efforts to maintain bipartisanship?
3. To what extent was institutional patriotism in the Senate a product of unfavorable judgments of the conduct of the House of Representatives and conflict with the goals of the White House?
4. Is the sense of having a proprietary interest in the well-being and reputation of the institution stronger in the Senate than in the House?
5. Finally, was the apparent reappearance of institutional patriotism in the Senate a momentary product of the impeachment context or a phenomenon likely to endure?

Bipartisanship's Opening Round: Gorton-Lieberman

Even before the House had taken its vote on impeachment, the bipartisan wheels in the Senate were beginning to grind. Senator Slade Gorton (R-WA) was on his way to a resort in Hawaii on December 7, 1998, and placed a call from the plane to a Democratic colleague, Joseph Lieberman of Connecticut. Gorton and Lieberman, both political moderates, had become close during their work on the V-chip legislation allowing parents greater control of their children's TV viewing habits. It is the kind of personal relationship that grows up readily in the more intimate confines of the Senate and often crosses party lines.

Believing that the Senate was not facing up to the problems posed by the upcoming impeachment trial, Gorton sought out Lieberman to craft a plan to end the trial quickly by holding a series of test votes after only two days of presentations by House manager and the president's lawyers. If two-thirds of the Senate voted to accept the House managers' allegation as true, the trial would proceed. If the number fell below sixty-seven, the trial would be over and the president acquitted (Baker et al. 1999).

The Gorton-Lieberman plan failed because it did not receive the unanimous consent required under Senate rules, and it appeared that a longer trial would be conducted. A number of senators had not wanted it to appear that the Senate was quickly and casually dismissing the work of the House. House managers were also asking the Senate to call as many as two dozen witnesses. The very issue of witnesses posed for the Senate the threat of a breakdown along partisan lines when it met on January 8, 1999.

Throughout the period of the House impeachment debate and the consideration of the House's action in the Senate, there were efforts, usually bipartisan in nature, to avert a full-scale Senate trial. These efforts took two forms: one was the kind of "straw vote" approach taken by Gorton and Lieberman and later by Robert C. Byrd, and the other was a vote of censure by the Senate that would put the body on record as disapproving Clinton's actions. Even after the Senate held the trial and failed to reach the two-thirds required to convict Clinton on the impeachment counts, Senator Dianne Feinstein attempted to offer a censure resolution.

Bipartisanship, Round Two: Kennedy-Gramm

If the Gorton-Lieberman initiative can be interpreted quite simply in terms of two moderate senators who were personally close sharing the common interest of sparing the Senate and the nation a bruising trial, the pairing of the names Kennedy and Gramm comes very close to being a political oxymoron. Yet it was a plan jointly sponsored by Senator Edward M. Kennedy (D-MA) and Phil Gramm (R-TX) that postponed the Senate's decision on witnesses and gave the institution time to resolve the thorny problem.

The agreement to defer the question of witnesses took place not where the Senate meets today but in the Old Senate Chamber, which had been last used in 1859. The decision to meet in this ornate room was made by Majority Leader Trent Lott. To further set the historical tone, Lott asked Democrat Robert C. Byrd, the Senate's unofficial historian and constitutional scholar, to deliver the opening remarks, which Byrd did by drawing on historical references ranging from the *Canterbury Tales* to the speeches of the great nineteenth-century senator Daniel Webster. Lott's role in setting the stage and reinforcing the image of the Senate's uniqueness played an important role in the outcome that was achieved.

Gramm did little more than propose to his colleagues that the decision to call witnesses be put off, and Kennedy did nothing more than second Gramm's proposal. But it was, perhaps, the fact that Kennedy the staunch liberal and Gramm the strong conservative had agreed on anything that caused some colleagues to proclaim it, somewhat hyperbolically, as "the Gramm-Kennedy Miracle" (Seelye and Alvarez 1999). That such a minor point of agreement should have been the occasion for such great celebration underscores the climate of apprehension in the Senate that the Senate would accompany the House in a descent into harsh partisanship.

In the aftermath of Gramm-Kennedy there was an outpouring of self-congratulation among senators and a few not-so-sly digs at the House. Senator Patrick Leahy (D-VT) said, "If we went to the rancor of the House, we'd have totally failed. . . . I think that most of us, Republicans and Democrats know the House failed miserably" (Clines 1999).

But Republican House members saw the Senate, in effect, as agreeing merely to disagree—as craven. Rep. Bob Barr (R-GA), a member of the Judiciary Committee, observed contemptuously of the senators, "How little interest, how little background they have to take on the tough issues" (Clines 1999).

The senators had actually accomplished something quite important. As one observer put it, "Senators seemed unanimous in the positive pleasure of letting the House, the White House, and the nation know today, at least, they had the backbone to go on record against partisanship in deciding the fate of the president" (Clines 1999).

The White House Chaos Theory versus Senate Patriotism

It appears, on the face of it, that the White House had little cause to fear a conviction in the Senate or even be concerned that a simple majority could be mustered for the articles of impeachment. Acknowledging this raises the question of whether the failure of the Senate to convict should, by itself, not have been perceived by the White House as a vindication of the president. It became apparent only after the trial, however, that the president aspired to a goal that he deemed even more desirable than acquittal, and that was stripping the entire process of its legitimacy by having the Senate dissolve into the same partisan rancor that had plagued the House. This was first suggested to me in an interview I conducted on March 12, 1999, shortly after the conclusion of the trial with Senator Phil Gramm (R-TX), who asserted, "It's clear and was clear from the beginning that the president had hoped to produce the same result in the Senate as he had in the House—a madhouse of partisan screaming that would totally discredit the whole process. That was his objective from the beginning, and it would end up with the Senate basically refusing to hold a trial."

I had dismissed this explanation as self-serving partisanship until a small item appeared in the *Washington Post* about a speech given by White House counsel Gregory Craig at Vermont Law School in April 1999. The article quoted Craig as saying that what the White House feared most was a bipartisan decision by the Senate to conduct a trial. The acrimony in the House, according to Craig's account, gave the White House hope that the Senate would follow suit and degrade the entire process (Kamen 1999).

Craig went on to say that "what happened in the House, we thought, was partisan, was unfair, and was illegitimate, and lo and behold we now have a unanimous Senate voting 100-to-nothing to proceed" (with the trial based on the Gramm-Kennedy proposal of January 8 to defer the witness question). Craig added, "This was actually a moment when the president's spirits were very low. He thought the partisan nature and the unfairness of the process had been lost and now we were beginning from scratch" (Kamen 1999).

The idea that the White House and the members of the U.S. Senate (including Democrats) were at odds received independent confirmation from journalists who covered both the White House and Congress during the impeachment. As one journalist, whom I interviewed on June 23, 1999, said, referring to the Kennedy-Gramm motion, "I wouldn't test Kennedy as to whether he was more loyal to the Senate or to the president. At that moment, what Kennedy did with Gramm, the White House hated, and said so."

Phil Gramm, when interviewed on March 12, 1999, echoed this opinion: "There were some Democrat [*sic*] senators who were more committed to the Senate than they were to the president. . . . What happened in the House was a planned riot. It's just that here [in the Senate] where senators couldn't even speak on the floor, getting that riot started was a lot harder. And the only way they could do what the Democrats had done for the president in the House was to set their own house on fire. And in the end, obviously, Democrats like Senator Byrd have more, infinitely more, commitment to the Senate than they did to the president." It was critical to verify this with sources independent of both the Senate and the White House, and journalists who covered both institutions seemed reasonable to turn to. Dan Balz, who covered the Lewinsky episode from the beginning for the *Washington Post,* provided evidence of the president's hope that the Senate would turn harshly partisan. "We knew that they weren't overly happy that bipartisanship was taking over because they loved the climate that was created in the House and anything that went against that was a problem for them because they had a clear strategy, which was to continue to make it a partisan fight, and anything that diluted that gave those guys at the White House heart failure" (interview, June 25, 1999).

Helen Dewar, Balz's colleague at the *Washington Post,* whose beat is Capitol Hill, confirmed Balz's appraisal. "Procedurally, everyone in the Senate was happy with that unanimous vote [on January 8, 1999] because they got over a hurdle that could plunge them into ugliness. But for the White House, it was scary. I think the thing was to maintain the unity of the Democrats. They saw that as their ultimate salvation. . . . I don't think they were thrilled that much by that moment when Ted Kennedy and Phil Gramm said, 'Aha!, we've got it.' I would assume that plunged them into total panic" (interview, June 23, 1999). The highest aspiration of the White House for a process tarnished by harsh

315

partisanship was at odds with the views of most senators that such a descent into partisan rancor would redound to the detriment of the U.S. Senate.

The senators to whom I spoke were unanimous in their opinion that the reputation of the Senate was inextricably tied to the manner in which the trial was conducted. For the majority, what this concern led them to was a belief that there had to be a proper trial and that witness testimony from some of the principals, in one form or other, had to be introduced. As Senator Thad Cochran (R-MS) put it, "I think we were all aware that we were going to be on trial just as the president was being put on trial and that it was a very important part of this process for us to be fair and to be seen as being fair, being thoughtful, and being serious minded about the obligations we had" (interview, June 10, 1999).

There was also an awareness that a full-dress trial with witnesses was in conflict with the president's optimal position that the Senate descend into partisan warfare and not proceed with a formal trial. Senator Jack Reed (D-RI) speculated, "Maybe [the White House] thought we would copy the House and make this bitterly partisan, you know, 'It's all politics, this guy is getting screwed, et cetera.' Frankly, I don't think that was ever going to happen. . . . Most of us said, 'Listen, the way to proceed is to initiate the trial. There would be a bad precedent if we didn't have a trial because then it would look as if we were picking and choosing what an is an impeachment process and what's not'" (interview, June 15, 1999).

Senator Chris Dodd (D-CT) also agreed that the White House wanted to avoid a full-dress trial and conceded that discrediting the process by partisan wrangling in the Senate "was part of it." But he stressed another factor: "There was the big fear over there, and that was that the witness they were most concerned about was Monica Lewinsky being interrogated in the well of the Senate. . . .This is where you'd have obviously the entire world focused on Monica Lewinsky describing in excruciating detail her sexual relationship with the president of the United States" (interview, June 14, 1999).

Whatever the motives ascribed to the White House, it became clear that in the minds of the senators I interviewed, the Senate was in the public spotlight and the reputation of the institution and its members was on the line. The maintenance of that reputation was increasingly seen as tied to the need for a trial.

Democrat Paul Sarbanes (D-MD) remarked: "I think that on occasions such as this a myth about the Senate becomes a reality, a self-realization on occasions of this sort. You hear everyone saying, 'This is clearly out of the ordinary. This is only the second time in history [that a president in on trial in the Senate]. You really have a tremendous responsibility. Don't you feel the weight of the nation pressing down on you?' You know, a lot of people rise to the occasion" (interview, March 19, 1999).

But if the reputation of the Senate was on the line, so, by extension, were those of the individual senators. Senator Chris Dodd (D-CT), however, reversed the order: "Well, to begin with they [the senators] were concerned with their own reputations, the reputation or their party and obviously, I'd like to believe, the reputation of the Senate" (interview, June 14, 1999).

The House As a Negative Role Model

What came across in the interviews more strongly and more consistently than any other view of the impeachment episode was the dismay with which senators viewed the House proceedings and the determination that the Senate not emulate the other body.

When asked the open-ended question "Why do you think things turned out the way they did in the Senate?" eight of the nine senators gave as their first response that they wanted to avoid what had happened in the House. It was the most striking pattern of response in all of the interviews. A sample of the initial responses to the question follows:

1. *Dodd*: "They [the senators] watched the House and they saw the public reaction to it. It was a living photograph of everything people think is wrong with American politics. . . . So you had the Senate watching that, and [it] made a sort of collective decision not to allow itself to be perceived as a reflection or a mirror-image of how the House had conducted itself" (interview, June 14, 1999).

2. *Sarbanes*: "So it came over to the Senate, and the members sort of said, 'Well, you know, we don't want to be perceived as being like the House because the perception of House out in the country and among the commentators was that they hadn't done a very good job with this'" (interview, March 19, 1999).

3. *Crapo*: "I was just coming over from the House, and having just experienced the intense hostility that arose over the issue there, on all sides, I was very much surprised that in the first meeting there was such an overwhelming effort to ensure that the issue was approached on the basis on principle" (interview, June 17, 1999).

4. *Reed*: "I think, first, we were all sobered by the example of the House, which was a train wreck. Institutionally [in the Senate] there was a consensus that cut across party lines that we were not going to engage in same type of process that leads to chaos and acrimony and, frankly, revulsion on the part of the American people as to what went on" (interview, June 15, 1999).

While the trial would continue for another five weeks, the tone set on January 8, 1999, seemed to chart a course that the Senate threatened, on later occasions, to abandon but never did. The Senate, it appeared, had developed a kind of collective will that it would avoid the extremes of partisanship that had taken place

317

in the House. And on the question of witnesses that turned out to be the thorni-
est problem facing the Senate, it was six Republican senators confronting Republican impeachment managers from the House who induced them to scale
down the witness list to three people. The testimony they would give would be
by deposition, not in live appearances in the Senate.

Institutional Patriotism and the Senatorial Stake

Another strong message that emerges from the interviews is that senators appear
to believe that they have a larger stake in the reputation of their institution than
do House members. One reason for this may be the greater dispersion of power
in the Senate. Whereas in the more hierarchical House, the distance, in power
terms, is much greater between the leaders and senior members on the one hand
and the recently elected members on the other, those distinctions in the Senate
are far less stark. It is, in a sense, more difficult for a senator to distance himself
from the actions of the smaller collectivity with its more even distribution of
power than it is for the single junior House member to repudiate the work of the
larger and less egalitarian body. The relatively high public profile of senators, as
compared the relative anonymity of most House members, also raises the stake
of any given senator in the prestige of the institution.

These factors were summed up in Senator Chris Dodd's reaction to the question of whether senators have a larger stake in the institution: "Yeah. Obviously.
It's a smaller group you're dealing with—100 people rather than 435—that in itself. Just the math has an impact. And the profiles of the people here are just
higher. In the House, out of 435 people you might have just 50 people, maybe,
who are high profile. The remaining 380 are just the ground troops" (interview,
June 14, 1999).

Senator Wayne Allard (R-CO), a recent House graduate, also agreed with the
idea of a greater individual stake in the institution but ascribed it to the longer
term and the greater intimacy of the Senate: "I usually knew the people in my
own party pretty well, and I worked hard to get to know some of the other
House members, but after each election you'd get a whole bunch of new ones
and you need to relearn again." Allard added, "I think one of the reasons they
get so rowdy over there is because they don't get to know each other on a personal basis" (interview, May 27, 1999).

Impressionistically, at least, there seems to be a greater sense of proprietor-
ship in Senators that expressed itself during the impeachment trial as a collective
desire to preserve the good name of the Senate. Because of this greater stake on
the part of individual senators, it would more difficult to preserve one's own reputation if the institution were to suffer disgrace.

Certainly among the journalists who cover Congress this greater tendency to identify with the institution and to derive personal payoffs from its good standing in the eyes of outsiders is seen as one of the defining characteristics of the Senate. Speaking of one House member who was elected to the Senate, Helen Dewar observed, "When he walked across that rotunda he became instantly a senator, talking about the revered traditions of the Senate and using all of the bizarre Senate rules and whatever, and talking about the Senate as the repository of all the stable things about American politics. There's a spirit and a pride. It's like a team. You sometimes expect to hear them chant, 'Yea, Senate!'" (interview, June 23, 1999).

It might be observed that the journalists who credit the Senate and its members, occasionally, for their virtues also consign them to collective disrepute for their shortcomings. From the media's point of view, the senator and the Senate may well be perceived as inextricable or even identical.

Institutional Kinship: A Brief Sighting or a Resurrection?

It is probably the case that institutional patriotism as a legislative folkway never declined as precipitously in the Senate as it did in the House. Greater polarization in the electorate and hence in the membership, more turnover both in leadership and in members, and the two more constant factors of shorter terms and greater disparities of power have contributed to the more serious erosion of this folkway in the House. It may be that senators are more decorous in their institution bashing than House members, but in the eyes of journalists, at least, there is a perception that senators are gentler critics. As *Los Angeles Times* congressional correspondent Janet Hook said, "Don't you just see it all over the place from just watching Congress in general? The House members aren't there as long. They're not so self-important, and they're just more independent contractors. Whereas with the senators, there's more a sense of the body that rises above the two parties" (interview, June 23, 1999).

But if institutional patriotism has not totally disappeared from the Senate, it often goes into hibernation for considerable periods of time. It is my conclusion, based on conversations with senators, that an unusual—even unique—combination of circumstances brought it out of hiding and placed it on conspicuous display during the early weeks of 1999.

With both the president and the House suffering disrepute after the conclusion of the impeachment, the Senate was presented with both a serious challenge and a unique opportunity. The threshold of satisfactory institutional behavior had been lowered so radically that it would not have taken a great deal to enable the Senate to emerge as uniquely untarnished among the three elective bodies of the national government. Simply conducting an orderly and dignified trial would, by comparison, have ennobled the Senate.

On this latter objective, as I have argued, the Senate and the White House were at odds. While the White House maintained an excellent intelligence operation and were well informed as to where senators stood at crucial times, they carefully, and astutely, avoided any appearance of tampering with the jury.

From the perspective of the White House, the evidence suggests that the critical question was not acquittal or conviction but whether there would be an orderly trial with witnesses in some form or a repetition of the partisan bloodbath that had taken place in the House. The latter was the president's preferred course.

For senators, and most notably the minority Democrats, there was a choice between giving the president his heart's desire, a partisan brawl that would cast the entire impeachment into disrepute, or an orderly trial that would have the happy result of causing the self-interest of senators and the well-being of the institution to coincide. The arcs of self-interest and collective action intersected.

The question of whether institutional patriotism has been reinvigorated is one that senators themselves seem reluctant to predict. Presumably, in those contexts in which external antagonisms are perceived as threatening both the senators and their careers and also the repute of the institution, patriotism will assert itself boldly. But even if the expression of Senate institutional patriotism is muted in more normal circumstances, it seems more capable of reasserting itself dramatically than that of the House of Representatives.

The wariness of senators about the future of institutional patriotism was captured by Mississippi Republican Thad Cochran. After reciting a list of hopeful signs that had appeared during the trial that, collectively, amounted to institutional patriotism, he added, "Whether it has a lasting impact, we'll see" (interview, June 10, 1999).

The bitter partisan wrangling in the late spring of 2000, when Democrats and Republicans battled over such things as whether germaneness was required on amendments to appropriations bills or whether the Senate should take any action at all on such bills until the House concluded its work, seemed to give support to Cochran's skepticism. But just as it seemed as if the institution was tied in knots, there seemed to be a kind of collective realization that, even in the heated atmosphere of an election year, things had gotten out of hand, and a dramatic reversal took place.

Senators, then, may not boast about the Senate and may even deride it publicly as a nursery of obstruction, but there comes a point in the Senate's darkest hours when a consensus seems to emerge that further deterioration must be avoided. Whether this reflects a fear of institutional damage or personal peril is difficult to determine. The impulse may vary from senator to senator, but if the effect, in either case, is institutional maintenance, the motives may be less important than the results.

Notes

1. For an excellent summary of the changes in the House wrought by Speaker Newt Gingrich, see Pfiffner (1999).
2. The choice of the ADA and Christian Coalition ratings as a indication of the philosophical polarization on the Judiciary Committee was made because some roll call voting scores, such as those of U.S. Chamber of Commerce or the AFL-CIO, tend to compile scores on economic issues. The jurisdiction of the Judiciary Committee deals more with the social issues of interest to the ADA and Christian Coalition, which are a better reflection of the split in the committee's membership.

· 16 ·

Explaining Impeachment: The Exceptional Institution Confronts the Unique Experience

Burdett A. Loomis

> Where else than in the Senate could have been found a tribunal sufficiently digni-
> fied, or sufficiently independent? What other body would be likely to feel confi-
> dence in its own situation to preserve, unawed and uninfluenced the necessary
> impartiality between an individual accused and . . . his accusers. —Alexander
> Hamilton, *Federalist 65*, quoted by Senator Joseph Biden (D-DE)

> Impeachment is the ultimate threat to the overreaching official whose unbridled
> self-interest or arrogant disregard for the public good renders him or her unfit to
> continue in . . . office. —Senator Robert C. Byrd (D-WV)

The U.S. Senate is an exceptional institution, like no other legislative body in
the world. What happens, then, when the members of such an institution exercise one of the most potent weapons in their arsenal, but one that has gone
untested in battle for 130 years?

This chapter will examine how U.S. senators ultimately came to terms with
impeachment as they decided upon the guilt or innocence of President Bill Clinton in February 1999. In particular, how did they explain their votes on the two
articles of impeachment? This is not, most assuredly, an analysis of the impeachment process, or even the trial. Rather, it offers a snapshot, taken at the end
of the trial, of how senators put behind them a process and a set of decisions that
they would have much rather avoided. From the outset, the conclusion was fore-
ordained, yet individual senators played their roles to the end. For most of them,
issuing a final statement on their respective votes represented closure. They, and
the Senate as an institution, could proceed to address other issues.

Many students of the Congress hoped that the impeachment debates and deliberation would offer, in Fenno's (1989b) felicitous phrase, a "window" on the Senate as its members engaged in self-conscious discussions of the role of the institution. Alas, although a few senators ruminated with some thoughtfulness, the great majority did not. In two separate, unrelated projects, researchers discovered few musings that encouraged viewing the Senate as an institution through the senators' public words, either uttered on the floor or reported in the media (Cook 1999 and this study).

Nevertheless, after sitting through the trial, listening to the evidence, and hearing the arguments, senators did have to vote on the articles of impeachment, and almost all of them offered public explanations of their position. If these texts provided no window on the Senate as institution, some shafts of light did filter through as senators explained their individual votes, sometimes in great, even excruciating, detail. Those explanations, mostly consisting of statements for the *Congressional Record,* make up the bulk of the data for this chapter. Given that legislators are professionals at the task of explaining their actions (Fenno 1978), it is worth examining how they reacted to a unique situation and how they chose their reference points—within the historical context of the U.S. Senate but also within the current context of the institution that has become increasingly partisan, even as it has burnished its reputation as a bastion of individualism.

The Exceptional Meets the Unique: Three Perspectives

In the wake of the Clinton impeachment trial, it is tempting to think of impeachment as just one more skirmish in the struggles for power between the parties and between the executive and legislative branches. At least in historical terms, nothing could be further from the truth.

The Senate has held just fifteen trials and convicted a mere seven individuals (all judges; see Byrd 1989). The two most important assessments of the Senate over the past forty years, those of Matthews (1960) and Sinclair (1989), do not mention impeachment, and as of the mid-1990s the leading texts on Congress devoted only a paragraph or two to the subject, largely in the context of removing judges (Davidson and Oleszek, 1994, 284; Smith, 1995, 314). And Swift's recent (1997) historical analysis of the Senate's early development contains no mention of impeachment. Thus, congressional scholars as well as senators must come to terms with the extraordinary politics of impeachment. For individual senators, holding an impeachment trial for a president was unique, although ten members (Biden, Byrd, Domenici, Helms, Hollings, Inouye, Kennedy, Roth, Stevens, and Thurmond) had served during the 1974 impeachment proceedings against President Richard Nixon.

Given the lack of direct context for addressing impeachment politics in the Senate, three bodies of scholarship offered assistance in understanding how individual senators approached their untested constitutional roles as both judges and jurors.

The first perspective derives from the observations by Sinclair (1999) and Ornstein, Rohde, and Peabody (1997), among others, that the Senate of the 1990s has become simultaneously more partisan and more individualistic. We might well expect that senators, framed by the clear partisanship of the impeachment process, would react to the unfamiliar circumstances of a presidential trial with their familiar partisan routines. At the same time, each senator would be responsible for providing his or her own explanation for the votes on the two articles of impeachment (perjury and obstruction of justice). Expectation: Republicans and Democrats would differ systematically, but there would be a considerable range of explanation among members of both parties.

A second perspective flows directly from Sarah Binder and Steven Smith's (1997) work on filibusters, in which they examine whether senators have historically engaged in filibusters as principled actions (the claim of many legislators) or as political behaviors, little different from many other tactics and strategies. The impeachment votes and their explanations offer an excellent opportunity to apply the Binder-Smith framework to a different set of decisions that invite the disjuncture of rhetoric and action. Expectation: Impeachment would confirm that principled rhetoric often papers over political motives.

A third framework hearkens back to Fenno's (1978) observation that explaining is one of the core behaviors of all legislators. The patterns that emerge among (a) the various kinds of explanations and (b) the kinds of senators who develop these explanations may generate some insights about how these elected officials defined their roles within a context that had few clear rules, norms, or precedents. Indeed, for many senators, defining the very idea of what was an impeachable offense remained an important issue well into President Clinton's trial. For at least some of them, the act of constructing the explanation for their votes may have been the first time that they understood themselves why they took the positions that they did. Expectation: A handful of core narratives would be developed as senators produced professional explanations that drew on various lines of scholarship, analogies, and experience.

Related to the notion of individual explanations was the possibility that one or more broad narratives would emerge from the analysis of the senators' statements. Legislators often shop around for explanations, trying to find a story that works for them (Loomis 1994). In this vein, one would expect to find patterns in the explanations—especially given the partisan nature of the process and voting, which implies that different groups of legislators in both chambers viewed the facts, the law, and the question of guilt in distinct ways.

The Data: Let 100 Flowers Bloom

In gathering the post-trial statements, I harbored some real hope that the senators would reflect not only on their votes and related reasoning but also on the nature of the process and, especially, on the role of the Senate in this historic undertaking. As noted, this was not the case, although on occasion a senator would offer some useful reflections. In that the outcome of the trial was not at issue, absent some earth-shattering new information, many senators simply did not think through how the Senate was acting, or at least such thoughts were not evident in their final, for-the-record statements. That is not to say that the legislators did not take the process, or their own roles in it, seriously. They did. Moreover, they expressed concerns about how the Senate would appear, especially in the wake of the visceral partisanship exhibited by many members of the House (Baker 1999). The House added to the confusion by proceeding in the absence of the nominal Speaker and the withdrawal of the putative Speaker, all in the context of a serious challenge to the majority leader a few days before the House voted to impeach. In the end, the House members of the 105th Congress unceremoniously dumped the impeachment trial on to the laps of the senators of the 106th Congress.

This was fresh in the minds of the members of the Senate as they prepared to vote (and explain) on February 12, 1999. The data for this chapter come from statements made within two or three days of February 12, and most were inserted into the *Congressional Record* of that day. There are also a few press releases in lieu of formal statements in the *Record.* Overall, 95 of 100 senators made some kind of public statement; these ranged in length from 130 words (Torricelli, D-NJ) to 31,000 (Biden, D-DE).[1]

My research assistant and I coded each statement on a number of dimensions, which we had framed after reading through the statements and taking extensive notes. Many of the variables report simple matters of fact (e.g., the mention of *Federalist #65*, in which Hamilton most seriously considers the impeachment issue). Other coding required interpretation (e.g., the extent to which, on a 1-to-9 scale, the overall statement reflected legalistic reasoning). We reconciled disagreements by rereading the statements and jointly recalculating a final score.

Most of the emerging patterns in the data were organized around partisan frameworks (see below), but there were a few more general trends. The great majority of senators based their ultimate judgments on their interpretation of what a broad "rule of law" required. Although many of the statements did emphasize partisanship and legalism, the senators, even when reaching diametrically opposed positions, drew on expansive "rule of law" interpretations to explain their votes. For example, Senators Patrick Leahy (D-VT) and Bob Smith (R-NH) demonstrated different elements of the "rule-of-law" emphasis in their respective statements. Drawing on his past experience, Leahy stated, "As a former prosecutor, one of the questions I asked is whether these criminal charges of perjury and obstruction would have been brought against Bill Jones rather then Bill Clinton. Experienced prosecutors, Republican and Democrat, testified before the House Judiciary Committee that no prosecutor would have proceeded based on the record compiled by Mr. Starr." The Republican Smith ranged farther afield in justifying his position, but his statement reflected a broad, rule-of-law perspective: "With a not-guilty verdict, you will tell the American people that perjury and obstruction of justice for the President are acceptable; that those who put their lives on the line for our Nation every day in our Armed Forces have a higher standard then the Commander in Chief; and that for everyone else in America who lose their jobs because of perjury and obstruction, that is not acceptable."

On specifics, two-thirds of the statements cited the Framers, and almost exactly the same number mentioned Monica Lewinsky. Most senators did mention or compliment the Senate leaders on their performance, but just a few (13 percent) compared the Senate favorably to the House. Seven in ten at least mentioned the House managers, and in general the senators adopted a neutral tone toward this group of Representatives. Fewer than one in four senators alluded to censure in any way. For the most part, the explanations come across as heartfelt, individualistic efforts to address a difficult subject, and most were framed— consciously or not—through highly partisan lenses.

In many ways, it was as if two different trials had been held in January and early February 1999, with Republican and Democrats participating in and observing separate events. One thing did unite them, however. Almost without exception the senators were happy to have their part of the process come to a definitive, if unsatisfying, end. In that sense, the statements can be seen as elements of exit strategies for both the individuals and the institution.

The Partisan, Individualistic Senate Takes up Impeachment

Although the transition from the collegial, clublike Senate of the 1950s to the more partisan and individualistic body of the 1990s did not occur suddenly, the changes have been profound. Sinclair's (1989) portrait of increased individualism in the 1980s remains apt, even enhanced, while Senate partisanship has grown apace in the 1990s. Writing in 1999, Sinclair noted that "the Senate parties in the 1990s are more internally homogeneous and more polarized than in previous decades" (5). If the threat of filibuster and the need to invoke closure are measures of individualism, the 1990s have seen the Senate move to a higher plateau on this dimension as well.

The basic evidence for these claims is straightforward. Both the percentages of party unity votes and the levels of party unity increased steadily from the

TABLE 16.1. The Growth of Partisanship in the Senate

		Party Unity Scores	
	Party Unity Votes	Dem.	Rep.
1954 –1960	41%	78.5%	80%
1961–1970	42%	74%	76%
1971–1980	42.5%	75%	72%
1981–1990	45%	83.5%	79.5%
1991–1998	57%	85%	85.5%

Source: Ornstein, Mann, and Malbin (1998, 210–213); *CQ Weekly*, January 9, 1999, 92–93.

TABLE 16.2. Cloture Votes (Total per Decade)

	Attempted	Successful
1950s	2	0
1960s	26	4
1970s	112	43
1980s	137	53
1990s (1991–98)	192	64

Source: Ornstein, Mann, and Malbin (2000, 164).

1950s through the 1990s (see table 16.1). Likewise, the willingness to engage in or threaten a filibuster became far more common.

Again, the changes from the 1950s through the 1990s were dramatic, as the number of cloture votes exploded during the 1970s and continued to rise in the following decades (Table 16.2). And since the 103rd Congress, more than half of the major measures that could have been subject to a filibuster were in fact the target of such an action (Sinclair 1999, Table 2).

The contemporary Senate is a place where partisan mechanisms and themes have grown in importance. Moreover, many senators' expectations of their floor leader, especially for members of the Republican majority, have become more like those one might find in the House, where holding the party team together is paramount. At the same time, senators have not been willing to grant their leaders enhanced powers to manage the flow of floor action (Sinclair 1999, 5). Similarly, even though the informal practice of "holds" has come under attack, especially when they are placed anonymously, party leaders continue to honor them because to do otherwise would be to attack the prerogatives of individual senators.

So the Senate has grown more partisan and more individualistic. What, then, would happen when the chamber turned to the impeachment trial, where there were three distinct pulls upon each senator? First, his or her party exerted an influence; second, the individual senator had to come to a decision on his or her own terms; and finally the Senate as an institution would be judged on its performance. The senators' statements in the wake of the impeachment offer varying amounts of information about how the action was seen in partisan, individualistic, and collective terms.

Partisanship: The Dominant Perspective

For all its early discussion of keeping the trial process as nonpartisan or bipartisan as possible, partisanship imbued impeachment from beginning to end in the Senate. Despite some early unanimous votes on procedural issues, senators viewed the proceedings through highly partisan lenses. Perhaps most striking was the overall tone of the explanations, which are addressed through several overlapping evaluations of the statements.

Legalism

The statements exhibited great variation in their reliance upon extensive legal reasoning. Although Democrats could and did make detailed legalistic arguments, as Senator Biden's 31,000-word statement attests, Republicans consistently emphasized the legalistic, caselike approach to impeachment (see Table 16.3). Most Democrats touched on legal aspects of the case but did not develop lengthy or detailed legalistic arguments; although some Republicans acted in a similar way, their modal response was considerably more legalistic. In general, they viewed the proceedings more like a court trial than did the Democrats.

Not only was the Republicans' overall approach more legalistic, but GOP senators developed distinct, party-based explanations as to (1) the facts of the case; (2) President Clinton's guilt; and (2) whether the acts, as charged, rose to the level of impeachable offenses. Republicans emphasized the facts and the president's guilt much more regularly than did Democrats (see Table 16.4). Only on the question of whether the acts rose to the level of an impeachable offense did Democratic senators approach the emphases provided by Republicans, and even there, on the central issue for most Democrats, Republicans addressed the matter in more detail.

TABLE 16.3. Partisanship and Legalism

	Low	Modest	High
Republican (51)	37% (19)	35% (18)	28% (14)
Democrat (44)	61% (27)	36% (16)	2% (1)

Note: Low = 1–3; Modest = 4–6; High = 7–9.

TABLE 16.4. Emphasis on Facts, Guilt, Impeachable Offense

		Low	Modest	High
Facts	Republicans (51)	49% (25)	20% (10)	31% (16)
	Democrats (44)	82% (36)	11% (5)	7% (3)
Guilt	Republicans (51)	25% (13)	49% (25)	25% (13)
	Democrats (44)	59% (26)	36% (16)	5% (2)
Impeachable Offense	Republicans (51)	20% (10)	51% (26)	29% (15)
	Democrats (44)	23% (10)	66% (29)	11% (5)

Note: Low = 1–3; Modest = 4–6; High = 7– 9.

TABLE 16.5. Senators Noting Framers and Scholars in their Arguments

		% Noting Scholars		
	% Noting Framers	0	1	2
Republicans (51)	57% (29)	88% (45)	2% (1)	10% (5)
Democrats (44)	80% (35)	68% (30)	14% (6)	18% (8)

Given that they were making a case for removing a president, arguably the most serious constitutional action that the Senate can take, the Republican senators' emphases on the overall legal case against President Clinton was appropriate. They framed their arguments in judicial, not political, terms. Thus, almost three Republicans in five (59 percent) mentioned Betty Currie, the president's secretary by name in that she was integral to the obstruction-of-justice charge (which most Republicans viewed as the stronger article). Only a quarter of the Democrats named Currie in their explanations.

In that almost all Democrats knew from the beginning that they were going to vote for acquittal, their explanations reflected this fact—and the related expectation that, in all likelihood, they were going to win. In this context, Democrats chose reference points quite different from those selected by their GOP colleagues. Although they did not construct legalistic narratives, for the most part, the Democrats did not ignore the Constitution. Quite the contrary. The Democratic senators employed arguments that emphasized both the Framers and contemporary constitutional scholars more than did those of the Republicans. Still, Republicans did not slight the Framers, as majorities from both parties mentioned them (see Table 16.5).

In contrast to the case-based legalisms of the Republicans, the Democrats made broader, rule-of-law arguments as to what should be considered an impeachable offense. Moreover, the Democrats placed the proceedings in a more thoroughly political framework than did their GOP counterparts. Democrats

TABLE 16.6. Partisanship/Electoral Nullification

	Partisanship		Electoral Nullification	
	Mentioned	**Mentioned & Emphasized**	**Mentioned**	**Mentioned & Emphasized**
Republicans (51)	27% (14)	4% (2)	16% (8)	0% (0)
Democrats (44)	64% (28)	25% (11)	57% (25)	27% (12)

TABLE 16.7. Impeachment Analogies: Percentages of Senators Making Analogy to Presidential and Nonpresidential Impeachments

	Nonpresidential Impeachments	Presidential Impeachments
Republicans (51)	45% (23)	16% (8)
Democrats (44)	23% (10)	48% (21)

both mentioned and emphasized partisanship to a greater extent than did Republicans. Likewise, they placed more emphasis on the potential nullification of the 1996 presidential election (see Table 16.6). Not only did senators from the two parties vote differently and explain themselves differently, but Democrats, at least, frequently argued that the process itself was partisan.

A couple more differences emerged in how to judge the president. First, aside from the evidence presented and the questions of constitutional law, a number of senators (more than 40 percent) used previous impeachments as guideposts for their reasoning. Most telling here were the analogies that the senators chose. Republicans tended to place President Clinton's actions within the context of non-presidential (judicial) impeachments (see Table 16.7), which had produced seven convictions, including that of Representative Alcee Hastings (D-FL), who subsequently won election to the House. Democrats, conversely, compared the Clinton impeachment to the actions taken against Andrew Johnson and Richard Nixon, to note either the partisanship of the process (as with Johnson) or the relative severity of the charges against President Nixon and the degree of his guilt. Parenthetically, the senators' statements almost completely ignored the sanctioning of Senator Robert Packwood (R-OR) for repeated sexual harassment episodes.

Second, the senators divided along party lines in how they addressed President Clinton's behavior. Only 43 percent of the Democrats labeled the president a liar, as opposed to 71 percent of the Republicans. Conversely, almost 7 of 10 Democrats (68 percent) explicitly denounced the president, while only 35 percent of the Republicans did so. Even as they were supporting their president with their votes, Democrats excoriated him more thoroughly in their explanations. For example, Senator Richard Bryan (D-NV) observed that although "the President's conduct is boorish, indefensible, even reprehensible, [it] does not threaten the Republic."

Democrats left no doubt that they disapproved of his actions, despite their unwillingness to convict him. Republicans found it much more important to depict Clinton as a liar, an integral element of the impeachment charges, than to denounce him. After all, what could a denunciation add to a vote in favor of conviction?

Given the party-based votes on the impeachment charges, the related explanatory patterns are scarcely surprising. Still, informative findings do crop up. For Republicans, the raw material of the independent counsel's investigation kept coming through: in their legalistic, fact-based emphases; in their extensive use of quotes from the Starr record; and in their focus on Clinton's oath of office as the chief constitutional officer of the nation (58 percent of Republicans noted this, compared to 9 percent of Democrats). Democratic senators did not ignore Starr, but their perspective generally moved them away from specifics and toward a broadly political (and democratic) view of impeachment. Democrats were more explicitly partisan, both in their unanimous votes on both articles and in how they ruminated publicly on their actions.

The Individualistic Senate: Wrinkles in the Partisan Fabric

Although the partisanship of the Senate stands as the major theme in the legislators' explanations, the institution's individualism emerges in any number of ways from the public statements. Most striking, perhaps, are the tremendous differences in their length. Despite some modest systematic differences between the parties (e.g., Republicans issued longer statements), the within-party variations were much greater. Some of these were predictable: Judiciary Committee members wrote more, on average, than did their colleagues. Thus, ranking member Joseph Biden (D-DE) with forty-four pages and Chairman Orrin Hatch with twenty-four pages led the pack. If they played their committee-based roles, so too did Sen. Arlen Specter (R-PA), who offered up a lengthy (twelve-page) articulation of his vote/explanation of "not proven," a position that won no converts.

Most Judiciary Committee members did compose fairly lengthy explanations, but some—notably those of Democrats—were brief. Even though she was a major player in the bid to censure President Clinton, Senator Diane Feinstein (D-CA) wrote a shorter than average explanation, and Sen. Robert Torricelli (D-NJ) took the prize for brevity, perhaps for the first and last time in his career, with a terse, 130-word statement.

Some noncommittee senators wrote at great length, in particular Sen. Fred

Thompson (R-TN), whose explanation drew from his unique perspective as a former Watergate counsel. Still, there were great variations. Nebraska Republican Chuck Hagel offered fewer than 600 words, while his neighbor, Sen. Sam Brownback (R-KS), wrote eight times that much.

Like Hagel, Senators John McCain (R-AZ) and Ben Nighthorse Campbell (R-CO) constructed brief explanations that highlighted their status as non-lawyers. More than any other senator, Campbell stressed his own background as it related to his decisions; his statement consisted of a set of loosely related anecdotes that set forth a simple standard—that elected officials, and especially presidents, should not lie. In the end, Campbell's reasoning came down to this: "I took a solemn oath—perhaps it is the only thing in common I share with [former senators] John F. Kennedy, Harry Truman, and Daniel Webster . . . —and that is why honoring it is all the more important to me. Simply speaking, the President did, too. And, so even though I like him personally, I find I can only vote one way. And that is guilty on both articles."

Given the thematic, partisan nature of many statements, Senate individualism often did not appear clearly in the explanations. Still, as Sen. Campbell demonstrated, the need to explain often brought out a unique perspective. Senator Mary Landrieu (D-LA), for example, began her statement by bowing to "Tom" [Daschle] and "Trent" [Lott], respectively, as she thanked her colleagues, and especially Senator Byrd, for a "timely refresher course" on the history of the U.S. Senate. Few other senators acknowledged that were such willing students. The timing of the Senate votes proved awkward for some legislators, most notably those first elected to the chamber in November 1998. Senator Blanche Lincoln (D-AR) started out, "As the youngest female senator in the history of our country, as a farmer's daughter raised on the salt of the earth with basic Christian values, and as a young mother whose first priority in life is my family and the well-being of the world they live in, I regret that my first opportunity to speak on the floor of this historic Chamber is under these circumstances. . . . You will find that I am not quite as eloquent, or as lengthy, as my predecessor [Dale Bumpers], but I will work on that." Although most of the statements would fit within a few patterns (see below), many, like Landrieu's, started out in the familiar territory of personal experience.

In one instance, the absence of a pattern demonstrated the individualistic nature of the institution: the extensive range of individual senators, past and present, who were mentioned in one or more of the statements. The speakers cast their nets widely in searching for reference points, and there was no consensus as to whom they should look. Aside from nodding toward the current floor leaders (Lott, Daschle) by several senators, only Senators Feinstein (four mentions) and Byrd (three) were cited in more than two statements. There was some superficial bipartisanship in the choices of Senate references. Democrats narrowly named Republicans more frequently, and Republicans overwhelmingly noted Democrats, past and present—ranging from Hubert Humphrey to Dale Bumpers. Icons (Henry Clay and Daniel Webster) received notice, as did a historic figure from the 1868 trial—Maine's Republican Senator William Fessenden, who was cited both by Senator Olympia Snowe (R-ME), naturally enough, and Senator Richard Durbin (D- IL).

Once senators moved beyond the case and the Constitution, the partisan patterns of explanation broke down, and nowhere more so than in the search for Senate referents. Given the lack of clear choices, the senators demonstrated highly individual approaches to finding relevant examples. In many ways, freighted with courtesy (thanking the leaders) and mythical figures (Webster), these parts of the statements were weak and ineffective, in contrast to some of the close legal reasoning that focused on the case or the Constitution.

Principled Rhetoric/Partisan Actions

Writing in 1997, Sarah Binder and Steven Smith offer a clear-headed analysis of the filibuster, in both historical and contemporary practice, in the U.S. Senate. Among their other findings, they conclude that, despite the rhetoric of "principle" that has surrounded the use of this tactic, filibusters have generally served partisan political ends, broadly defined (201 ff). Although an impeachment vote differs from a cloture vote in various specifics (sixty-seven required, as opposed to sixty, and the great difference in frequency of such votes), some core similarities do exist. First, both demand supermajorities, and second, a great deal of hand-wringing about principle accompanies an institutional action larded with partisan politics.

The 1999 impeachment debates and votes often strained the limits of credulity. Senator after senator argued that he or she had an open mind as the trial began, only to cast votes along highly partisan lines on February 12. As noted, Democrats exceeded Republicans in denouncing the president, but they voted unanimously for his acquittal. Conversely, many Republicans seemed to wrestle with their consciences, but they voted in overwhelming numbers, albeit not unanimously, for conviction. In many ways the "legalistic" arguments of the Republicans and the broad "rule-of-law" sentiments of the Democrats camouflaged the intense partisanship that dominated the issue in both House and Senate. As Eric Uslaner (1999) observes, the contemporary Senate may be a bit more restrained than the House, but it "is not a bastion of either civility or moderation." Rather, as partisanship has increased, "members [of the Senate have] reserved their bile for legislators of the other party" (160).

The expression of partisanship was generally restrained in the postimpeachment statements, but, especially among Democrats, it remained an underlying theme. Moreover, the structure of explanations (see below) was dominated by partisan dimensions. We are left, then, to ponder how genuine were some senators' explanations. The five Republicans who split their votes offer the best illustrations—and perhaps the most heartfelt, although a "no" voted could well be tactical.[2] For example, noting that the Framers set a "high bar" for removing a president, Senator Fred Thompson (R-TN) argued that the facts "clearly demonstrated" that the president had obstructed justice but that "unlike articles in previous impeachments, the specific statements alleging perjury were not spelled out." Rather, the "allegations of several criminal acts were lumped together," and the rules as to notice had not been observed. For Thompson, the perjury charges failed to conform both to legalistic form and to the broader rule of law.

Among those who voted to convict on both counts, Senator Robert Bennett (R-UT) developed the one of the most extensive narratives of a principled decision. He recounted a strategy of choice that moved him from leaning toward innocent on perjury and undecided on obstruction to eventual guilty votes on each article. In the end, the central question governing his votes was asked by presidential counsel Charles Ruff: "Would [the crime] put at risk the liberties of the people?" Bennett convinced himself it would—in direct contrast to the reasoning of other senators, most notably Senator Ted Stevens. In fact, Senator Stevens (R-AK) wins the award for candid, even principled, reflection. He voted to convict only on the obstruction charge, but more important he publicly placed his actions in a broader political context: "While I believe the President violated his oath, it does not necessarily follow that he must be removed. For myself, if I knew my vote would be the deciding vote here, I would not vote to remove this President, despite his unlawful acts. He has not brought the level of danger to the nation which, in my judgment, is necessary to justify such an action."

In the end, senators from both parties knew what the outcome would be—very much like most cloture votes. They framed their argument with that knowledge, only occasionally admitting the political nature of their votes. One can only wonder how many other senators might have acted differently if the result had been in doubt. Principled action might well have given partisanship a run for its money.

Structuring the Explanations: The Obvious and the Less So

Partisanship dominated the explanations of most senators, sometimes on the surface, but mostly as the framework for their words. Many Republicans developed long, legalistic explanations that treated the president much like a defendant in a criminal case, with conviction requiring proof "beyond a reasonable doubt." They set a high standard and then argued that the president had exceeded it.

Democrats, conversely, developed a "rule-of-law" explanation that could, for

TABLE 16.8. The Structure of Senators' Explanations

	Components							
Major Contributing Variables	I (Republican/ Legalistic)	II (Democrat/ Partisan)	III Junior Senators	IV Trust/ Senate Const'l Role	V (Senate-Oriented)	VI (Protecting the Constitution)	VII (Listening to the Public)	VIII (Senate Oath)
(Bold = .500 + Ital. = .400–.499 Plain = .300–.399)	**Legalism** **Direct Quotes** **Emphasis on Facts** **Guilt Discussion** **Impeachable Offense? Party** **Currie** **Jordan** **Lewinsky** **Guilt on Art. 2** **Length** *Guilt on Art. 1* *Nonpresidential Analogy* *(-) Partisan Emphasis* *Presidential Oath*	**(-) Guilt on Art. 2** **(-)Guilt on Art. 1** **Party Framers** **Presidential Impeachment Analogy** *(-) Tone>House* *Electoral Nullification* *Federalist #65* *Scholars* Starr House-Senate Differences	**(-)Years in Senate** **1st Term** **(-) Chair/or Ranking Member** *Years in House* *Observation on Distinction Between Chambers*	**(-) Denounce Clinton Trust** **Role of Senate in Protecting Constitution** *Senate Role Noted* *Presidential Oath*	**(-)Sep. of Powers** *Partisan Emphasis* Trust	**Protect the Constitution** *Sense of History*	**Censure Desired** *Nat'l Public Opinion* *(-) Nullification* *(-) Jordan* *(-) Currie* *(-) Lewinsky*	**Senate Oath** Length

Eigenvalues

Component	% of variance	Cumulative %
I	16.435	16.435
II	11.020	27.455
III	6.974	34.429
IV	5.868	40.296
V	4.659	44.955
VI	4.359	49.314
VII	4.170	53.484
VIII	3.518	57.002

some senators, include technical guilt on one or both of the issues. But in context, removal from office represented a severe penalty that did not fit the crime. They revisited constitutional issues and found the standard for impeachment unmet (see Table 16.8).

In an examination of the ninety-five statements, these two party-based explanations stand out, but many other themes can be heard underlying the dominant partisan melodies. Some legislators did think seriously about the potential damage done to the Constitution, or to the Senate, or to the electoral process. To locate these less well-defined, supplementary explanations, factor analysis was employed to tease out some less obvious themes. No claims are made here as to any conclusive explanatory power in this analysis. Nor are the factors employed in any further analysis. Still, the method does locate several dimensions that offer nuanced additions to the dominant partisan motifs.

The first two factors make up most of the partisan variation. The "legalism" element of the most powerful component is extremely strong, and the other variables combine to lay out the prototypical Republican explanation for conviction. The second component defines the Democrats' partisan, rule-of-law approach to impeachment—again, the core anti-impeachment argument that emphasizes both scholarly and, to an extent, Senate-as-institution sets of explanations.

The remaining components are considerably less powerful than the first two, but they open up other explanatory dimensions in that none of them relate, even weakly, to the party variable. In a sense, these dimensions do illustrate the individualism that lurked behind the partisan voting patterns and statements. The third dimension easily wins the label of Junior Senators with House Experience, in that its major components include (1) years in the Senate (negative); (2) first-term status; (3) not serving as a committee chair or ranking member; (4) years of House experience; and (5) the observation of House-Senate differences in the process (with the Senate being judged more favorably). The fourth dimension (Trust) emphasizes the issue of trust as embodied in doubts about the ability to trust the president, especially in light of his oath of office, even though denunciation of him is strongly negatively related. This dimension emphasizes the role of the Senate in protecting the Constitution. The focus is narrow and oriented toward the implications of taking the oath of office.

The fifth dimension (Senate-oriented), although statistically a bit stronger than the three other, remaining components, is less well organized. Central is a lack of consideration of separation-of-powers issues; rather, the Senate itself and its actions are most significant. The sixth dimension (Protecting the Constitution) is much more straightforward, as the core elements are (1) historical concerns with precedents being set and (2) the general notion of protecting the Constitution.

The seventh component (Listening to the Public) incorporates elements of national public opinion (reflecting Clinton's high job ratings) and a desire to vote on censure, a compromise position oriented toward public opinion. The eighth component (Senate Oath) is organized around the simple notion that the senators took a separate oath as jurors at the beginning of the trial. Without making too much of these minor components in the factor analysis, their existence suggests that, despite their partisan lenses, senators did view impeachment in a number of other, reasonably coherent ways.

The Senate's role and historical precedent were worthy of consideration, as were both senatorial and presidential oaths. In the end, thirty-eight senators articulated the sentiment that history would be an important judge of how the Senate conducted itself in the trial and reached its outcome. Senator Dodd felt so strongly about the need to record this process and individual members' reasons for their votes that he made an explicit request for senators to add to the record for future reflection. Senators from all perspectives can be found among the thirty-eight who believed that history will be the ultimate judge of the impeachment process, but, as we might have expected, even this was shaped by the partisanship that dominated the process. President Clinton's supporters expressed their fears that removing the president for his actions would result in a weakened presidency. As Dodd observed, "I revere the presidency and I wish all future occupants of the Oval Office to inherit a strong, independent, and 'energetic' office. I fear the precedent of this impeachment case will come to haunt us."

This stands in contrast to the Republicans' general use of historical concerns. Senators Grassley (R-IA) and Smith (R-NH) linked the arguments that Clinton had broken the rule of law and seriously abused the public's trust. Such abuse, they stated, had effects beyond the White House by creating cynicism and mistrust of elected officials in general. Consequently, they argued, history will be the final judge and jury not only of the Senate's actions but of President Clinton's as well.

In many ways, Senator Connie Mack (R-FL) may have best summed up the senators' overall concerns about how history would view the impeachment process in the context of the institution's actions: "I am proud of the United States Senate and how it conducted itself during this process. Despite extraordinary difficulty, we did our job according to the Constitution and to the best of our ability. I am hopeful that through this process we have provided future generations with enough information to make an informed judgment of this President's actions."

Explanation and Beyond

Although some lawmakers did ruminate on the roles of the Senate as an institution and the Senate vis-à-vis both the House and the president, the fact remains that little direct understanding of the chamber flows from their explanations. However solemnly the senators viewed their duty as jurors, they could scarcely wait for the trial to end, and their explanations, while usually well crafted, were often mechanical—especially those that developed extensive, legalistic arguments. Moreover, partisanship dominated the statements, even though many subthemes resonate in the background.

The Senate's partisanship, however, was framed differently than that of the House. In part this derived from the more individualistic nature of the Senate and its smaller size, which calls attention to the actions of each individual member. In addition, House members acted in a very different context, and many of them felt little need to offer elaborate explanations for their actions. By rushing impeachment through the chamber in a lame-duck, pre-Christmas session, Republican leaders essentially rounded up the votes and got out of town. More than 40 Representatives would not be returning for the 106th Congress, and for most House members, representing homogeneous constituencies, the impeachment vote was not all that controversial. Indeed, only one House member—Representative James Rogan (R-CA), who served as one of the thirteen managers in the Senate trial—found himself in any electoral difficulty because of his actions on impeachment.

In the end, the Senate was faced with an impeachment trial, to be sure, but it did not truly confront the possibility of conviction, given the charges and the information at hand. In response to Kenneth Starr's legalistic approach and his expansive view of his role, it was scarcely surprising that Republicans picked up on his legalism and Democrats saw him as upsetting the balance in the rule of law. A closer vote might well have made for more introspection on both an individual and an institutional basis. But with the result never in doubt, a partisan perspective offered most senators a safe, reliable explanatory framework.

Notes

My thanks to Chad Kniss and Heather Hoy for their assistance.
1. This contrasts to the 1868 impeachment of Andrew Johnson, when 30 of 54 senators placed statements in the *Record.*. My thanks to Chris Deering for this fact.
2. The five, all of whom voted against the perjury charge and for obstruction, were Senators Gorton (R-WA), Sessions (R-AL), Stevens (R-AK), Thompson (R-TN), and Warner (R-VA).

*Concluding Thoughts on
Senate Exceptionalism*

· 17 ·

Seeing the House and Senate Together: Some Reflections on the Research on the Exceptional Senate

David W. Rohde

Dick Fenno, in his remarks that kicked off the conference as well as this volume, noted that when he began studying Congress the balance of research was Senate centered. In contrast, when I started graduate school the House was the nearly exclusive target of then current research. Few people were focused on the Senate, and virtually none on both chambers simultaneously. Five years later, as I began my American Political Science Association Congressional Fellowship, I and others were convinced that the Senate was a very different institution from the one that Huitt and Mayhew had studied and described. Consequently, Norm Ornstein and I embarked on a large-scale project (later joined by Bob Peabody) that sought to take a fresh look at the Senate. We wrote a number of papers and articles that addressed some aspects that particularly interested us and seemed significant,[1] although we never completed the book that we had originally planned, and our work considered the Senate only. (The task of offering a full reconsideration of our picture of the Senate was taken on by Barbara Sinclair, resulting in her prize-winning book [1989].)

Immediately after this, however, I also turned back to studying the House and concentrated mainly on that body in the ensuing years. In these brief comments I want to reflect on how much has been learned about the Senate in recent years, as reflected in the excellent set of papers in this volume. In particular, I want to argue that certain features of this recent work have been (and should continue to be) especially productive of new knowledge. I also want to say a few things about the thrust of future research, not in an effort to dictate what everyone should do but instead to argue that certain paths could be quite interesting and useful. I intend to pursue some or all of those paths myself; perhaps I can entice others to do so as well. I'll begin by briefly considering some of the findings and analysis of the individual chapters. For convenience in discussion, I will group them as they were grouped at the conference.

Elections

The most striking thing to me about the three papers on elections is that all three provide evidence of a prominent role for ideology in the electoral process. Kahn and Kenney show that campaigns can shape and inform voters' perceptions of the ideological positions of incumbents and that the voters can infer ideological information from campaign statements. Erikson finds that the voters' "mood"— the liberalism-conservatism of public policy preferences—has a substantial impact on the partisan division of *both* the House and the Senate. Abramowitz provides us with another perspective on the ideological polarization of the electorate, which many other analysts have noted. Also, his analysis indicates that the impact of ideology on congressional voting has increased from the Carter years to the present in both House and Senate voting but that the increase has been noticeably greater in the latter than the former.

Regarding this work, I would first note that one comment at the conference contended that voters indicate that they don't like ideology or partisanship. This is true of a large segment of the electorate—those clumped around the center. But voters—and particularly activists—toward the extremes often press for candidates and officeholders to be more partisan and to pursue ideological agendas. This was the essence of the "Republican revolution" in the wake of the election of 1994. The polarization of activists and its effect on the primary process provide, I think, a missing link in the explanation of the transformation of national elections and political institutions—namely, the increase in intraparty homogeneity and interparty conflict—over recent decades.[2] When southern Democratic primaries were dominated by conservatives, and when northeastern GOP primaries included significant numbers of moderates and liberals, we saw a substantial amount of overlap between the parties in the preferences of representatives and senators elected. Now, when in nearly every race across the country the Democratic candidate is noticeably to the left of the district's median and the Republican is noticeably to the right, overlap is little or nonexistent. And it is important to note that this effect can be driven, as Tom Mann noted at the conference, by a very small segment of the electorate, like the ideological activists in increasingly low-turnout primaries. Party polarization in the electorate and in governmental institutions are each both cause and effect—a continuing interaction along the lines discussed by Carmines and Stimson (1989). The results of this interaction lead to the ideological effects found in the electoral papers.

Representation

Another point I want to make about the election papers is that the Abramowitz and Erikson studies get substantial analytical leverage from the decision to analyze data from both House and Senate elections. This is also true of the Alford-Hibbing paper. This imaginative paper shows us many important things. Certainly the demonstration that the system has changed away from the Framers' expectation that the House would be the more responsive body, electorally speaking, to one of electoral convergence is very interesting. Also striking is the comparison of the swing ratios in the two bodies, with the Senate being considerably more responsive to shifts in voters' decisions. In the conclusion the authors begin to address the connection between the electoral changes they demonstrate and the operation of the respective chambers and impact on policy outcomes. It is certainly remarkable that in the impeachment debate (as well as in other significant policy areas since 1994), the House overrode the clear public preference, while the Senate was more responsive. I hope the authors and others will follow up on these ideas, for I think they offer a promising agenda for research.

Wendy Schiller's paper offers a nice counterpoint to the important role played in the other papers by partisanship and ideology. She shows that even in this highly partisan era, senators build and maintain idiosyncratic constituencies. They try to build support in areas where their colleague does not already have heavy support, and Schiller shows that voters do respond to these efforts.

The Sellers paper is important in understanding the link between members' preferences and policy outcomes. Members of Congress operate in an inherently multidimensional policy context. They can choose to emphasize one or the other of these dimensions in their decisions. Party leaders try to get members to focus on the issues on which their party has an advantage and to get members on those issues to decide on the partisan dimension. Success by leaders in these efforts will result in stronger patterns of partisanship in congressional voting, enhancing the intraparty homogeneity and interparty conflict discussed above. Voting takes on an increasingly unidimensional pattern, stratified along party lines, as shown in the Poole and Rosenthal (1997) analyses. This study helps us to properly interpret the Poole-Rosenthal results by reminding us that the patterns are not only the result of the "pristine" personal or electorally induced preferences members bring into the body. They are also the consequence of all of the influences within the body that can alter those preferences or affect whether the preferences are revealed in actual votes.

Historical Perspectives

I want to second a remark made at the conference by Barbara Sinclair to the effect that it is shocking how much we did not know about the history of the

343

Senate and how much these papers add to our knowledge. The work by Gamm and Smith (in the current study and the larger project of which it is a part) is both fascinating and illuminating. They argue that unlike the patterns that have been found in studies of the House, developments in party organization in the Senate are not linked to variations in the policy distance between the parties. These results, tentative though they may be, help us to see again the import of institutional context in comparing the two chambers. The authors argue convincingly that the Senate's maintenance of individual and minority rights has limited the potential and payoff for the majority party to delegate strong powers to leaders, even when the preferences of the parties are very different. The majority just cannot extract the same kinds of policy benefits that the House majority can.[3] They show, however, that innovations in organization are linked to close electoral competition. They spring, as Gamm and Smith say, from political weakness. I would note that on this point the two chambers may not be so different. The organizational innovations of the Gingrich speakership certainly stem in part from his desire, and that of the GOP rank and file, to try to maintain majority status in a closely divided environment. Further, the innovations adopted by the reform Democrats in the 1970s were motivated by a different kind of weakness—the close division in preferences between the "national Democrats" and the conservative coalition and the contextual advantage that the existing committee structure conferred on the latter. This analysis reminds us that due to differences in existing organizational structure, similar causal forces can have different effects, and similar effects may have different causes.

Both the Canon-Stewart paper and the Cooper-Rybicki paper show us again the analytical benefits of comparisons between the House and Senate. The Canon-Stewart paper begins to flesh out a picture of the historical development of the partisan influence over the committee system in the Senate, and it makes comparisons to similar analysis conducted for the House. The authors find that from this perspective the patterns for the two chambers were similar, and they provide a persuasive argument as to why this is so. On the other hand, they find differences between the chambers regarding the geographic distribution of more desirable committee assignments, and the reasons for this are not clear. Unlike the case of the committee system, the Cooper-Rybicki analysis shows that the development of rules and procedures regarding bill introduction differed notably between House and Senate. Here, as in the Gamm-Smith study, institutional context looms as central to understanding what happened, both in general and in comparing the chambers. All in all, these studies show us again that individual motives, institutional rules, and political context interact in complex ways.

344

Influences on Policy and Outcomes

In these studies we see again the advantages of analysis that include both the Senate and the House. In Larry Evans's project, the comparison is largely implicit at this point, as the approach is modeled on John Kingdon's (1973) path-breaking study of vote decisions in the House.[4] I believe that this fascinating project, of which we get only the initial glimpse here, has the potential to have as great an impact as Kingdon's. To be sure, the necessarily limited number of senators and votes that can be studied means that we will not get the entire story of senators' vote decisions from this approach, but I believe it will give us novel and critical insights. We see already, for example, some important ways that party leaders can be influential in shaping what I have termed the "operative" preferences (Rohde 1991, 41) of members, and this reinforces the point made above about the interpretation of the Poole-Rosenthal results. The roll call votes that we analyze are not only the consequence of personal and voter-induced preferences that members bring to the chamber immediately after election. They are also influenced in various ways by subsequent forces.

The project of which Barbara Sinclair's paper is a part is further along, and it provides us with some solid and important results. While the final outcomes of the legislative process are not the only thing we should be interested in, surely they are some of the most important. Sinclair's project sheds important light on those outcomes, demonstrating the import of institutional rules and changing political context. We see that the Senate's rules on filibusters make that institution more of a roadblock to passage than the House, but we also see that the frequency with which this has occurred has increased over time as the political context has become more partisan. The likelihood that major proposals will become law has declined over time. We also see some indication that divided government does influence whether proposals become law. I eagerly await further results from this project.

Frances Lee gives us a detailed look at the role of the Senate in distributive politics, and the solid results are partly a consequence of the consideration of legislative characteristics of both the House and Senate. Of particular note is the perhaps unexpected finding that committee representation does not have a significant impact on the allocation of surface transportation funds. (This result is particularly puzzling given how desirable service on the House committee is. It is the largest House committee, and its membership increased from sixty-three in 1994 to seventy-five in 1999, while many other committees decreased in size.) The results do, however, demonstrate again the importance of the particular relationship between a given committee and its parent chamber (see Fenno 1973).

Impeachment

The last two papers are appropriately Senate specific, as they examine that body's discharge of its solitary responsibility in one of the most dramatic political decisions of our time: whether President Clinton was to be convicted on the House's impeachment charges. With any luck, this will be a unique event, not repeated in our lifetimes. Yet as these two studies show, we can draw useful information about the Senate from these events that will enhance our more general understanding of the institution. In the Loomis study, I thought it was interesting how a vote that almost perfectly matched the ordering of senators on the dominant dimension of the Poole-Rosenthal NOMINATE scores yielded such a mutidimensional set of explanations. I also think that Loomis's point that both the decisions of senators and the pattern of their explanations were shaped by the foreknowledge of the outcome is particularly important. I have long thought that a roll call study that contrasted very close votes with others that didn't fit that category could be very illuminating.

In the Baker study, though we get a more limited number of viewpoints expressed, the subject is not public explanations of individual decisions but answers to questions designed to elucidate the causes of the result. I would just raise two points. First there is the issue that Baker addresses at the end: assuming that this is really an instance of the old norm of institutional patriotism being revived, does it have any implications for the future? It seems to me, watching the Senate during the year and a half since the acquittal, that there is precious little evidence that these events have mitigated to any degree the acid partisanship and political conflict directed at the next election that have come to characterize the body. And second, I wonder to what degree even the limited display of institutional patriotism was made possible only because the result was never in doubt.

Senate Exceptionalism and Future Research

In the remainder of my comments, I want to say a few things about future research. One of the central issues of interest to those involved with the "New Institutionalism" thrust in political science is the attempt to understand the impact of institutional arrangements on behavior and outcomes. To do this, our research must include variation in those institutional arrangements. That is, if institutional structure is to be an independent variable in our work, then that structure must *vary*. We cannot know if the Senate is exceptional in some significant way unless it is compared to something. I regard it as one of the most promising signs in the current body of work, as I have emphasized in my remarks above, that so many of the works in this collection compare the Senate to the House, or to itself over time. This is also true of other recent work. For example, while I may have disagreements with the theoretical structure of Keith Krehbiel's (1998) pivotal politics theory, it is clearly a major contribution to our understanding of the legislative process because of the way it deals centrally with the effects that the different institutional arrangements of the House, Senate, and presidency have on outcomes.[5]

A consideration of the House and Senate together could shed light on a wide range of interesting questions. I will note just a few. For example, we in the legislative politics subfield have not paid a great deal of attention to Fenno's (1986) call for a focus on sequence in the study of politics. He argued for the importance of sequence in both the electoral and legislative contexts and noted that many aspects could be considered "interpretive sequences, negotiating sequences, voting sequences, and career sequences" (14). And while he was arguing for the use of observation as a technique for exploring sequence, it is surely not the only technique for doing so.[6]

One aspect of sequence that I find particularly interesting, and on which the simultaneous consideration of House and Senate could shed light, is the fact that on tax and appropriations bills (and many other instances) the House moves first. On the money bills this is the result of constitutional rule and tradition, respectively. In other cases it is a matter of happenstance or deliberate strategy. Of what consequence is this? Are the proponents (or opponents) in one chamber or the other advantaged by this sequence? Is it easier (or more difficult) to alter the status quo because of it, or does it change more or less? Is deadlock more likely in one instance or the other? (This last question, in particular, is interesting in the context of Barbara Sinclair's analysis discussed above.) I don't know the answer to these, and related, questions, but I think it would be interesting—and potentially important—to think it through theoretically and then to assess the theoretical conclusions empirically. And to do that, we would have to gather evidence on how both chambers process each piece of legislation and try to determine whether who the first mover was made a difference.

A second and potentially related issue involves conference committees. It always strikes me as quite remarkable how little work has been done on this aspect of the legislative process, particularly compared to the (justifiable) attention lavished by political scientists on the standing committees of the two houses. Remarkably, the last large-scale consideration of conference committees (Longley and Oleszek 1989) is out of print.[7] We just don't know a lot about conference committees, and in particular we don't know whether and how their patterns of operation have changed in the current era of strong partisanship.

Shepsle and Weingast (1987) argued that the conference process offered majorities on the committee of jurisdiction that saw their bills altered on the floor in ways that they didn't favor the opportunity to exert an "ex post veto." That is, the conference could possibly alter the bill's content to move it back toward the preferred position of the committee. (For a contrary argument, see Krehbiel 1987.) If this was a possible device for committees in the past, at least on some occasions, then possibly in the current era it is another device that can potentially be used by majority-party leaders to achieve their party's legislative goals. That is, leaders who saw bills altered on the floor against the preferred outcome of the majority might seek to use conferees as delegates to change the bill back to (or closer to) the original position. (See Kiewiet and McCubbins 1991, chap. 6, for argument and evidence on this point with regard to appropriations bills.) This is only one of many questions of interest that new research on conference committees could address.

A final example (although there could be many others) also involves partisanship. I have written about how the area of foreign and defense policy in the House was transformed from one frequently (albeit not always) characterized by bipartisanship to one that was often intensely partisan (Rohde 1994). We know that the Senate has special constitutional powers related to foreign policy and that as a consequence senators often assert that they and their chamber have primacy on these matters. Has the Senate been affected differently than the House in this issue area, even though we know that it has exhibited a general trend toward greater partisanship over the last forty years that parallels that in the House (see Rohde 1992)? Surely we have anecdotal evidence that might lead us to say no—from the vote in the fall of 1981 on the sale of AWACS, to the conflict over the commitment of troops to the Persian Gulf in 1991, to the Senate's rejection last year of the Comprehensive Test Ban Treaty. All of these were sharply partisan conflicts. We do not, however, have as detailed a consideration of the Senate patterns as we do on the House, although a coauthor and I are seeking to rectify this imbalance.

Notes

1. See, for example, Peabody, Ornstein, and Rohde (1976) on presidential candidacies; Ornstein, Peabody and Rohde (1977) and chapters in subsequent editions of *Congress Reconsidered* on the Senate generally; and Rohde, Ornstein, and Peabody (1985) on Senate norms.

2. See Aldrich and Rohde (2001) for a discussion and summary of some relevant evidence.

3. I have elsewhere termed this contrast "policy partisanship" versus "process partisanship." See Rohde (1992).

4. It's unfortunate that we will not have a parallel contemporary analysis of the House be-

cause it will be difficult to determine whether differences from Kingdon's results are the consequence of institutional differences or changes over time.

5. See Aldrich and Rohde (2000).

6. A recent work in which sequential considerations are central to the analysis is Cameron (2000).

7. A more recent but more limited analysis is Van Beek (1995).

· 18 ·

Making Sense out of Our Exceptional Senate: Perspectives and Commentary

Lawrence C. Dodd

The essays contained in this volume mark a turning point in the study of the U.S. Senate. Long considered the world's greatest deliberative body, and the object of classic studies during the early postwar years by analysts such as Huitt (1961a, 1961b), Matthews (1960), Ripley (1969b), and White (1956), the Senate nevertheless has taken second place in contemporary empirical research to its larger sister chamber, the U.S. House of Representatives. The broad-ranging research projects reported here and the freewheeling discussion at the Vanderbilt conference where these projects were presented make clear that the study of the Senate is no longer an isolated or antiquated phenomenon. Bruce Oppenheimer's excellent introduction that frames these essays and David Rohde's probing assessment of the research directions represented by them point to a strong, innovative, and collective research effort now underway among legislative scholars to explore and illuminate senatorial politics. My role here is to conclude with some thoughts about the broader dialogue that took place at the conference itself with respect to how best to understand and interpret Senate politics, and to speak to the overarching topic of the conference—Senate exceptionalism. In doing so I will focus on one observation that ran throughout much of the discussion at the conference.

The recurring thematic undercurrent was the elusiveness of the Senate as an institution. On the first night, in his keynote address, Richard Fenno opened the conference with a stimulating and reflective overview of his experience and observations across forty years exploring the Senate and interviewing senators. Summing up, Fenno noted that what impressed him most, in retrospect, was how difficult it was to "find the Senate." While we can get a relatively clear understanding of individual members, unlocking a clear and systematic patterning to the Senate itself is more problematic. Two days later the conference closed with a story by Ross Baker in which he shared the observation of a long-term Washington lobbyist who confessed that while he almost always thought he pretty much knew what was happening in the House, he generally had an undercurrent of apprehension about the more "mysterious Senate"—never really believing that he knew what to expect there.

Between Fenno and Baker came numerous other commentators testifying to the surprising and distinctive character of Senate behavior when contrasted with the House or other legislatures and to the consequent difficulty in interpreting or assessing it. This discussion is illustrated most vividly by Barbara Sinclair's suggestion that policy making in the Senate—given its exceptional institutional characteristics, which virtually mandate supermajoritarian coalitions—is so different from that found in the House and elsewhere as to make theories and explanations derived from study of such majoritarian legislatures untenable when applied to the Senate. In fact, Sinclair suggests, the difficulties created for the Senate by its organizational complexities and supermajoritarian character are so unique, and would seem so debilitating, as to raise fundamental questions about how and why the Senate is able to operate effectively at all. Sinclair's observations serve to highlight the concern raised by Alford and Hibbing at the end of their essay as to whether the contemporary Senate is capable of playing its most distinctive constitutional role, the moderating of congressional politics and the conserving of stable representative government.

My effort here, building on the observations of Fenno, Baker, Sinclair, Alford and Hibbing, and others, is to argue that the Senate may well be such a truly exceptional institution that in fact it does require a new form of theoretical analysis if we are to understand it and appreciate its continuing role in American politics.

I

The Senate has proven an elusive institution, I suggest, because the exceptional characteristics of the Senate, operating in combination, have created an institutional context so distinctive that the theoretical lenses needed to see and comprehend the Senate are qualitatively different from the rational-choice lenses that have proven so useful in the study of the U.S. House. In raising this possibility I build on recent empirical and conceptual advances within social psychology.

For several decades, the social sciences have debated how best to understand human behavior.[1] One dominant school of thought maintains that individuals and groups can best be studied from a microeconomic perspective that stresses the primary role of rational-choice calculations in shaping individual and group behavior. According to such a perspective, individuals share common and relatively stable perceptions of the fundamental values and social choices at stake in society and politics; social and political conflict emerges primarily as individuals seek to maximize their personal self-interest in the common pursuit of similar personal goals and social benefits. This approach to politics—which can be characterized as substantive or objective rationality because it assumes general agreement on the interests at stake in social and political life—is illustrated by the work of Downs (1957), Riker (1962), and Olson (1965). In contrast to rational choice, an alternative school of thought argues that social relations are best understood as a process of adaptive social learning. According to this perspective, individuals and groups have quite distinct and often transient perceptions of the values, goals, empirical conditions, and self-interest concerns that dominate social life.

While individuals may each pursue their perceived self-interest, their perceptions of goals, conditions, and interests may be substantially different, so that they lack a shared substantive understanding of the world by which to comprehend each other, interact and negotiate among themselves, and develop expectations about group and institutional behavior. To operate in a world of "multiple realities," social actors devote much of their effort to deciphering each other's worldviews and developing mutually acceptable working arrangements that accommodate their divergent perceptions and substantive orientations. This perspective—which can be characterized as procedural or bounded rationality because it acknowledges that individuals do engage in rational calculations but not necessarily from within the same substantive perspectives on the world—is illustrated by the work of Simon (1985), Berlin (1996), March and Olsen (1989, 1995), Padgett and Ansell (1993), Tilly (1997), and Vickers (see Adams, Forester, and Catron 1987).

Scholars have generally approached this debate as an all-or-nothing choice and have chosen to stress either a rational-choice or an adaptive learning perspective as the appropriate way to understand society and politics. The early success of political scientists in using rational-choice analysis to develop some powerful parsimonious explanations of political behavior—particularly their success in applying rational choice to the study of legislative behavior—seemed to suggest that a rational-choice perspective was the appropriate approach to politics. Now the growing recognition of the elusiveness and distinctiveness of Senate behavior serves to reopen this debate and does so at a time when the dichotomous choice between a rational-choice and a social learning perspective is increasingly being questioned.

During the 1990s, on the basis of a range of conceptual advances and empirical observations, leading social psychologists such as Michigan's Karl Weick came to the position that both forms of behavior are prevalent in the world.[2]

People are not exclusively narrow rational-choice calculators, preoccupied with self-interested pursuit of a few common and fundamental goals, nor are they exclusively adaptive learners continually crafting and recrafting social arrangements in ways that satisfy divergent styles and multiple perspectives on reality. Rather, they are complex social actors who at times tilt toward shared forms of rational calculation that yield relatively simple, continuous, and predictable group behavior patterns and at other times tilt toward adaptive social action that can yield complex, continually evolving, and idiosyncratic behavior patterns. Which way individuals tilt in their behavioral orientation depends heavily on the context within which they find themselves and the process of sense making—that is, the process of comprehending the context—that best helps them operate within it. This "context-dependent" understanding of human behavior, and its implications for conceptualizing and studying the House and Senate, can be grasped by considering two "ideal types" of social context and the "sense-making" orientation associated with each.

II

Some contexts—type I contexts—are highly structured. Such situations have well-defined organizational arrangements that dominate social life; a large and relatively continuous membership that is divided into clearly identifiable and relatively homogenous subgroups composed of distinctive and predictable types of members; clearly etched status hierarchies among members and organizational positions that serve to create generic roles and organizational goals that predominate group life; formalized rules and procedures that extensively regulate members' organizational activity; and shared identities and characteristics among groups of members that simplify and clarify the character of social life. These and other characteristics generate a regularized world in which a relatively high degree of certainty can exist about how organizational processes will proceed across time, about how participants will behave in their various generic roles and collective activities, and about the consequent outcomes that are likely to characterize collective action or inaction in such contexts.

Because structured contexts yield considerable certainty about organizational processes and group behavior, individuals operating in a structured context can reasonably believe that the principles and social patterns that they have learned through organizational socialization and experience provide a reliable framework through which to make sense out of ongoing events. In other words, structured contexts allow members to develop a shared belief system, based on commonly understood organizational principles and behavior patterns, and to use that belief system for comprehending social life. Little time must be devoted to interpreting, deciphering, reinterpreting, or adapting to social dynamics.

Rather, relying on this common belief system, individuals can devote their time and energy to fulfilling the roles they are expected to play and pursuing the individual goals appropriate to such roles. This approach to social life—which Weick calls "belief-driven" sense making—is particularly compatible with the theories of "substantive rationality" that characterize a rational-choice approach to social and political analysis. To explain behavior in a structured context characterized by belief-driven sense making, scholars primarily need to decipher the limited set of shared beliefs that participants hold about the structure of social life and to replicate the calculus that participants use as they determine how best to pursue their roles and goals within that regularized and continuous structure.

Much of the way contemporary scholars approach politics, and certainly the predominant way legislative scholars have approached Congress and other representative institutions, assumes the existence of highly structured contexts likely to generate belief-driven sense making and substantive rationality. In particular, there have been good reasons to assume that the U.S. House is a highly structured or "institutionalized" chamber in which members are socialized into a broadly shared understanding of House politics and pursue shared electoral, organizational, and political goals in a common and calculated manner (Polsby 1968; Asher 1973). Thus, for example, its large size and significant legislative role have fueled the demand for a specialized committee system, relatively strong party organizations, and a formalized system of rules and procedures, thereby helping generate a highly structured politics. Policy specialization among and within committees has helped create generic roles that simplify and regularize House politics. The requirement for reelection every two years creates a common electoral focus among members that facilitates and simplifies their political understanding of each other.

A relatively well-defined status hierarchy of power within and across committees and party organizations structures progressive ambition within the House so that the dominant organizational goals preoccupying its members are relatively clear. The close linkage of personal power in the House with membership in the majority party serves to further simplify and structure House politics. Finally, the fact that the distinctive constitutional power of the House lies in its special role in initiating revenue legislation means that the organizational life of the House is shaped by the annual debates and struggles over taxing and spending, a factor that introduces a strong and routinized regularity to House politics year by year. These and other factors have helped generate a House politics that can be deciphered by participants and scholars in a relatively systematic, straightforward and sustained manner.

The result has been a variety of studies of Congress, based heavily and sometimes entirely on House-centered data or illustrations, that use rational-choice analysis to explain differing aspects of congressional politics. Thus, Mayhew

(974b), Fiorina (1977b), and Arnold (1979) show how members' rational pursuit of reelection drives organizational structure, constitutional service, and congressional-bureaucratic relations. Fenno (1973) demonstrates how members' pursuit of reelection, good public policy, and chamber influence explains the operation and decisions of congressional committees. Cox and McCubbins (1993) and Arnold (1990) argue that strategic maneuvering for majority-party status helps structure committee politics and chamber policy making. And my own work (Dodd 1986) assesses how member concern for personal power conflicts with partisan and institutional power in ways that generate electoral realignments and institutional reform.

An underlying if unspoken assumption of such studies has been that an explanatory strategy that could deliver such systematic results in House-centric studies also provides the way of understanding the Senate, at least once one corrects for the fact that an institution of fewer members would necessarily generate somewhat less statistically powerful results. In point of fact, as the studies in this volume indicate, close examination of the Senate increasingly suggests that it is less a fuzzy shadow of the House and more a different type of institution altogether, with behavior patterns distinctly different from the House. To understand how this could be, it may be useful to recognize, as the work of Weick and others suggests, that social context can shift so dramatically as to actually induce different processes of human sense making and different patterns of human interaction. This can be seen by considering a second type of context.

III

The second type of context—type II—consists of situations that are highly fluid. Such situations can in many ways look like structured contexts, in the sense that there exist systematic organizational arrangements, a stable membership, and some meaningful formal rules. The critical reality in fluid contexts, however, is that the orderliness and regularity of organizational arrangements and rules, and the ways they serve to evoke a simplified and generic reality, are offset by additional conditions and characteristics of the context that complicate, confuse, and even subvert the straightforward operation of the institution. Such additional conditions can include a multiplicity of tasks that a social group must perform to fulfill its social roles and maintain its authority, with the multiplicity of tasks complicating the focus of social life; the unpredictable timing and overlap among tasks, making it difficult to create orderly procedures and rules that easily regulate group life; circumstances that allow individual members to perform a multiplicity of roles and to do so in idiosyncratic and innovative ways that limit the existence of regularized and specialized generic roles; the existence of a small and highly distinctive membership characterized by idiosyncratic motives, goals, and aspirations, thereby limiting the existence of a simple set of identifiable "types" of members that could simplify social life; and arrangements or conditions that allow circumstances external to the organization to dramatically and erratically influence member motives, organizational tasks, or governing activities.

The more complicated and confusing the organizational context is, the less likely it is to generate a continuous and generic structured reality—characterized by clarity and certainty about organizational life—and the more likely it is to generate instead a discontinuous and idiosyncratic fluid reality—characterized by confusion and uncertainty. Because there is no continuous, simple, and generic reality that predominates in such fluid social settings, the real and consequential arrangements that tend to matter are often informal, improvised, and transient behavior patterns that members develop to facilitate the functioning of the organization in response to shifting environmental conditions. As a result, there is no simple substantive understanding of such fluid contexts that members can learn through socialization or experience and use to interpret social life on a continuing and confident basis. Belief-driven sense making and strategic pursuit of interests within a shared substantive understanding of a highly structured reality are thus of limited value.

To function effectively, members in fluid contexts must learn to engage in "action-driven" sense making designed to discover the shifting nature of a complex social reality. Such action-driven sense making includes continuous experimental "action probes" by members designed to discover what the salient conditions of the moment are; extensive social networking designed to understand the distinctive values, goals, and styles of other members of the organization; extensive intragroup communication designed to "update" social awareness in the face of shifting tasks and environmental pressures; and the improvisation of new social relationships and governing strategies that help individuals and groups satisfy their divergent values, styles, and interests while also ensuring the operation of the organization itself as it confronts new circumstances.

The success and power of an organization confronted by highly fluid and permeable contexts, in other words, lies in the long-term and continuing ability of members to improvise social relations within the organization in ways that enable it to adapt to its highly dynamic and unpredictable environment. The tasks for scholars studying fluid contexts is to recognize the complex and shifting conditions that characterize such contexts and to identify the adaptive processes through which participants shape and reshape organizational politics in response to such fluidity. It is difficult enough for scholars to decipher politics in relatively static and structured contexts; it is considerably more challenging to grasp the nature of politics when it is subject to such perpetual change and adaptive transformation, so that the study of organizations in type II fluid contexts is a substantial challenge.

IV

The question confronting congressional scholars is whether there are sufficient reasons to believe that the Senate is best seen as a fluid context so that sustained attention to reconceptualizing senatorial politics, and exploring theories of adaptive process, would seem worthwhile. It seems to me that there are.[3] For example, the Constitution gives to the Senate a greater range of critical governing tasks than is the case for any other major legislature in the world; these include not only a central role in legislation and oversight, and a shared role with the House in the impeachment and conviction of judicial and executive officials, but also critical roles in advice and consent over treaties and over executive, judicial, and ambassadorial nominations; these multiple tasks create an inherent complexity of focus and unpredictability of timing into Senate life. These broad responsibilities then must be handled by a relatively small number of members—two per state for a total of 100 in the contemporary chamber—so that individual members must play a multiplicity of crosscutting roles for the chamber to manage these tasks; these multiple roles undercut the existence of simple and generic characterizations of senatorial life.

The small size and broad responsibilities of the Senate, moreover, create strong pressures for informal procedures and supermajoritarian decision rules, pressures that undercut the existence of the sort of highly structured majoritarian and partisan politics seen in the contemporary U.S. House and that induce fluid cross-partisan coalitions and moderating compromise. The difficulty of developing a simple, generic, and structured understanding of Senate life, and thus the need for ongoing adaptive learning among members, is reinforced by a variety of additional factors: these include the existence of staggered six-year terms for senators and vast differences in the population sizes of senate constituencies, as the research of Lee and Oppenheimer (1999) and the chapter by Lee in this volume (chapter 15) demonstrate; the periodic involvement of senators in campaigns for the presidency, as stressed by Ornstein, Peabody, and Rohde (1985); and the multiple sources of power and career advancement within the Senate that senators enjoy (Matthews, 1960; Ripley, 1969b; Sinclair, 1989). These varying conditions introduce substantial differences in the career goals and political calculations across members year by year so that ongoing informal contact and communication among members are needed for them to understand and respond to each other's distinctive political and career considerations.

These and other conditions would seem, in combination, to create a fluid and action-driven politics within the Senate characterized by multiple realities,

procedural rationality, widespread social networking, perceptual and role adjustment, and ongoing organizational adaptation. These expectations of adaptive
learning on part of senators are supported by the pioneering Senate narratives of
Richard Fenno, in which he reports on observations of five senators across a
decade of Senate life.[4] Fenno's observations suggest a world in which senators
proceed, and succeed, not so much according to the pursuit of specific goals, the
mastery of specific roles, and the calculation of specific foreseeable career paths,
but according to their capacities to comprehend a shifting reality, redefine their
roles and goals, and reconstruct political alliances in response to changing times
and circumstances, and to do so in nongeneric and idiosyncratic ways largely
unforeseen by themselves and others.[5] The expectations of adaptive organizational change are reinforced by Barbara Sinclair's (1989, 2001) broad and dynamic portrait of the Senate across forty years, a portrait that discloses a Senate
shifting dramatically from a clubby and closed world of courtly gentlemen to a
busy and competitive world of policy entrepreneurs and then most recently to a
world of partisan warriors; these changes appear to be explained by the ability of
its members to craft and recraft its internal life in response to shifts in its external environment and to do so somewhat informally, without dramatic structural
upheaval or political revolution.

Finally, the sense of a highly fluid and adaptive Senate would seem to be
greatly reinforced by the essays in this volume. For example, the research reported by Abramowitz (chapter 3), Alford and Hibbing (chapter 6), Erikson
(chapter 5), Kahn and Kenney (chapter 4), Schiller (chapter 7), and Sellers
(chapter 8), in combination, portrays an *institution* so extraordinarily visible and
powerful that its members (1) actually experience issue voting and competitive
elections when running for reelection; (2) must work both to build highly particularistic electoral coalitions and to coordinate partisan media efforts in order to
gain a margin of electoral comfort; and (3) confront regular alterations in their
chamber's ideological and partisan majorities and in governing arrangements
because of their electoral circumstances. These patterns, taken together, tend to
make the Senate much more permeable to outside pressures and developments,
and thus to generate a less predictable internal environment, than is generally the
case for the highly structured House.

The work of Larry Evans (chapter 13) portrays *senators* who are so distinct
in their constituent and political concerns that they must forego cueing off one
another when voting and instead develop elaborate staff-based systems to guide
them in policy decision processes. This staff-based decision process reinforces
the idiosyncratic nature of individual senators, making them extremely sensitive
to their unique political circumstances. It also magnifies the unpredictable quality of Senate life.

The essays by Sinclair (chapter 12) and Baker (chapter 15) portray a *policy process* so fragile that the Senate continually operates on the verge of institutional collapse. The Senate appears to avoid this outcome only through the continual construction of new voting alliances in response to the demands of shifting and somewhat unpredictable minorities. It also relies on a deep norm of institutional loyalty that, in moments of extraordinary conflict and tension such as the conviction vote on a president, can introduce shared concern for the institution among an otherwise highly idiosyncratic body of senators. These and numerous other findings point to distinctive qualities of Senate life that are at variance with our expectations derived from the study of the U.S. House and analogous legislatures and that would seem more compatible with the complex and dynamic expectations of a highly fluid world of adaptive learning.

V

The thrust of these observations is to suggest that the Senate has proven elusive because the theories of substantive rationality that legislative scholars have learned to use in extensive study of the highly structured House of Representatives inhibit our ability to comprehend the fluid patterning of senatorial politics. Our problem is not a lack of information about the Senate or research on senatorial politics per se but a lack of appropriate theory. As the essays in this volume indicate, scholars are generating a rich body of Senate research. Our problem in seeing the Senate lies in the implicit theoretical frames we bring to it, frames crafted for very different institutional contexts. To see the patterning across new and existing research, and how it fits together to make sense of Senate politics, we need to shift away from theories of substantive rationality, which assume the existence of a regularized, stable, and predictable structure to institutional politics, and toward theories of adaptive learning and procedural rationality, which more nearly anticipate a transient, erratic, idiosyncratic, and improvisational political world.

In raising this possibility, I am not suggesting that senators are not rational individuals capable of identifying and pursuing self-interest: essays such as the one by Bert Loomis in this volume (chapter 6) and research by scholars such as Brady and Volden (1998), and Krehbiel (1998) make clear that senators are fully capable of assessing and pursuing self-interest. Nor am I suggesting that the Senate lacks substantial elements of structural commonality with the House and analogous legislatures. The Senate is, in fact, a classic American legislature, composed of professionalized office staffs, powerful committees, meaningful party caucuses, and consequential leadership structures; empowered by constitutional roles and delegated prerogatives; and guided by formal rules, traditions, and precedents. Moreover, as the essays by Gamm and Smith (chapter 11),

Cooper and Rybicki (chapter 10), and others make clear, these various arrangements play significant roles in the politics of the Senate.

What I am proposing is that the focus of senatorial politics is so complex, erratic, and uncertain across time, and the focus of rational action generally so varied and idiosyncratic senator by senator, that the predominant concern of Senate life is a crafting, learning, and recrafting of the transient social arrangements that enable it to operate effectively. Such arrangements must respect the broad organizational rules and structure of the chamber and certainly will involve an embrace of substantive rationality when arrangements generate a highly structured moment of political choice. But within these broad parameters, and between these moments of structured choice, senators must continually improvise and adapt an evolving set of interpersonal relationships, personal routines, political alliances, and group norms. It is this process of improvisation and adaptation that enables senators to address the distinctive combination of constitutional tasks, political circumstances, policy problems, and individual ambitions that preoccupy them across time.

Insofar as fluidity is the hallmark of Senate politics, it may well be theories of procedural rationality, satisficing, social learning, social networking, and organizational adaptation that provide us the greatest capacity to comprehend it, rather than theories of substantive rationality and institutional equilibrium. This possibility suggests that considerable debate may be in order over how best to study the Senate in its own right—a debate the essays in this volume should serve to stimulate. Such a debate requires us to grapple self-consciously with the deep theoretical assumptions and expectations that we have brought to legislative analysis over the past several decades—assumptions of institutionalized structure, generic roles, identifiable legislative types, common strategic calculations, and regularized political processes—and to imagine the alternative assumptions and theoretical patterns appropriate to a fluid legislative world. As we image such a world, we may more clearly see it. Moreover, an additional and critical concern of such debate must be with the significance that the contrasts between a structured House and a fluid Senate have for the broader functioning of the Congress and the national government. In particular, the perception of such a fluid Senate presented here necessarily forces us to wonder whether and how the Senate today fulfills its most basic constitutional responsibility to moderate and conserve stable representative government.

One possible way to understand how the Senate successfully fulfills its moderating role may lie in recognizing the extraordinary—perhaps even exceptional—ways that the differing institutional contexts and organizational dynamics of the House and Senate fit together so as to facilitate the long-term operation of both chambers. Thus, the House may provide the stabilizing structure and regularity that helps introduce a necessary degree of order and predictability onto bicameral politics during periods of "normalcy," when a dominant policy regime pervades national politics. In so doing the House also defines political and programmatic boundaries that serve to limit and constrain senatorial innovation and improvisation. For its part, the ongoing improvisational quality of senatorial politics may introduce and legitimize political and policy innovations that help generate some degree of congressional responsiveness to social change, despite the highly structured, stable, and more insulated character of the House.

The ongoing process of procedural and policy innovation in the Senate can help keep it more contemporaneous in its focus than the more routinized and insulated House, so that radical change proves less necessary and appealing in the Senate during periods of national crisis and so that moderation in the face of such crises appears more politically viable. Simultaneously, the sustained experience of the Senate with difficulties in governing may generate norms such as institutional patriotism and cross-partisan compromise that in moments of national crisis help the Congress as a whole maintain a degree of adaptive equilibrium. The extensive experience of the Senate with uncertainty and adaptive learning may induce a deep belief among legislators and citizens alike in the ability of representative assemblies to confront governing difficulties and emerge revitalized and re-empowered. Such experience may also allow members of the Senate to face system crises with more confidence and to be more open to learning effective strategies for addressing institutional crises than House members accustomed to a routinized politics of "normalcy." Finally, the very experience of life in the Senate may enable senators to provide Congress and the nation with broad perspective and steady judgment, guided by the firsthand knowledge that individuals and groups of differing values, goals, and worldviews can nevertheless work together, learn to accommodate divergent understandings, and find areas of common ground and collective cooperation even in troubled times.

When crises challenge the viability of our bicameral Congress—moments so often driven by the tendency of citizens to embrace "political revolution" as the primary way to induce change within our highly insulated House—the conserving, moderating, and stabilizing roles of the Senate come to the fore.[6] Accustomed to improvisation amidst uncertainty and buoyed by norms of institutional loyalty, a fluid and permeable Senate that appears to operate exceedingly close to the edge of collapse during periods of normalcy may possess precisely the capacities for adaptive learning, experienced judgment, policy moderation, and foresightful leadership that are necessary to cushion and constrain destabilizing change induced by the House. In doing so, the Senate necessarily engenders within the nation an appreciation for the power and purpose of its representative institutions, sustaining popular support for Congress in periods of upheaval and confusion. If this interpretation is true, then the Senate may be an exceptional institution indeed, and a truly essential partner in the successful operation of our bicameral Congress.

Notes

1. Examples of this debate within political science are found in the point/counterpoint between William Riker (1982) and Herbert Simon (1985) in the *American Political Science Review;* in Almond (1990), in Green and Shapiro (1994), and in the extensive discussion of Green and Shapiro's book in *Critical Review,* Vol. 9, 31–32, Winter-Spring, 1995. The distinction between substantive and procedural rationality is developed in Simon (1985, 294–98).

2. See, for example, Karl E. Weick (1995, 1979). Other important statements about the role that context and process can play in shaping the nature of rationality and human sense making can be found in Bendor (2001), particularly his suggestion that substantive or objective rational choice is most prevalent when the "game" of politics has narrowed to a few clear strategies and choices, whereas bounded rationality is more prevalent in situations characterized by complexity and multiple paths of action; in Dreyfus and Dreyfus (1986), which suggests that the use of narrow strategic or substantive rationality is primarily confined to simple contexts characterized by easily learned rules and procedures, whereas advanced patterns of procedural rationality and sophisticated or expert learning more nearly characterize complex settings that cannot be managed by simple rules and procedures; and in Flyvbjerg (2001), particularly his extensive discussion of Dreyfus and Dreyfus in chap. 2 and of the varied ways that "context counts" in chap. 4.

3. For a more extensive discussion of the general characteristics of the Senate and how they contrast with the House, see Baker (1989) and Oleszek (1996).

4. I refer here to Fenno (1988, 1990, 1991a, 1991b, 1992). Also instructive for seeing the Senate as a fluid institution composed of individualistic and idiosyncratic senators is Fenno's (1986) presidential address to the American Political Science Association.

5. For a more extensive discussion of the implications of Fenno's narratives for a social learning perspective on the Senate, see Dodd (1992). As that article indicates, the ideas developed in the current essay derive in many ways from reading and reflecting on Fenno's Senate narratives. Also critical has been the distinction that Fenno (1973) makes between "corporate committees," which typify key House committees, and "permeable committees," which appear to typify all Senate committees. Fenno's analysis there suggests the existence, even within an elaborate committee system, of a highly fluid and porous politics within the Senate and thus to support the applicability of theories of adaptive learning to it.

6. The periodic tendency of the Congress to experience sudden, unforeseen, and destabilizing upheavals, illustrated by the experience of the "Republican Revolution," is discussed in Dodd's "Re-Envisioning Congress" (2001), with the logic and illustrations of that essay largely based on the politics of the House. The thrust of the current essay is to suggest that the incremental and adaptive learning processes that "Re-Envisioning Congress" sees as critical to the power and survival of Congress during such crises may derive heavily from the distinctive politics of the Senate. Across time, then, the differ-

ential politics of the two houses may well generate a kind of cybernetic patterning to bicameralism, out of which emerges a dynamic equilibrium between them. Thus, the institutionalized structure of the House provides considerable stability to the Congress in "normal" times, helping to keep the Senate in check and moderated in its action innovations. Yet eventually the institutionalized structure of the House is up-ended by political revolution that comes in response to new social conditions, a revolution that focuses on the House because of its more insulated and less responsive politics. During such periods, the House must undergo substantial procedural, structural, and policy adjustment to "catch up" with the Senate and the social and political world at large. In these adjustment periods, the Senate, being more in tune with and adapted to national currents, may play a special stabilizing, moderating, and conserving role that gives the House some critical time and substantive guidance as it innovates a new policy and structural equilibrium. This interpretation would seem consistent with Mayhew's observations that the Senate generally produces more innovative action than the House, particularly in periods when a dominant regime politics exists in national government. But in periods of extraordinary upheaval such as the Civil War/Reconstruction, the Progressive Era/World War I, the Depression/World War II, and possibly the contemporary period, the House drives legislative innovation while the Senate shifts into a less action-driven and more moderating stance. See Mayhew (2000, 130–35); see also Carmines and Dodd (1985).

REFERENCES

Abramowitz, Alan I. 1980. "A Comparison of Voting for U.S. Senator and Representative." *American Political Science Review* 74: 633–40.

——. 1988. "Explaining Senate Election Outcomes." *American Political Science Review* 82: 385–403.

Abramowitz, Alan I., and Jeffrey A. Segal. 1986. "Determinants of the Outcomes of U.S. Senate Elections." *Journal of Politics* 48: 433–39.

——. 1990. "Beyond Willie Horton and the Pledge of Allegiance: National Issues in the 1988 Elections." *Legislative Studies Quarterly* 15: 565–80.

——. 1992. *Senate Elections.* Ann Arbor: University of Michigan Press.

Achen, Christopher. 1978. "Measuring Representation." *American Journal of Political Science* 22: 475–510.

Adams, Guy B., John Forester, and Bayand Catron. 1987. *Policymaking, Communication, and Social Learning: Essays of Geoffrey Vickers.* New Brunswick, N.J.: Transaction Books.

Ahuja, Sunil. 1994. "Electoral Status and Representation in the United States Senate: Does Temporal Proximity to Election Matter?" *American Politics Quarterly* 22: 104–18.

Aldrich, John H.. 1995. *Why Parties?* Chicago: University of Chicago Press.

——. 1997. "Does Historical Political Research Pose Any Special Methodological Concerns?" *Political Methodologist* 8: 1, 17–21.

Aldrich, John, and David Rohde. 1995. *Theories of the Party in the Legislature and the Transition to Republican Rule in the House.* Political Institutions and Public Choice Working Paper 95-05. East Lansing: Institute for Public Policy and Social Research, Michigan State University.

——. 1997. "Balance of Power: Republican Party Leadership and the Committee System in the 104th House." Paper presented at the annual meeting of the American Political Science Association, Chicago, September.

——. 1997–98. "The Transition to Republican Rule in the House: Implications for Theories of Congressional Politics." *Political Science Quarterly* 112: 541–67.

——. 1998. "Measuring Conditional Party Government." Paper presented at the annual meeting of the Midwest Political Science Association, Chicago, April.

——. 2000. "The Consequences of Party Organization in the House: The Role of the Majority and Minority Parties in Conditional Party Government." In *Polarized Politics,* edited by Jon Bond and Richard Fleisher. Washington, D.C.: Congressional Quarterly Press.

——. 2001. "The Logic of Conditional Party Government: Revisiting the Electoral

Connection." In *Congress Reconsidered,* 7th ed., edited by Lawrence C. Dodd and Bruce I. Oppenheimer. Washington, D.C.: Congressional Quarterly Press.

Alesina, Alberto, and Howard Rosenthal. 1994. *Partisan Politics, Divided Government, and the Economy.* New York: Cambridge University Press.

Alexander, DeAlva Stanwood. 1916. *History and Procedure of the House of Representatives.* Boston: Houghton Mifflin.

Alford, John R., and David W. Brady. 1987. "Personal and Partisan Advantage in U.S. House Elections: 1840–1986." Paper presented at the annual meeting of the Southern Political Science Association, November, Charlotte, N.C.

Alford, John R., and John R. Hibbing. 1981. "Increased Incumbency Advantage in the House." *Journal of Politics* 43: 1042–61.

Almond, Gabriel. 1990. *A Discipline Divided: Schools and Sects in Political Science.* Newbury Park, Calif.: Sage Publications.

Alvarez, R. Michael, and Jason L. Saving. 1997. "Congressional Committees and the Political Economy of Federal Outlays." *Public Choice* 92: 55–73.

Amacher, Ryan C., and William J. Boyes. 1978. "Cycles in Senatorial Voting Behavior: Implications for the Optimal Frequency of Elections." *Public Choice* 33: 5–13.

Anagnoson, J. Theodore. 1980. "Politics in the Distribution of Federal Grants: The Case of the Economic Development Administration." In *Political Benefits,* edited by B. S. Rundquist. Lexington, Mass.: Lexington Books.

_____. 1982. "Federal Grant Agencies and Congressional Election Campaigns." *American Journal of Political Science* 26: 547–61.

Anderson, Gary M., and Robert D. Tollison. 1991. "Congressional Influence and Patterns of New Deal Spending, 1933–1939." *Journal of Law and Economics* 34: 161–75.

Ansolabehere, Steven, Roy Behr, and Shanto Iyengar. 1993. *The Media Game: American Politics in the Television Age.* New York: Macmillan.

Arnold, R. Douglas. 1979. *Congress and the Bureaucracy: A Theory of Influence.* New Haven, Conn.: Yale University Press.

_____. 1990. *The Logic of Congressional Action.* New Haven, Conn.: Yale University Press.

Asher, Herbert B. 1973. "The Learning of Legislative Norms." *American Political Science Review* 67: 499–513.

Atlas, Cary M., Thomas W. Gilligan, Robert J. Hendershott, and Mark A. Zupan. 1995. "Slicing the Federal Government Net Spending Pie: Who Wins, Who Loses and Why." *American Economic Review* 85: 624–29.

Bacon, Donald C. 1991. "Joseph Taylor Robinson: The Good Soldier." In *First among Equals: Outstanding Senate Leaders of the Twentieth Century,* edited by Richard A. Baker and Roger H. Davidson. Washington, D.C.: Congressional Quarterly Press.

Baker, Peter, Juliet Eilprin, Guy Gugliotto, John F. Harris, Dan Morgan, Evia Pianin, and Daniel Van Drehle. 1999. "The Train That Wouldn't Stop." *Washington Post,* National Edition. February 22.

Baker, Richard A., and Roger H. Davidson. 1991. "Introduction." In *First among Equals: Outstanding Senate Leaders of the Twentieth Century,* ed. Richard A. Baker and Roger H. Davidson. Washington, D.C.: Congressional Quarterly Press.

Baker, Ross K. 1989. *House and Senate.* New York: Norton.

———. 1998. "Factors Influencing the Political Relationships of Same-State Senators." Working Paper.

———. 1999. "Examining Individualism vs. Folkways in the Aftermath of Impeachment." Paper presented at the Norman Thomas Conference on Senate Exceptionalism, Vanderbilt University, October 21–23, Nashville, Tenn.

Barone, Michael, and Grant Ujifusa. 1999. *The Almanac of American Politics 2000.* Washington, D.C.: National Journal.

———. 1997. *The Almanac of American Politics 1998.* Washington, D.C.: National Journal.

Barone, Michael, Grant Ujifusa, and Douglas Matthews. 1973. *The Almanac of American Politics 1974.* Boston: Gambit.

Barry, John M. 1989. *The Ambition and the Power.* New York: Penguin.

Bartels, Larry M. 1988. *Presidential Primaries and the Dynamics of Public Choice.* Princeton, N.J.: Princeton University Press.

Baumgartner, Frank, and Bryan D. Jones. 1993. *Agendas and Instability in American Politics.* Chicago: University of Chicago Press.

Bendor, Jon. 2001. "Bounded Rationality in Political Science." *The International Encyclopedia of the Social and Behavioral Sciences.* Oxford, England: Pergamon.

Berlin, Isaiah. 1996. "On Political Judgment." *New York Review of Books,* October.

Beth, Richard. 1995. "What We Don't Know about Filibusters." Paper presented at the annual meeting of the Western Political Science Association, Portland, Ore., March 15–18.

Bickers, Kenneth N., and Robert M. Stein. 1996. "The Electoral Dynamics of the Federal Pork Barrel." *American Journal of Political Science* 40: 1300–26.

Binder, Sarah. 1997. *Minority Rights, Majority Rule: Partisanship and the Development of Congress.* New York: Cambridge University Press.

Binder, Sarah A., and Steven S. Smith. 1997. *Politics or Principle: Filibustering in the United States Senate.* Washington, D.C.: Brookings Institution.

Biographical Directory of the American Congress, 1774–1971. 1971. Washington, D.C.: U.S. Government Printing Office.

Born, Richard. 1979. "Generational Replacement and the Growth of Incumbent Reelection Margins in the U.S. House." *American Political Science Review* 73: 811–17.

Box-Steffensmeier, Janet M., Laura W. Arnold, and Christopher J. W. Zorn. 1997. "The Strategic Timing of Position Taking in Congress: A Study of the North American Free Trade Agreement." *American Political Science Review* 92: 324–38.

Brady, David W. 1988. *Critical Elections and Congressional Policy Making.* Stanford, Calif.: Stanford University Press.

Brady, David W., Richard Brody, and David Epstein. 1989. "Heterogeneous Parties and Political Organization: The U.S. Senate, 1880–1920." *Legislative Studies Quarterly* 14: 205–23.

Brady, David, Kara Buckley, and Douglas Rivers. 1999. "The Roots of Careerism in the U.S. House of Representatives." *Legislative Studies Quarterly* 24: 489–508.

Brady, David W., and David Epstein. 1997. "Intraparty Preferences, Heterogeneity, and the Origins of the Modern Congress: Progressive Reformers in the House and Senate, 1890–1920." *Journal of Law, Economics, and Organization* 13: 26–49.

Brady, David W., and Bernard Grofman. 1991. "Sectional Differences in Partisan Bias and Electoral Responsiveness in U.S. House Elections, 1850–1980." *British Journal of Political Science* 21: 247–56.

Brady, David, and Craig Volden. 1998. *Revolving Gridlock: Politics and Policy from Carter to Clinton.* Boulder, Colo.: Westview Press.

Brandes Crook, Sara, and John R. Hibbing. 1997. "A Not-So-Distant Mirror: The 17th Amendment and Congressional Change." *American Political Science Review* 92: 845–53.

Brians, Craig Leonard, and Martin P. Wattenberg. 1996. "Campaign Issue Knowledge and Salience: Comparing Reception from TV Commercials, TV News, and Newspapers." *American Journal of Political Science* 40: 172–93.

Brown, William S. 1991. *Introductory Econometrics.* New York: West Publishing Company.

Bullock, Charles S., III. 1973. "Committee Transfers in the United States House of Representatives." *Journal of Politics* 35: 85–120.

———. 1976. "Motivations for U.S. Congressional Committee Preferences: Freshmen of the 92nd Congress." *Legislative Studies Quarterly* 1: 201–12.

———. 1985. "U.S. Senate Committee Assignments: Preferences, Motivations, and Success." *American Journal of Political Science* 29: 789–808.

Bullock, Charles, III, and David W. Brady. 1983. "Party, Constituency, and Roll Call Voting in the U.S. Senate." *Legislative Studies Quarterly* 8: 29–43.

Bullock, Charles S., III, and John Sprague. 1969. "A Research Note on the Committee Reassignments of Southern Democratic Congressmen." *Journal of Politics* 31: 493–512.

Burdette, Franklin L. 1940. *Filibustering in the Senate.* Princeton, N.J.: Princeton University Press.

Byrd, Robert C. 1989. *The Senate 1789–1989.* Vol. 2, *Addresses on the History of the United States Senate.* Washington, D.C.: U.S. Government Printing Office.

———. 1993. *The Senate, 1789–1989.* Vol. 4, *Historical Statistics, 1789–1992.* 100th Cong., 1st sess. S. Doc. 100-20. Washington, D.C.: Government Printing Office.

Calvert, Randall L. 1987. "Coordination and Power: The Foundation of Leadership among Rational Legislators." Paper presented at the annual meeting of the American Political Science Association, Chicago. April.

Cameron, Charles M. 2000. *Veto Bargaining*. New York: Cambridge University Press.

Campbell, James E. 1996. *Cheap Seats: The Democratic Party's Advantage in U.S. House Elections*. Columbus: Ohio State University Press.

Canon, David T., and Charles Stewart III. 1998. "The Development of the Senate Committee System, 1789–1879." Paper presented at the annual meeting of the American Political Science Association, September 3–6, Boston.

———. 2001. "The Evolution of the Committee System in Congress." In *Congress Reconsidered*, 7th ed., edited by Lawrence C. Dodd and Bruce I. Oppenheimer. Washington, D.C.: Congressional Quarterly Press.

Canon, David T., and Martin Sweet. 1998. "Informational and Demand-Side Theories of Congressional Committees: Evidence from the Senate, 1789–1993." Paper presented at the annual meeting of the American Political Science Association, September 3–6, Boston.

Carmines, Edward G., and Lawrence C. Dodd. 1985. "Bicameralism in Congress: The Changing Partnership." In *Congress Reconsidered*, 3d ed., edited by Lawrence C. Dodd and Bruce I. Oppenheimer. Washington, D.C.: Congressional Quarterly Press.

Carmines, Edward G., and James A. Stimson. 1989. *Issue Evolution: Race and the Transformation of American Politics*. Princeton, N.J: .Princeton University Press.

Carsey, Thomas M., and Barry Rundquist. 1999. "Party and Committee in Distributive Politics: Evidence from Defense Spending." *Journal of Politics* 61: 1156–69.

Chernick, Howard A. 1979. "An Economic Model of the Distribution of Project Grants." In *Fiscal Federalism and Grants-in-Aid*, edited by P. Mieszkowski and W. H. Oakland. Washington, D.C.: Urban Institute.

Clarke, Peter, and Susan Evans. 1993. *Covering Campaigns: Journalism in Congressional Elections*. Stanford, Calif.: Stanford University Press.

Clarke, Peter, and Eric Fredin. 1978. "Newspapers, Television, and Political Reasoning." *Public Opinion Quarterly* 42: 143–60.

Clines, Francis X. 1999. "One Senate, Indivisible (For Now)." *New York Times*, January 9.

Cohen, Richard E. 2000. "A Congress Divided." *National Journal*, February 4. http://www.cloakroom.com.

Connelly, William F., and John J. Pitney Jr. 1994. *Congress' Permanent Minority?* Lanham, MD: Rowman & Littlefield.

Conover, Pamela J., and Stanley Feldman. 1989. "Candidate Perception in an Ambiguous World: Campaigns, Cues, and Inference Processes." *American Journal of Political Science* 33: 912–40.

Converse, Philip E. 1962. "Information Flow and Stability of Partisan Attitudes." *Public Opinion Quarterly* 26: 578–99.

———. 1964. "Nature of Belief Systems in Mass Publics." In *Ideology and Discontent*, edited by David Apter. New York: Free Press.

Cook, Timothy E. 1998. *Governing with the News*. Chicago: University of Chicago Press.

———. 1999. "Senators and Reporters Revisited." Paper presented at Robert J. Dole Institute Conference on Civility and Deliberation in the U.S. Senate, July 16, Washington, D.C.

Cooper, Joseph. 1970. *The Origins of the Standing Committees and the Development of the Modern House.* Houston, Tex.: Rice University Studies.

———. 1977. "Congress in Organizational Perspective." In *Congress Reconsidered,* edited by Lawrence C. Dodd and Bruce I. Oppenheimer. New York: Praeger.

———. 1981. "Organization and Innovation in the U.S. House of Representatives." In *House at Work,* edited by Joseph Cooper and G. Calvin Mackenzie. Austin: University of Texas Press, 1981.

Cooper, Joseph, and David W. Brady. 1981a. "Institutional Context and Leadership Style: The House from Cannon to Rayburn." *American Political Science Review* 75: 411–25.

———. 1981b. "Toward a Diachronic Analysis of Congress." *American Political Science Review* 75: 988–1006.

Cooper, Joseph, and Cheryl D. Young. 1989. "Bill Introduction in the Nineteenth Century: A Study of Institutional Change." *Legislative Studies Quarterly* 14: 67–105.

Cooper, Joseph, and Garry Young. Forthcoming. "Party and Preference in Roll Call Voting in the House of Representatives." In *Essays on the History of Congress,* edited by David Brady and Mathew McCubbins. Stanford, Calif.: Stanford University Press.

Cover, Albert D. 1977. "One Good Term Deserves Another: The Advantage of Incumbency in Congressional Elections." *American Journal of Political Science* 21: 523–42.

Cox, Gary W., and Matthew D. McCubbins. 1993. *Legislative Leviathan.* Berkeley: University of California Press.

Dalager, Jon K. 1996. "Voters, Issues, and Elections: Are the Candidates' Messages Getting Through?" *Journal of Politics* 58: 486–515.

Damon, Richard E. 1971. "The Standing Rules of the U.S. House of Representatives." Ph.D. diss., Columbia University.

Davidson, Roger H., and Walter J. Oleszek. 1977. *Congress against Itself.* Bloomington: Indiana University Press.

———. 1994. *Congress and Its Members,* 4th ed. Washington, D.C.: Congressional Quarterly Press.

Dion, Douglas. 1997. *Turning the Legislative Thumbscrew: Minority Rights and Procedural Change in Legislative Politics.* Ann Arbor: University of Michigan Press.

Dodd, Lawrence C. 1986. "The Cycles of Legislative Change." In *Political Science: The Science of Politics,* edited by Herbert F. Weisberg. New York: Agathon.

———. 1992. "Learning to Learn: The Political Mastery of U.S. Senators." *Legislative Studies Newsletter,* November. No pag.

———. 2001. "Re-Envisioning Congress: Theoretical Perspectives on Congressional

Change." In *Congress Reconsidered,* 7th ed., edited by Lawrence C. Dodd and Bruce I. Oppenheimer. Washington, D.C.: Congressional Quarterly Press.

Dodd, Lawrence C., and Bruce I. Oppenheimer. 1997. "Congress and the Emerging Order: Conditional Party Government or Constructive Partnership?" In *Congress Reconsidered,* 6th ed., edited by Lawrence C. Dodd and Bruce I. Oppenheimer. Washington, D.C.: Congressional Quarterly Press.

Downs, Anthony. 1957. *An Economic Theory of Democracy.* New York: Harper and Row.

Drew, Dan, and David Weaver. 1991. "Voter Learning in the 1988 Presidential Election: Did the Debates and the Media Matter?" *Journalism Quarterly* 68: 27–37.

Dreyfus, Herbert, and Stuart Dreyfus. 1986. *Mind over Machine: The Power of Human Intuition and Expertise in the Era of the Computer.* New York: Free Press.

Drury, Allen, 1963. *A Senate Journal: 1943–1945.* New York: McGraw-Hill.

Ehrenhalt, Alan. 1986. "The Senate: World's Least Effective Saucer." *Congressional Quarterly Weekly Report* 44: 583.

Elling, Richard. 1982. "Ideological Change in the U.S. Senate: Time and Electoral Responsiveness." *Legislative Studies Quarterly* 7: 75–92.

Elving, Ronald D. 1995. "Less Accommodation in a Partisan Era." *Congressional Quarterly Weekly Report,* April 15.

Endersby, James W., and Karen M. McCurdy. 1996. Committee Assignments in the U.S. Senate. *Legislative Studies Quarterly* 21: 219–33.

Erikson, Robert S. 1971. "The Advantage of Incumbency in Congressional Elections." *Polity* 3: 395–405.

———. 1978. "Constituency Opinion and Congressional Behavior: A Reexamination of the Miller-Stokes Representation Data." *American Journal of Political Science* 22: 511–35.

———. 1990. "Roll Calls, Reputations, and Representation in the U.S. Senate." *Legislative Studies Quarterly* 15: 623–42.

Erikson, Robert S., Michael B. MacKuen, and James A. Stimson. 1998. "What Moves Macropartisanship? A Response to Green, Palmquist, and Schickler." *American Political Science Review* 92: 901–12.

———. 2002. *The Macro-Polity.* New York: Cambridge University Press.

Erikson, Robert S., and Gerald C. Wright. 1980. "Policy Representation of Constituency Interests." *Political Behavior* 2: 91–106.

———. 1997. "Voters, Candidates, and Issues in Congressional Elections." In *Congress Reconsidered,* 6th ed., edited by Lawrence C. Dodd and Bruce I. Oppenheimer. Washington, D.C.: Congressional Quarterly Press.

Evans, C. Lawrence. 1991. *Leadership in Committee.* Ann Arbor: University of Michigan Press.

———. 1999. "Legislative Structure: Rules, Precedents, and Jurisdictions." *Legislative Studies Quarterly* 24: 605–45.

Evans, C. Lawrence, and Walter J. Oleszek. 1997a. "Analyzing Party Leadership in Congress: An Exploration." Paper presented at the annual meeting of the Midwest Political Science Association, Chicago, April.

———. 1997b. *Congress under Fire: Reform Politics and the Republican Majority.* Boston: Houghton Mifflin.

———. 1999. "The Procedural Context of Senate Deliberation." Paper presented at the Robert J. Dole Institute Conference on Civility and Deliberation in the U.S. Senate, July 16, Washington, D.C.

Evans, Daniel J. 1988. "Why I'm Quitting the Senate." *New York Times Magazine,* April 16, 1988.

Evans, Diana. 1994. "Policy and Pork: The Use of Pork Barrel Projects to Build Policy Coalitions in the House of Representatives." *American Journal of Political Science* 38: 894–917.3

Feldman, Stanley, and Pamela J. Conover. 1983. "Candidates, Issues and Voters: The Role of Inference in Political Perception." *Journal of Politics* 45: 811–39.

Fenno, Richard F., Jr. 1966. *The Power of the Purse.* Boston: Little, Brown.

———. 1973. *Congressmen in Committees.* Boston: Little, Brown.

———. 1978. *Home Style: U.S. House Members in Their Districts.* Boston: Little, Brown.

———. 1982. *The United States Senate: A Bicameral Perspective.* Washington, D.C.: American Enterprise Institute.

———. 1986. "Observation, Context and Sequence in the Study of Politics." *American Political Science Review* 80: 1–15.

———. 1989a. *The Making of a Senator: Dan Quayle.* Washington, D.C.: Congressional Quarterly Press.

———. 1989b. "The Senate through the Looking Glass: The Debate over Television." *Legislative Studies Quarterly* 14: 313–48.

———. 1990. *The Presidential Odyssey of John Glenn.* Washington, D.C.: Congressional Quarterly Press.

———. 1991a. *The Emergence of a Senate Leader: Pete Domenici and the Reagan Budget.* Washington, D.C.: Congressional Quarterly Press.

———. 1991b. *Learning to Legislate: The Senate Education of Arlen Specter.* Washington, D.C.: Congressional Quarterly Press.

———. 1992. *When Incumbency Fails: The Senate Career of Mark Andrews.* Washington, D.C.: Congressional Quarterly Press.

———. 1996. *Senators on the Campaign Trail.* Norman: University of Oklahoma Press.

———. 1997. *Learning to Govern: An Institutional View of the 104th Congress.* Washington, D.C.: Brookings Institution.

Ferejohn, John A. 1974. *Pork Barrel Politics.* Stanford, Calif.: Stanford University Press.

———. 1977. "On the Decline of Competition in Congressional Elections." *American Political Science Review* 71: 166–76.

Fiorina, Morris P. 1977a. "The Case of the Vanishing Marginals: The Bureaucracy Did It." *American Political Science Review* 71: 177–81.

———. 1977b. *Congress: Keystone of the Washington Establishment.* New Haven, Conn.: Yale University Press.

———. 1989. *Congress: Keystone of the Washington Establishment.* New Haven: Yale University Press.

———. 1992. *Divided Government.* New York: Macmillan.

———. 1996. *Divided Government.* 2d ed. Boston: Allyn and Bacon.

———. 2001. "Keystone Reconsidered." In *Congress Reconsidered,* 7th ed., edited by Lawrence C. Dodd and Bruce I. Oppenheimer. Washington, D.C.: Congressional Quarterly Press.

Fleisher, Richard, and Jon R. Bond. 2000. "Partisanship and the President's Quest for Votes on the Floor of Congress." In Jon R. Bond and Richard Fleisher, eds., *Polarized Politics.* Washington, D.C.: Congressional Quarterly Press.

Flyvbjerg, Bent. 2001. *Making Social Science Matter.* New York: Cambridge University Press.

Foley, Michael. 1980. *The New Senate.* New Haven, Conn.: Yale University Press.

Foley, Michael, and John E. Owens. 1996. *Congress and the Presidency: Institutional Politics in a Separated System.* New York: St. Martin's Press.

Fox, Harrison W., and Susan W. Hammond. 1977. *Congressional Staffs: The Invisible Force in Lawmaking.* New York: Free Press.

Franklin, Charles H. 1991. "Eschewing Obfuscation? Campaigns and the Perceptions of U.S. Senate Incumbents." *American Political Science Review* 85: 1193–1214.

Frohlich, Norman, Joe Oppenheimer, and Oran Young. 1971. *Political Leadership and Collective Goods.* Princeton, N.J.: Princeton University Press.

Gamm, Gerald, and Kenneth A. Shepsle. 1989. "Emergence of Legislative Institutions: Standing Committees in the House and Senate, 1810–1825." *Legislative Studies Quarterly* 14: 39–66.

Gamm, Gerald, and Steven Smith. 2000. "Last among Equals: The Senate's Presiding Officer." In *Esteemed Colleagues: Civility and Deliberation in the U.S. Senate,* edited by Burdett Loomis. Washington, D.C.: Brookings Institution.

———. 2002. "Policy Leadership and the Development of the Modern Senate." In Matthew McCubbins and David Brady, eds., *New Directions in Studying the History of the U.S. Congress.* Stanford: Stanford University Press.

Gelman, Andrew, and Gary King. 1990. "Estimating Incumbency Advantage without Bias." *American Journal of Political Science* 34: 1142–64.

Gertzog, Irwin, 1995. *Congressional Women: Their Recruitment, Integration and Behavior.* 2d ed. Westport, Conn.: Praeger.

Gilfry, Henry. 1909. *Senate Precedents from the First Congress to the End of the Sixtieth Congress, 1789–1909.* Washington, D.C.: Government Printing Office (s.Doc. 61-5).

Gilligan, Thomas W., and Keith Krehbiel. 1990. "Organization of Informative Committees by a Rational Legislature." *American Journal of Political Science* 34: 531–64.

Gist, John, and Carter Hill. 1984. "Political and Economic Influences on Bureaucratic Allocation of Federal Grants: The Case of Urban Development Action Grants." *Journal of Urban Economics* 16: 158–72.

Goldenberg, Edie N., and Michael W. Traugott. 1984. *Campaigning for Congress.* Washington, D.C.: Congressional Quarterly Press.

Goss, Carol F. 1972. "Military Committee Membership and Defense-Related Benefits in the House of Representatives." *Western Political Quarterly* 25: 215–33.

Graber, Doris. 1993. *Mass Media and American Politics.* Washington, D.C.: Congressional Quarterly Press.

_____. 1997. *Mass Media and American Politics.* Washington, D.C.: Congressional Quarterly Press.

Green, Donald P., and Ian Shapiro. 1994. *Pathologies of Rational Choice Theory.* New Haven, Conn.: Yale University Press.

Grofman, Bernard, Thomas L. Brunell, and William Koetzle. 1998. "Why Gain in the Senate but Midterm Loss in the House? Evidence from a National Experiment." *Legislative Studies* 23: 79–90.

Groseclose, Timothy, and Charles Stewart III. 1999. "The Value of Committee Seats in the United States Senate, 1947–91." *American Journal of Political Science* 43: 963–73.

Gryski, Gerard. 1991. "The Influence of Committee Position on Federal Program Spending." *Polity* 23: 443–59.

Hall, Richard. 1996. *Participation in Congress.* New Haven, Conn.: Yale University Press.

Hall, Richard L., and Bernard Grofman. 1990. "The Committee Assignment Process and the Conditional Nature of Committee Bias." *American Political Science Review* 84: 1149–66.

Harlow, Ralph. 1917. *History of Legislative Methods in the Period before 1825.* New Haven, Conn.: Yale University Press.

Hatfield, Mark O. 1997. *Vice Presidents of the United States, 1789–1993.* 104th Cong., 2d sess. S. Doc. 104-26. Washington, D.C.: U.S. Government Printing Office.

Haynes, George H. 1938. *The Senate of the United States: Its History and Practice.* Boston: Houghton Mifflin.

Herrera, Richard, Thomas Epperlein, and Eric R. A. N. Smith. 1995. "The Stability of Congressional Roll Call Indexes." *Political Research Quarterly* 48: 403–16.

Herrnson, Paul S. 1995. *Congressional Elections: Campaigning at Home and in Washington.* Washington, D.C.: Congressional Quarterly Press.

Hibbing, John R. 1984. "The Liberal Hour: Electoral Pressures and Transfer Payment Voting in the United States Congress." *Journal of Politics* 46: 846–65.

Hibbing, John R., and John R. Alford. 1990. "Constituency Population and Representation in the U.S. Senate." *Legislative Studies Quarterly* 15: 581–98.

Hibbing, John R., and Sara Brandes. 1983. "State Population and the Electoral Success of U.S. Senators." *American Journal of Political Science* 27: 808–19.

Hird, John A. 1991. "The Political Economy of Pork: Project Selection at the U.S. Army Corps of Engineers." *American Political Science Review* 85: 429–56.

History, Rules, and Precedents of the Senate Republican Conference, 105th Congress. 1997.

Hoadley, John F. 1986. *Origins of American Political Parties: 1789–1803.* Lexington: University Press of Kentucky.

Holt, W. Stull. 1933. *Treaties Defeated by the Senate.* Baltimore, Md.: Johns Hopkins University Press.

Hooton, Cornell G. 1997. "Politics versus Policy in Public Works Grants: A Critical Test of the Simple Model." *American Politics Quarterly* 25: 75–103.

Huddy, Leonie, and Nayda Terkildsen. 1993. "Gender Stereotypes and the Perception of Male and Female Candidates." *American Journal of Political Science* 37: 119–47.

Huitt, Ralph K. 1961a. "Democratic Party Leadership in the Senate." *American Political Science Review* 55: 333–44.

———. 1961b. "The Outsider in the Senate." *American Political Science Review* 55: 566–75.

———. 1965. "The Internal Distribution of Influence: The Senate." In *The Congress and America's Future,* edited by David Truman. Englewood Cliffs, N.J.: Prentice Hall.

Huitt, Ralph. 1990. *Working within the System.* Berkeley, Calif.: Institute for Governmental Studies.

Iyengar, Shanto, and Donald Kinder. 1987. *News That Matters: Television and American Opinion.* Chicago: University of Chicago Press.

Jackman, Simon. 1994. "Measuring Electoral Bias: Australia, 1949–93." *British Journal of Political Science* 24: 319–57.

Jacobson, Gary C. 1987. "The Marginals Never Vanished: Incumbency and Competition in Elections to the U.S. House of Representatives, 1952–1982." *American Journal of Political Science* 31: 126–41.

———. 1992. *The Politics of Congressional Elections.* New York: Harper Collins.

———. 1993. "The Misallocation of Resources in House Campaigns." In *Congress Reconsidered,* 5th ed., edited by Lawrence C. Dodd and Bruce I. Oppenheimer. Washington, D.C.: Congressional Quarterly Press.

———. 1997. *The Politics of Congressional Elections.* New York: Longman

Jones, Charles O. 1961. "Representation in Congress: The Case of the House Agricultural Committee." *American Political Science Review* 55: 358–67.

———. 1976. "Senate Party Leadership in Public Policy." *Policymaking Role of Leadership in the Senate.* Compilation of papers prepared for the Commission on the Operation of the Senate, 94th Cong., 2d sess. Washington, D.C.: U.S. Government Printing Office.

Jung, Gi-Ryong, Lawrence W. Kenny, and John R. Lott, Jr. 1994. "An Explanation for Why Senators from the Same State Vote Differently So Frequently." *Journal of Public Economics* 54: 65–96.

Kahn, Kim F. 1996. *The Political Consequences of Being a Woman: How Stereotypes Influence the Content and Impact of Statewide Campaigns.* New York: Columbia University Press.

Kahn, Kim F., and Patrick J. Kenney. 1997. "A Model of Candidate Evaluations in Senate Elections: The Impact of Campaign Intensity." *Journal of Politics* 49: 1173–1205.

———. 1999. *The Spectacle of U.S. Senate Campaigns.* Princeton, N.J.: Princeton University Press.

Kamen, Al. "What's So Bad about Partisanship?" *Washington Post,* National Edition, May 3.

Kieweit, D. Roderick, and Mathew McCubbins. 1991. *The Logic of Delegation: Congressional Parties and the Appropriations Process.* Chicago: University of Chicago Press.

Kinder, Donald R. 1978. "Political Person Perception: The Asymmetrical Influence of Sentiment and Choice on Perceptions of Presidential Candidates." *Journal of Personality and Social Psychology* 36: 859–71.

King, David. 1997. *Turf Wars: How Congressional Committees Claim Jurisdiction.* Chicago: University of Chicago Press.

King, Gary. 1989. *Unifying Political Methodology: The Likelihood Theory of Statistical Inference.* New York: Cambridge University Press.

King, Gary, and Andrew Gelman. 1991. "Systematic Consequences of Incumbency Advantage in U.S. House Elections." *American Journal of Political Science* 35: 110–38.

Kingdon, John W. 1973. *Congressmen's Voting Decisions.* Ann Arbor: University of Michigan Press.

———. 1978 *Congressmen's Voting Decisions.* 2d ed. New York: Harper.

———. 1989. *Congressmen's Voting Decisions.* 3d ed. Ann Arbor: University of Michigan Press.

———. 1999. *America the Unusual.* New York: Worth.

Klein, Joe. 1998. "The Soul of the New Machine." *New Yorker,* June 1, 45.

Krasno, Jonathan S. 1994. *Challengers, Competition, and Reelection: Comparing Senate and House Elections.* New Haven, Conn.: Yale University Press.

Kravitz, Walter. 1974. "Evolution of the Senate's Committee System." In *Changing Congress: The Committee System,* edited by Norman Ornstein. Annals of the American Academy of Political and Social Science, vol. 411. Philadelphia: American Academy of Political and Social Science.

Krehbiel, Keith. 1987. "Why Are Congressional Committees Powerful?" *American Political Science Review* 81: 929–35.

_____. 1991. *Information and Legislative Organization*. Ann Arbor: University of Michigan Press.

_____. 1998. *Pivotal Politics: A Theory of U.S. Lawmaking*. Chicago: University of Chicago Press.

Kromkowski, Charles. 1999. "The Bond of Union: Rules of Apportionment, Constitutional Change, and a General Theory of American Political Development, 1700–1870." Ph.D. diss., University of Virginia.

Krosnick, Jon A. 1988. "Psychological Perspectives on Political Candidate Perception: A Review of Research on the Projection Hypothesis." Paper presented at the annual meetings of the Midwest Political Science Association, Chicago, April.

_____. 1990. "Expertise and Political Psychology." *Social Cognition,* 8: 1–8.

Krosnick, Jon, and Laura Brannon. 1993. "The Impact of the Gulf War on the Ingredients of Presidential Evaluations: Multidimensional Effects of Political Involvement." *American Political Science Review* 87: 963–75.

Larson, Stephanie Greco. 1990. "Information and Learning in a Congressional District: A Social Experiment." *American Journal of Political Science* 34: 1102–18.

Lau, Richard R., and David O. Sears, 1986. *Political Cognition*. Hillsdale, N.J.: Lawrence Erlbaum Associates.

Leary, Mary Ellen. 1977. *Phantom Politics: Campaigning in California*. Washington, D.C.: Public Affairs Press.

Lee, Frances E. 1998. "Representation and Public Policy: The Consequences of Senate Apportionment for the Geographic Distribution of Federal Funds." *Journal of Politics* 60: 34–62.

_____. 2000. "Senate Representation and Coalition Building in Distributive Politics." *American Political Science Review* 94: 59–72.

Lee, Frances E., and Bruce I. Oppenheimer. 1999. *Sizing up the Senate : The Unequal Consequences of Equal Representation*. Chicago: University of Chicago Press.

Levitt, Steven D., and James M. Poterba. 1999. "Congressional Distributive Politics and State Economic Performance." *Public Choice* 99: 185–216.

Levitt, Steven D., and James M. Snyder, Jr. 1995. "Political Parties and the Distribution of Federal Outlays." *American Journal of Political Science* 39: 958–80.

Lewis-Beck, Michael. 1980. *Applied Regression: An Introduction*. Newbury Park, Calif.: Sage Publications.

Lijphart, Arend. 1984. *Democracies: Patterns of Majoritarian and Consensus Government in Twenty-One Countries*. New Haven, Conn.: Yale University Press.

Lipset, Seymour Martin. 1996. *American Exceptionalism: A Double-Edged Sword*. New York: Norton.

Lodge, Milton G., and Ruth Hamill. 1986. "Partisan Schema for Political Information Processing." *American Political Science Review* 80: 505–19.

Londregan, John. 2000. "Estimating Legislator's Preferred Points." *Political Analysis* 8: 35–56.

Longley, Lawrence R., and Walter J. Oleszek. 1989. *Bicameral Politics: Conference Committees in Congress.* New Haven, Conn.: Yale University Press.

Loomis, Burdett, 1988. *The New American Politician.* New York: Basic Books.

_____. 1994. *Time, Politics, and Policy: A Legislative Year.* Lawrence: University Press of Kansas.

Luntz, Frank I. 1988. *Candidates, Consultants and Campaigns: The Style and Substance of American Electioneering.* Oxford, England: Basil Blackwell.

MacKuen, Michael B., Robert S. Erikson, and James A. Stimson. 1989. "Macropartisanship." *American Political Science Review* 83: 1125–42.

_____. 1992. "Question-Wording and Macropartisanship." *American Political Science Review* 86: 475–81.

Madison, James. 1987. *Notes of Debates in the Federal Convention of 1787.* New York: Norton.

Madison, James, Alexander Hamilton, and John Jay. 1965. *The Federalist Papers.* New Rochelle, N.Y.: Arlington House.

Maltzman, Forest. 1997. *Competing Principals: Committees, Parties, and the Organization of Congress.* Ann Arbor: University of Michigan Press.

Manley, John. 1970. *The Politics of Finance.* Boston: Little, Brown.

Mann, Thomas, and Raymond Wolfinger 1980. "Candidates and Parties in Congressional Elections." *American Political Science Review* 74: 617–32.

March, James G., and Johan P. Olsen. 1989. *Rediscovering Institutions: The Organizational Basis of Politics.* New York: Free Press.

_____. 1995. *Democratic Governance.* New York: Free Press.

Martis, Kenneth. 1989. *The Historical Atlas of Political Parties in the United States Congress, 1789–1989.* New York: Macmillan.

Matthews, Donald. 1960. *U.S. Senators and Their World.* Chapel Hill: University of North Carolina Press.

Mayer, William G. 1993. "Trends: Trends in Media Usage." *Public Opinion Quarterly* 57: 593–611.

Mayhew, David R. 1974a. "Congressional Elections: The Case of the Vanishing Marginals." *Polity* 6: 295–317.

_____. 1974b. *The Electoral Connection.* New Haven, Conn.: Yale University Press.

_____. 2000. *America's Congress: Actions in the Public Sphere, James Madison through Newt Gingrich.* New Haven, Conn.: Yale University Press.

McConachie, Lauros G. 1898. *Congressional Committees: A Study of the Origins and Development of Our National and Local Legislative Methods.* New York: Thomas Y. Crowell.

McDonald, Michael P. 1999. "Representational Explanations of Ideological Polarization of the House of Representatives." *Extension of Remarks,* July.

McLeod, Jack M., and Daniel McDonald. 1985. "Beyond Simple Exposure: Media

Orientations and Their Impact on Political Processes." *Communication Research* 12: 3–34.

McSweeney, Dean, and John E. Owens, eds. 1998. *The Republican Takeover on Capitol Hill.* New York: Macmillan.

Milburn, Michael. 1991. *Persuasion and Politics.* Pacific Grove, Calif.: Brooks/Cole.

Miller, James, 1986. *Running in Place: Inside the Senate.* New York: Simon and Schuster.

Miller, Warren E., and J. Merrill Shanks. 1996. *The New American Voter.* Cambridge, Mass.: Harvard University Press.

Miller, Warren, and Donald Stokes. 1963. "Constituency Influence in Congress." *American Political Science Review* 75: 45–56.

Mughan, Anthony, and Samuel C. Patterson. 1999. "Senates: A Comparative Perspective." In *Senates: Bicameralism in the Contemporary World,* edited by Samuel C. Patterson and Anthony Mughan, 333–49. Columbus: Ohio State University Press.

Munger, Michael C. 1988. "Allocation of Desirable Committee Assignments." *American Journal of Political Science* 32: 317–44.

Munger, Michael C., and Gary M. Torrent. 1993. "Committee Power and Value in the U.S. Senate: Implications for Policy." *Journal of Public Administration Research and Theory* 3: 46–65.

Munk, Margaret. 1974. "Origin and Development of the Party Floor Leadership in the United States Senate." *Capitol Studies* 2 (Winter): 23–41.

Neal, Steve. 1991. "Charles L. McNary: The Quiet Man." In *First among Equals: Outstanding Senate Leaders of the Twentieth Century,* edited by Richard A. Baker and Roger H. Davidson. Washington, D.C.: Congressional Quarterly Press.

Niemi, Richard G., and Patrick Fett. 1986. "The Swing Ratio: An Explanation and an Assessment." *Legislative Studies Quarterly* 11: 75–90.

Oleszek, Walter J. 1971. "Party Whips in the United States Senate." *Journal of Politics* 33: 955–79.

———. 1991. "John Worth Kern: Portrait of a Floor Leader." In *First among Equals: Outstanding Senate Leaders of the Twentieth Century,* edited by Richard A. Baker and Roger H. Davidson. Washington, D.C.: Congressional Quarterly Press.

———. 1996. *Congressional Procedures and the Policy Process.* Washington, D.C.: Congressional Quarterly Press, 1996.

Olson, Mancur. 1965. *The Logic of Collective Action.* Cambridge, Mass.: Harvard University Press.

Oppenheimer, Bruce. 1985. "Changing Time Constraints and the Congress: Historical Perspectives on the Use of Cloture." In *Congress Reconsidered,* 3d ed., edited by Lawrence C. Dodd and Bruce I. Oppenheimer. Washington, D.C.: Congressional Quarterly Press.

———. 1996. "The Representational Experience: The Effect of State Population on Senator-Constituency Linkages." *American Journal of Political Science* 40: 1280–99.

Ornstein, Norman J. 1981. "The House and the Senate in a New Congress." In *The New Congress,* edited by Thomas E. Mann and Norman J. Ornstein. Washington, D.C.: American Enterprise Institute Press.

———. 1997. *Campaign Finance: An Illustrated Guide.* Washington, D.C.: American Enterprise Institute Press.

Ornstein, Norman J., Thomas E. Mann, and Michael Malbin. 1994. *Vital Statistics on Congress, 1993–1994.* Washington, D.C.: Congressional Quarterly Press.

———. 1998. *Vital Statistics on Congress, 1997–1998.* Washington, D.C.: Congressional Quarterly Press.

———. 2000. *Vital Statistics on Congress, 1999–2000.* Washington, D.C.: American Enterprise Institute Press.

Ornstein, Norman J., Robert L. Peabody, and David W. Rohde. 1977. "The Changing Senate: From the 1950s to the 1970s." In *Congress Reconsidered,* edited by Lawrence C. Dodd and Bruce I. Oppenheimer, 3–20. New York: Praeger.

———. 1985. "The Senate through the 1980s: Cycles of Change." In *Congress Reconsidered,* 3d ed., edited by Lawrence C. Dodd and Bruce I. Oppenheimer. Washington, D.C.: Congressional Quarterly Press.

Owens, John E. 1998. "Congress and Partisan Change." In *Developments in American Politics 3,* edited by Gillian Peele, Christopher J. Bailey, Bruce Cain, and B. Guy Peters. New York: Chatham House.

Padgett, John F., and Christopher Ansell. 1993. "Robust Action and the Rise of the Medici, 1400–1434." *American Journal of Sociology* 98: 1259–1319.

Page, Benjamin I. 1996. *Who Deliberates?* Chicago: University of Chicago Press.

Peabody, Robert L., Norman J. Ornstein, and David W. Rohde. 1976. "The United States Senate as a Presidential Incubator: Many Are Called, but Few Are Chosen." *Political Science Quarterly* 91 (Summer): 237–58.

Petrocik, John R. 1996. "Issue Ownership in Presidential Elections, with a 1980 Case Study." *American Journal of Political Science* 40: 825–50.

Pfiffner, James P. 1999. "President Clinton, Newt Gingrich, and the 104th Congress." In *On Parties: Essays Honoring Austin Ranney,* edited by Nelson W. Polsby and Raymond E. Wolfinger. Berkeley, Calif.: Institute of Governmental Studies Press.

Pitkin, Hanna. 1967. *The Concept of Representation.* Berkeley: University of California Press.

Plott, Charles R. 1968. "Some Organizational Influences on Urban Renewal Decisions." *American Economic Review* 58: 306–21.

Polsby, Nelson. 1968. "The Institutionalization of the U.S. House of Representatives." *American Political Science Review* 62: 144–68.

Poole, Keith T., and Howard Rosenthal. 1991a. "Patterns of Congressional Voting." *American Journal of Political Science* 35: 228–78.

———. 1991b. "On Dimensionalizing Roll Call Votes in the U.S. Congress." *American Political Science Review* 85: 955–60.

_____. 1997. *Congress: A Political-Economic History of Roll Call Voting.* New York: Oxford University Press.

Pothier, John T. 1984. "The Partisan Bias in Senate Elections." *American Politics Quarterly* 12: 89–100.

Price, David E. 1972. *Who Makes the Laws?* Cambridge, Mass.: Schenkman.

Price, H. Douglas. 1977. "Careers and Committees in the American Congress: The Problem of Structural Change." In *The History of Parliamentary Behavior,* edited by William Ayderlotte. Princeton, N.J.: Princeton University Press.

Rahn, Wendy M. 1993. "The Role of Partisan Stereotypes in Information Processing about Political Candidates." *American Journal of Political Science* 37: 472–96.

Ray, Bruce. 1980a. "Congressional Promotion of District Interests: Does Power on the Hill Really Make a Difference?" In *Political Benefits,* edited by B. S. Rundquist. Lexington, Mass.: D. C. Heath.

_____. 1980b. "Federal Spending and the Selection of Committee Assignments in the U.S. House of Representatives." *American Journal of Political Science* 24: 494–510.

Remington, Thomas, and Steven Smith. 1995. "Theories of Legislative Institutions and the Organization of the Russian Duma." *American Journal of Political Science* 42: 545–72.

Rahn, Wendy M. 1993. "The Role of Partisan Stereotypes in Implementation Processing about Political Candidates." *American Journal of Political Science* 37: 472–96.

Rich, Michael J. 1989. "Distributive Politics and the Allocation of Federal Grants." *American Political Science Review* 83: 193–213.

Riddick, Floyd M. 1941. *Congressional Procedure.* Boston: Chapman and Grimes.

_____. 1971. "Majority and Minority Leaders of the Senate: History and Development of the Offices of the Floor Leaders." 92nd Cong., 1st sess. S. Doc. 92-42.

_____. 1980. *History of the U.S. Senate Committee on Rules and Administration.* S. Doc. 96-27. Washington, D.C.: Government Printing Office.

Riddick, Floyd, and Alan Fruman. 1992. *Riddick's Senate Procedure: Precedents and Practice.* S. Doc. 101-28. Washington, D.C.: U.S. Government Printing Office.

Riker, William H. 1955. "The Senate and American Federalism." *American Political Science Review* 49: 452–69.

_____. 1962. *The Theory of Political Coalitions.* New Haven, Conn.: Yale University Press.

_____. 1982. "The Two Party System and Duverger's Law: An Essay on the History of Political Science." *American Political Science Review* 76: 753–66.

_____. 1986. *The Art of Political Manipulation.* New Haven, Conn.: Yale University Press.

_____. 1996. *The Strategy of Rhetoric: Campaigning for the American Constitution.* New Haven, Conn.: Yale University Press.

Ripley, Randall B. 1969a. *Majority Party Leadership in Congress.* Boston: Little, Brown.

_____. 1969b. *Power in the Senate.* New York: St. Martin's.

Robinson, George Lee. 1954. "The Development of the Senate Committee System." Ph.D. diss., New York University.

Robinson, Michael J., and Dennis K. Davis. 1990. "Television News and the Informed Public." *Journal of Communication* 40: 106–19.

Rohde, David W. 1991. *Parties and Leaders in the Post-Reform House.* Chicago: University of Chicago Press.

———. 1992. "Electoral Forces, Political Agendas, and Partisanship in the House and Senate." In *The Postreform Congress,* edited by Roger H. Davidson, 27–47. New York: St. Martin's Press.

———. 1994. "Partisanship, Leadership, and Congressional Assertiveness in Foreign and Defense Policy." In *The New Politics of American Foreign Policy,* edited by David A. Deese, 76–101. New York: St. Martin's.

Rohde, David W., Norman J. Ornstein, and Robert L. Peabody. 1985. "Political Change and Legislative Norms in the United States Senate." In *Studies of Congress,* edited by Glenn R. Parker, 147–88. Washington, D.C.: Congressional Quarterly Press.

Rohde, David W., and Kenneth A. Shepsle. 1987. "Leaders and Followers in the House of Representatives: Reflections on Woodrow Wilson's *Congressional Government.*" *Congress and the Presidency* 14: 111–33.

Rosenstone, Steven J., and John Mark Hansen. 1993. *Mobilization, Participation, and Democracy in America.* New York: Macmillan.

Rothman, David J. 1966. *Politics and Power: The United States Senate, 1869–1901.* Cambridge, Mass.: Harvard University Press.

Rundquist, Barry S. 1978. "On Testing a Military Industrial Complex Theory." *American Politics Quarterly* 6: 29–53.

———, ed. 1980. *Political Benefits.* Lexington, Mass.: Lexington Books.

Rundquist, Barry S., and David E. Griffith. 1976. "An Interrupted Time-Series Test of the Distributive Theory of Military Policy-Making." *Western Political Quarterly* 29: 620–26.

Salisbury, Robert H., and Kenneth A. Shepsle. 1981. "Congressman as Enterprise." *Legislative Studies Quarterly* 6: 559–76.

Satz, Debra, and John Ferejohn. 1994. "Rational Choice and Social Theory." *Journal of Philosophy* 91: 37–87.

Scharpf, Fritz. 1997. *Games Real Actors Play: Actor-Centered Institutionalism in Policy Research.* Boulder, Colo.: Westview Press.

Schickler, Eric. 2000. "Institutional Change in the House of Representatives, 1867–1998: A Test of Partisan and Ideological Balance Models." *American Political Science Review* 94: 269–89.

———. 2001. *Disjointed Pluralism: Institutional Innovation and the Development of the U.S. Congress.* Princeton, N.J.: Princeton University Press.

Schiller, Wendy J. 2000. *Partners and Rivals: Representation in U.S. Senate Delegations.* Princeton, N.J.: Princeton University Press.

Sellers, Patrick J. 1997. "Fiscal Consistency and Federal District Spending in Congressional Elections." *American Journal of Political Science* 41: 1024–41.

———. 1998. "Strategy and Background in Congressional Campaigns." *American Political Science Review* 92: 159–72.

———. 1999. "Promoting the Party Message in the U.S. Senate." Paper presented at the annual meeting of the Midwest Political Science Association, Chicago, April.

Sellers, Patrick, and Brian Schaffner. 1999. "More Than Reelection: Senators and the News Media, 1985–1998." Paper presented at the annual meeting of the Midwest Political Science Association, Chicago, April.

Shepsle, Kenneth A., and Barry R. Weingast. 1987. "The Institutional Foundations of Committee Power." *American Political Science Review* 81: 85–104.

Simon, Herbert. 1985. "Human Nature in Politics: The Dialogue of Psychology with Political Science." *American Political Science Review* 79: 293–304.

Sinclair, Barbara. 1983. *Majority Leadership in the House.* Baltimore, Md.: Johns Hopkins University Press.

———. 1989. *The Transformation of the United States Senate.* Baltimore, Md.: Johns Hopkins University Press.

———. 1995. *Legislators, Leaders, and Lawmaking.* Baltimore, Md.: Johns Hopkins University Press.

———. 1997. *Unorthodox Lawmaking: New Legislative Processes in the U.S. Congress.* Washington, D.C.: Congressional Quarterly Press.

———. 1999. "Coequal Partner: The U.S. Senate." In *Senates: Bicameralism in the Contemporary World,* edited by Samuel C. Patterson and Anthony Mughan, 32–58. Columbus: Ohio State University Press.

———. 2001. "The New World of U. S. Senators." In *Congress Reconsidered,* 7th ed., edited by Lawrence C. Dodd and Bruce I. Oppenheimer. Washington, D.C.: Congressional Quarterly Press.

Smith, Eric R. A. N., Richard Herrera, and Cheryl A. Herrera. 1990. "Measurement Characteristics of Congressional Roll-Call Indexes." *Legislative Studies Quarterly* 15: 283–95.

Smith, Margaret Chase, 1972. *Declaration of Conscience.* Garden City, N.Y.: Doubleday.

Smith, Steven S. 1989. *Call to Order: Floor Politics in the House and Senate.* Washington, D.C.: Brookings Institution.

———. 1993. "Forces of Change in Senate Party Leadership and Organization." In *Congress Reconsidered,* 5th ed., edited by Lawrence C. Dodd and Bruce I. Oppenheimer. Washington, D.C.: Congressional Quarterly Press.

———. 1995. *The American Congress.* Boston: Houghton Mifflin.

———. 2000. "Positive Theories of Congressional Parties." *Legislative Studies Quarterly* 25: 193–217.

Smith, Steven S., and Christopher J. Deering. 1990. *Committees in Congress.* 2d ed. Washington, D.C.: Congressional Quarterly Press.

Smith, Steven S., and Marcus Flathman. 1989. "Managing the Senate Floor: Complex Unanimous Complex Agreements since the 1950s." *Legislative Studies Quarterly* 14: 349–74.

Smith, Steven S., and Gerald Gamm. 2001. "The Dynamics of Party Government in Congress." In *Congress Reconsidered,* 7th ed., edited by Lawrence C. Dodd and Bruce I. Oppenheimer. Washington, D.C.: Congressional Quarterly Press.

Sorauf, Frank J. 1998. "Political Parties and the New World of Campaign Finance." In *The Parties Respond: Changes in American Parties and Campaigns,* 3d ed., edited by L. Sandy Maisel. Boulder, Colo.: Westview Press.

Squire, Peverill. 1989." Challengers in U.S. Senate Elections." *Legislative Studies Quarterly* 14: 531–47.

———. 1992. "Challenger Quality and Voting Behavior in U.S. Senate Elections." *Legislative Studies Quarterly* 17: 247–64.

Squire, Peverill, and Eric R. A. N. Smith. 1996. "A Further Examination of Challenger Quality in Senate Elections." *Legislative Studies Quarterly* 17: 247–64.

Starobin, Paul. 1987. "Speed Limit Stays a Roadblock for Highway, Mass Transit Bill." *Congressional Quarterly Weekly Report,* January 24, 169–70.

Stein, Robert M., and Kenneth N. Bickers. 1994. "Congressional Elections and the Pork Barrel." *Journal of Politics* 56: 377–99.

———. 1995. *Perpetuating the Pork Barrel: Policy Subsystems and American Democracy.* New York: Cambridge University Press.

Stewart, Charles III. 1992. "Committee Hierarchies in the Modernizing House, 1875–1947." *American Journal of Political Science* 36: 835–56.

———. 1995. "Structure and Stability in House Committee Assignments, 1789–1947." Paper presented at the annual meeting of the Midwest Political Science Association, Chicago, April.

———. 1999. "The Inefficient Secret: Organizing for Business in the U.S. House of Representatives, 1789–1961." Paper presented at the annual meeting of the American Political Science Association, September.

Stewart, Charles, III, and Timothy Groseclose. 1998. "The Value of Committee Seats in the House, 1947–1991," *American Journal of Political Science* 42: 453–74.

Stewart, Charles, III, and Barry R. Weingast. 1992. "Stacking the Senate, Changing the Nation: Republican Rotten Boroughs, Statehood Politics, and American Political Development." *Studies in American Political Development* 6 (Fall): 223–71.

Stimson, James A. 1991. *Public Opinion in America: Mood, Cycles, and Swings.* Boulder, Colo.: Westview Press.

———. 1999. *Public Opinion in America: Mood, Cycles, and Swings.* 2d ed. Boulder, Colo.: Westview Press.

Strahan, Randall. 2002. "Leadership in Time: The Nineteenth Century House." In *New Directions in Studying the History of the U.S. Congress,* edited by David Brady and Mathew McCubbins. Stanford, Calif.: Stanford University Press.

Strom, Gerald S. 1975. "Congressional Policy Making: A Test of a Theory." *Journal of Politics* 37: 711–35.

Stubbs, Walter. 1985. *Congressional Committees, 1789–1982: A Checklist.* Westport, Conn.: Greenwood Press.

Swanstrom, Ray. 1985. *The United States Senate.1789–1801.* S. Doc. 99-19. Washington, D.C.: U.S. Government Printing Office.

Swift, Elaine. 1997. *The Making of an American Senate: Reconstitutive Change in Congress: 1787–1841.* Ann Arbor: University of Michigan Press.

Taylor, Andrew. 1997. "Clinton Signs 'Clean' Disaster Aid after Flailing GOP Yields to Veto." *Congressional Quarterly Weekly Report,* June 14, 1362.

———. 1999. "Parties' Post-Veto Game Plan: Do Nothing Rather Than Yield." *Congressional Quarterly Weekly Report* 57: 1921–22.

Thomas, Martin. 1985. "Election Proximity and Senatorial Roll Call Voting." *American Journal of Political Science* 92: 96–111.

Tieffer, Charles. 1989. *Congressional Practice and Procedure.* Westport, Conn.: Greenwood Press.

Tilly, Charles. 1997. *Roads from the Past to the Future.* Lanham, Md.: Rowman and Littlefield.

Tufte, Edward R. 1973. "The Relationship between Seats and Votes in Two-Party Systems." *American Political Science Review* 67: 540–47.

U.S. Bureau of the Census. 1988. *Statistical Abstract.* Washington, D.C.: U.S. Government Printing Office.

Uslaner, Eric M. 1999a. "Is the Senate More Civil Than the House?" Paper presented at the Robert J. Dole Institute Conference on Civility and Deliberation in the U.S. Senate, July 16, Washington, D.C.

———. 1999b. *The Movers and the Shirkers.* Ann Arbor: University of Michigan Press.

Van Beek, Stephen D. 1995. *Post-Passage Politics.* Pittsburgh, Pa.: University of Pittsburgh Press.

Vincent, Carol Hardy, Paul S. Rundquist, Richard C. Sachs, and Faye M. Bullock. 1996. "Party Leaders in Congress, 1789–1996: Vital Statistics." CRS Report for Congress, updated 12 November. Washington, D.C.: Congressional Research Service.

Waterman, Richard. 1990. "Comparing Senate and House Election Outcomes: The Exposure Thesis." *Legislative Studies Quarterly* 15: 88–114.

Watkins, Charles L., and Floyd M. Riddick. 1964. *Senate Procedure: Precedents and Practices.* 88th Cong. S. Doc. 44. Washington, D.C.: U.S. Government Printing Office.

Weick, Karl E. 1979. *The Social Psychology of Organizing.* New York: McGraw-Hill.

———. 1995. *Sensemaking in Organizations.* Thousand Oaks, Calif.: Sage Publications.

Weingast, Barry R. 1998. "Political Stability and Civil War: Institutions, Commitment, and American Democracy." In *Analytic Narratives,* edited by Robert Bates, Avener

Greif, Margaret Levi, Jean-Laurent Rosenthal, and Barry Weingas. Princeton, N.J.: Princeton University Press.

Weingast, Barry R., and William J. Marshall. 1988. "The Industrial Organization of Congress; or, Why Legislatures, Like Firms, Are Not Organized as Markets." *Journal of Political Economy* 96: 132–63.

Weissberg, Robert. 1978. "Collective vs. Dyadic Representation in Congress." *American Political Science Review* 72: 535–47.

Westlye, Mark C. 1991. *Senate Elections and Campaign Intensity.* Baltimore, Md.: Johns Hopkins University Press.

White, William S. 1956. *Citadel: The Story of the United States Senate.* New York: Harper and Brothers.

Whiteman, David. 1995. *Communication in Congress.* Lawrence: University Press of Kansas.

Widenor, William C. 1991. "Henry Cabot Lodge: The Astute Parliamentarian." In *First among Equals: Outstanding Senate Leaders of the Twentieth Century,* edited by Richard A. Baker and Roger H. Davidson. Washington, D.C.: Congressional Quarterly.

Wilson, Woodrow. 1885. *Congressional Government: A Study in American Politics.* Boston: Houghton Mifflin.

Wood, B. Dan, and Angela Hinton Andersson. 1998. "The Dynamics of Senatorial Representation, 1952–1991." *Journal of Politics* 60: 705–36.

Wright, Gerald C., Jr., and Mark B. Berkman. 1986. "Candidates and Policy in U.S. Senate Elections." *American Political Science Review* 80: 567–90.

Zaller, John R. 1992. *Nature and Origins of Mass Opinion.* New York: Cambridge University Press.

Zhao, Xinshu, and Steven H. Chaffee. 1995. "Campaign Advertisements versus Television News as Sources of Political Issue Information." *Public Opinion Quarterly* 59: 41–65.

CONTRIBUTORS

Alan Abramowitz is the Alben W. Barkley Professor of Political Science at Emory University.

John Alford is professor of political science at Rice University

Ross Baker is professor of political science at Rutgers University

David Canon is professor of political science at the University of Wisconsin, Madison.

Joseph Cooper is professor of political science at Johns Hopkins University.

Lawrence C. Dodd is Manning Dauer Eminent Scholar Chair at the University of Florida.

Robert S. Erikson is professor of political science at Columbia University.

C. Lawrence Evans is professor of government at the College of William and Mary.

Richard Fenno is Kenan Professor of Political Science and Distinguished University Professor at the University of Rochester.

Gerald Gamm is chair of the Department of Political Science and associate professor of political science and history at the University of Rochester.

John Hibbing is the Foundation Regents University Professor of Political Science at the University of Nebraska-Lincoln.

Kim Fridkin Kahn is professor of political science at Arizona State University.

Patrick J. Kenney is professor of political science at Arizona State University.

Frances E. Lee is associate professor of political science at Case Western Reserve University.

Burdett A. Loomis is professor of political science at the University of Kansas.

Bruce I. Oppenheimer is professor of political science at Vanderbilt University.

David W. Rohde is University Distinguished Professor of Political Science at Michigan State University.

Elizabeth Rybicki is a research fellow at the Brookings Institution.

Wendy J. Schiller is associate professor of political science at Brown University.

Patrick Sellers is associate professor of political science at Davidson College.

Barbara Sinclair is Marvin Hoffenberg Professor of American Politics at UCLA.

Steven S. Smith is Kate M. Gregg Professor of Social Sciences, professor of political science, and director of the Weidenbaum Center at Washington University in St. Louis.

Charles Stewart III is professor of political science and Associate Dean of the Humanities, Arts, and Social Sciences at MIT.

386

INDEX

Hook, Janet, 319
Hooton, Cornell, 286
hostage-taking, 247, 250
Hormel, James, 250, 255
House-initiated pattern, 91–92. *See also*
House-truncated pattern; Senate-
truncated pattern
House Rules Committee, 190
House-truncated pattern, 92. *See also*
House-initiated pattern; Senate-
truncated pattern
House-Senate comparisons:
apportionment, 288; Appropriations,
292–300; campaigns, 34, 47, 65;
committees, 157–58, 259;
constituencies, 70–73; distributive
politics, 284; elections; 4, 8, 70–79,
82, 88–107; function, 14, 104–5, 107;
ideology, 8; incumbency, 34–44, 177,
342; in general, 213, 341–63; powers,
4; roll call votes, 264–65, 279–80;
rules, 214, 260; of scholarship, 4, 9,
11–12, 179–80, 341, 359
Huddy, Leonie, 52
Huitt, Ralph, 6, 12, 244, 341, 350
Humphrey, Hubert, 249, 333
Hyde, Henry, 308, 309

Inter-university Consortium for Political
Science Research (ICPSR), 233
ideology: and campaigns, 48–53, 342;
effects of seniority, 61–62; ideological
balancing, 8, 79–83 (*see also* Divided
Congress; Divided government);
ideological divergence, 34; ideological
groups, 38; ideological mood, 73, 75;
ideological polarization, 31–39;
ideological portrayals, 45–65;
ideological position, 40, 50; ideological
realignment, 31–39, 40, 46, 47;
ideological voting, 34, 39–43; liberal-
conservative, 55–59; and partisanship
8, 41–42, 73–74; Senate elections, 8,
342
impeachment, 10–11, 305–38, 345–46

incentives, 244–46, 287
incumbency: and campaigns, 46–65; and
House elections, 177; and ideology,
51–52; and information, 62; and
Senate elections, 34–44, 342; and
swing ratio, 101; vote-share,128–29.
See also challenger
Indianapolis Star, 17
indirect elections, 93, 103. *See also* direct
elections
individualism, 305–20, 324, 326
information, 263–69
informational theory, 286
Inhofe, James, 255
Inouye, Daniel, 321
institutional patriotism, 305, 310–12,
314–20. *See also* folkways; norms
Intensive Communications Unit, 275
interest groups, 33, 246. *See also*
advocacy groups
inter-party distance, 342. *See also* party
polarization
intra-party cohesiveness, 32, 43, 44, 280,
342. *See also* party unity; party voting
intra-party competition, 233, 342
Irrigation Committee, 176
issue advocacy campaigns, 33. *See also*
campaigns
issue consistency, 52–53, 56–57
issues, 8, 43, 49–50, 52–53, 138, 245,
267, 270, 280; issue positions, 60–62,
134–35
Iyengar, Shanto, 49, 132

Jackson, Andrew, 97, 221–22
Jacobson, Gary C., 51, 54, 73, 101, 133,
290
Javits, Jacob, 33
Jay, John, 89
Jeffords, James, 33, 266, 276–77
Johnson, Andrew, 310, 330
Johnson, Lyndon, 35–38, 41–42, 220, 246
Jones, Bryan D., 136
Jones, Charles O., 6, 212
Jones, James K., 219

PARLIAMENTS & LEGISLATURE SERIES

General Advisory Editor
Samuel C. Patterson, Ohio State University, USA

Editorial Board
Janet Box-Steffensmeier, Ohio State University, USA
David W. Brady, Stanford University, USA
Gary W. Cox, University of California, San Diego, USA
Erik Damgaard, University of Aarhus, Denmark
Carlos Flores Juberias, University of Valencia, Spain
C. E. S. Franks, Queen's University, Canada
John R. Hibbing, University of Nebraska, USA
Keith Jackson, University of Canterbury, New Zealand
Gerhard Loewenberg, University of Iowa, USA
Werner J. Patzelt, Dresden Technical University, Germany
Thomas F. Remington, Emory University, USA
Suzanne S. Schüttenmeyer, University of Potsdam, Germany
Ilter Turan, Istanbul Bilgi University, Turkey